GILDED YOUTH

GILDED YOUTH

Three Lives in France's
Belle Époque

KATE CAMBOR

Farrar, Straus and Giroux

New York

Farrar, Straus and Giroux
18 West 18th Street, New York 10011

Distributed in Canada by Douglas & McIntyre Ltd.
Printed in the United States of America
First edition, 2009

Chapter 1, "Tuesday Lessons," originally appeared in the *New England Review*.

Library of Congress Cataloging-in-Publication Data
Cambor, Kate, 1975–
   Gilded youth : three lives in France's Belle Époque / Kate Cambor. —
1st ed.
      p.   cm.
   Includes bibliographical references and index.
   ISBN: 978-0-374-16230-6 (hardcover : alk. paper)
   1. Daudet, Léon, 1867–1942. 2. Charcot, Jean, 1867–1936. 3. Hugo,
Jeanne, 1869–1941. 4. France—Bibliography. 5. France—History—
1870–1940. 6. France—Politics and government—1870–1940. I. Title.

DC342.C36 2009
944.081'30922—dc22
                                                        2008049221

Designed by Jonathan D. Lippincott

www.fsgbooks.com

1 3 5 7 9 10 8 6 4 2

For my parents, Kathleen and Glenn,
and my brother, Peter

We are a cursed generation, which is fated to experience its coming-of-age as a series of frightening and grand events whose repercussions will pervade the remainder of our lives.

—Paul Valéry (1922)

Contents

GILDED YOUTH

Introduction

To the child, lover of maps and engravings,
The universe is a match to his vast appetite.
Oh! how grand the world is under the brightness of lamps!
How insignificant it appears when it is but a memory!
—Charles Baudelaire, "The Voyage,"
Les Fleurs du Mal (1857)

To any passerby on the street, it looked like another lively evening at the Café du Croissant, a popular hangout for journalists whose offices dotted the busy rue Montmartre neighborhood. By nine p.m. the café was crowded with patrons, and the animated sounds of chatting and music drifted through the large open windows into the sultry night. Suddenly the evening was pierced by the sound of two gunshots, then silence, then a single scream: "They've shot Jaurès!" The news exploded through the streets of Paris like an electric shock. It was July 31, 1914.

Jean Jaurès, a fifty-five-year-old socialist deputy, had seemed like France's last chance for avoiding the impending war. His prominent beard and hulking frame were well known throughout the country: for the better part of the last thirty years he had been the leading figure of French socialism, tirelessly wielding his fiery oratorical skills and political acumen in defense of those most in need. His fame had reached new heights in 1895, with his impassioned defense of brutalized miners during the infamous Carmaux strike, and then again a few years later when he entered the political maelstrom of the Dreyfus Affair, first on behalf of the accused Jewish captain and then of his illustrious defender, the writer Émile Zola. But after a lifetime of striding fearlessly and confidently into the political and economic battles of the day, the aging socialist now watched helplessly as the very bonds of international socialism that he had devoted his life to maintaining evaporated before the intoxicating call of nationalism. His public efforts to prevent France from becoming embroiled in what he called "wild Balkan adventures" had provoked ire from many corners. The nationalist and royalist journalists Léon Daudet and Charles Maurras had been most visible and venomous in their attacks on the socialist deputy, denouncing him as a traitor, a spy, and an enemy of the state. But even friends and former admirers had begun to turn on Jaurès for his obstinate refusal to support the war. His former protégé, the young writer Charles Péguy, was so incensed that he declared the only way to stop the socialist leader was to drown out his voice with drumrolls, just as foes of the French Revolution had been silenced on their way to the guillotine.

Jaurès had spent the entire day of July 31, 1914, walking up and down the corridors of the Chamber of Deputies, pleading with various ministers and deputies to show restraint in the face of mounting international pressure to enter into the European conflict on the side of France's ally Russia, which had been readying for war since the June assassination of Archduke Franz Ferdinand by Serbian nationalists in Sarajevo. Returning, disappointed and depleted, to the offices of the socialist newspaper *L'Humanité*, Jaurès had announced to his staff his intention of writing a new "J'accuse" in a last, desperate attempt to turn the tide of history by appealing to the public, as Zola had done with such success during the Dreyfus Affair. But first his friends, who understood how much recent events were weighing down their mentor, insisted they all retire to the Café du Croissant to unwind and make plans. They clustered around a table next to the window, leaning into one another and the food as they strained to hear over the din. As they talked no one noticed the pale young man with a beard and flowing tie lurking on the sidewalk just outside: Raoul Villain, a sometime follower of the nationalist doctrines of Charles Maurras, Léon Daudet, and their royalist and nationalist group, the Action Française. With a history of mental instability, he had been stalking Jaurès for weeks, waiting for his moment to rid France of a man the Action Française had declared an enemy of the state. As dessert was served, one of Jaurès's companions pulled out a photograph of his daughter to show the deputy. Jaurès complimented the proud father and had turned back to his tart when suddenly the screen at the window behind them came crashing down and a figure emerged from the dark shadows. Villain took aim and fired two bullets into the back of his target's head. A bleeding and unconscious Jaurès slumped to the side as the café exploded into panic and confusion. Villain was immediately arrested. By the time the doctor arrived, Jaurès was already dead. The crowd that had begun to form outside the café watched, aghast, as the white-hung stretcher carried the body into the ambulance. A strange, sad silence descended upon the rue Montmartre. As the car with its bloody cargo began to move away, the onlookers erupted into an angry howl of sound and sadness. "Jaurès! Jaurès! Jaurès! Jaurès forever!" To other observers the event had more immediate significance. "They've killed Jaurès! This means war."

The news of Jaurès's death appeared in the Paris papers the following day, Saturday, August 1. Later that afternoon the German and French governments gave the orders to begin general mobilization, which would go into full effect the following day at noon. By evening, in Paris and cities throughout France, groups of young men, reservists from all classes, could be seen marching off toward the railway stations as civilians waved and cheered, assuring them, and one another, that the boys would swiftly return victorious. Many greeted the prospect of war not with fear but rather with a sense almost of relief—now they finally had the chance to have their revenge against the country that had laid siege to Paris some forty years earlier and stolen two provinces in the east. France's defeat in 1871 had sent a generation of Frenchmen into a tailspin of soul-searching and bitterness that only a mighty military victory could remedy.

Their nightmare had begun on July 19, 1870, when the French

emperor Napoléon III declared war on Prussia after years of escalating political tension between the two nations. The other German states quickly joined on Prussia's side of the conflict, and soon French forces found themselves outnumbered and outmaneuvered by the vastly superior military might of their foes, led by the brilliant strategist and statesman Otto von Bismarck. A series of crushing German victories in the east of France culminated in the battle of Sedan on September 2, 1870, when Napoléon III and his entire army were captured. When the news of Sedan reached Paris, the crowds proclaimed a republic and a government of national defense was formed. The Prussian army next laid siege to Paris. Despite enduring a punishing winter during which famine conditions quickly developed, the beleaguered Parisians held out until January 8, 1871. On January 28, 1871, ten days after the proclamation of the unification of the German states, an armistice between the two nations was signed. In addition to paying a steep indemnity to the victors, the new French government also agreed to cede Alsace and much of Lorraine to the new German empire. Parisians, who had withstood the Prussian army for four months, were outraged at the ease with which their countrymen from the provinces had given in to Prussian demands. On March 18, 1871, they rose up in opposition to the new French government, thus beginning a bitter civil war that lasted until mid-May and left painful scars in the national psyche. In the decades that followed, the nation nursed a deep-seated resentment and a desire to expunge the memory of that humiliating, humbling debacle. So when offered a chance, in the summer of 1914, to settle the score with their neighbors to the east, most Frenchmen welcomed it.

The same day of the order for general mobilization—August 1—the ultranationalist Action Française circulated a statement denying that Jaurès's assassin was affiliated with their movement. Still, fearing reprisals and unwilling to take any chances, forty-seven-year-old Léon Daudet abruptly left Paris for Touraine with his younger brother Lucien in order to avoid possible retaliation. If Léon publicly denied any responsibility, he certainly shed no tears for the fallen politician. While Jean Jaurès had been desperately trying to cobble together a plan for peace, Léon Daudet and his collaborators at the Action Française had been fanning the flames of war. Léon had long declared Jaurès to be a menace, someone who needed to be "eliminated." But he had said that of many men—German agents were everywhere, Léon and his colleagues warned their anxious followers, an unlikely alliance of erstwhile aristocrats dismayed by the demands of democracy, nervous shopkeepers looking for scapegoats for their economic woes, and loutish adolescent hoodlums spoiling for a fight. Léon had never been afraid of creating controversy—on the contrary, he thrived on it personally and had built a career on it professionally. He had begun early, attacking in his 1894 novel *Les Morticoles* his mentor and family friend Jean-Martin Charcot as well as the medical profession for which Léon had once been destined. As he progressed in his career, he gradually took aim at anyone and everyone he considered "unpatriotic": the more prominent the politician, the more insulated the captain of industry, the more zealously Léon pursued him, and the more pride he felt when he saw his target topple. And now, as the nation cast its gaze anxiously to the east, his accusations of widespread disloyalty and collusion with the German enemy had begun to seem accurate, even prescient.

Léon stared out the car window into the murky night while his brother, Lucien, slept fitfully beside him. He felt torn and annoyed. Few looking into that darkened vehicle would have guessed that this middle-aged man was one of France's most controversial political instigators. With his bushy handlebar mustache, fleshy cheeks, and ever-expanding girth—the last the unavoidable and highly publicized result of too many excessive nights on the town—Léon possessed an air of bonhomie. His love of words was almost Rabelaisian. They tumbled forth over one another, sometimes generously, sometimes with adolescent cruelty, in his pamphlets and editorials and in the mediocre novels he insisted on writing. But to truly understand Léon's force, his sheer vitality, one had to see him in his element, onstage before an audience. It was here, haranguing and cajoling his onlookers into feverish states of outrage and ardor, convincing them of Jewish conspiracies, socialist menaces, and the possibilities of royalist redemption, that he demonstrated the power of words— the power to incite the people to fear and to despise, the power to galvanize. This was also the Léon Daudet of the dueling field, a place that his penchant for merciless ridicule and slanderous accusations had compelled him to visit on numerous occasions. But there were consequences for leading such an uncensored and unbridled life, consequences that weighed on him now, motoring toward his family home in Touraine. The public, he knew, was fickle, and yesterday's act of patriotism could quickly become tomorrow's act of treason in the hands of a fellow journalist. And now, to be away from the capital at a time like this, when war was imminent, felt foolish and small for a man so accustomed to being at the center of the action.

A flash of lights and the sound of metal straining against metal were the last impressions Léon had before he was catapulted from the car. His vehicle had been struck by an oncoming truck. Landing in a nearby ditch, Léon lay on the ground, stunned, as blood poured from a large wound in his head. Lucien, who had escaped with only a few minor cuts and bruises, rushed over to his prostrate brother. Luckily, a few moments later, a car drove up: it was the Princess de Broglie, a vivacious redhead known for her antics on the Parisian social circuit, who was on her way to her château in the Loire valley. The car's driver and the two Daudet brothers were bundled into her highness's limousine and swiftly taken to the nearby town of Artenay, a sleepy hamlet tucked into the rolling hills and wheat fields of La Beauce, twenty kilometers from Orléans. The town physician, Dr. Naudet, had been making his final preparations before joining his regiment and departing for the war when the bedraggled and injured party arrived at his door. How ironic that this young man, about to join an international conflict that would lead to unspeakable carnage, should be attending to the fractured skull of a portly, middle-aged man whose columns and speeches had greeted the prospect of war with such blind enthusiasm. Once he had washed the gaping wound with alcohol and closed it with twenty-two stitches, Dr. Naudet warned that there was nothing to do but wait. Léon slipped into unconsciousness and did not awaken for more than three weeks. The day after attending to his notorious patient, Dr. Naudet joined other men from his village and left for the capital, where trains took them east toward the Germans and, presumably, victory. As mothers and fathers throughout Europe bravely bade farewell to their sons, Léon's family continued to keep watch over him, praying that he would wake up. And eventually, defying the doctors' grim predictions, he finally emerged from his slumber. Then he could only rest and recover. How frustrating to be immobilized, cut off from his friends and colleagues in Paris, from news of what was occurring even as his country mobilized for war. He was too old, in any case, to be drafted and too weak for the moment to engage in his usual rhetorical battles against France's innumerable foes. And so Léon watched from his bedroom window as the once quiet country roads filled with cars carrying worried, weary Parisians fleeing the capital as word spread of the advancing German army. He watched and he waited and he planned his return.

Hundreds of miles from the family home where the Daudets cared for Léon and waited anxiously for news from Paris, forty-seven-year-old Jean-Baptiste Charcot stood on the bridge of his three-mast ship, plowing toward the waters off Iceland, as he gave the orders to change course and return to Cherbourg. With his dark eyes and trim figure, a full mustache bristling upon his upper lip and a beard expertly groomed into a well-defined point, Jean-Baptiste managed to convey an air of both vigor and stateliness. He had just received word that his country was going to war, so there was no question but that he and his men must return home. Not only was the ship's crew—Jean-Baptiste and his officers were leading a team of student sailors training to become captains—now needed for France's defense, but their ship, the famed *Pourquoi-Pas?*, which had withstood many treacherous Antarctic icebergs and unforgiving Atlantic swells, could surely be useful in defending French shores. "Honor and country": that was the ship's motto, and at no other time had those words stirred such emotion in each of them. But even as all thoughts turned south, toward France and a continent on the brink of international calamity, Jean-Baptiste could not help looking back toward the Arctic waters they would no longer enter that summer. No doubt he was recalling his own first trip to the region, when he had visited the desolate island of Jan Mayen in the Arctic Ocean in 1902, at the age of thirty-five. It had been his initiation into the strange and haunting world of the polar regions—an untouched and natural place palpably in the sway of forces at once solitary and grandiose, sinister and glorious. Jean-Baptiste felt the call of these unimagined lands for the rest of his life. Now, as the distance grew between him and these northern waters, he wondered if he'd ever find his way back to the ends of the earth.

That summer of 1914 had begun calmly enough. Of course, Jean-Baptiste was aware of the rumors and tensions. Even in the muted, dusty hallways and thickly paneled rooms of the Yacht Club in Paris, where Jean-Baptiste spent much of his time organizing his scientific projects and promoting Arctic exploration, conversations about the impending trouble had intruded on all other talk. The appearance of the famed explorer, who had led France's first Antarctic expedition in 1903 and another in 1908, always produced admiring stares and hushed tones from club members and visitors alike, and now everyone was eager to hear his opinion about the best course for France. But all the talk of politics, of foreign premiers and territorial squabbling, of munitions and troop movements, had never been his domain. In fact, Jean-Baptiste had looked forward to his summer voyage aboard the *Pourquoi-Pas?* as a chance to escape— even if only for a short while—these Continental woes. He knew by now that another Antarctic expedition was out of the question—he was too old, even too tired for such punishing tests of human endurance. But there was still so much to see and discover, and the icy waters between Iceland and Greenland provided fertile, if slightly more modest, ground for a noted scientist and explorer like himself. For the past two years, with a caution engendered by age, he had devoted himself to his new position as captain of an educational mission training young student sailors to handle themselves on the open sea, held aboard the ship that had successfully weathered a trip to Antarctica and back. Only seven years earlier, the *Pourquoi-Pas?* had been unveiled as the fastest, proudest vessel ever to face the Antarctic challenge. Jean-Baptiste had spared no expense when building her. She was 460 tons and 40 meters long—a sleek, three-mast ship made entirely of oak and crowned by an intricate web of ropes and beams and sails. She traveled at seven knots in good conditions with her 550-horsepower steam engine, eleven knots with sails on the open sea. Jean-Baptiste had insisted that she be able to stand up to the extreme conditions of Antarctic exploration, so everything was made three times as strong as on an ordinary ship of the same tonnage. Beyond these structural achievements, Jean-Baptiste was most proud of the ship's two laboratories, filled with beakers and workbenches, and of its library, which boasted a collection of almost two thousand literary and scientific works.

The *Pourquoi-Pas?* was *his* ship, the grown-up realization of the childhood dreams that had kept him awake at night as a young boy. Now Jean-Baptiste found something at once comforting and exciting in watching these young sailors learn their trade on the ship that had seen him through so much in previous expeditions. His men, especially those who had risked everything to share Jean-Baptiste's dream of Antarctic exploration, had always been the real heart and soul of the enterprise. He had taken care of them as if they were his own sons. And yet, as Jean-Baptiste listened to them now, yelping and cheering at news of the war, flushed as they imagined the *boches* they would kill, the glory that would be theirs, he felt them slipping away from him. All dreams of exploration had left their heads. They had quit the laboratories and observation posts. Their only thoughts were of speedily returning home, not to their families, but to war. Honor and country—perhaps *they* were right, perhaps it was time to put away Arctic dreams. Jean-Baptiste hoped to do his duty in the upcoming conflict, but he could not help but feel that this would be a war for the young and naive. As he watched his men's faces, now turned expectantly toward France, he struggled with a mixture of feelings. Paternal pride. A touch of annoyance. Foreboding.

What, after all, did they know of war? He barely knew of it himself, just fleeting memories from his childhood: the sight of a maid's rushed packing; the sound of fingers fumbling with the enclosures of trunks; the pressure of his mother's hand on his head warning him to be quiet and still; the sound of carriage wheels and the clanging of horse hooves on cobblestones as the family was sent away from Paris, from the shelling and the inexorable advance of Prussian armies in 1870. These young sailors, these boys, knew nothing yet of the precariousness of life—something Jean-Baptiste had only truly begun to grasp in Antarctica. Even there, in the most untouched places, one could not escape the dangerous encroachments of the modern world or the relentlessness of men. How many seals had they killed when their own provisions had run out? What about the whalers at Deception Island, whose mechanized slaughter had filled the bay with the carved-out carcasses of those massive creatures and a foul odor of death and decay? These were just animals, but their defenselessness before the voracious needs of man had troubled him. "Why is man bound to do evil as soon as he visits any place?" he had asked himself in his journal on December 30, 1908. If nature can seem cruel, men can be even crueler, and those brief moments of violence he saw in Antarctica—violence in which he himself was sometimes forced to engage—almost left him at a loss. And now they were steering the *Pourquoi-Pas?* back to France and to new opportunities for violence toward other men. His students' enthusiasm in the face of these opportunities made him feel nervous, weary, frightened—and, yes, rather old.

As the *Pourquoi-Pas?* steamed toward France, a woman sat alone in her large, ornate apartment at 171, rue de la Pompe in Paris's sixteenth arrondissement. Heavy velvet curtains were closed against the late-afternoon sun that should have been streaming in through the large double windows. The woman, quite still in the darkness, was unaware that the city had been transformed into a vortex of activity. But if tension and excitement were palpable in the streets outside, a heavy stillness pressed upon the woman inside the apartment, who was dressed in black. Jeanne Hugo had always been told that she was beautiful. Her grandfather, the famed Victor Hugo, had immortalized her as *Jeanne au pain sec* ("Jeanne with toast"), the delightful, curious creature who had returned a light to the aging writer's eyes. She could not count the number of times she had been photographed or had her portrait made, the perfect image of pretty, childlike devotion. As she grew up, her beauty only deepened. Her thick chestnut hair and lively blue eyes had won her many admirers by the time she was just a teenager. Her brother Georges's friends—Léon Daudet, Philippe Berthelot, and Jean-Baptiste Charcot—had gone to great lengths to charm her. She naturally delighted in the attention, as any young girl would. But anyone watching her in that somber room today, as the world rushed toward war, would have seen only a shadow of that former beauty. The young belle who had danced and sparkled her way through the most elegant parties and sumptuous salons of turn-of-the-century Paris had been replaced by a pensive forty-five-year-old woman with graying hair. Her figure, which had once been admiringly described as ample, had now passed over into plump, and her eyes, which had once shone so brightly, now stared vacantly.

She had the air of someone defeated. After just eight years of marriage, she had buried her third husband, Michel Negreponte, in early April. He had been her great love, and his death left her feeling utterly alone. The two had met when she was just a teenager. It had been at the elegant home of the great Ferdinand de Lesseps, architect of the Suez Canal triumph, whose son had met and married Michel's mother, a Greek-Egyptian heiress. Jeanne and Michel, who was then a Greek cadet studying at the military academy of Saint-Cyr, had danced several dances. Their connection had been instant and electric. But her mother had wished other things for her—marriage to a Frenchman from a great family, someone with connections and roots. Jeanne had been steered into a friendship with and then marriage to Léon Daudet. Léon had moved in the same exclusive circles as the young Hugos and their mutual friend, Jean-Baptiste Charcot. The match of these two great literary names—Daudet and Hugo—was widely celebrated as the triumphant merging of two great republican dynasties. But neither marriage nor the birth of a son could sustain the troubled couple. They divorced a few years later. Jeanne found comfort with her childhood friend Jean-Baptiste Charcot, and soon he admitted that he had always loved her from afar and now wished to marry her. She explained to him that her heart belonged to another. In spite of her confession, he still wanted to marry her, hoping that his love and devotion would be enough to sustain them both. That marriage, too, collapsed—his frequent absences at sea widened the gulf that had existed between them from the beginning. It was only at the age of thirty-six that she finally found her way back to the young officer whom she had met at a party so many years earlier. He, too, had married and divorced—a Greek actress named Eugenia Antoniadis—but he had never forgotten the young woman with the angelic face and grand reputation who had so surprised him by announcing, imperiously, proudly, that she was the granddaughter of Victor Hugo. Fate had dealt her a cruel blow in taking him from her before they had a chance to grow old together. And now, as the sons of France were mobilized, she remained locked in her grief, unable to move, unwilling to imagine that any international crisis could be as annihilating as her own private loss.

During that summer of 1914, when the whole of Europe plunged with terrifying enthusiasm into a ghastly experiment with modern warfare, Léon Daudet, Jean-Baptiste Charcot, and Jeanne Hugo found themselves caught awkwardly at the sidelines—a place they were not accustomed to being. They had grown up at the pinnacle of Third Republic achievement, power, and success. Their understanding of the world and their place in it had been molded by conversations with presidents and philosophers, pioneers of the arts and sciences. They had attended the most glamorous parties and vacationed at the most fashionable European resorts, moving through the upper echelons of Parisian society with the self-assurance of favored heirs apparent. Their fathers (or, in the case of Jeanne Hugo, grandfather)—the wildly popular writer Alphonse Daudet, the world-renowned neurologist Jean-Martin Charcot, and the immortal Victor Hugo—had cast long shadows not merely over their own children but over an entire generation of Frenchmen. Alphonse Daudet, Jean-Martin Charcot, and Victor Hugo each helped to redefine their respective fields and in doing so ushered their countrymen with confidence toward the final years of the nineteenth century. As children, Léon, Jean-Baptiste, and Jeanne had observed these men courted by emperors, entertained at the most exclusive salons, praised as heroes and national treasures by their contemporaries. But the passing of the torch from one generation to the next did not happen smoothly: growing up in the refracted glow of their families' celebrity, Léon Daudet, Jean-Baptiste Charcot, and Jeanne Hugo would forever struggle with the burden of their gilded youth and with the pressure of inheriting a legacy of greatness that was not their own.

As offspring of three of the greatest representatives of nineteenth-century French achievement, Jeanne Hugo, Léon Daudet, and Jean-

Baptiste Charcot were poised, more than most, to take advantage of the promises of the dawning century. For that reason they also felt most keenly the disappointment and disorientation of a generation who discovered that the faith in science and progress that had so sustained their elders would prove inadequate for modern life. Léon, Jean-Baptiste, and Jeanne belonged to a generation that lived through extremes: from the genteel certitude of the Belle Époque to the nightmare of World War I, from the turbulence of the interwar years to the sound of German soldiers marching through the streets of Paris and the beginnings of World War II. Their lives offer a remarkable window into the hopes and disillusionments of a generation and into the universal challenges that emerge between the dreams of youth and the realities of aging, between the aspirations for greatness and the fears of mediocrity.

Léon Daudet, Jean-Baptiste Charcot, and Jeanne Hugo grew up with certain expectations, inherited and self-imposed, about themselves and their world. These expectations would be challenged, and even overturned, as private demons and international events collided. Childish fantasies gave way to adult compromises as triumphant marriages ended in divorce, careers were cast aside, and politics led to ostracism, exile, and even war. The new generation of writers and politicians around them were engaged in a battle of epic and Oedipal proportions; at stake was nothing less than the heart and soul of Mother France. Forced to confront their own anxieties of influence, Léon, Jean-Baptiste, and Jeanne stumbled from their gilded youth at the height of Third Republic society into the disparate domains of right-wing politics, polar exploration, and domestic self-confinement. Their very personal quests for self-discovery took place in the most elegant salons of Paris and in the streets of Buenos Aires, on the shores of Antarctica, and in the fishing communities of Brittany, and were bound up in the great debates of the day about the power of science, the role of religion, the fate of the nation. The growing pains experienced by a generation of French men and women are reflected in the life stories of these three young people. Their time together, and the subsequent choices they made in their lives afterward, offer an illuminating glimpse into the possibilities and frustrations of growing up in the public eye at the dawn of the last century.

ONE

Tuesday Lessons

Homo sum: humani nihil a me alienum puto.
(I am human: I consider nothing human foreign to me.)
—Terence, *Heauton Timoroumenos*
(The Self-Tormentor) (163 B.C.)

The child's attitude to its father is colored by a peculiar ambivalence. —Sigmund Freud, *The Future of an Illusion* (1927)

On October 13, 1885, a young man with a well-groomed beard and a foreigner's heavy coat stepped out of the train and onto the busy platform at the Gare du Nord in Paris. Letting the other travelers hurry past him, he stood still for a moment, waiting for his ears and eyes to adjust to the strangeness of this foreign destination. Sigmund Freud was twenty-nine years old and had left everything behind, sensing with some strange certainty that his future would begin here, hundreds of miles away from his adored fiancée, Martha, and beautiful Vienna, with its familiar *Kaffehaüser* and imposing Ringstrasse. He could have remained at home and begun the predictable, respectable career that most young physicians longed for and that he would be required to pursue if he wished to marry. But instinctively he knew that he needed something that Vienna could not offer him. For there, in Paris, shone the great name of Charcot.

Who had not heard of the illustrious neurologist Jean-Martin Charcot, or of his famed Tuesday lessons? Each week at his Salpêtrière hospital, he presented for study his ailing patients, who these days were most often hysterical women. He discussed their symptoms—irrational ramblings and convulsive spasms, for example—before a rapt and eclectic audience of curious scientists, skeptical journalists, and chic socialites. Freud had heard tantalizing accounts of these sessions, of writhing bodies brought into submission under the piercing, all-seeing gaze of the great doctor. As a testament to the Frenchman's considerable power and influence, he was even known as the "Emperor of the Salpêtrière."

Yet for all these accolades, Charcot was also considered something of a maverick. He had been among the first to treat hysteria as a knowable neurological disorder, despite its vague symptoms that seemed to have no discernible physiological source and despite the fact that many of his contemporaries still dismissed such sufferers—often women—as malingerers. Such courage . . . such confidence—the young Freud was bowled over at the thought of such achievement. And so, hoping that with so innovative a teacher he would find the training and inspiration he needed to launch his own career, Sigmund Freud entered the swirling commotion of the French capital. "For years, I only dreamed of Paris," he later recalled, "and the extreme happiness that I felt in posing my foot for the first time on these cobblestones seemed to me to guarantee the realization of my other desires."

Freud's first weeks in the City of Lights, however, proved disappointing and bewildering. He felt lazy and out of sorts, and, in letters home to his most intimate confidante, Martha, he fretted about the high prices and the exhausting, frenetic pace of Parisian life. His hotel in the fifth arrondissement was small and cramped. His accent and limited knowledge of the French language made the simplest conversation difficult. After failing to make a waiter at a café understand his request for *du pain* ("some bread"), Freud was too embarrassed to ever go back there. As he waited for his first meeting with the great Charcot, Freud restlessly toured the capital, seeking shelter among the antiquities of the Louvre from the city of strangers and from his own gawky foreignness. To stave off his mounting sense of inferiority, Freud savagely noted the symptoms of that pathology unique to the French: their "miserable megalomania," which caused them to mount theater performances that lasted four hours and meals that lasted five or six, and bred a misplaced idealization of revolutionary activity. But there was something else, something about the city and its inhabitants that struck him as uncanny and alien. "I think they are all possessed by demons," he confided to Martha. "The French are a people of psychical epidemics, of historical mass convulsions, and they have not changed since the time of Victor Hugo's *Notre-Dame de Paris.*" Freud felt that great poet, who had died only a few months earlier, had captured something elemental and unsettled about the capital. At first glance Paris seemed to him like a city flush with possibility. Everywhere he looked, there was something to catch his eye, from the dance halls and cafés lining the *grands boulevards*, to the Luxor obelisk in the center of the place de la Concorde, or the impressive array of goods at the new department stores. People were whisked to and fro in the elaborate system of streetcars and omnibuses, and many were already talking with excitement about the centennial celebration of the French Revolution that would take place four years later at the Universal Exposition. But while Hugo had embraced the volatility of the capital, Freud was unnerved by it. Underneath the frenetic exuberance, one could just make out a dull throb of anxiety. Nor was he alone in thinking that something was afoot in Paris: specialists of the day only half-jokingly called Paris "the hysteria capital of the world."

But as he slowly settled into a routine, Freud found himself warming to certain benefits of Parisian living: the coffee, he allowed, was excellent, as were the dramatic talents of the sublime Sarah Bernhardt. The cathedral of Notre Dame left the most lasting impression upon him. And a week after his first visiting the church, Freud breathlessly invoked it in another letter to Martha as a metaphor for his own evolving relationship with his new mentor, Jean-Martin Charcot, under whom he had begun studying:

> I am now quite comfortably installed, and I think that I am changing greatly. I will tell you in great detail what is causing this change. Charcot, who is one of the greatest doctors and

whose genius is only limited by his sanity, is quite simply in the process of demolishing my ideas and my plans. I leave his course as if I was leaving Notre-Dame, full of new ideas about perfection. But he exhausts me, and when I leave him, I no longer have any desire to do my own work, which seems so insignificant . . . Will the seed produce any fruit? I don't know; but all that I do know is that no other man has ever had so much influence on me.

Like a man intent on heralding his own mythology, Jean-Martin Charcot enjoyed telling his students about his origins. They in turn would whisper these stories to one another before lectures or after making patient rounds, and in this way the contours of their teacher's life and those of the scientific discipline that he was building became virtually indistinguishable.

He was born in Paris on November 29, 1825, to Simon-Pierre Charcot, a twenty-seven-year-old carriage builder and artisan, and Jeanne-Georgette Saussier, who was not quite seventeen. His first years occurred against the backdrop of the political turmoil of the final days of the Restoration and the revolts of 1830, most famously immortalized by Victor Hugo in *Les Misérables.* His family was of modest means, and Jean-Martin lived with his parents and three brothers in a lively section of Paris near the *grands boulevards* on the Right Bank. It was a pleasant childhood, marred only by the death of his mother when Jean-Martin was just fourteen years old. Yet he was a stern child, who already showed signs of that cold, taciturn disposition for which he would later become famous, preferring to spend his time alone reading and drawing than playing with friends. In 1843, when he was eighteen, he finished his secondary schooling and was faced with the prospect of choosing a career either in art or in medicine, ultimately deciding to become a physician, with its promise of greater economic and social advancement.

At the time, the field of medicine was enjoying a newfound prestige in light of doctors' prominent role in the July Revolution of 1830 and in fighting the cholera epidemic in 1832. "No lifestyle that I know," gushed the author of *The French As Viewed by Themselves,* a popular book published while Jean-Martin was in school, "is more varied, more complete, than that of the medical professor. To advance the interests of science and his own fortune, to have a clientele and an audience, to be obliged to reveal a thousand secrets in the name of art, but never breaching the trust of his patients . . . He sees all aspects of pain . . . a palace, and a leper asylum, this is his world."

To be both master over and witness to the sick and diseased—*this* was what young Jean-Martin wanted for himself. And so he began his training at the School of Medicine in Paris, the Faculté, at the center of the city, off the rue de l'École de Médecine. A thin, pale young man, with long black hair and a small black mustache, Charcot spent most of his free time sketching scenes from the Latin Quarter rather than mingling with the other students, many of them fellow children of the lower and middle bourgeoisie who had enthusiastically embraced the credo of upward mobility captured in the exhortation of statesman François Guizot: "Enrich yourself!" In 1853 he presented his doctor's thesis, in which he differentiated between the symptoms and lesions of gout and those of chronic rheumatism. For the next ten years, Charcot steadily and tirelessly worked his way up through the ranks of the medical hierarchy until he had built himself an impressive enough portfolio in teaching and research to earn a hospital post in 1862. At the age of thirty-seven, he was nominated to the Salpêtrière clinic in Paris, and he accepted a chaired position there in 1882.

Charcot had first entered the Salpêtrière as a student on January 1, 1852, passing through the great arched gateway that allowed the visitor, in a single glance, to take in the entire grand facade, along with its imposing dome, reminiscent of the Hôtel des Invalides. But behind this grand exterior lay a dark and grubby institutional history: originally built as an arsenal in 1634, the Salpêtrière had been transformed by a royal edict in 1656 into a public hospital or asylum to shelter destitute women and prostitutes. Treatment of the inmates ranged from neglectful to outright abusive: the most disturbed of its inmates—those restricted to the wing for insane women—often had their feet and hands bound by chains and their bodies confined in large iron rings affixed to the walls. Some were kept in pits, which, during winter, were invaded by rats. In September 1792 the Salpêtrière entered a gruesome chapter when a revolutionary mob notoriously stormed the gates and raped and massacred forty-five female prisoners and a few prison chaplains, whom the mob suspected of aiding a counterrevolutionary plot. It was not until 1800 that the inmates' iron shackles were replaced with straitjackets. As the nineteenth century progressed, the Salpêtrière eventually became the largest asylum in Europe, housing anywhere from five to eight thousand inhabitants.

While most medical practitioners saw the Salpêtrière as a place to be avoided, a "Versailles of misery" rather than a site of scientific innovation, Charcot, who had by now turned exclusively to the study of neurological disorders, saw its large and diverse patient population as providing an excellent opportunity for the comparative study of disease. It was nothing less, he declared, than an immense "living pathological museum." When Charcot returned to the Salpêtrière in 1862 as an attending physician, his first step, undertaken with his colleague Alfred Vulpian, was to attempt an inventory of the massive patient population, which was divided into two primary categories of inpatients. The psychiatric section contained the insane, *les aliénés*, who numbered between one and two thousand. Another three thousand patients, mostly elderly women suffering from chronic disorders of the nervous and musculoskeletal systems, were also housed there. He and Vulpian roamed the wards together, beginning the arduous task of compiling, for the first time in that institution's history, detailed medical case histories, which would allow physicians to follow the patients and, upon death, relate their clinical record with autopsy findings. They heard stories of lifelong suffering and slow, painful decline; they saw hands gnarled into claws futilely grasping at the thin bed sheets, limbs akimbo. Surrounded by the disarray of a misunderstood and mislabeled population of Paris's most diseased and crippled bodies, Charcot was determined to transform the hospital from a "a prison and an asylum of unwanted womanhood" into one of the great clinical research centers in the world. And he did.

To wrest order out of the chaos before him, Charcot turned the clinical observation of his patients into a kind of divining art form. Doctors at the School of Medicine in Paris had already begun, for the first time, to correlate clinical symptoms in living patients with anatomical lesions identified during postmortem examinations. In this way they were able to determine that jaundice pointed to an ailment of the liver, while frothy sputum was frequently a sign of cardiac or pulmonary distress. Charcot went one step further, placing primary importance on the close observation of his *living* subjects: "It is not on an inert corpse," he wrote, "that one can chart the incessant movements that life, with its infinite variations of movements, impresses on all parts of the human body." He called his method the "anatomo-clinical" method. Working under the supposition that each patient's external symptoms related to some kind of internal state of deformation and degeneration in the form of anatomic lesions, Charcot concluded that these lesions were responsible for such previously enigmatic afflictions as epilepsy, multiple sclerosis, strokes, and other neurodegenerative conditions. His penetration of disease required the ability to comprehend, in a single glance, an essential image of the inner disorder from a variety of superficial appearances, a skill that he had honed during his earlier years as an aspiring artist. He was able to trace the origin of these disorders further still due to recent developments in cellular pathology. He used a new microscope developed by Rudolf Virchow, a German doctor who, in 1858, had advanced cell theory by demonstrating that tissues were composed of cells that maintained a normal order unless disrupted or destroyed by disease states. Over the years Charcot expanded the facilities of the Salpêtrière to facilitate his increasingly complex forays into neurological diseases, adding a laboratory with the latest microscopic equipment and both outpatient and inpatient services. There was also a museum of pathologic anatomy, with an attached studio for modeling and photography. All day, every day, doctors and interns in each of these departments threw themselves into documenting and cracking the code of unknown diseases that appeared daily as cruel and vengeful scourges on the bodies of their victims.

For Charcot, as for other men of science in his generation, the classification of disease—in his case, of *les maladies nerveuses*—was as important as its treatment. Their methods held out the tantalizing possibility of a complete knowledge of the human being, including mysteries of the brain and nervous system. Because these areas had previously been so shrouded in ignorance, Charcot's zeal for applying new technologies and knowledge to the field resulted in its becoming one of the most dynamic areas of modern medicine in the 1870s and 1880s. His approach and dedication came to be seen as ultimate proof of the kind of insight medicine could bring to the human condition.

In the twenty years between his arrival at the Salpêtrière and his nomination as the first Professor of Diseases of the Nervous System at the Faculty of Medicine, the first position in the world to be devoted to clinical neurology, Charcot essentially founded the field of modern neurology. His reputation grew through the publication of a series of studies and his innovative teaching techniques. The general public was made aware of the medical breakthroughs occurring at the Salpêtrière in reviews such as *Iconographie Photographique de la Salpêtrière* and *Nouvelle Iconographie de la Salpêtrière*. In these journals, which were even discussed and debated in the newspapers and popular novels of the day, readers were presented with case histories of Charcot's patients, ghoulish photographs of naked men and women with distended bellies, bulging joints, and spasmed limbs, feebly propped up with pedestals or umbrellas, juxtaposed with bland descriptions of the symptoms in the most current medical language.

It was into this heady world that Sigmund Freud ventured when he arrived in Paris to study with Charcot in the fall of 1885. He first caught a glimpse of the professor's genius through his teaching courses and lectures. By the time Sigmund Freud had arrived in Paris, Charcot was in the habit of giving his weekly Friday clinical lecture in a cavernous lecture hall at the Salpêtrière, which could hold four hundred people. As visitors entered from the rear and walked past the wooden benches, their attention was instantly drawn to the low platform at the front, where they saw statues of patients in contorted, anguished poses, plaster casts of bulbous deformities, and multicolored anatomic drawings of brains and spinal cords, which were carefully laid out like so many altar icons. As a backdrop to this staging was a gigantic painting of Philippe Pinel breaking the irons from the wrists and ankles of the insane in 1795, a not-so-subtle reminder that the upcoming display was only the most recent step in a long and lofty history of noble medical liberation. The doors flung open and Charcot entered swiftly and resolutely, a force of nature. With his low forehead and pronounced jowls, his cold, penetrating gaze and stocky body, Charcot bore more than a passing resemblance to Napoléon. He was followed in formal procession by his entourage of physicians and interns who assisted him in running the school of the Salpêtrière. Staring out at the audience assembled before him, Charcot took a deep breath and immediately launched into his formal presentation of whatever specific neurological disease—Parkinson's, hysteria, multiple sclerosis, or paralysis—was on the agenda. While most doctors who lectured at the time relied on knowing asides and rhetorical flourishes, Charcot's lectures were stripped of all unnecessary affectation or ornament. He spoke precisely, carefully, as if to ensure that no one would misunderstand him. Freud, who had already been won over by the master's energy and lively intellect, quickly stopped attending other doctors' lectures, so convinced was he that they had little more to offer than "well-constructed rhetorical performances." Charcot threw himself entirely into these talks, mimicking different clinical signs—the mask of facial paralysis, the spasmodic muscular rigidity of a patient suffering from Parkinson's disease—or, when words began to fail him, turning to graphic diagrams, enlargements of microscopic examinations, statuettes, actual anatomical specimens, and the new technology of photography to make himself clear.

Freud found these lectures to be wholly absorbing, calling them "a little work of art in construction and composition," particularly the way in which the great master would explain in vivid detail his train of thought. In thus revealing his doubts and hesitations, Charcot seemed to reduce the gulf between teacher and pupil. His lectures were based on exhaustive, interminable research—from the latest medical journals in French, German, and Italian, to clippings from newspapers or books that had caught his eye, to notes he made during his extensive readings in literature, art, and history. Patients were wheeled out onto the platform—sometimes alone, sometimes in groups—where they were questioned, examined briefly, and held up as examples of one disease or another. He liked to bring out groups of patients with slightly different problems to compare and contrast. Or sometimes he would bring in three or four examples of patients suffering from the same disease, in order to show the breadth of clinical expression for common disorders. Prognosis of the patient was usually discussed after he or she had left the room, or it was given in Latin. The medical advances accomplished in those lectures were truly breathtaking. Charcot and his students were working on the cutting edge of neurological research, foraying into diseases like multiple sclerosis, tabetic arthropathies, and amyotrophic lateral sclerosis (ALS)—all pathological conditions so recently identified that they were frequently ignored in the textbooks of the period. And the skill with which he diagnosed and distinguished specific neurological disorders recalled to Freud nothing less than Adam identifying and naming the animals.

In addition to these clinical lectures, Charcot began holding more informal lectures—the famed Tuesday lessons—in 1882, drawing on the most interesting cases from his outpatient service and aimed at initiating students into the difficulties of diagnosis and practice. By the time Freud had arrived in Paris, Charcot was increasingly devoting these public lectures to "hysterical" conditions like Parkinson's and epilepsy, which could not be obviously linked to any specific anatomical lesion, and had therefore been relegated to the unidentified category of *névroses*: disorders that involved the nervous system but could not yet be classified. In the mid-1870s, the work on hysteria at the Salpêtrière first leaped to public notice with the publication of the first three volumes of *Photographic Iconography of the Salpêtrière* under the editorship of Charcot's assistant, Désiré-Magloire Bourneville. These books drove the reality of hysteria home with their graphic pictures of those suffering from various neurological diseases and those in the throes of hysteric episodes. Accompanying the photos were various tables, graphs, and other statistics that conferred upon hysteria the status of objective disease, while its more prurient aspects—case studies with salacious sexual details and accounts of delirious fantasies—were delivered with a flair that recalled the newspaper *faits divers* that fed the baser, voyeuristic appetites of the general public.

Although one of the oldest identified mental disorders, with a recorded history going back to ancient Egypt and Greece, hysteria had been largely ignored by medical practitioners until the nineteenth century. However, in the final decades of that century, hysteria became a visible, if not notorious, affliction, and French men and women saw a rapid rise in the number of diagnosed hysterics: in Charcot's clinic at the Salpêtrière, they were coming in at a rate of one a day. The victims of hysteria were predominantly working-class, young, unmarried women, who, it was widely believed, had acquired the disease hereditarily and were now experiencing outbreaks due to some sort of "dynamic lesion" or psychologically traumatic event that had acted as an agent provocateur. The chief symptoms of hysteria were convulsions, spasmodic seizures, and feelings of strangulation. Faintings and swoonings, paralysis, coughing, and trancelike states were also frequently involved. It was a particularly frustrating disease at a time when the practitioners of science were bent on classification and were more comfortable with the idea that each disease had fixed and identifiable defining marks. But Charcot, astoundingly and elegantly, subsumed the seemingly random symptoms under positive laws. He argued that, based on his attentive and repeated observations, the symptoms of hysterical attacks revealed themselves on a completely predictable basis. Charcot believed it to be a real and curable malady, the primary cause of which lay in hereditary degeneration of the nervous system.

These presentations were responsible for popularizing Charcot's theories and for cementing his reputation in the larger public. While Charcot saw his work as making illness and disease more knowable, and hence more manageable, others were worried about the implications of what he was discovering. At the time, the relationship between the central nervous system and human behavior was increasingly being explored in literary, artistic, and legal circles as a growing number of laypeople began relying on a neurological vocabulary of hysteria, degeneration, and heredity to explain crime and social deviance for the nation as a whole. To many, these forces seemed to be overpowering the older values that had served as the backbone of Victorian sense and sensibility—family, religion, and social hierarchy—only to be replaced, or so announced the front pages of mass circulation newspapers, by divorce, the occult, and dangerous class warfare. Rapid industrialization and the rhythms of urban living were creating new stresses that now seemed to be overwhelming the nervous system. Doctors found themselves diagnosing more cases of "melancholy," "neurasthenia," and, of course, "hysteria," which they declared a direct result of the cacophonous nature of urban life, while social reformers and politicians ominously warned of a variety of modern epidemics—of syphilis, of alcoholism, of delinquency—that seemed symptomatic of the nation's rotten core. So it was unsurprising that the audience attending Charcot's Tuesday lessons, along with Sigmund Freud and the other students and doctors, also included journalists and public officials, as well as hospital dignitaries and youthful interns, curious bourgeoisie and personalities from the stage. The philosopher Henri Bergson, the sociologist Émile Durkheim, the writers Guy de Maupassant and Edmond de Goncourt, the actress Sarah Bernhardt—all were frequent attendees at these star-studded presentations. There would also routinely be representatives from around the world—the United States, Germany, even Japan—all eager to witness for themselves the great doctor's virtuosic gift for observation and analysis.

Laypeople watching the young women suffering from attacks— loss of consciousness, rigidity, foaming at the mouth, violent or tear-ridden outbursts, and delusions—found them chaotic and inexplicable, but Charcot and his colleagues underscored that they were as predictable and orderly in evolution as other diseases. He cut through everything that he deemed superficial or irrelevant to the diagnosis—often these were sordid details of emotional and physical abuse or painful personal history—and watched for signs of the physical elaboration of the four main periods of a hysterical attack: epileptic, "clown," *grands mouvements*, and *attitudes passionnelles*.

It was thus, during one of his Tuesday lessons, on February 7, 1888, that he had a young woman suffering from hysteroepilepsy brought into the amphitheater on a stretcher. Having identified her three hysterogenic points—on her back, under her left breast, and on her leg—Charcot instructed the intern to touch one of them, immediately provoking an attack.

"Now, here we have the epileptoid phase," Charcot calmly began, calling attention above his patient's groans and squeals to her arched back.

"Now here comes the phase of emotional outbursts, which fuses with the back arching . . ." he continued, noting how, thus far, the attack resembled true epilepsy. In order to identify the attack as a truly hysterical one, Charcot instructed the intern to compress the ovarian region. The attack ceased and resumed again only when the compression was released.

As the young woman began contracting and contorting, Charcot turned to the audience and continued talking.

"Mother, I am frightened . . ." the female patient called out.

"Note the emotional outburst," he continued. "If we let things go unabated, we will soon return to the epileptoid behavior."

"Oh! Mother."

"Again, note the screams," Charcot steadily observed. "You could say it is a lot of noise over nothing," he added drily. "True epilepsy is much more serious and also much more quiet."

And with that he nodded quickly to an assistant, who swiftly and smoothly removed the quivering patient and brought out a new one.

These young hysterics and Charcot's capacity to decipher their symptoms as they passed various dissociative twilight states of consciousness left an indelible impression on the young Freud and would have important implications for his own theory of the unconscious. He found the energy and intellectual excitement coiled within the sixty-year-old scientist electrifying, and he found himself daring to hope that some of this greatness might be passed on to him. Charcot's antitheoretical streak—"Theory is fine," he would growl, "but that doesn't prevent facts from existing"—led the Frenchman to trust his careful observation of his patients over the opinions of experts or the abstract assumptions of medical textbooks. From the mid-1880s, when Charcot began to discuss "autosuggestion," or self-hypnotism, as a mechanism for the mind-body interaction in hysteria, he incorporated a psychological dimension into what had originally been a purely somatic conception of the disease. It was Charcot's use of hypnosis in an attempt to discover an organic basis for hysteria that stimulated Freud's own interest in the psychological origins of neurosis. Freud recalled hearing him say that the greatest satisfaction a man could have was to see something new . . . to recognize it as new. By being willing to see hysteria as something real and new that could be treated by appealing to the laws of reason and the new technologies of science and medicine, Charcot had thrown the whole weight of his authority behind a disease that had, up to this point, been studiously ignored. In Freud's mind this was nothing short of a smaller version of the "act of liberation" Pinel had committed when he freed the inmates of the Salpêtrière from their chains.

On January 19, 1886, Freud first attended one of Charcot's famed soirées at his opulent mansion on the boulevard Saint-Germain, where the most fashionable and notable representatives of arts and letters, science and society, regularly gathered: the famed scientist Louis Pasteur, statesmen like Léon Gambetta and Pierre Waldeck-Rousseau, Charcot's patient and friend the emperor of Brazil, and writers such as Alphonse Daudet, Théodore de Banville, Jules Claretie, Edmond de Goncourt, and Émile Zola, among others. Freud was so nervous that he devoted the entire day to preparing for his debut, spending fourteen francs on the barber and on new clothes for the occasion (white gloves, white tie, and even a new shirt). Wracked by anxiety, he even took a little cocaine to "untie my tongue" on his way out the door of his hotel room. When he arrived at his destination, Freud marveled at the elegantly appointed salon in Charcot's home, which was like another world for him—the stained-glass windows and walls hung with heavy silken tapestries and exquisite artwork, the cabinets crammed with Hindu antiques and Chinese artifacts.

Although he could seem quite severe and imposing, Charcot was also a very social person and liked nothing better than to open up his home on Tuesday nights when, after a family dinner with a few select guests, the Charcots entertained with large receptions from October until May. It did not have the same formal function as some of the other salons, like the Daudets' gatherings on Thursdays, where artistic and literary relationships—and even movements—were forged. But it allowed Charcot's students to mix with their professors and other notable personalities, while sampling the delightful culinary offerings provided by Mme Charcot. The conversation was always sparkling and wide-ranging, tripping easily from science to art to politics. For Sigmund Freud these gatherings offered something entirely new and unexpected—most notably a fascinating glimpse at his mentor's family and domestic life.

Jean-Martin Charcot had devoted the same determined energy to cultivating his domestic empire as he had to his professional life.

In 1864, at the age of thirty-nine, Charcot had married Augustine Durvis, a twenty-seven-year-old widow with a seven-year-old child, Marie. Augustine was herself the daughter of a prominent and wealthy clothier in Paris who also collected paintings. She was a pleasant-looking woman, a skilled cook, and a talented painter and potter. She brought 450,000 francs to the marriage, as well as the prospect of inheriting all her father's estate and a portion of her grandparents' estate. Charcot, by contrast, only brought to the marriage 29,000 francs and a half-interest in a country house north of Paris. Mme Charcot was devoted to her husband and constructed a life around making sure he wanted for nothing. A year after they married, the Charcots welcomed a daughter, Jeanne, into the world; then, in 1867, came their son, Jean-Baptiste. The Charcot family was a close-knit unit. Jean-Martin doted on his children, frequently taking them on trips or going on long walks with them. He was a great animal lover, and there were always dogs of all sizes running about the Charcot home; for a while, Charcot even had a little monkey from South America, which had a place of her own near him at the dining table, where she would sit on a child's high chair with a bib while the family enjoyed leisurely, sumptuous meals together. At night the Charcots often retired together to a workshop in the house, where Jean-Martin painted and his wife and the girls worked with clay, leather, metal, and glass. Mme Charcot was an avid artist and patron of the decorative arts whose work was also displayed in contemporary art exhibits.

Like any family, of course, they had their struggles. Jean-Baptiste, although devoted to his father, was a headstrong child who early on developed a fascination for all things maritime. Sailor suits, toy boats, and books about exploration and navigation were the supplies for his most ardent dreams. Jean-Martin initially chalked up such ideas to typical childlike enthusiasms. But as time passed, he witnessed his son's interest in the sea intensifying, passing from mere fancy to a veritable obsession. Jean-Martin was strenuously opposed to his son's youthful ambition to become a sailor—any son of his must follow in his footsteps and become a doctor, he frequently reminded Jean-Baptiste. And Jean-Baptiste knew in his heart of hearts that his father's wishes would prevail. In any case, disobeying or disappointing his father was a thought Jean-Baptiste could scarcely fathom. But while Sigmund Freud was eagerly soaking up Charcot's lessons, hardly able to believe his good fortune at being able to enter the great professor's private circle, Jean-Baptiste took up his medical studies with some reluctance.

Among Charcot's close friends—and patients—was the famous author Alphonse Daudet, whom Freud had an opportunity to meet at one of the soirées. "A magnificent face! . . . a resonant voice, and very lively in his movements," Freud observed. Daudet was a great favorite of Charcot, who preferred ending his Tuesday evenings conversing exclusively with the writer as the doctor's young disciples savored midnight chocolate and buttered toasts and attempted to eavesdrop on the lively exchange between the two friends. Yet Daudet was far from thriving; Charcot had taken over his care a short time earlier, having warned the author in May 1882 that he was most definitely sick with tertiary syphilis manifesting as tabes dorsalis, the result of the degeneration of nerve cells and fibers in the spinal cord. Gradually, patients suffering from this form of syphilis could expect to experience an increased inability to control their movements— one could pick out the victims of the disease by their distinctive shuffling walk—before general paralysis would set in. Alphonse was fifteen years younger than Charcot and had arrived in Paris at the age of seventeen, when Charcot was already well embarked on his medical career. They eventually became neighbors—the Charcots had lived since 1884 at 217, boulevard Saint-Germain and the Daudets since 1885 around the corner at 31, rue de Bellechasse—and the two families came together almost every Thursday, while Alphonse and his wife, Julia, would attend almost every Tuesday night salon hosted by the Charcots. Alphonse had attended Charcot's class presentations at the Salpêtrière between 1882 and 1884, fascinated by the great doctor's keen ability to analyze based on close observation. "A beautiful mind, respectful of literature. His analytic sense is close to mine," Alphonse wrote of his physician and neighbor. Jean-Martin was no less fascinated by Alphonse, once telling the latter's son Léon, "When I chat with Daudet, I feel like I'm under a microscope." Yet Alphonse also felt an uneasy fellowship with Jean-Martin's patients, felt drawn to the parade of human misery whose spasmodic trembling and grimaces of pain so closely echoed his own physical distress. From where he stood, it seemed as if his friend Jean-Martin and he existed on opposite ends of the continuum of health and disease.

The friendship between Jean-Martin Charcot and Alphonse Daudet trickled down to their sons Jean-Baptiste and Léon, who were inseparable from an early age. As a boy Léon often ran over to the Charcots' home to play with Jean-Baptiste and Jeanne. The children chased each other from room to room, dashing through the anteroom where Charcot's gaunt, ill patients waited to be seen. American millionaires and Polish princes were reduced by illness to the role of desperate supplicants. If the Charcot household "was hell for mental suffering," Léon later remembered, "it was a paradise for youth." While Léon was early on exposed to the dangers of illness, Jean-Baptiste Charcot grew up inculcated with the belief that illness could be contained or even mastered. Sigmund Freud was not the only one to be seduced by Jean-Martin Charcot's seemingly limitless ability to recognize and understand disease. In so many ways, young Jean-Baptiste also came to look on his father's abilities as nearly godlike. He spent his childhood surrounded by doctors, by his father's reputation for being able to cure—not even the sight of his father's patients, with their tears and spasms and disfigurations, could mar the harmonious interior of the Charcot family *hôtel particulier*. Jean-Martin bestowed order and reason on his son's world, managing to keep the dangerous specter of irrationality and chaos at bay. For the rest of his life, Jean-Baptiste continued to believe in the supreme nobility of science and of the leading role his father had played in it.

For Léon, however, it was different. He felt considerable ambivalence, even suspicion, when confronted with tales of Charcot's medical prowess—perhaps because he never felt entirely shielded from the threat of disease even in the great doctor's presence. Like his father, he felt curiously aware of those on the receiving end of Charcot's genius, remembering about his time playing with Jean-Baptiste:

Ataxics and melancholiacs squirmed on thirteenth-century Baroque prayer stools, those with muscular atrophy rested their scrawny arms on griffins, serpents, and gargoyles. Imagine Hell and all its suffering in an old antique shop, the spectrum of all pathological curses lodged in a setting from Victor Hugo. This spectacle along with our noisy games must have made the experience seem like a nightmare for those millionaires from Germany, Russia, America, Poland, England, and Turkey who came faithfully and humbly to obtain their prescription for bromide, strychnine, or a thermal cure at Lamalou from the king of neurologists . . .

And when Léon came home from playing with the Charcot children, he returned to the illness of his own father, whose struggle with nervous and muscular disorders associated with late-stage syphilis was a constant shadow over an otherwise happy family life for Léon and his two siblings. Subjected by Jean-Martin Charcot and an array of eminent doctors to a barrage of excruciating yet ultimately ineffective treatments—being suspended for a full minute by his chin and taking injections of fluid extracted from bull testicles were only two of the worst ones—Alphonse became obsessed with his own physical deterioration and began a journal of observations about his illness, which was published after his death as *La Doulou* (*In the Land of Pain*). Watching his father's inexorable decline into a twilight of morphine and pain, the adolescent Léon developed his own obsession with heredity and degeneration and first had the idea that he himself would study medicine in the dual hope of trying to save his father and to avoid becoming him.

Had Léon admitted his anxieties to Professor Charcot, he would not have found much reassurance, for the professor was firmly in the camp of those who believed that neurological disorders were passed on within a family by hereditary transmission. Hysteria, epilepsy, a predisposition to alcoholism, retardation, or syphilis . . . each of these was a member of that dark *famille névropathique* and, thus, a form of degeneracy. Of course, he found that his patients usually attempted to deny this basic truth, which is why he placed such little stock in the family histories his patients attempted to present to him. "It is instinctive, almost a Darwinism," he declared, "for families to hide from themselves and from others their neurological problems. They are the family blemishes. Man does not like fatality.

Instinctively, he searches for another explanation, an accident or chance occurrence, rather than accept that this disease is passed on within his family by hereditary transmission." If this view of human life guided by unforgivable rules seemed harsh, it was nonetheless a view that Charcot had found buttressed by his extensive research in philosophy and literature as well as in medicine. After a lifetime of work dedicated to unlocking the secrets of disease, of liberating men from ignorance about the human body, Charcot had come to the conclusion that our grim destinies were inescapable, already written onto our very cells and tissues. And he found himself continuing to return to a favorite quotation of his: "Man is in the hands of the gods, like a fly in the hands of children. They play with it until they crush it."

In his focus on heredity and, specifically, in his belief that hysteria, along with most neurological and mental diseases and many other chronic diseases, was essentially the result of familial inheritance, Charcot was merely following in the footsteps of a school of thought that used the concept of degeneration to explain mental pathology and physical disease. The theory of degeneration was first introduced by a French psychiatrist named B. A. Morel in the 1840s and became a kind of catchall explanation for everything from criminality to genius. In Morel's view, an organism may adapt to a pathological environment but would conceal this pathology as an aptitude or tendency. In subsequent generations, however, the pathology would reveal itself as a worsening physical or nervous disorder. The end result of degeneration was nothing less than sterility and, finally, death. Cesare Lombroso, an Italian criminologist and physician, furthered the discussion with the publication of his famous 1864 work *Genius and Madness*, followed by his *Genius and Degeneration* in 1887. Taking as examples such figures as Leopardi, Tasso, Byron, Napoléon, Zola, and Poe, Lombroso argued that the nervous sensibility could be so highly developed in geniuses that it was almost a kind of illness, that aesthetic production could, in fact, be stimulated by a kind of psychosis. The young psychiatrist and clinician Valentin Magnan, who had been trained at the Salpêtrière, was primarily responsible in France for the adaptation of organic theories of degenerative mental illness to the neurological science of the day. He even collaborated with Charcot on several publications. It was a powerful theory that only gained more ground as the 1880s progressed. But to a boy like Léon, anxiously watching his ailing father, such theories simply smacked of guilt by association.

With the lessons of Charcot still tumbling about in his brain and a photograph of Notre Dame tucked into his suitcase, Sigmund Freud left Paris on February 28, 1886 (just nine months after Victor Hugo's death), knowing what the new century would require him to do. And on Easter Sunday, April 25, 1886, the *Neue Freie Presse* in Vienna ran a small announcement that would have a lasting impact on the century to come: "Herr Dr. Sigmund Freud, Docent for Nervous Diseases at the University, has returned from his study trip to Paris and Berlin and has consulting hours at [District] I, Rathhausstrasse No 7, from 1 to 2:30."

TWO

The Group of Five

Our acts make or mar us, we are the children of our own deeds.
—Victor Hugo

Dinner at Riche's with Flaubert, Zola, Turgenev, Alphonse Daudet. A dinner of people of talent who esteem each other—and that we would like to make monthly in the coming winters.
—Edmond de Goncourt (April 14, 1874)

News that Victor Hugo had taken ill was announced on May 18, 1885. Hugo had been sick for days, since May 14, when he had dined with his family and Ferdinand de Lesseps, the mastermind behind the Suez Canal and a lifelong friend of the poet and novelist. One can only imagine what the two men talked about when they had been left alone. Perhaps they chatted about old age (Hugo was eighty-three and Lesseps only three years younger) or about their families (both were devoted grandfathers). They would certainly have talked about Lesseps's recent induction, with Hugo's support, into the Académie Française; or perhaps Lesseps confided in the poet about his latest and most difficult project to date: the construction of the Panama Canal. But if Lesseps was still engaged in wrestling with the world, Hugo had largely retired from it, especially since the death of Juliette Drouet, his longtime mistress, in 1882. Since then he mostly passed his days writing in solitude or spending time with his two grandchildren, Georges and Jeanne, whose playful insouciance he had so movingly captured in his bestselling collection of poems, *The Art of Being a Grandfather*. And so the conversation between the two old men drifted between past and future until eleven p.m., when Hugo bade Lesseps farewell and went to bed. In the middle of the night he complained of feeling ill, and the family doctor, Émile Allix, was immediately summoned. Despite his ministrations, Hugo's condition worsened, and the news spread through the capital. For four more days, the nation held its breath, waiting and praying that the poet would recover. Reporters kept a round-the-clock vigil in front of his residence at 130, avenue d'Eylau, eager for any news his doctors might give them, sure that the slightest cough, change in temperature, or sickbed utterance could be spun into a riveting anecdote for their readers. Cardinal Guibert, archbishop of Paris, arrived in the hopes of obtaining the great man's last confession and was politely yet promptly turned away by the family. "Victor Hugo is expecting death but does not desire the services of a priest."

That the prospect of Victor Hugo's death should inspire such drama was entirely to be expected. He was a superstar before the age of superstars, a literary figure whose personal and political life had attained mythic proportions in his country and among his contemporaries. Part poet, part prophet, part politician, Victor Hugo had commanded the public's attention for the better part of his life, even during his exile to the craggy outpost of Guernsey following the coup d'état in 1851, when President Louis-Napoléon seized control of the government, specifically targeting liberal members of the National Assembly, of which Hugo was one. If at various moments over the past half century he had served as a stark reminder of the political divisiveness that tore France apart with such dismal regularity, in his later years Hugo had become something else—a living testament to national reconciliation after the horrors of the Franco-Prussian War and the Paris Commune, a memorial to the healing power of love. In his life, as in his works, he seemed to embody the very century he lived in, capturing the doubts, contradictions, and aspirations of those long hundred years. Throughout his full life, he had charged from one extreme to another: a former monarchist turned ardent republican, an anticlerical spiritualist and advocate of human rights, an admirer of Napoléon I and staunch critic of Napoléon III, an opponent of the Commune and a defender of the Communards, a scandalous womanizer and a devoted grandfather: he was something for everyone. In his work he had become the conscience of a nation, writing prophetically and powerfully about what was most base and most sublime in the human heart.

More than anything, people wanted to know about the poet's last moments of life, the final prophetic statement or gesture. Many journalists, determined to maintain his aura of greatness, reported that even in his dying breaths there were flashes of literary genius. One newspaper claimed he managed a flawless recitation of Spanish poetry—in Spanish. Another confidently announced that he uttered the prophetic alexandrine, "Here we have the struggle 'twixt day and night." Most accounts agree, though, that in the end, his very final words were reserved for his beloved grandchildren, Jeanne and Georges.

Since the death of their own father in early childhood, Victor Hugo had been a towering figure in Jeanne and Georges's lives, a nearly omnipotent presence. They had become his companions, his children, replacing those he had already lost: Léopoldine in 1843, then François-Victor in 1873, and Charles, the children's father, to apoplexy in 1871. Hugo's youngest child, Adèle, had been trapped in her own private hell of madness for the past seventeen years, confined to an asylum. So, in his bereavement, Hugo had adopted his grandchildren as his own, finding in their childhood the inspiration he needed to fuel the creative embers that old age and a lifetime of political battles had left weak and cooling. Out of their games and unabashed enthusiasm, he created a parable about second chances, about the redemption of an old man through the innocence of youth. And now they stood at his deathbed, his adolescent creations, watching as the person who had dominated, had *invented* their lives, slipped away. Georges, eighteen years old, was so overwrought that he kept bursting into tears and fleeing the room to hide. But his younger sister, sixteen-year-old Jeanne, remained there, trembling, with cheeks hollowed by weariness, keeping watch.

Episodes of their lives together played through her mind. She recalled the request that her "papapa" had made four years earlier: "Remember everything for me." They had been at the second-floor window of their home as a huge throng of people flocked below to celebrate his seventy-ninth birthday. It was February 27, 1881, a cold, slate-gray day. A chill wind whipped through Paris. She remembered that there had been flowers everywhere, wagons and trucks full, sent from as far away as Nice, all for her grandfather's birthday. The streets were also filled with children—over 50,000 of them marched at the head of the procession of 500,000 men and women jubilantly crying out, "Father!" On that day, after standing at the balcony for some time, her grandfather had briefly returned inside to warm himself, and when he reappeared at the open window, the crowd roared with delight at seeing him again. For two hours, despite the cold, Victor Hugo remained, smiling and gesturing as throngs of Parisians filed by him, singing songs, cheering for him, waving banners with the names of some of his books and characters scrawled across them: "Gavroche," "Cossette," and *The Art of Being a Grandfather*. The streets echoed with the cries: "Long live Hugo!" "Long live the glory of France!" "Long live the Republic!"

Eleven-year-old Jeanne and thirteen-year-old Georges stood on either side of him, also waving to the crowd, throwing kisses, celebrities in their own right, shining in their grandfather's reflected glory. As she so often did, Jeanne instinctively reached out to take his hand and was stunned by the sound of sobbing. When she looked up, she saw tears streaming down her papapa's face, dampening his white beard. "Remember everything for me," he'd whispered.

And now, as he lay dying, her grandfather had yet another request. Summoning Jeanne and Georges to his bedside, he kissed them each on the forehead and said, tenderly, "Be happy! Think of me. Love me. My darlings . . ." But his very last words were directed at his favorite, his granddaughter, Jeanne: "Adieu, Jeanne, adieu."

Although not her father, this man more than any other had given birth to her, had made her what she was—*Jeanne au pain sec*, the granddaughter of a nation, who was honored each year on her birthday with gifts from schoolchildren as if she were a princess. She had passed her whole life in his presence, living to please and entertain him. She had been adored and spoiled by him and had been his muse. She could not imagine being happy without him, nor loving anyone as much as she loved him.

When death finally claimed Victor Hugo at around 1:30 a.m. on May 22, men and women throughout the nation joined together in a shared display of grief and respectful devotion the likes of which none had ever seen. Journalists obsessively recorded every feature of the prestigious and famous admirers who came to pay their final respects. A special envoy was sent on behalf of the municipal government and the Chamber of Deputies. The great actress Sarah Bernhardt dramatically appeared at the Hugo home dressed completely in white and brought with her an immense crown of white roses. Mourning visitors left calling cards on a table outside the residence and waited in line for hours to sign the official register, hoping to inscribe their names onto this moment in history. The press hungrily seized on every detail of his final will and testament: his decision to leave half of his fortune to Adèle, his insane, institutionalized daughter—his only remaining living child—and the rest to Jeanne and Georges, as well as his gift of fifty thousand francs to the poor. Hugo had requested, in a gesture at once grandiose and lachrymose, that his body be conveyed to his grave in a pauper's hearse with no religious rites. But although he had asked to be buried with his wife at the cemetery in Villequier, the government decided instead to have a state funeral and place his remains in the Panthéon. Editors and politicians around the globe rushed to expound on the significance of his passing. "The death of Victor Hugo is an event which touches the whole civilized world," the *Times* of London intoned.

For eight days Hugo's embalmed corpse remained in his bed, his face preserved in an expression of noble beatitude, while his survivors and his government haggled over funeral arrangements. Every morning for those eight days, Jeanne had gone into the cold, quiet room of her papa to kiss his lifeless hand and sit beside him. In the muted light of the early morning, his features looked gentle and peaceful, almost normal. Only the feel of his hand, rigid and unresponsive, and the sounds of weeping from the rooms beyond prevented her from imagining that he might soon wake up and smile at her as he had done so many other mornings. Soon they would take him to lie in state under the Arc de Triomphe, where his public could come and be close to him for one last night before he was buried. He had promised, shortly before his death, "You might never see me again, but I will always be there, near you, nearer to you than I am right now." And yet he seemed so far away.

Out of the dark, mourning house and into the early morning day, pallbearers took her grandfather as Jeanne and her brother and mother followed. As they placed him in the pauper's hearse, she felt a kind of panic at the thought that he was leaving her forever. She closed her eyes; in her mind she begged him for some sign. It was just as the driver urged the horses forward that Jeanne glimpsed a sudden flash as a small silver star fell from the funeral sheet covering the coffin. Jeanne bent down, scooped it up, and closed her fingers tightly around it. For her entire life, she kept this talisman, this confirmation that she and her grandfather shared a bond of such strength as to defy death.

The funeral procession began at noon with a twenty-one-gun salute and the melancholy music of Chopin's funeral march and set off down the Champs-Élysées, through the most elegant addresses in Paris: place de la Concorde, boulevard Saint-Germain, boulevard Saint-Michel. A few anarchists waved red flags, but for the most part the masses remained quiet and calm. On that warm, fine day, over two million people filled the city, some to watch, others to participate. Anyone with a claim to intellectual or political distinction was permitted to walk in the procession. In addition to the usual range of state, city, departmental, and communal officials, there were also delegations representing a motley assortment of associations and special interests: from the Ligue des Patriotes to shooting and gymnastics organizations; from various societies of freethinkers to a committee of Creoles from Martinique and Guadeloupe. The procession was so long that by the time the head had arrived at the Panthéon for the final ceremony, the rear had not yet left the Arc de Triomphe. In all, it lasted over eight hours, an event not to be forgotten, a defining moment in the life of Third Republic France.

Eighteen-year-old Léon Daudet spent the entire week following the poet's death offering solicitous attention to his good friend

Georges and his pretty younger sister, Jeanne. But Léon found the funeral itself grandiose and rather pompous—or at least that is how he remembered it in his memoirs, *Fantômes et Vivants*, in 1914. He was nonetheless touched by the sincere grief of his two friends. He was moved to see how openly they wept for their grandfather "without any concern about protocol or vanity." Léon marched in the procession with the Hugo family members and intimate relations, while his father, Alphonse Daudet, stood among other writers, poets, and savants assembled to honor the great man. The day's events had placed a great deal of strain on the elder Daudet, who was suffering from an illness for which there seemed to be no cure. He was terrified to find himself growing weaker and weaker, at times even unable to control his limbs. Before the funeral Alphonse had been incapable of signing his name to the guest register because his hands were shaking so. "Surrounded, watched—it was terrible," he wrote in the diary he had recently begun. Luckily, Léon had been there to guide his hand, although the father could not help but feel embarrassed and annoyed that he'd been reduced to such reliance on his son.

He had just begun treatments for his syphilis, administered by his friend and neighbor, Dr. Jean-Martin Charcot. He dreaded those examinations, felt humiliated having to expose his naked body to the painful probing and clinical assessment of his friend. But Charcot was his last chance; he had no choice but to submit. Throughout the funeral Alphonse had wondered if there was any hope that he could ever be rid of this disease or if he, too, would join the list of men—Maupassant, Flaubert, Baudelaire, Jules de Goncourt—who had limped about town with the debaucheries of their youth written on their rotting, syphilitic bodies.

During the funeral Jean-Martin Charcot stood among his colleagues with his customary air of implacable, watchful distance. He sensed the fervor of the crowd, the connection existing between them and this man they had come to idolize. He hadn't known Hugo personally but had admired his work, his eye for the sublime and the debased, his almost unhinged artistry. He'd heard the stories about the great man's daughter, Adèle, who'd returned from halfway around the world—the Caribbean, perhaps?—her mind shattered beyond repair. The family had hidden her away as soon as she was back on French soil, an impulse he understood. Charcot had frequently observed that, out of a kind of instinct, families often hid from themselves and tried to hide from others the *tares nerveuses* that stain them. How interesting to think of a family of such extremes—polar opposites, really: a genius and a madwoman.

Several blocks away, Charcot's son, Jean-Baptiste, stood with his mother and sister watching the procession from a balcony overlooking the street. Eighteen years old, tall and athletic, with the sort of dark and exotic features that made women blush, Jean-Baptiste looked down on the crowds with a mixture of awe and envy. He had never before witnessed such an outpouring of emotion, such a sense of national solidarity. But all thoughts of the immortal poet faded when he saw his friend Léon Daudet walking by with the members of the Hugo family. How lucky, Jean-Baptiste thought, to be able to enjoy such intimacy with Georges and especially with Jeanne Hugo. He, like everyone, knew about her unusual life with the great poet. Today she looked so alone, so vulnerable—he felt an almost overpowering wish to comfort her.

In a few months, he and Léon Daudet would begin medical school together. It was, he knew, a privilege—his sister, also named Jeanne, would have given everything to become a doctor. But privately he despaired of ever being able to live up to his father's reputation. Part of him just wanted to board the next ship to sea and begin life in a strange place with no name and no expectations, to make a future for himself that was his own. But Jean-Martin Charcot had made it clear that his son would become a doctor, and Jean-Baptiste could no more defy his father than his father's patients could.

The Hugos, the Daudets, the Charcots—three famous, prestigious families whose fates were about to pass into the hands of a younger generation: Jeanne, Léon, and Jean-Baptiste. Brought together by the shared burden of their families' fame and reputation, these three young people would face friendship, courtship, marriage, children, divorce, and finally death. To their domestic dramas and intimate heartaches were added expectations of professional and personal greatness—the price one paid for growing up in the bright lights of fame in fin-de-siècle France.

Once Victor Hugo's funeral ceremony was over, Alphonse Daudet and Léon met up at the Café de la Rotonde at the place de l'Observatoire with Alphonse's friends Émile Zola and Edmond de Goncourt and a few others. They were all unusually quiet—still processing the spectacle they had just witnessed, still unsure as to what impact the old man's passing would have on them all. Alphonse, who was always fragile in appearance, was looking particularly tired. Even Zola, who always had something to say, sputtered and sighed like a disconsolate child.

Eighteen-year-old Léon had known them all since he was small, and he now considered a few of them, like Edmond de Goncourt, friends of his own. Some of the people in his father's circle of intimate acquaintances were artists. Others were politicians and many were members of that most elite and splendid upper echelon of Parisian society. But it was the writers who impressed Léon the most, and four in particular stood out: Zola, Edmond de Goncourt, Flaubert, and the Russian writer Ivan Turgenev. For as long as Léon could remember, these men had loomed in the background, acting as a sort of steadfast intellectual constellation for him and his father. When Léon was younger, he had watched the five of them come together for regular gatherings at his family's home or had witnessed his father's pleasure as he prepared to go out to meet them. Even when they were not physically present, their works and ideas informed many of the lengthy conversations between father and son in Alphonse's book-lined study. For, during several years in the 1870s and 1880s, these five men came together at regular intervals to relax and to enjoy one another's company and also to reflect upon the body of work that they had created—or were still creating. Although they self-deprecatingly christened their little club the "Group of Five," or, jokingly, the "Group of Hissed Authors" in reference to the poor reception their works had received when they were adapted to the stage, they in fact represented the leading lights in contemporary literature. At a time of changing literary tastes and cultural upheaval, their dinners together held out the possibility for companionship and understanding for five men whose artistic ideals often put them at odds with their contemporaries and joined them in a fruitful, and sometimes frustrating, web of camaraderie and competitiveness. And to young Léon, at least for a time, they all seemed like giants.

No man stood taller in little Léon's eyes than his beloved father. His devotion to Alphonse was worshipful, fueled by a love both filial and fraternal. Alphonse would shut Léon in his dressing room with him so that they could discuss some topic, occasionally interrupting himself mid-sentence, jabbing his comb through the air to emphasize a point or dunking his head in a basin full of water "in order to clear up our ideas." These were precious, heady hours for Léon, who would be swept up in the intensity and enthusiasm of his father's larger-than-life spirit. But they did not limit their time together to literary discussions. When not deep in the thralls of some translation or expounding on the greatness of Shakespeare, Alphonse could be found swooning over the music of Bizet, Massenet, or Reynaldo Hahn or gesturing enthusiastically at the latest Realist and Post-Impressionist paintings by Millet or Cézanne—his critical evaluation often delivered with a profanity-laced exuberance that delighted his son and horrified his wife. By the time Léon was ten, Alphonse had already begun instructing his son in the ways of swordsmanship; a few years later, he began sharing with Léon his views on women and lovemaking. For example: "The man who, having made a night of it, has not washed himself or made his toilet, is capable of performing the most frightful follies, and is incapable of the meanest train of argument."

But by far the most important lesson Alphonse gave Léon was an appreciation of life and literature—or rather that ineffable bond between the two. Writing informed Alphonse's vision of the world. He took note of everything he saw, from the earnest ultimatums of children to the silky murmurs of ardent lovers in the park. He jotted them all down in little notebooks he kept with him at all times, so that these direct impressions of even the most mundane expressions of human emotion could be transferred into one of his works and confer upon it a greater degree of authenticity. For Léon it was his father's own natural goodness, his soulful intelligence, that enabled him to transmute what would otherwise be a banal, even forgettable sketch of some passing interaction and render it in such a way that it reverberated in the reader's soul. In Léon's eyes his father soared even higher in this capacity than the great Flaubert.

But where Léon saw only perfection, others found flaws. He had heard his father and his friends speak peevishly about the frequently savage reviews of their works by the critics—critics who would not pardon them for their Realism, which departed from the notion of art as it had been bequeathed to the world by Victor Hugo. As Daudet, Zola, and their fellow Realists understood it, French literature had been a stifling procession of classical works until men like Hugo and Alfred de Musset had come along to give them gems such as *Les Orientales* (1829) and *Contes d'Espagne et d'Italie* (1830). These works pulsated with a new energy and dynamism in language that stressed strong emotion, subjectivity, the quest for freedom, and communion with nature. But by the time Zola and the others began to dip their own toes in literary waters, poems about nature and melodramas set in the Middle Ages seemed spiritually out of touch with the scientific flavor of late-nineteenth-century French culture. Victor Hugo remained a revered figure in their eyes, but they were no longer interested in emulating his style. They wanted to create a new way of writing about the world. Secretly, they hoped to replace him.

The five of them—Alphonse Daudet, Gustave Flaubert, Edmond de Goncourt, Émile Zola, and Ivan Turgenev—had all known one another with varying degrees of intimacy before their regular dinners began in the spring of 1874. In the past, men of their ilk would have sought refuge in the famous dinners at Magny's, a well-known Left Bank haunt of writers, artists, and intellectuals of all persuasions, which had begun in 1862 with the gathering of François Veyne, physician to the artistic set, the writer Théophile Gautier, the Goncourt brothers, Flaubert, and the famous critic Sainte-Beuve. George Sand was also eventually made a regular invitee—she was the only woman to be admitted into the group. It was at one of these meetings, on February 28, 1863, that Flaubert and the Goncourts met Turgenev for the first time. The Magny's group met twice a month and intensely debated and discussed everything under the sun—politics, the state of education, the meaning of the word "progress," the state of literary criticism. But eventually these dinners had become too popular, too overrun with politicians and socialites, devolving into tedious social gatherings attended by mediocre literati and hangers-on with vague artistic pretenses. So when Alphonse Daudet, Émile Zola, Edmond de Goncourt, Ivan Turgenev, and Gustave Flaubert decided to start meeting regularly, they hoped they would find something more intimate, more honest—the chance to speak with like-minded writers with absolute candor.

Their first official meeting as a group occurred on April 14, 1874, at Café Riche, the popular haunt of artists and lawyers not far from the Opéra Garnier. The opening of Flaubert's play *The Candidate* had taken place the month before and had bombed so badly that Edmond de Goncourt, who attended the performance, could only describe the audience's reaction to the play as "funereal." As he recorded in his journal—a catty and alarmingly comprehensive account of his and his brother Jules's social universe, which was published posthumously, much to the dismay and outrage of those who appeared in it—the mood of the audience members began with pity, gradually developed into disappointment, and crescendoed into a cruelly vocal display of schadenfreude that not even respect for the venerable talents of the great Gustave Flaubert could keep at bay. After the performance, Goncourt sought out the author in the wings, only to find his friend standing alone on a deserted stage— the actors, no doubt eager to place as much distance between themselves and the lingering aftertaste of such a theatrical flop, had fled. The sight of the great, hulking writer brought low by a work of his own creation, Goncourt confessed, "was both sad and a little surreal, like a total retreat, a collapse . . ."

Upon seeing Goncourt, Flaubert shook himself and attempted to muster an air of relaxed disinterest in the proceedings. But the failure stung: a few days later, he sent Alphonse Daudet a despairing note, confiding in him that even one of the administrators of the theater, a man who had a vested interest in the play being a success, had booed him. Daudet knew what he was feeling, since the theatrical adaptation a few years earlier of his novella *The Arlésienne* enjoyed only a few performances before the production was shut down. Each of the members of the Group of Five, in fact, knew firsthand about theatrical failure: Goncourt's *Henriette Maréchal* had been derided when it opened, while Zola's recent adaptation of *Thérèse Raquin* for the stage had been roundly savaged by the critics. Only Turgenev could not point to a theatrical rout on the Paris stage, although he swore that he had been booed, and almost lynched, in Russia. That was good enough for the others, as they all agreed that there was only one way to respond to such a public humiliation—a feast!

But though they all tried to laugh off the harsh reviews and tepid public reception, such rejection hit a nerve and spoke to the underlying precariousness of their situation in the literary world. Zola best captured that anxiety in his review of *The Candidate* for *Le Sémaphore de Marseilles*, in which he railed against the lack of artistic sensibilities of his fellow Frenchmen. "I feel tears rising, it seems to me that I am bogged down in all this contemporary stupidity," he explained, despairing of a public that clamored only for vaudeville.

Towering above the rest of the assembled writers at Café Riche, Gustave Flaubert, with his massive Norman frame, leonine mustache, and teeth blackened from years of taking mercury to ward off the gradual encroachment of syphilis, was the acknowledged master of the group. The "hermit of Croisset" still enjoyed the solitude of provincial life more than the fêtes and fanfare of Paris. Since the wild success of *Madame Bovary* in 1857, when he was thirty-five, the author, now aged fifty-two, had achieved a level of public acclaim and recognition that, as a young man, toiling away in the obscurity of his family estate outside of Rouen, he could never have imagined. Despite the failure of *The Candidate*, Flaubert was inarguably one of the nation's most illustrious living writers. *Madame Bovary* was both hailed and reviled for ushering in a new kind of writing style, which some termed "Realism" and which ostensibly turned away from the emotionalism and pageantry of Romanticism in search of accurate, objective, detailed, and unembellished depictions of nature or of contemporary life.

Next to him sat his close friend, the Russian writer Ivan Turgenev, whose similarly hulking body and high-pitched, sonorous voice led Goncourt to describe him famously as "the sweet giant, the amiable barbarian, with his white hair falling in his eyes, the deep crease across his brow, like a plowed furrow." With his childlike voice, Goncourt continued, Turgenev charmed everyone whom he met "with this mixture of naiveté and finesse—the seductiveness of the Slavic race, elevated in him by the originality of a superior spirit, by an immense and cosmopolitan knowledge." The son of a retired cavalry officer and a wealthy and, by most accounts, sadistic mother, Turgenev had been raised on an extensive estate as a member of the landed gentry in rural Russia. He attended university in both Moscow and St. Petersburg and then spent four years at the University of Berlin. This plunge into the turbulent waters of European cultural life was, for the young Russian, a life-altering experience. He returned to Russia a changed man, convinced of the superiority of the West and the unsustainable nature of Russian feudal society, and determined to set his views on paper. In works like *The Diary of a Superfluous Man* (1850) or *A Month in the Country* (1855), he captured the uneasy aimlessness of men of his generation. Most famously, in 1852, he published the short-story cycle *A Sportsman's Sketches*, a stark portrait of landowners' mistreatment of their peasants, which, according to legend, actually inspired Czar Alexander II to liberate the serfs. When the first collected edition appeared, Turgenev was jailed for a month in St. Petersburg, then given eighteen months of enforced residence at his family estate. Upon his release Turgenev finally left his native Russia, eager to taste once again the freedom and culture of the European continent. There he met and fell in love with the singer Pauline Viardot, to whom he would remain hopelessly devoted for the rest of his life. He also began writing the sorts of careful character studies for which he would later be known. In novels like *Rudin* and *Home of the Gentry*, he wrote with wry nostalgia about his own generation, "the men of the forties," who had been rendered irrelevant by the Russian defeat in the Crimean War (1854–56). In their stead a new generation of Russian intelligentsia emerged—younger, more radical, less inclined to nuance. This conflict between generations was most powerfully evoked in *Fathers and Sons*, the tale of a brooding young nihilist, Yevgeny Bazarov, and his struggle against the older 1840s liberals. Turgenev considered the work his masterpiece and was severely disappointed at its only modest success. Feeling restless and disillusioned, he began writing several shorter pieces and continued to travel. By the time he joined the Group of Five, he had been bouncing around the major cities and spa resorts of Europe for a few years, delighting all who met him.

By far the most alluring figure that night at Café Riche was the thirty-four-year-old Alphonse Daudet. Daudet had been born in 1840 in Nîmes, in an area of Languedoc that borders on Provence. He came from a family of wealthy bourgeoisie brought low by economic crisis. After trying his hand at teaching, which he loathed, Daudet had moved to Paris in 1857 at the age of seventeen to write. His trajectory was that of countless other provincial would-be literati, newly arrived in the capital. Seeking to scale the heights of Olympus, these young idealists often ended up among the more sordid shadows of bohemia. "A literary life was the sole object of my dreams," he recalled about his first year in the capital. "Sustained by the boundless confidence of youth, poor but radiant, I passed the whole year in my attic versifying." Daudet struggled in obscurity for several years before his first major work, *Letters from My Mill*, appeared in a Parisian paper in 1866 under the pseudonym Marie-Gaston, and was published in book form in 1869. In 1872 he wrote the famous *Prodigious Adventures of Tartarin de Tarascon*, and the three-act drama *The Arlésienne*. But it was *Young Fromont and Old Risler* (1874) that really took the world by storm, making him the most commercially successful of the Group of Five. Critics fell over themselves in praise of the young author, declaring him to possess a rare understanding of both the pathos and the hilarity inherent in the human condition that sparkled in his characters, who seemed remarkably real and typical. Alphonse was a bit embarrassed about his success, especially when in the company of his friends. But he was also grateful for the opportunity to provide for his growing family: in addition to Léon, Alphonse and his wife, Julia Allard, had two other children—Lucien, born in 1883, and Edmée, born in 1886.

Sitting next to Alphonse was his friend and sometime competitor, thirty-four-year-old Émile Zola. Anxious, brilliant, and obdurate, Zola had been born in Paris but was raised in Aix-en-Provence in southern France, the son of a civil engineer of Italian descent. After moving to Paris to complete his high school training, he lived in abject poverty while looking for employment—legend later had it that he had subsisted during these lean years by eating sparrows trapped outside his attic window. After finally getting a job as a clerk at a publishing firm, he supplemented his income by writing articles on various subjects—mostly reviews of books and plays—for different newspapers. He wrote fiction late into the night. Zola's first novel, *Claude's Confession*, was published in 1865; soon after he left his job as a clerk to become a full-time freelance journalist. By the time of the first dinner of the Group of Five in 1874, Zola was well on his way to gaining both the bourgeois respectability and literary recognition he so craved: he had married Alexandrine-Gabrielle Meley, who had been his companion and lover for almost five years, and had already begun work on the series of novels *La Fortune des Rougon* (The Rougon Family Fortune) that, he hoped, would one day rival Balzac's *La Comédie Humaine*.

And finally, there was Edmond de Goncourt—the difficult dandy who, unbeknownst to his friends, was recording the minute details of his active social life in the diary he had started with his beloved brother, Jules. At fifty-two, Edmond belonged to the generation of Flaubert and Turgenev, and like those two, he considered himself well past his literary prime. But he had been a source of outrage and contention as a young man: in 1852 he and his brother had been arrested—although later acquitted—for "outrage against public morality," due to their citation of some vaguely erotic Renaissance verses in one of their articles. Their specialty was the meticulous reconstruction of social environments, both past and present, in which, with a coolly clinical eye, they gathered mountains of detritus from their avid collecting. Their 1864 novel *Germinie Lacerteux* had been one of the first works of Realist literature. It was based on the double life of their plain, seemingly upstanding servant, Rose, who stole their money to pay for nocturnal orgies and men. The book caused quite a scandal when it was published, although it also quickly earned a devoted following: Émile Zola was one of the novel's earliest and most enthusiastic admirers. But Edmond and Jules's success was overshadowed by Jules's death in 1870, of complications from advanced syphilis. The loss of his brother, best friend, and companion was a horrible blow for Edmond. He never fully recovered, and by 1874 his literary output had become negligible.

The group that first came together on April 14, 1874, was both predictable and unlikely. Although of vastly different temperaments, they shared a common frustration with the current state of literary affairs. Each had embraced a style of writing that privileged close observation over melodramatic excess and that sought to convey an accurate and objective approximation of "real life," even if it meant exploring subjects deemed insufficiently heroic or even downright sordid. They used these dinners together to compare and to commiserate—and to blow off some steam. During the course of their first dinner, as Goncourt recounted in his diary, the conversation began with a lengthy discourse on the special aptitudes of the constipated in literature and swiftly gave way to a consideration of the mechanics of the French language. Turgenev had much to say on this topic, complaining that the French language was being wielded like a blunt instrument by nervous and high-strung wordsmiths, who had sadly drained the language of its gorgeous gift of approximation. This was a subject in which Flaubert, in particular, was keenly interested. *Madame Bovary* had changed the way a generation of Frenchmen thought about their native tongue. As a young man, Flaubert had been full of the Romantic fervor of other members of his generation, fed on a tempestuous diet of Hugo sonnets and tales of exotic travels to the Orient. A friend, the poet Louis Bouilhet, warned him of his exaggerated deference to lyricism, and suggested he write a "down-to-earth" novel in the style of Balzac. The young Flaubert initially blanched—Balzac, how crass!—and then reluctantly set about writing the story of Eugène Delmare, a country doctor in Normandy, who died of grief after being deceived and ruined by his wife, Delphine. Over the next five years, Flaubert developed a new attitude toward writing, one that was ruthless in its pursuit of an unrelenting objectivity. He meticulously, almost obsessively, recorded every trait or detail that might illuminate the reality of his characters. In an attempt to master his subject, Flaubert filled notebook upon notebook with minute observations—the creaking sound of carriages, the instantly recognizable swoosh of crinoline. He then painstakingly organized these observations, certain that only the most precise and authentic coordination of these details with his narrative would be able to capture the essential truth of the subject and touch the reader's consciousness through his senses.

In Flaubert's own estimation, his was a struggle against words, an effort to reanimate language with a lyricism and resonance that it otherwise lacked. The result was electrifying. When the finished novel was published by his old friend Maxime Du Camp in the *Revue de Paris* from October 1 to December 15, 1856, *Madame Bovary* produced a scandal. The government found it to contain many passages that were "an outrage to public morals," and the matter was referred to criminal court. After a sensational obscenity trial, Flaubert was finally acquitted on February 7, 1857, with a reprimand. But the work and its author were hailed as signs of a new age in literature. Growing up, Léon was taught to revere his father's friend as a "king," and he later recalled being thoroughly surprised when one day he overheard the writer Barbey d'Aurevilly attacking Flaubert. He had not thought such a thing was possible. Realism was the order of the day, despite Flaubert's protestations to the contrary that he was, and would forever be, "an old, enraged Romantic." Indeed, such inconsistencies frequently drove his would-be followers a bit crazy. Zola was initially shocked to find that Flaubert, whom he had imagined as staunchly and unrepentantly modernist, had enjoyed histrionic outbursts in which he declared, in his booming voice, "that the modern did not exist, that there were no modern subjects."

Flaubert's Realism was in fact Romanticism tempered by pessimism, the pessimism of a generation that had witnessed the abortive revolutions and bitter disappointments of 1848. His quest for absolute "impersonality" (achieved only when the author, hoping to capture certain truths about observed life and society, rigorously and incessantly maintains his position outside his work) led his close friend George Sand, for instance, to reproach him for not intervening in his novels with his own personal convictions. "It seems to me that your school is not concerned with fundamentals—that is, it stops too close to the surface," she wrote him, adding, "We are human beings, first and foremost. At the heart of every story, of every fact, we seek the man." He promptly protested: "As for my 'lack of convictions,' alas! I am only too full of convictions. I am constantly bursting with suppressed anger and indignation. But my ideal of Art demands that the artist reveal none of this, and that he appear in his work no more than God in nature. The man is nothing, the work everything! . . . I aim at *beauty* above all else."

Yet it would seem that the general public did not embrace Flaubert's ideal of art, and the author's pessimism was only further enhanced by the cool reception that greeted the work he considered his masterpiece—*Sentimental Education*. In *Sentimental Education* Flaubert described the love of an insipid young man, Frédéric Moreau, for an older woman, set against the backdrop of the revolution of 1848 and the founding of the Second French Empire. He wanted it to be a "moral history" of the men of his generation, a subtle study of the materialism and moral poverty of Frenchmen since the abortive revolution, a time marked, in Flaubert's eyes, by "unending lies," "false politics," "false literature," and "false credit." The critics almost universally panned *Sentimental Education*, with its impartial contempt for every miserable, flawed character that sputtered and sighed on its pages. His friends around the dinner table, Turgenev and the others, had all suffered similar disappointments, where their artistry and insight were mistaken for misguided, tactical fumblings. Art, he concluded, lay in the arena of personal relationships, the character of feelings, nature—but certainly not politics. The other writers at the table that night—Zola, Goncourt, and Daudet—agreed.

A few months after the first dinner of the group at Café Riche, Alphonse wrote to Goncourt about his assessment of the evening: "Voilà, a dinner deadly for letters! . . . Flaubert as the head, Turgenev the foot, me the belly . . . And you absolutely pinched . . . Conclusion: life is extremely stupid and Paris deucedly grand."

And thus began the Group of Five. In subsequent meals, they talked freely and openly about everything and anything, their tongues and spirits enlivened by the excellent food and wine. "We opened our minds to one another without flattery and without any conspiracy of mutual admiration," Alphonse dreamily reminisced later on:

Ah! We were not easy to provide for and the restaurants of Paris no doubt remember us. We often changed our meeting-place. Sometimes it was at Adolphe and Pelé, behind the Opera; sometimes in the square of the Opera Comique; then at Voisin's whose cellar could meet any emergency and reconcile all tastes. We were wont to sit down to table at seven o'clock, and at two o'clock we had not finished. Flaubert and Zola dined in

their shirtsleeves; Tourgueneff lounged on the divan; the wait-
ers were turned out—a needless precaution since Flaubert's
"roar" could be heard from roof to cellar of the house—and
we talked literature . . .

Sometimes they spoke of one another's work—Flaubert was then
working on his *Temptation of Saint Anthony*, while Zola was hard at
work on *The Fault of Abbé Mouret* and Alphonse was beginning his
novel *Jack*. And when they tired of talking about literature, they
discussed love and women, death and illness. The older men would
complain about their rheumatisms; the younger ones would complain about money.

At dinner on January 25, 1875, Goncourt noticed that Zola
could not take his eyes off the food. Turning to the younger man,
Goncourt asked, "Zola, you wouldn't happen to be a gourmand?"
Zola admitted that food was one of the few pleasures in his otherwise bleak existence, and began to tick off a list of the horrible facts
of his childhood, the bitter disappointments of his daily life, the insults constantly hurled at him, and the sort of quarantine that people had put around his works. "A pariah, that's what I am . . . a
pariah," he repeated balefully several times. Goncourt was incensed
by this excessive display of neurotic self-pitying. "It is strange what
a whiner that fat, pot-bellied young fellow is, and how quickly he
falls into a melancholy mood."

Despite his claims to the contrary, Émile Zola was, in fact, just
beginning to embark on a truly extraordinary career. After too many
years of toiling away in obscurity, he was finally making a name for
himself after the publication of books like *Thérèse Raquin* (1867)
and *The Belly of Paris* (1873). His essays and reviews on art and literature for newspapers were also garnering attention. And when he had
sent *La Fortune des Rougon* to Flaubert in 1871, he received this
welcome response:

*I have just finished your dreadful and splendid book. I'm still
giddy after reading it. It's strong! Very strong!*
You have a noble talent and you are a valuable man!

*Send me a line to say when I can come to see you, to talk at
length about your book.*

Gustave Flaubert

The Group of Five dinners were among the happiest memories
of Zola's life. He would leave them trembling with the fever of
ideas, in an agitated ferment that would last for days at a time. Or
they would all issue together worn, and with a great world-sorrow
weighing upon their breasts, Zola accompanying Flaubert through
the dark streets, because of the latter's horror of going home alone
in the rue Murillo. They would stop at every corner to philosophize
in the morning hours in soft and urgent tones. Flaubert at his door
would kiss him on both cheeks and have the last word: "All has been
said before us, my dear friend. We have nothing left but to say the
same things, only in a more beautiful form if that is possible . . ."

On January 7, 1876, the group came together at the Daudets'
house for a gay and charming dinner of bouillabaisse and Corsican
pâté. Léon was delighted by the giant Flaubert, who arrived at the
door, saying laughingly to his host, "Hello Alphonse, how do I
seem? . . . Still young, aren't I?" and who bent down to kiss the little
boy with a great laugh and spoke in a fierce, strong voice. Alphonse
presided over the table wearing his customary black velvet jacket.
Turgenev, who had been suffering once again from gout, arrived in
his slippers and benignly padded about the room, while Zola only
had eyes for the bouillabaisse and Goncourt simply watched and listened, already eager to run home and preserve the memory of the
scene in his journal. They sat elbow to elbow, Flaubert thumping his
fists against the table with such enthusiasm that Mme Daudet
squirmed nervously in her seat.

Léon looked on in wonder as his beloved father became magnified by the conspiratorial laughter he shared with the enormous
Flaubert. He loved to listen to his father hold forth. The sound of his
voice was truly enchanting—everyone said so—with so many different inflections and gentle nuances. He was truly a great romancer,
not only with women but with everyone, his seductiveness render-
ing even the most obdurate opponent in a debate immediately more
amenable. And at these gatherings, particularly at the dinners with

his four friends, he often forgot about the pain that had gradually crept into his life. The same was not true in other situations. Just as Alphonse excelled at the tête-à-tête or in the animated conversations of a dinner table or in a small salon, he hated public speaking and became cross and nervous for hours beforehand. Léon had also taken to watching his father more closely, scanning his face to see when a wince of pain contracted his fine features, just for an instant, before he quickly composed himself once again and smiled reassuringly at his family, who alone among the diners sensed that something was amiss. This pain, this physical weakness, was the one chink in his father's armor, the one sign to Léon that his father was not superhuman.

Alphonse Daudet and Flaubert had known each other for several years. Upon the publication of Alphonse's third book, *The Prodigious Adventures of Tartarin de Tarascon*, in 1872, Flaubert generously wrote the young writer a glowing note: "It's purely and simply a *masterpiece*! That's the word that springs to my lips, and I'll not take it back. I began *Tartarin* on Sunday at midnight, and finished it at 2:30! Everything, absolutely everything, kept me entertained, and I burst out laughing several times." A few years later, in a note of praise he sent to Alphonse about *Jack*, Flaubert told the younger man, grandly: *"Testiculos habes, et magnos."* Alphonse was one of the favorite guests at Flaubert's regular Sunday gatherings. As Guy de Maupassant, another guest, later remembered, the young writer brought with him a breath of fresh air, reminding the other guests of Paris at its gayest and most lively. "In a few words," Maupassant explained, Daudet "sketches amusing silhouettes and touches everyone and everything with his charming irony, so southern and personal; the delicacy of his wit is enhanced by the charm of his face and gestures, by the polished perfection of his anecdotes." Léon Daudet later remembered how happy these afternoons made his father, how he returned home with more energy, often going straight to his study to write. Alphonse spoke tenderly to his son Léon about the splendid displays of literary camaraderie at these gatherings:

We kept the best of ourselves for those meetings. One would think to himself: I shall tell them this; or else, I shall read that page and take their advice on it. No truckling, no servility! Neither pupils nor masters, but comrades; respectful to the older men, warming themselves in the reflection of their glory and proving by their choice that in our profession there is something else besides money and vanity.

But of all the members of the Group of Five, Alphonse Daudet was closest to Edmond de Goncourt. The two had first been drawn together on December 5, 1865, at the raucous premiere of the play Edmond had written with his brother, *Henriette Maréchal*. It was also there that Alphonse had first met his future wife, Julia Allard, who was attending the performance with her parents. Alphonse and Edmond then formally met on March 16, 1873, at one of Flaubert's gatherings. At first Edmond was not so sure about the young Daudet couple—after visiting the couple at Champrosay, a little village on the banks of the Seine where Julia's family had property and where Julia, Alphonse, and their son Léon were staying. Goncourt, ever the aesthete, was decidedly disappointed by the banality of the furnishings and decorations of the house. But he was fascinated by the Daudets themselves, who seemed to him the perfect image of domestic bliss, and he decided in due course to become a mentor to the younger writer, opening for him the doors to some elite social venues. For his part, Daudet helped keep Edmond culturally relevant, introducing him to all the young writers of note—Pierre Loti, Maurice Barrès, Paul Bourget—and kept the older man in stitches with his droll impersonations and high-flying anecdotes of bohemian indulgence. Edmond's affection for Alphonse was eventually extended to Léon, whose development as a young man with a precocious intellect interested the older man greatly.

And so this merry fivesome continued until Saturday, May 8, 1880, when Goncourt's servant, Pélagie, who was in the middle of asking his master if he was going to M. Flaubert's the following day, placed in front of Goncourt a telegram with two words: "Flaubert dead!" He had suffered an apparent heart attack that day at his home in Croisset. His four friends were devastated. Goncourt recorded in his journal, "I felt that a band sometimes slackened, but inextricably knotted, secretly attached us to each other. And today,

I remember with a certain emotion the trembling tear at the edge of his eyelashes when he kissed me and said *adieu* on his doorstep six weeks ago." Turgenev was at his home in Russia when he heard the news. "It is not just that a remarkable talent has left, but also a most wonderful man," the grieving friend explained, adding, "He was the center of all our lives." Daudet, Zola, and Goncourt made their way to Rouen for the funeral with heavy hearts. The ceremony itself was drab and tawdry, hardly befitting such a great man of letters, Zola thought. Only a small crowd attended to pay final respects to Flaubert, and by and large the citizens of Rouen watched the funeral procession wind its way through the town with undisguised uninterest. The final humiliation came when they attempted to lower Flaubert's coffin into his grave, only to discover that the gravediggers had miscalculated and dug a pit that was too small. They handled the box clumsily, getting it stuck on a slant, head down, so that it was impossible to either raise or lower. Oddly enough, the same macabre misadventure had occurred at the burial of Flaubert's sister thirty-four years before. Flaubert had watched in horror as the gravediggers had first shaken the casket and then pulled and stomped on it in the hopes of forcing the box with its precious cargo down into the ground. Now it was his niece, Caroline, who wrung her hands and groaned at the grisly sight. Finally Zola cried, "Enough, enough!" and the decision was made to let the gravediggers finish the job after the mourners had left.

On March 6, 1882, the remaining four members of the Group of Five met again. The loss of their friend hit them hard, and, despite their best efforts, they found themselves repeatedly coming back to the subject of death. Daudet admitted to feeling persecuted, to having his view of life poisoned by his illness so that he never moved into a new apartment without his eyes seeking out the place where his coffin might one day be placed. Although no one would say it aloud, they all understood that Daudet had the most reason to worry about his demise. Zola explained how, when his mother died in their home in Médan, they discovered that the stairs were too small, so they had to remove her body by the window. Now, he confessed, whenever his eyes came to rest upon that window, he found himself wondering if he or his wife would pass through it first. The others could see the absolute terror in his eyes as he described his haunting feeling that death was out there waiting for him. Turgenev scoffed that such morbid thoughts were familiar to him as well but that he simply pushed them away when they began to weigh too heavily upon him, making a little gesture with his hand to illustrate his point. Their dinner continued in this melancholy vein, and soon they found themselves reproaching the young people of the day who, they concluded with some bitterness, viewed nature not directly, as they had all attempted to do, but through the books of their predecessors. They didn't use to feel so old, but now it was increasingly difficult not to feel that the best was behind them.

From then on, they met less and less. Daudet was increasingly preoccupied with his health, while Turgenev was busy traveling. Goncourt quietly seethed while Zola attained new heights of literary celebrity with the critical and commercial success of works like *L'Assommoir* and *Germinal.* Their Group of Five was replaced by other cohorts: there was "The Five"—the writers Henry Céard, Léon Hennique, Paul Alexis, and Guy de Maupassant, who pledged their allegiance to Zola and began meeting with him every Thursday in 1882. Already by 1877 they had announced their status as the next generation of Realists at a dinner in honor of Goncourt, Zola, and Flaubert, which featured such dishes as a "purée de Bovary" soup, a salmon-pink trout "à la Fille Elisa," truffled chicken "à la Saint-Antoine," and liqueur "de l'Assommoir." "Here is the new army forming," Goncourt wryly observed in his journal. A few years later yet another group of five emerged, this time five young self-styled Naturalists who published a "Manifesto of the Five" in *Le Figaro* expressing their disenchantment with—nay, disgust at—Zola: "To the young it seemed that after leading the charge he backed away, like those revolutionary generals whose brains become the valets of their stomachs . . ."

But for the remaining members of the original Group of Five, the memory of their time together remained an important touchstone, a reminder of a time when each of them had found their ideal audience and had felt truly understood. As Edmond de Goncourt observed in his journal, on April 25, 1883:

Our old friend Turgenev is a real man of letters. He has just had a cyst removed from his stomach, and he told Daudet, who went to see him a few days ago: "During the operation I thought of our dinners and I searched for the words with which I could give you an exact impression of the steel cutting through my skin and entering my flesh . . . something like a knife cutting through a banana."

Two years later, in March 1885, Charpentier published Zola's *Germinal*. It was hailed as a masterpiece; critics declared it to be the final, definitive triumph of Naturalism over Romanticism. A few months later, Victor Hugo was dead. Zola, who twenty-five years earlier, when he was just beginning his writing career, had sent the great poet a seven-hundred-line poem in the hopes of obtaining a verdict as to whether he should continue writing, now found himself offering his condolences to Victor Hugo's grandson, Georges. "I insist upon telling you now, as you grieve, that all hearts have, like your own, been broken. Victor Hugo was my youth, I am fully cognizant of what I owe him."

Léon had grown up at the center of this changing of the guard. He had been presented to Victor Hugo as a boy, just as bishops are sent to Rome to receive the papal benediction. He had then listened to Alphonse and his friends come together to despair about the indifference of the public for new literature and changing artistic mores. He took great pride in knowing that, along with Zola and Flaubert, Goncourt and Turgenev, his father was part of something unconventional, important, and new. What Léon learned from Alphonse was that writing required a certain boldness, bordering on recklessness. "There is the courage of the author to be considered, which consists in accomplishing his mission to the very end. The bold are always victorious. The timid ones always remain incomplete," Léon would later explain in a biography he wrote about his father. Léon watched the Group of Five debate and argue, and he was struck by his father's ability to persuade, to overpower people with the intimate harmony of his thoughts. He saw how writing, for Alphonse, was merely an extension of living. Indeed for Alphonse, whose body could no longer be counted on, it was a lifeline. Sitting there at the café after Victor Hugo's funeral with his father, Émile Zola, whose hair had recently been described by a journalist as standing up "like quills upon the fretful porcupine," and a handful of other writers, Léon could not help but wonder if he would one day find a similar passion and his own circle of like-minded men.

THREE

Hauteville House

I am delighted with my little daughter. Here at last is a work of mine which has a prospect of life.

—Victor Hugo to Charles Nodier (July 28, 1830)

Two paths are open to me. What does it matter? If I have a life, it will be great; if I have a death, it will be great.

—Adèle Hugo (March 28, 1852)

———⊃⊂———

A few weeks after the madness of Victor Hugo's funeral, eighteen-year-old Léon Daudet accompanied his friends, sixteen-year-old Jeanne and her eighteen-year-old brother, Georges Hugo, to their grandfather's house of exile on the island of Guernsey, off the coast of England. Léon had known them since he was ten years old, when his parents formally introduced him to the poet and then allowed him to play hide-and-seek with the two famous grandchildren. Léon and Georges had quickly become fast friends, attending the same schools and associating with the same group of young men, of which Jean-Baptiste Charcot was also a member. At Hauteville House they were joined by Jeanne and Georges's mother, Alice, her second husband, the prominent leftist politician Édouard Lockroy, and various trustees of the Hugo estate. All were charged with the task of sorting through the great man's belongings. Léon could scarcely believe that he was there, handling the papers and books that had once belonged to a literary god, whom he had been raised to worship. He had hesitated only for a moment at the thought of leaving his father. But Léon was also secretly, ashamedly, relieved at the idea of having some respite from that diseased world of doctors and morphine shots, the feverish nights and the agonizingly long days. By this point Alphonse's pain had quietly infiltrated every facet of the family's life, worming its way into even the most banal daily interaction— a walk to the park, the timing of dinner, the receiving of guests. Illness now had left a dull residue on everything in Léon's world. When Georges had asked him to come along to Hauteville House, Léon, who wanted to breathe healthy air and stretch his legs, had convinced himself that he simply could not say no. Perhaps he hoped that in focusing his attention on his friends' mourning for the loss of the one true father figure in their lives, he just might keep the certainty of his own father's demise at bay, at least for a time.

To all of the poet's intimates assembled there that summer, the house seemed darker, more ominous than it had before. At least when Victor Hugo had been alive, it had radiated with the determined purposefulness that had characterized all the poet's movements. In his absence the coherence of that rarefied environment, of the very lives once lived in those rooms, could almost be said to falter. To know Victor Hugo was to be held in thrall to him, and this was especially true for his grandchildren, whose lives had been oriented toward him, had been lived through him, since their birth. Georges did his best to maintain the sort of briskly efficient air to which he supposed young men of his station and temperament conformed. Having Léon there with him certainly made things easier. It was more difficult for Jeanne, who had taken her grandfather's death very hard and now spent much of her time on the island near her mother, finding comfort in the familiar rustle of her skirts and soothing whiff of eau de toilette. Yet everywhere Jeanne went, there were reminders of the life they had once led with him.

The Hugos had owned Hauteville House since 1855, when the exiled poet had installed his entire family there. Before Victor had chosen the house as the site of his exile and the incubator of his artistic vision, it had stood vacant for nine years—would-be tenants, it was locally reported, had been chased away by the ghost of a woman who had been killed there. At first glance it appeared to be just another plain-looking three-story house with fourteen Georgian windows that looked onto the street. But the building's unassuming exterior hid a jewel-like interior, where Victor's aesthetic eclecticism and taste for gothic excesses were in full show. The walls were covered in heavy tapestries, and every room was crammed with keepsakes and mementos from the poet's life and works—a Sèvres dinner service given to him by Charles X in 1825, a canvas by the political theorist Benjamin Constant, Gobelins tapestries, Japanese frames, Breton furniture, carved figurines made by the poet himself, Mexican panels. His favorite spot by far in the entire house was an eighteen-by-ten-foot "crystal palace," which had been built on to the roof and which had outside walls and a glass ceiling. Victor called it, in English, the "look-out," and it was here, in blinding light and heat, that he toiled away at his writing. He wrote standing up and while staring past the lush garden and out at the changeable sea and the rocky Channel Islands before him. Victor Hugo embraced the drama of exile with characteristic gusto and prowled the rooms and the grounds with the air of a clan chieftain, presiding with patrician sternness over his wife and three children, his longtime mistress Juliette Drouet (who had been installed in a house called La Fallue farther up the street), and the dozen or so exiles who had followed him to Guernsey.

In the weeks spent in Guernsey following Victor Hugo's death, Léon and Georges woke up each morning and set to work organizing and cataloging the library. They found all sorts of treasures. There was an extensive and motley assortment of books—on navigation, the Catholic counterrevolutionary movement during the French Revolution, the Middle Ages, Shakespeare, folklore, conscription under Napoléon I. They found daguerreotypes of Hugo and his family, bundles of letters—to "Toto," to "little Adèle," "for Vacquerie." They even found a large stash of condoms, size large, which, Léon later revealed to Goncourt, they had a hard time disposing of without being caught by the watchful mother of Jeanne and Georges. Sometimes in the afternoon, the three young people would roam about the great house, exploring its mysteries: revolving walls, hiding places, crates filled with Chinese porcelain figures, tantalizingly locked cabinets, mysterious séance tables. With its themed rooms stuffed with knickknacks, a jumbled array of unusual furniture, and walls covered with cryptic maxims—*"Absentes absunt"* over one armchair, *"Ego Hugo"* on the back of another, and "Be in fear of error" engraved on the door of a small lavatory—the house was the perfect site for adolescent antics and imagination. Sometimes the three young friends climbed up to the very top of the house, their favorite spot, and stared out at the sea, willing the swirling water to release whatever secrets it had whispered to the great poet. In the early evenings, they went for long walks, ranging across the wild, windswept landscape. Georges and Léon would sometimes leave Jeanne home, so they were free to troll for local girls, although increasingly Léon found much of his attention being focused on the lovely Jeanne, who had developed from a large-eyed and rather roly-poly little girl to a ravishing young woman. Jeanne noticed the way he looked at her with the satisfied indifference of a young girl accustomed to such attentions.

Jeanne was universally acknowledged to be a lovely girl. Journalists and commentators rapturously reported on her tender sweetness and her growing beauty. She was "ingenuous, rosy simplicity itself," with her "soft, grey kindly eyes" and "sweet candor and composure," which, it was hypothesized, must surely be the result of the freedom and devotion she enjoyed under her grandfather's watchful, loving gaze. People were struck by her unfussy, outgoing nature, her ability to mingle with strangers of all ages. One British journalist described his visit to the Hugo family on Guernsey during the summer of 1878. After solemnly making a speech to the revered poet, the journalist's attention was then demanded by nine-year-old Jeanne, who wished to relate to him a detailed biography of her pet cat. "All were interested in the narrative, which was told with great animation," the journalist explained, "and while the story proceeded Victor Hugo stood behind the child and kept pressing her hair with the palms of his hands." Such love and encouragement from her grandfather had helped Jeanne to develop, as she grew up, an easy, quiet self-assurance that, when coupled with her alluring good looks and famous family name, made for an intoxicating object of interest and perhaps even desire. But in the days following her grandfather's death, she had felt as if she had been thrown off her axis. She longed for that feel of his hand on her head to steady her and to guide her toward whatever was supposed to come next.

What was nothing more than an exotic and well-loved vacation destination to Léon, Jeanne, and Georges had served as something of a gilded cage for Victor and his wife and children. The Hugos' journey into exile on this remote and craggy island in the English Channel had begun in 1851. The political situation in France had been deteriorating at an alarming rate as President Louis-Napoléon's conservative government began clamping down on its critics. That summer Victor's two sons, twenty-five-year-old Charles and twenty-three-year-old François-Victor, were imprisoned for articles they had published in their journal, *L'Événement*—one against the death penalty, the other on the right of asylum—and sentenced to prison for six and nine months, respectively. Even then, Victor was unable to distinguish his sons' actions from his own, insisting at Charles's June 11 court hearing, "The real guilty party . . . is I, I who, for twenty-five years, have fought despite all forms of irreparable penalties! I who, for twenty-five years, have defended on every occasion the inviolability of human life! This crime . . . I committed it well before my son." While his sons languished in prison, Victor scribbled and fumed and carried on as he usually did. He was caught completely off-guard when, early on the morning of December 2, leading legislators were dragged from their beds and arrested, while Louis-Napoléon announced a drastic revision of the 1848 constitution, extending the presidential term to ten years and sharply limiting the legislators' powers. In a hastily drawn-up plebiscite, 92 percent of the population supported the changes; the only resistance occurred in the working-class quarters of Paris, where for two days, violent fighting occurred between opponents of the coup and the army, and in some of the "red" holdouts in some southern and central portions of the country. Before order was restored, several hundred protesters had been killed and twenty-six thousand arrested, ten thousand of whom were shipped off to Algeria or beyond. As Louis-Napoléon's authoritarian government swiftly took over, Victor Hugo and many other republican politicians fled the country. While most of them eventually returned after a short period, Hugo would remain abroad for nineteen years, only returning to Paris triumphantly in 1870, after the defeat of Louis-Napoléon (now Napoléon III) by the Prussians. His political persecution and subsequent flight into exile had earned Hugo the sympathy and admiration of people around the world and thrust him into a (self-declared) role of universal political martyr. One of the people most impressed with his actions was his twenty-one-year-old daughter, Adèle, who wrote to him in Belgium, where he had initially fled, "You were very great and also extremely heroic and you are admired and esteemed by the entire world. I am very proud to be your daughter."

Victor decided to move the family from Belgium, where he had initially sought refuge, to Jersey in the Channel Islands, even though no one in the family apart from his son François-Victor spoke English, the weather was horrible, and the island itself seemed particularly isolated. The exiled party consisted of Victor and his wife, Adèle; Victor's devoted mistress, Juliette Drouet; his son François-Victor; and Adèle, his only remaining daughter. His other son, Charles Hugo, also traveled into exile and, like his father, was followed to Jersey by his mistress. Auguste Vacquerie, a family friend and confidant, also joined the family. Initially, the novelty and glamour of their newfound status as celebrity political refugees filled their expectant waiting on their rocky outpost in the turbulent English Channel. But as weeks slipped into months, and months became years, the isolation began taking its toll on Victor's family. The situation only deteriorated when, in October 1855, they were forced to leave Jersey due to the poet's politics, which were deemed too disruptive by the locals. He decided to move the family from Jersey to a grand house on the even smaller and more remote island of Guernsey, two and a half hours to the north. Mme Hugo and her children attempted to muster some enthusiasm for the move—she told her daughter to pretend she was a real princess in a castle in her grand new home—but the reality was far more difficult. As Victor settled into a natural rhythm of writing all morning, followed by a walk to Fermain Bay and time spent observing the ebb and flow of the tide, his children, especially Adèle, now twenty-five, seemed to languish. Victor was unable to understand their difficulty, describing his three remaining children, "Charlot, Toto and Dédé" as "great, proud souls. They accept their solitude and exile with gay, severe serenity." He insisted that each member of the family undertake some creative activity. François-Victor set to work translating Shakespeare into French and helping his father with all English correspondence, although, as time passed, he began to sense that he, too, was "stagnating" in the company of "Lord Spleen and Lady Nostalgy." Charles, also bored and restless, longed for the freedom of his previous surroundings and sought escape and amusement during increasingly long holidays full of gaming and women on the Continent.

Adèle, the youngest, struggled in both body and soul. Shortly after their arrival on Guernsey, she fell gravely ill. Her family kept a vigil after the doctor announced there was a chance she would not make it through the night. To celebrate her recovery, Victor composed a poem, "To My Daughter Adèle," in which he imagined the two of them bound together in a sacred bond of tears and devotion. She eventually recovered but increasingly bristled at the stringent expectations of filial obeisance. She became obsessed with the feminist writings of George Sand, deciding that marriage was tyrannical and resenting the narrow-mindedness of purportedly liberal men like her father, whose lofty views on human emancipation failed to extend to members of her sex. Such quibblings could easily have been explained away as a mere rebellious phase of a precociously intelligent young woman. But Adèle had begun to display signs that she was more than just precocious.

As the daughter of the most celebrated writer in the world, Adèle took her first steps before an illustrious company of men and women—artists, musicians, and writers from across Europe who came, at regular intervals, to pay homage to and admire Victor Hugo. She was an accomplished pianist and composer and early on displayed the same felicity with the written word that had so graced her father. And all this talent, this thirst for creative expression, was housed in a figure of almost uncanny beauty—Balzac described her at thirteen as the most attractive woman that he had ever seen. As she neared adulthood, this bright, vivacious young woman, who confidently exchanged ideas with the crème de la crème of European intellectual society, seemed destined for a brilliant marriage and a formidable life. In an 1853 letter to her sister, Mme Hugo proudly boasted about her daughter's accomplishments and her stature in Jersey society, declaring her to be "a young miss, speaking a little English, knowing her poets, making her fingers travel brilliantly along the piano." The only thing that worried Adèle senior about her daughter was the latter's fragile health—and her absolute resistance to marriage. Adèle declared there was no question of "losing my name and giving myself a master, I who am so proud to call myself Mlle Hugo, I who am so free, so quietly happy in my interior."

Yet even before she arrived at Guernsey, there were signs of trouble. Adèle had grown up in the shadow of her elder sister, the beloved Léopoldine. It was in September 1843, when Léopoldine, who was then twenty years old and three months pregnant, and her husband of seven months, Charles Vacquerie, tragically drowned in a boating accident on the Seine, that Adèle's world first started to become unglued. Victor Hugo, who had been traveling in Spain with Juliette, first learned about the deaths while flipping through a newspaper at a café in Rochefort. He was devastated by the news: his "Didine" had been his favorite, part daughter, part confidante, whose adoration replaced the indifference of her mother and to whom he promised, in letter upon letter, eternal love and devotion. Victor's wife was so upset that she refused to come to the funeral, instead staying at home and stroking the cut hair of her dead daughter.

No member of the family was the same after the accident, but young Adèle felt the loss most keenly. She was only thirteen when her older sister died, and desperately—if vainly—attempted to comfort her family by being as deserving and good as her perfect older sister. But she herself was inconsolable, consumed with morbid thoughts of death and the afterlife. The cult of Léopoldine became a family affair: ten years later the Hugos set out their dead girl's favorite dress, which she had worn the day she drowned, and believed that she was trying to contact them from the dead at nightly séances.

Adèle's penchant for romantic fervor was already in evidence at the tender age of sixteen, when she fell in love with Auguste Vacquerie, the younger brother of Charles Vacquerie, her sister's husband, in perhaps another attempt to remain connected to her deceased older sister. Adèle was young and desperate for affection, yearning for the intense array of emotions and sensations that caused the heroes and heroines of her father's writing to shatter exquisitely. When the stolen kisses with Auguste in the moonlit garden did not seem quite enough, she was willing to go further. The caresses deepened as she drew him closer to her and willed herself to be transformed by the experience. But afterward, things were unchanged. She felt neither exquisite nor sublime. She was still trapped in the stultifying monotony of her world, an afterthought for the men around her, an unusual but fundamentally ornamental member of her father's entourage. Then she met an older sculptor, Jean-Baptiste (Auguste) Clésinger, who touched her differently—she grandly declared that he was quite like Victor Hugo. Their affair was brief, passionate, soaring—at least, that is what Adèle thought, until Clésinger left her for Solange, the adolescent daughter of the writer George Sand.

As the biographer Graham Robb has observed, "The spirit of Victor Hugo and the body of a twenty-six-year-old, nineteenth-century woman was a disastrous combination." And indeed, as she grew older, Adèle's chafing at the constraints of her sex and position only grew. Even before exile Adèle was desperately bored by the insipid sameness of social life in Paris, the false, stilted formalities designed to choke off any real emotion. Her loneliness became increasingly apparent to those who knew her, even to strangers. During a lunch at the restaurant Robelin, the composer and musician Eugène Vivier remarked to her, "You are an extraordinary woman. I am certain, without having seen you before, that you are not at all ordinary. You have no friends among the young women of your age."

"No," she replied bleakly, "I have none."

By the time she and her family had installed themselves in the Channel Islands, her isolation was near complete. The dazzling young Parisian woman began fading away—almost imperceptibly at first, but then more forcefully. Her raven hair, which had always served as such an alluring contrast to her pale, porcelain skin, was now pulled back tightly in a careless bun while her features first sank and then hardened where they had fallen. Where once she had displayed a graceful, youthful generosity and piety, she increasingly seemed to give herself over to an uneasy restlessness, withdrawal, and neurosis. Not even her brother Charles could coax a smile from his sister in any of the many photo sessions to which he subjected the family. He had developed a mania for photography and liked nothing better than aiming his camera at anything that did or did not move. Each plate showed the same sad Adèle, a withdrawn damsel in distress, gradually becoming older and more taciturn, her face and figure becoming heavy and slack until she looked like one of those spinster aunts hovering with pathetic resignation in the background of family photos.

Victor did not understand what had become of his charming and obedient little girl and became increasingly critical of Adèle, despairing of her willfulness and self-centeredness. Mme Hugo always rushed to her daughter's defense in the face of such paternal remonstrances, once pointedly chiding her husband that since it was customary for an honest man to compensate a mistress for giving the best years of her life to him, why would the man not do the same for a daughter? Adèle's dejection gradually took more elaborate and disturbing forms. She spent hours listening to the sea and listlessly fingering tunes at the piano. She had fevers and constipation and would lie prostrate for days on end, her eyes fixed in a deathly stare. Or was it simply that her mettle had wilted under the stale monotony of exile life, surrounded by dominating and indifferent men? In a 1857 note to her husband asking for permission to visit Paris with her daughter, Mme Hugo confessed her worries about Adèle: "I see my daughter become sad again because life, here, is always the same. Not a diversion, not an accident, not a new face; the existence that this child is leading could go on for a certain time, but if the exile lasts a long time this existence is impossible." While he and his sons had their various projects, she continued, "my daughter alone loses her life, she is disarmed, powerless." She continued in this vein in yet another letter, explaining: "A little garden and some needlework are not enough to satisfy a twenty-six-year-old girl." She added:

> You said this morning at breakfast that your daughter *loves no one but herself.* I did not want to respond because our children were there and because it was not a good thing to say. Adèle has given you her youth without complaint and without asking for gratitude, and you find her selfish. Now, Adèle

may indeed have become cold and may display a certain dryness, but what right do we have to ask her, when she has been deprived of all the joys of the heart, to be like other young women? Who knows what she has suffered and what she continues to suffer when she sees her future flee before her, when she adds up the years and realizes that tomorrow will be just like today?

Victor relented, and for the next few years, Adèle and her mother were allowed an annual four-month holiday away from Guernsey. He may even have been relieved to see her go. There were rumors—both whispered and published—that Victor was not in fact her father. People speculated that young Adèle, with her strange, sad beauty, was the product of the amorous coupling of her mother and Saint-Beuve, a family friend and France's leading literary critic. Some said that Victor had come to believe the rumors, that he viewed the child as an embodiment of all his doubts about his wife's faithfulness. In any case, despite these sojourns away from the island, Adèle continued to fall in on herself. Her mother continued to plead her case to Victor Hugo, reminding him in another letter in April 1859, "You are a father and you must feel as I do the necessity of a renewal for Adèle. In this almost monastic existence that we lead, Adèle lives inside herself. She thinks, and her often false ideas, unable to be modified by the exterior current, become scoria." Her father and mother increasingly wondered why she wouldn't marry, although suitors abounded.

Then, in 1861, when Adèle was thirty-one, her family learned about her fascination with Albert Andrew Pinson, a young English lieutenant colonel whom she met while living on Jersey when he was, briefly, stationed there. With nothing else to occupy her time and attention, Adèle had become consumed with thoughts of the young Englishman. In a letter to her father, on December 20, 1861, she explained the romantic beginnings of their love with appropriately Hugolian flourishes. She told of how he had first witnessed her reading on a terrace and how, although she had been so absorbed in her book that she failed to notice him, he was already instantly in love with her. As if their individual feelings could not sufficiently explain the great import of what had happened, Adèle also described their love in terms of world-historical significance: "He was a royalist and British. He was the past. Whom did he love? A woman of the future, a republican, a Frenchwoman. Who cares! The Republic and France appeared to him in my form, and thus he found the Republic more beautiful than the royalty and France higher than England." According to Adèle, Pinson had refused all sorts of enticements to leave Jersey because, ultimately, "of what importance was the army, career, ambition! His career was to love me; his ambition, to see me . . ." The only reason he had stayed away, Adèle continued, was that he felt he had to prove himself before he could become her husband and a member of the Hugo family. And so he waited and worked and strove to become worthy, all the while keeping the image of the young girl reading in his head and his heart. And only then did he ask for her hand in marriage.

It was a story of which Victor could not fail to approve—romantic and grandiose. The old man was indeed moved and consented to the match. On Christmas Day 1861, Pinson came to spend a few hours at Hauteville House, but he did not formally ask Victor for his daughter's hand. His manner seemed so vague—Victor found him to be truly inscrutable—next to the strident assertions of Adèle. And then the next day he left for Canada with his regiment. Victor and his wife assumed that the love would slip off into nothingness, but Adèle secretly had other plans in mind. In 1863 she turned thirty-three. She had turned down five suitors, and her parents had resigned themselves to the fact that she would remain a spinster forever. On June 2 she left Guernsey to join her mother in Paris. She never arrived. Soon after, her brother François-Victor received a letter from England informing him that his sister was en route to marry Lieutenant Pinson. Then, in July, they received a letter from New York informing them that Adèle had crossed the Atlantic and was on her way to Halifax, Nova Scotia, where Pinson was stationed with his regiment. A few months later, she announced her marriage to Pinson, but then, in a letter to her brother François-Victor, admitted that she needed more money to pay her landlord. The marriage, it seemed, was a complete fantasy. Victor's narcissism could only allow for one possible explanation for such willfulness: "She hates me," he declared.

Perhaps someone should have anticipated Adèle's desperate leap out of the family's reach. She had certainly meditated upon it before. A year prior to her flight in 1863, she wrote the following paragraphs in her diary:

> It would be an incredible thing if a young woman, who is so enslaved that she cannot even go out to buy paper, went to sea and sailed from the Old World to the New to be with her lover. This thing I shall do.
>
> It would be an incredible thing if a young woman, whose only sustenance is the crust of bread her father deigns to give her, had in her possession, four years from now, money earned by honest toil, money of her own. This thing I shall do.

Victor was mystified by Adèle's behavior. Why would she sneak away when he and Mme Hugo had already consented to the marriage? Was this "awful little English ruffian" even her husband? In the hope of silencing the wagging tongues of people who had already caught wind of this sad, strange story, Victor placed an announcement in the local newspaper claiming that the wedding had taken place in Paris on September 17, 1863, and, for added effect, included after his name a formal list of his honors and titles: Officer of the Legion of Honor, former Peer of France, former Representative, member of the Académie Française, Knight of the Order of Charles III of Spain, and so on. Perhaps he hoped that the combined authority of his name and achievements would compel people to accept his daughter's unorthodox path to matrimony. But soon thereafter François-Victor dropped an even greater bombshell: Adèle had confessed to him that she was not married, but rather had gone to Halifax to force the lieutenant to marry her. In order to do so, she had explained to her brother, she would need five thousand francs so that she could pay for him to be hypnotized. The money, she assumed, could come from their father as an advance on her dowry.

The family then got news that Adèle's behavior had become even more erratic—she had taken to wandering the wintry city in flimsy gowns and had stopped eating. Hugo could not help but be reminded of his brother Eugène as anxiety over his daughter's increasingly tenuous hold on sanity consumed his thoughts. His frustration with Adèle faded to concern, and he eagerly began planning her return to the family bosom and thinking about how he would dedicate himself to making things up to her. He wrote to his wife on December 1, 1863:

> The poor child has not yet known happiness. It is time that she did. I want her to. I will throw her parties at Hauteville House. I will invite all the great intellects. I will dedicate books to Adèle. I will make her the crown of my old age. I will celebrate her exile. I will make up for everything. If an idiot can have the power to dishonor her, Victor Hugo will have the power to glorify. Later, when she is cured and smiling, we will marry her to an honest man.

But the family had to wait for the happy reunion. In the meantime the close-knit Hugo clan began falling apart. First, thirty-eight-year-old Charles, tired of living in his father's shadow, finally left the island. In October 1865 he married an eighteen-year-old orphan, Alice Lehaene, who had been raised by her godmother, the wife of Jules Simon, a notable French *député* and a member of the republican opposition. The marriage did not mean that Charles had settled down: he had always acted like a spoiled child and continued to run through his money in expensive hotels and gaming parlors. Even loyal and steadfast François-Victor finally left home for good. His fiancée, a local girl named Emily de Putron, died of tuberculosis in January 1865. François-Victor left Guernsey right after his father's funeral oration and traveled to Brussels with his mother, who herself did not return to the island for two years.

Meanwhile, Adèle was still in pursuit of the ever-elusive Pinson. When his regiment was sent off to Barbados she followed it, continuing her routine of wandering the streets in inappropriate attire—sometimes an elegant gown, sometimes men's clothing—in the hope of running into her love. In 1869 Pinson and his regiment left Barbados, but by then Adèle was so lost to reality that she did not even realize it and stayed behind, roaming the streets and sinking further and further into the yawning hole of mental illness. Finally, a freed slave known as Mme Baa took her in.

In 1868 Victor finally left Guernsey to join his ailing wife in Brussels. On August 24 she suffered a heart attack, and she died three days later without ever seeing her second daughter again. She was buried at Villequier, as she had wished, next to her first daughter, Léopoldine. A grieving Victor Hugo accompanied his wife's coffin to the border but no farther—his exile was ongoing. But even in the midst of their mourning, there was also reason to celebrate. Eleven days before, Alice Hugo, Charles's wife, had given birth to a son, Georges. Meanwhile, the hated empire that had forced Victor into exile seemed dangerously on the edge of collapse, weakened from within by a series of strikes and scandals and an economic depression and from without by the threat of Bismarck's Prussia. At the same time, an easing of press restrictions had unleashed a tidal wave of new publications, which eagerly took swipes at the despised emperor Napoléon III.

Jeanne Hugo was born on September 29, 1869. One of her first acts upon meeting her illustrious grandfather was to grab his finger—a gesture that greatly moved the old man, who felt as if a connection with his own daughters had been reestablished. She made her first appearance at Hauteville House with her family—father Charles, mother Alice, and brother Georges—in the summer of 1870, when she was almost a year old. Soon after their arrival, war broke out between France and Prussia. On August 15 Victor left Guernsey for Southampton, accompanied by Charles, Alice, his grandchildren, three maids, his mistress, Juliette, and her nephew. From there they went to Waterloo, then to Dover, and finally to Brussels on the evening of August 17. The French army ultimately surrendered at the battle of Sedan on September 2, and Napoléon III was captured. He was formally deposed two days later, and a republic was proclaimed on September 4. The following day, Victor boarded a train for Paris, his first time back in his homeland in nineteen years. When the Prussians laid siege to the capital shortly thereafter, Victor was there, with his sons and his grandchildren.

As conditions in the besieged city worsened, Victor slowly became reacquainted with the city he had left behind so many years earlier. While others sank into despair, he kept himself busy with frequent sexual trysts and with hours spent observing his two grandchildren, Georges and Jeanne—Jeanne in particular. In his diaries, reports of Jeanne's progress were interspersed with accounts of the growing deprivation facing the city's inhabitants:

> October 22—Little Jeanne has imagined a way of puffing out her cheeks and raising her arms in the air that is adorable . . . We are eating horsemeat in every style. I saw the following in the window of a cookshop: *Saucisson chevaleresque.*
>
> November 27—Pâtés of rat are being made. They are said to be very good . . .
>
> January 2—This morning we lunched on wine soup. The elephant at the Jardin des Plantes has been slaughtered. He wept. He will be eaten. The Prussians continue to send us 6,000 bombs a day . . .
>
> January 30—Little Jeanne is still poorly and does not play. Mlle Périga brought me a fresh egg for Jeanne . . .
>
> February 13—Yesterday, before dinner, I read to my guests . . . two pieces of poetry which will form part of *Paris Besieged* ("To Little Jeanne," and "No, You Will Not Take Alsace and Lorraine").

The siege lasted for a little over four months, from mid-September 1870 to the end of January 1871. Then the moderate republican government of national defense sought an armistice with the newly proclaimed German empire. The Germans insisted on a triumphal entry into Paris in the peace terms. Parisians, who had borne the brunt of the Prussian attack, were bitterly resentful and were particularly angry that, as part of the terms of the armistice, the enemy would be allowed to march triumphantly into the capital.

In February 1871, Victor Hugo was elected to the National Assembly, whose job it was to negotiate the terms of surrender with Bismarck, and headed to Bordeaux, where the government would be located. When it became clear that the new government would betray the people of Paris first, and most symbolically, by moving the Assembly not back to Paris but to Versailles, the traditional seat of the monarchy, Victor resigned in a huff. On March 13, while the Assembly was packing up for Versailles and Victor was at a restaurant, waiting for his son Charles to join him, he received word from a messenger that a cabdriver who had been taking Charles to the Café de Bordeaux had opened the door of the cab upon their arrival to find Charles dead, the victim of a heart attack followed by massive hemorrhaging—the apparent result of a lifetime of obesity and overindulgence. He was forty-four. "It isn't normal," the grieving father told Edmond de Goncourt, who had come to Paris to offer his condolences, "two bombshells in one life." On that same day, Adolphe Thiers, who had just been named head of the provisional government, ordered a small detachment of troops to the Parisian neighborhood of Montmartre to seize cannon that had been used by the National Guard during the Prussian siege of Paris. Women at the local market warned the neighborhood, and the troops, who refused to fire on the crowd, were quickly surrounded. The mob, furious at the new government's recent capitulation to the Prussians while they, the Parisians, had endured a four-month siege, took their anger out on the troops, seizing two generals, lining them up against a wall, and shooting them. Thiers then ordered his troops to surround the capital, thus beginning a second siege of Paris. Socialists and left-wing Parisians of all stripes banded together to form the "Paris Commune" in defense of their city. The funeral procession for Charles Hugo was forced to take a long and circuitous route to Père Lachaise Cemetery as the barricades went up throughout the city.

During the next two months, while the standoff continued, Hugo was in Brussels to settle the affairs of his late son Charles. As politics was never far from his mind, Hugo also attempted to use his celebrity to lobby the Belgian government to offer asylum to other Frenchmen fleeing persecution in the wake of the "bloody week" following the final assault on Paris by government troops and the subsequent collapse of the Commune. Alice, Jeanne, and Georges remained by his side. On the night of May 27, 1871, an angry mob gathered outside of Hugo's residence at the place des Barricades, calling out, "Death to Victor Hugo! Down with Jean Valjean!" while trying to break down the doors. Suddenly a sharp rock came crashing through the window in his granddaughter's room, and two-year-old Jeanne, who had been sick for days, began screaming in terror. Never one to miss an opportunity for mythic self-rendering, Hugo used this incident for a poem, "Brussels.—the Night of May 27." The next day, Hugo was officially expelled from the country and was forced, with his mistress Juliette Drouet, Alice, and his two grandchildren in tow, to travel to Luxembourg for what would be his fourth exile experience.

If 1871 was indeed *l'année terrible*, as the aptly chosen title for Hugo's poetic account of the Commune and the violent reprisals of the "bloody week" suggested, 1872 was not much better. First, Victor failed to be reelected to the National Assembly: having been out of the country during the bloody Commune, his calls for unconditional amnesty and the abolition of the death penalty were out of step with the recriminatory, post-traumatic anger of those who had fought on either side. A month later, on February 12, an aged and vacant Adèle arrived in the capital with her Barbadian chaperone, Mme Baa. François-Victor visited his sister first. She failed to recognize him. Victor arrived the following day. "I saw Adèle. My heart is broken."

When Adèle had run off from her family, she had still been a young woman, a haughty, unstudied beauty whose reputation preceded her. But she came back as a broken forty-one-year-old; her hair, which had been cropped close because of her inability to care for it, now hung slack and unkempt, her face lined and tanned by the tropical sun. She claimed to hear the voice of her dead sister, Léopoldine, but seemed unable to connect with people around her as her fingers listlessly picked at the threads of her worn dress. She was confined to an expensive nursing home at Saint-Mandé, situated just outside of Paris, run by Mme Rivet, daughter of the noted alienist Alexandre-Jacques-François Brière de Boismont and wife of Gustave Rivet, a close friend of Victor Hugo. It was a well-appointed home that offered excellent care in a beautiful setting on the border of the Bois de Vincennes and, according to *Le Figaro*, was a place that "everyone knows." Room and board cost 2,400 to 5,000 francs per year, depending on the number of rooms and servants one desired. Adèle was confined there—with the occasional trip to the opera or the theater—for the remainder of her life. Several years later a journalist who was visiting Mme Rivet's asylum came upon the great poet's last living child and was astounded by her girlish appearance. She carried herself well, he explained, reasoning correctly and seemingly understanding others, remembering everything. Yet, the journalist continued, she was unmistakably unwell. At the table she would seize a piece of meat and stash it away in her pocket or she would suddenly start to waddle strangely or begin balancing herself for no reason on one foot and then the next. Sometimes she could only concentrate on picking up, one by one, the pebbles of a long alley.

When he was in Paris, Victor would visit her occasionally. Sometimes he would bring along his mistress, Juliette, whose own daughter, Claire, had been buried in the cemetery nearby. They also sometimes brought young Jeanne and Georges. On August 7, 1873, Victor wrote in his journal, "At 1h ½ we went to Saint-Mandé. JJ and me, her to see her daughter, me to see mine, in their tombs, alas! I found Ade in the same moral state, but physically better, fattened up and more attractive. She kissed Georges and Jeanne." His two grandchildren did not know what to make of this strange older relative— Georges later told his son, Jean, that when he did occasionally visit his aunt, she confused the generations, taking him for his father, Charles. Did Adèle think that Jeanne was her long-departed sister, Léopoldine? Who did Jeanne think this strange old woman was?

The remaining Hugo clan made yearly pilgrimages to Hauteville House, usually during the summer, when Victor could swim in the sea and the children could run about in the garden. While Adèle remained at Saint-Mandé, sinking deeper and deeper into the darkness, Victor continued his ways, living as vigorously and viciously as he ever did: writing—finishing up his final novel, *Ninety-Three*, and beginning the poems that would make up the series *The Legend of the Centuries* (1877)—and falling in love and in lust with his mistress's servant, Blanche Lanvin. Edmond de Goncourt dined with the Hugos in April 1873 and observed Victor the poet "full of life and *joie de vivre*, overflowing with vitality." In comparison, Victor's son François-Victor was failing from renal tuberculosis. "Next to his son's agony, the obliviousness of his powerful and rugged good health is painful to behold," Goncourt pointedly observed of the aging poet. A few months later, Edmond de Goncourt once again found himself reflecting on the particular family romance of the Hugos, conflating rumor and reality when he mused, "About this father, about this genius, about this monster—about this first daughter drowned, about this second daughter kidnapped by an American and returned insane to France—about these two sons, one dead, the other dying—about this Mme Hugo, adulterous with her son-in-law . . . A TRAGIC FAMILY . . . that is the title of the Hugo family."

Hugo's grandchildren, at least, were thriving, and he delighted in the development of little Jeanne and Georges. "I played in the garden with the little ones, who are adorable. Jeanne said to me, 'I left my knickers at Gaston's place.' Gaston is her boyfriend, five years old," he wrote on July 31. When François-Victor died on Christmas Day 1873, Victor Hugo wrote, "Another break in my life, and a supreme break at that. I have no one else before me than Georges and Jeanne." From then on the three of them would be even more tightly bound together. There was no mention of Adèle, who had been reduced to a simple, anonymous obligation.

Victor and his remaining entourage—Juliette, Alice, Georges, and Jeanne—moved into two apartments at 21, rue de Clichy in Paris, dwelling in the one he shared with his daughter-in-law and grandchildren, receiving visitors from throughout Europe in the rooms belonging to Juliette. Although he was, by that time, a millionaire, he had chosen for his family apartments located on a busy street chockfull of secondhand furniture shops and fading cafés. For the next several years, this address was *the* desired destination for the glitterati of Europe. Few who arrived at Victor Hugo's famed rue de Clichy residence for the first time knew what to expect, so exaggerated was the poet's reputation. A personal invitation to attend dinner at Victor Hugo's home, where his longtime mistress and the poet would preside over the overheated salon, hung in red satin and boasting a large bronze elephant, had the social significance of a royal audience. But to the surprise—and even outrage—of many, instead of enjoying an intimate tête-à-tête with the immortal poet, they found themselves seated next to a cherubic six-year-old, Hugo's granddaughter, Jeanne. Hugo would alternately lecture his guests or ignore them completely, absorbed in drawing pictures for Jeanne and her older brother, Georges, or popping whole oranges into his mouth as they laughed and clapped in delight. And when Jeanne fell asleep at the dinner table, her cheek resting against her plate, a chicken bone clasped in her plump child's fist, Victor Hugo sternly instructed the other guests, all writers and statesmen of considerable importance, not to disturb the sleeping child. When she finally awoke, Jeanne and Georges sleepily scrambled down from their places and solemnly made the tour of the table, interrupting elevated conversations to bid each guest a formal good night. Ordinarily children would never even have been present at such a gathering, but at their grandfather's table, Jeanne and Georges were always the guests of honor.

He immortalized his grandchildren in a series of poems that became de rigeur reading for French children throughout the nation. He had written poems about his other children—Léopoldine, especially, and an homage to his sons, *Mes Fils*, in 1874. But *The Art of Being a Grandfather*, which was published in 1877, was different. Eschewing the Sturm und Drang of his earlier political or romantic poems, the morsels in *The Art of Being a Grandfather* celebrate simply and directly the pure, unconstrained delight and naturalness of being a child. "To Jeanne," "Jeanne Sleeping," "Jeanne with Toast"—these poems explored a new side of love for Hugo, the unconditional and unparalleled adoration between a grandfather and his granddaughter. The French public was won over by it, and the work made Jeanne a star. In one single, grand gesture, Victor Hugo had regained his footing as France's most beloved writer and had found an appropriately appreciative admirer of his fatherly affections. He may have already lost Adèle forever—she was busy reliving her daring escape from her family's clutches and her amorous exploits from within the confines of an asylum—but he had little Jeanne. She sent him touching infantile notes, expressing her distress at having to be apart from him during vacations yet also excitedly relating to him her adventures, and ended by telling him that she kissed him "with all her heart." He oversaw her education—keeping tabs on her progress in spelling (she was very bad) and her progress in other subjects (one tutor complained that she was "too playful" to make much real progress). Later she sent him notes from her travels with her brother, her mother, and her new stepfather, Édouard Lockroy. There was so much to tell him: the elegant beaches at Lake Como, the mosquitoes in Venice, the lovely view of Vesuvius. She sent him copies of her most recent schoolwork. Written in awkward schoolgirl French, riddled with spelling and grammar mistakes, Jeanne's earnest essays solemnly promised to help "all the sick and the poorest people" and to give out lots of money and do as much good as she'd like.

Jeanne and Victor Hugo both found in each other the perfect audience. Growing up with him, Jeanne felt completely protected by his love. Her adoration for him, meanwhile, was total and unwavering. The only hint she had about the darker side to her grandfather's mythical heroism was the story of her aunt Adèle, who had chafed so against the constraints in that hothouse exile environment and had run away, only to be returned to France years later, broken and insane. Jeanne grew up with the image of her aunt's vacant stare, her grandfather's unhappy silences, and whispered accounts of the insanity that, some claimed, ran through the entire Hugo family and even fueled the creative genius of Victor himself. But such things were hardly discussed, and Adèle became nothing more than a pregnant pause in family stories, a sigh, a moment of regret for a life whose debut had been so promising. After all, there had never been any reason for Jeanne to trouble herself with inconvenient stories from a distant past when she could be the heroine in the fairy tale of her grandfather's making. With his death, however, a new chapter in Jeanne's life was about to begin.

FOUR

Babies of the Republic

The "modern young man" is complex . . . He is at once a skeptic and a mystic, ambitious and blasé, egotistical and charitable, cruel and sweet, etc. One could match to his intentions a long suite of adjectives that are allowed to be together . . . One of the most surprising traits of the "modern young man" . . . is the impatience with which he wishes to live. Does he carry within himself the obscure foresight of a catastrophe by which he feels menaced, war or revolution, and hurries himself because there is little time left? Or, more importantly, does he have the instinct that everything passes with tenfold speed and that one must seize the goals at the very moment one perceives them, for fear of losing them?

—Édouard Rod, *Le Figaro* (1890)

One evening in May 1890, in the prestigious second arrondissement, four elegantly dressed young men, returning from a lively evening of good food and better wine, came upon an old man on the boulevard des Capucines, across from the Grand-Hôtel. The man reproached them for their rowdy behavior, and one of the young men set upon him with his cane. Others quickly joined in, and soon a full-out brawl was under way. Such scuffles were not infrequent on the late-night streets of the capital, and the young offenders were duly arrested and taken to the police station, where they would presumably be released not long after with a reprimand.

At first the young men indignantly refused to give their names. But when they did, it became clear that they were not just any foursome of idle young playboys. The four men, who had by this point sobered up enough to admit to their true identities, were, in fact, Georges Hugo, Léon Daudet, Jean-Baptiste Charcot, and Philippe Berthelot, son of the renowned chemist and former minister of public instruction Marcellin Berthelot.

That representatives of such illustrious families should be caught up in such a drunken public disturbance was exactly the sort of sordid tidbit with which the press enjoyed titillating their readers. The next day, the major Paris dailies reported a shameful incident involving "sons of notable families." The ever-eloquent Séverine, a fierce socialist journalist, wrote scathingly of these "papa's boys," these "nothings," these "babies of the Republic" who aspired to social greatness. As Léon Daudet would later recall about the event and its journalistic aftermath: "We were spared neither admonitions nor remonstrance nor a tirade on the degenerate abortions of glorious and hardworking families that squander the paternal or grand-paternal heritage." The families in question were in an uproar: the Daudets and Hugos at the audacity of the papers for exaggerating the youthful shenanigans, the Charcots at the foolishness of their son for dragging the family name into the mess in the first place (although, by at least one account, Charcot had to suppress an indulgent smile when he first saw the newspaper story). Five years after Victor Hugo's funeral, the young heirs of the Republic had found themselves woefully adrift.

Public reaction was so great precisely because these young men were supposed to represent the best and brightest of their generation, carrying with them the expectations not only of their prominent families but also of the close observers of French society. They had grown up shielded from the pressures of many of their generation, their childhoods spent cosseted by nannies and tutors, shuttling back and forth between well-appointed apartments and gracious country retreats or posh resorts on the Riviera or in Italy. As offspring of famous men, they possessed a self-consciousness about their position not shared by their peers, who had never known the near constant presence of fawning hangers-on, never experienced the jolt of recognition upon seeing newspaper profiles of their famous parents in print. When they grew older, such luxuries and consideration took on new importance as they became aware that people whom they had merely regarded as jovial family friends were, in fact, people of great importance—the tastemakers and opinion-shapers of the nation. But the pressure to succeed—to meet if not to surpass expectations—was sometimes simply too great. And, inevitably, parental expectations and adolescent yearnings alternately merged and clashed in an ever-shifting struggle between duty and desire.

For young men like Léon and Jean-Baptiste, the training for a life of distinction had begun early. In those days a boy's education could define him for the rest of his life. Léon had always been quite serious when it came to his studies. His father had instilled in him a love for the classics—Horace and Virgil, Montaigne, Rabelais, and Shakespeare. But he found even greater inspiration in contemporary writers. He adored Flaubert, whose loud laugh and frequent presence at his parents' home in the Marais was the source of many fond memories and whose death shook him considerably. And he had grown up in awe of the great Victor Hugo. Léon had developed an exuberant and careless love of beauty from his father and an appreciation for order, on display in his carefully organized notebooks, meticulous blotting paper, and bright, shiny inkpot, from his mother. These methodical predispositions only flourished as he made his way up along the path of well-heeled education. Léon's first tutor, when he was nine years old, was Gustave Rivet, an ardent republican and friend of Victor Hugo, who had recommended him to Alphonse. Léon had always been an impatient, headstrong child, but with Rivet, he learned the importance of thinking before he acted and experienced for the first time the savory satisfaction of being able to sit there with some bit of text and, all by himself, struggle through to clarity, to make his own sense of the words on the page. These early studies were reinforced by his parents, with his mother taking him regularly to see the classics at the Comédie-Française and his father giving him private tutorials about French literature.

When Léon was a little older, he studied as a partial boarder at the Lycée Charlemagne. Sometimes Alphonse would walk with him from the place des Vosges (where they lived at number 18) down the rue des Francs-Bourgeois, eventually crossing the rue de Rivoli, through the narrow rue Saint-Paul to the lycée on the rue Charlemagne. They would talk about writing and philosophy, the latest plays or the latest social gossip. In the afternoons it was his mother, Julia, who came to fetch him, walking him back through the ghetto with its foreign smells and exotic characters, asking her son questions about his day. Léon was an excellent student: he was always first in his class in French and made up for his lack of any true mathematical skill with a diligence and dedication to his studies that impressed his teachers. Next it was on to Louis-le-Grand, the venerable old high school in the Latin Quarter, which counted among its illustrious alumni Molière, Voltaire, and Victor Hugo, and which was located five minutes from the family's new apartment on the avenue de l'Observatoire. It was here, during an awards ceremony in 1880, that the great historian Ernest Renan took Léon aside and hissed in his ear, "We will make something of you." Léon Gambetta, the great politician and future prime minister, said the same thing a short time later while dining at the Daudets' home. It was a very important thing to hear, for both Léon and his proud parents, coming as it did from two of the most prominent men of the Third Republic. Léon would later remember this time of adolescent intellectual discovery with considerable fondness, heady years spent reading Kant and Spinoza, and first hearing about a new theory called evolution, which was then being hotly debated in cafés and in newspaper columns throughout the city. Philosophical discussions weren't held in a vacuum. They were treated by educators and politicians alike as a useful opportunity for political indoctrination: thus Kant's search for the *noumène*, the divine within the self, could be held in opposition to the divine in the churches, and an analysis of *Critique of Pure Reason* might go hand in hand with a tribute to Léon Gambetta. When the boys were feeling naughty, they snuck off to read Baudelaire's *Les Fleurs du Mal,* which had been condemned when it appeared in 1857 for its "immorality."

In the winter of 1884, Alphonse's *Sapho* began to be serialized in the new *Écho de Paris.* At the end of May, his publisher, Georges Charpentier, sold it with a first run of eighty thousand copies. The success was instantaneous and overwhelming, and sixteen-year-old

Léon found himself praised with even greater vigor simply for being the son of the illustrious Alphonse Daudet. The Daudets' enjoyment of his newfound popularity, however, was short-lived—Alphonse's syphilitic symptoms worsened dramatically. What had begun with sores and a painfully swollen testicle had settled permanently in his body, sometimes asserting itself as agonizing rheumatism and, most recently, as an increasing inability to control his limbs. His friend Jean-Martin Charcot saw him and diagnosed tabes dorsalis. There would be many more hazy days of morphine and pain, he was told, although Charcot also recommended he go to the baths at Lamalou-les-Bains, a popular spa in the south for people in similar predicaments. But when he arrived at the spa, instead of a respite from his illness, he found a grotesque parade of fellow sufferers.

As Alphonse wasted away, Léon grew more and more into his own. He was the picture of adolescent health, with his dark complexion, strong nose, and dark brown hair. He had a stocky, athletic body, the result of hours spent in fencing and boxing lessons. And beneath his ruddy, pugnacious exterior lay a remarkably curious and occasionally quite subtle intellect. Both Léon and Jean-Baptiste—and the generation they grew up in—were, in many ways, being trained to take over the world that their fathers had created. This world was buttressed by a hard-won faith in the human capacity for progress. Champions of reason and science, their fathers had believed that the world was knowable, explainable, and this vision had eventually seeped into the politics, economics, and literature of the day. And how could they not feel confident? In their lifetime the vicious cycle of revolutions had finally been broken, while wealth and talent had replaced birth and noble title as the requirement for social and political achievement. Faith in positivist thought from earlier in the century had been transformed into a veritable cult of science, whose aim it was to drive away the last vestiges of religious superstition and ignorance and to explain the secrets not only of nature but of man himself. Innovations in science and technology, from the invention of the microscope to the expanding network of railroads, pushed back the frontiers of human existence. Yet beneath the confident pronouncements, the stirring toasts and the glasses raised to a starry future forged out of science and steel, there were worries, an unsettling sense that nipping at the corners of this well-wrought plan for the future were forces beyond their control. As the century came to a close, a growing number of challenges to that confidence of the older generation emerged. Perhaps things were just changing too quickly. Or perhaps it was an uncertainty bred from defeat for a nation still reeling from the trauma of 1870, when Prussian men and Prussian guns were flung at a proud yet unprepared France. Her confidence had been shaken further still by the internecine fighting of the Commune. In the years that followed, Frenchmen sought a reason for their country's weakness, and they concluded that it had become too porous, too dependent on the fruits and labors of other, mightier countries, primarily Germany.

Both Léon and Jean-Baptiste were directly touched by the fall-out from the war. While thinkers like Fustel de Coulanges and Ernest Renan debated French reliance on German thought at academic conferences and in the august pages of the learned *Revue des Débats*, a teenage Léon found himself soaring to new heights—and plunging to new lows—in the thrall of thinkers like Kant and Schopenhauer. One of Léon's teachers at Louis-le-Grand, Auguste Burdeau, was himself the translator of several works by Schopenhauer, and introduced his impressionable young pupils to the complicated, often convoluted ideas of the German philosopher. Men of his father's generation, men like his father's friend Charcot, had announced that, with reason and science, it was at last possible for men to explain and to master the world. By the time Léon and Jean-Baptiste had entered adolescence, this older, hopeful message of human progress and self-sufficiency had faded somewhat. Herbert Spencer's notion of the Unknowable power behind the visible world and Eduard von Hartmann's "spirit" joined Schopenhauer's pessimism as the hot topics to be discussed in lecture halls and cafés. Léon and his cohort were consumed with uncertainty. Years later he blamed his former teachers for introducing him to ideas that "fought within ourselves the good national sense and the traditions of method and measure inherited by our fathers." While in school, a classmate declared to him one evening that he was planning on killing himself "because the world is bad in itself." Léon decided to tell their supervisor, who called for the desperate young man to come to him. After lecturing him, he sent the boy home to his family for a few days. When the pupil returned, he was "cured." Léon, however, was not so sure.

Alphonse noticed a change in his son. One evening when Léon was about seventeen years old, he burst into tears, demanding to know from his mother and father if life was truly how German pessimism said it was and, if so, was it really worth living. Alphonse thought deeply about his son's anguish, writing in his notes, "The sadness, the alarm of my dear son who just began studying philosophy and reading the books of Schopenhauer, Hartmann, Stuart Mill, Spencer. Terror and disgust of living; the doctrine is gloomy, the professor despairing, the classroom conversations desolate. The futility of everything appears to these lads and devours them." Wouldn't it be better, he wondered, to lie to them a little longer, to let life itself—not lessons—disillusion them, removing piece by piece the false trappings and masks of society? As much as Alphonse may have wanted to maintain certain illusions for his son, though, the world around them was rapidly changing, to the consternation of many. Despite Jean-Martin Charcot's absolute faith in his ability to keep the darkness at bay, scientific discoveries were challenging the way people understood the world, daily revealing it to be far more complicated than they had imagined. Cells, it was determined, formed the basis for life, and new "particle theories" revealed the complexity of motion, light, and matter. Social theorists began studying the effects of rapid social change in industrial society. The Paris Metro was unveiled in 1900, and electric lamps now dotted the city. Scientific progress devalued formerly cherished assumptions and created insecurities. Alphonse may have wished to shield his Léon, but neither fathers nor sons in fin-de-siècle France could avoid the changes to their world.

Jean-Baptiste's educational upbringing, meanwhile, was far less fraught. He had spent nine years at the noted liberal school École Alsacienne, on the avenue de Vavin near the Luxembourg Gardens. The school had been founded in 1873 by a group of Alsatian Protestants, who had chosen to leave their home when the Prussians invaded in 1870 and who had wished to give their children a French education unhampered by the conservative religious traditions in other lycées. It boasted small classes, so that the children could have individual attention; and rather than doling out specific punishments, teachers appealed to the children's sense of honor and responsibility. Modern languages were spoken and sung, and art was studied by visits to museums. While Léon had a tendency for introspection and was greatly preoccupied by intellectual pursuits, Jean-Baptiste already showed his penchant for action and adventure. He was not a particularly gifted student, and the only prize that he won during those years was for good camaraderie. Rather than pore over his books, he preferred being outside, playing rugby or fencing, or writing swashbuckling adventure stories featuring plucky heroes headed to exotic destinations like Patagonia or Canada. He founded an illustrated weekly paper when he was eleven, which featured columns with puzzles, cartoons, and songs, and even a serial entitled "Revenge," the story of a three-mast schooner sailing for Patagonia. He was an active, energetic, optimistic child, who excelled at sports and loved school vacations. He and his family would go to the Jardin d'Acclimatation, where the guardian allowed the Charcots access to the Lac Saint-James and the island in the middle of it. He would spend his days playing Robinson Crusoe, fighting off savages and ferocious wild animals, imagining feats of bravery and remarkable displays of cunning that would set him apart from his peers. When his family went on vacation to Ouistreham in Normandy, Jean-Baptiste's first visit was to the harbor to find his friends the fishermen, who taught him how to navigate through the swift currents of the channels. It was there that he learned how to sail, and first took pride in the ability to orient himself in strange, unknown places, to master his environment.

At a young age, he already had dreams of becoming an explorer, but his father would hear nothing of such folly. "One must always have in mind that a goal needs to be achieved, an ideal realized," his father patiently explained. "Now, for you, the ideal is to acquire in the world a good and honorable position, to excel at something." Jean-Martin told his son that it would be absurd for him not to follow him into a field in which he could be his son's guide and support. It would be the opposite of Jean-Martin's own experience, working alone, without patrons, as a young doctor from a family without means or connections. Jean-Baptiste struggled against his father's pronouncement, enlisting the help of his mother, pleading, cajoling, but to no avail. He felt frustrated, stifled, and wished—not for the first time—that he had a less illustrious name to live up to. Proud of his father's name, he studied hard with the goal of becoming a doctor like him. But he always worried that "being the son of Papa, I would always be taken for a papa's boy." He resigned himself to his future, figuring that with his salary as a doctor he could, at the very least, save up enough money to buy a yacht to use on his vacations.

If his father firmly denied Jean-Baptiste's wish to become an explorer, he nonetheless encouraged him and his siblings to travel and learn something of the world. During the summer vacations, Mme Charcot would remain in the comfortable opulence of the summer home in suburban Neuilly while her husband and the children traveled. They went to Wales in 1883, and then Belgium and Holland. A few years later, it was a trip to Venice in 1886 and then another to Spain and Spanish Morocco in 1887. "With their imagination and their naturally sensitive 'nature,' they will always know how to amuse themselves anywhere," their father wrote back to his wife with satisfaction. These trips were instructive for Jeanne and Jean-Baptiste, too. They were impressed at how their father was recognized everywhere, and Jeanne, writing to her mother, noticed that the women could not keep their eyes off her handsome brother. Jean-Baptiste was also becoming quite the prankster. One time he pulled up to the entrance of the Château de Madrid, a fashionable restaurant in Paris, in the gardener's cart drawn by a donkey named Saladin. Another time he was seen rowing in a small boat on the Lac Saint-James accompanied by an elegant young lady. Suddenly the crowd on the bank witnessed Jean-Baptiste stand up and hurl the young lady into the lake. The police were called, but he burst out laughing: the victim was only a scarecrow wearing his sister's best hat. The passionate nature that drew him to tales of dangerous quests and exotic travel was also on display in Jean-Baptiste's affairs of the heart. Tension erupted when he informed his father that he had fallen madly in love with and wished to become engaged to one of the daughters of Léon Gérôme, a painter and member of the Institute. "One doesn't marry at twenty-three. One first finishes one's studies," Jean-Martin had insisted, and so Jean-Baptiste refused to eat with the rest of the family, preferring to dine alone in his room. At around the same time, Charcot's daughter, Jeanne, who had developed a passionate crush on Léon Daudet, made the shocking declaration that she found it completely natural for a woman in society to live in concubinage with a man if she truly cared for him. After being roundly upbraided by her father, Jeanne, too, insisted on being served meals in her room, leaving Jean-Martin and his wife to eat alone. But really these were halfhearted rebellions at best—Jeanne and Jean-Baptiste worshipped their father too much to ever truly go against his wishes. Their mother, while sympathetic to their heartache, firmly supported the will of her husband. There were few, after all, who would dare to challenge him in earnest.

Whether they were still too young to fully grasp the intellectual and cultural revolutions just beginning to stir around them, or whether they were simply too cocooned by their own privileged status, neither Jean-Baptiste nor Léon had to cast about too far to find a future profession. When it was time for them to turn to a career, they both made the sensible choice of medicine. In those days doctors enjoyed considerable prestige in French society and were seen as being at the forefront of the most exciting scientific advances. There were, of course, other, more personal reasons for the choice. If his father's expectations pushed Jean-Baptiste to medical school, then Alphonse Daudet's illness sent Léon down that path—the constant pain, the morphine injections, and, in particular, those miserable trips to spas peopled by those suffering from the same sort of degenerative disease as his father. Despite the beauty of their surroundings and the comfortably appointed furnishings of the lodgings, these spas had a decidedly desperate quality to them, with well-dressed wraiths wandering through the grounds, their jerky, maladroit movements revealing the extent to which they had been betrayed by their bodies. For young Léon the sufferers often seemed like foreign beings, maniacs and hypochondriacs who had given their doctors absolute preeminence and whose nervous disorders had developed into a sort of perpetual worry, occasioned by years of being poked and prodded and analyzed *ad nauseam*, and of spending wakeful nights pondering the horrors of heredity and the inevitable arrival of death. Although Léon had also considered following in his father's footsteps and taking up a career as a writer, he ultimately chose to devote himself to unlocking the mysteries of illness, to exorcising the suffering of his father.

And so these two friends, who had grown up on opposite sides of disease and decay and yet shared a similar sense of obligation to their study, entered medical school together. In October 1885, a few months after the whole world had stopped and marked the passing of Victor Hugo, Léon and Jean-Baptiste began their medical studies. They were surrounded by men they had always known, esteemed doctors, whose cool and confident ministrations had been dished out at relatives' bedsides and whose most grisly anecdotes had later become fodder for the idle chatter at glittering dinner parties and salons. And yet if Léon and Jean-Baptiste had begun their medical studies with the hope of gaining access to a privileged and enlightened— even noble—profession, they were quickly disappointed. The light-filled fantasy of medicine's nobility was quickly replaced with the reality of dilapidated hospices, sleep-deprived students, and somber, waning patients. Years later Léon still remembered the odor of dirty feet and carbolic acid that wafted up from the unswept floors to mix with the heat and the flies and the chemical fumes that circled around the patient beds like so many vultures. When he finally began seeing his own patients at the Hôtel-Dieu, during his second year, his very first suffered from cancer, and the smell of her deteriorating body was so horrible that Léon nearly vomited. At night he would stumble back to the hostel where he took his meals and stare at his plate with a mixture of horror and disgust. The sights and smells of the hospital had induced in him a perpetual sense of nausea.

Jean-Baptiste also had a difficult time in medical school. Everyone knew who he was, and he frequently felt people scanning his face to see if they could discern any likeness with his famous father. His teachers expected him to excel over the other students, expected him to take to medicine as fish took to swimming. He responded to these assumptions with a mixture of annoyance and trepidation. The classes were difficult, but he enjoyed the science, finding that his courses exposed him to a more rich and comprehensive view of the world. But he found his time with patients trying—with their various illnesses and complaints, they were extreme opposites of his own robust self. He did enjoy the camaraderie of the school, which allowed him and the other students to recover from long days in the hospital with raucous parties and elaborate practical jokes.

Their days were spent immersed in their studies—practical courses of botany and chemistry on the rue Vauquelin, studies in physics at the Sorbonne. Léon loved most studying anatomy at the lab of the physiologist Nestor Gréhant in the Jardin des Plantes, hidden in the greenery, while an old dog, which had been the subject of countless experiments, barked around them like the "dog of Faust." If they had worked in another field—law or finance, perhaps—the discrepancy between greatness of mind and the limitations of the body might not have appeared so vast, so dwarfing to these young men. But every day they were confronted with the entire gamut of illness and despair.

In March 1886 Léon was working in the surgery service of Professor Paul Tillaux when several Russian peasants who had been bitten by a rabid wolf were brought in. They had been sent by the Russian government to be treated by the great Louis Pasteur, who had recently and controversially declared that he had discovered a treatment for rabies. For eight days Léon, Jean-Baptiste, and the other student doctors helped with the observations of the Russian peasants, watching each day as Pasteur himself administered the injections of his serum, while newspapers in Paris and around the world breathlessly awaited each triumphant installment. On the ninth day, one of the peasants succumbed to rabies and was quickly removed to isolation. But his cries were heard throughout the hospital, and Léon could see on the faces of the Russian's companions the horrified expressions at the thought of what lay in store for them as well. They tried stopping up their ears, with large, coarse, scarred fingers, but with each day that passed, another would be struck by the same symptoms. Day after day the hospital staff saw their condition deteriorate, watched the men foaming at the mouth, eyes bulging, scraping desperately at the walls, rolling on the floor, begging for help. Eventually, according to Léon, Tillaux and Pasteur consulted with the pharmacist, who prepared pills for those beyond hope. One by one the men were held down as doctors held the jaw, coaxed open the mouth, and slid the deadly relief down the tongue, stroking the neck gently yet firmly as the chemicals and powders dissolved into the surrounding tissue and juices. Silence fell like a shroud as everyone wept in horror. Medicine, both Léon and Jean-Baptiste were learning, could be a sinister art.

While Léon and Jean-Baptiste were learning the tools of medicine firsthand, the elder Charcot continued to monitor the health of Alphonse, whose condition had deteriorated to the point where he could no longer administer his own morphine. There were days when both Léon and Alphonse would be in the Salpêtrière as Alphonse stiffly submitted himself to increasingly painful and experimental treatments, such as the Sayre suspension, in which he was hung up, some of the time by the jaw alone, for several minutes, causing excruciating pain. No wonder he had dreams in which he was Christ on the cross. While Alphonse's frail body underwent such dubious "treatments," his son Léon and the other interns, clad in white aprons and hats, moved in and out among patient beds. As Léon's medical knowledge grew, he took on more responsibility for his father's care. In August 1886 he accompanied his father to a cure at Lamalou, armed with an array of syringes and morphine. The trip did Alphonse no good. Alphonse put on a brave face for his family, but to his friend Edmond de Goncourt he confessed his darkest thoughts: his absolute "terror" at the thought of disgusting the people whom he loved, his thoughts about suicide and about putting an end to all the suffering. As Alphonse became more dependent on morphine, Léon would take to sneaking into his father's office while the rest of the house was asleep, and replacing some of the morphine with distilled water, noting with both relief and guilt that his father "never suspected this filial treachery."

But beyond the suffering of his father, which pained Léon as nothing else could, he was interested, if not obsessed, with this disease for other reasons. At the time, the School of Medicine in Paris, like most schools of medicine in Europe, was deeply concerned with the idea of heredity as a way of explaining the etiology and transmission of illness. Theories of heredity were fed by the growing interest in the theory of Darwinism and the trendy fixation on degeneration.

Jean-Martin Charcot had used this theory to explain the appearance of neurological disorders. And the famed syphilographer Alfred Fournier, who was one of Léon and Jean-Baptiste's teachers, was developing the theme of hereditary syphilis . . . and the idea of "heredos," offspring of men and women suffering from the primary infection of the disease who have inherited certain hereditary defects stemming from the initial infection. In class Léon would watch the deformed faces of children and adolescents with flattened heads and sunken jaws in a flush of horror. Would the disease that had ravaged his father's health reveal itself in his own seemingly healthy body, Léon fretted, or would it pass over him entirely, only to reveal itself in future generations of Daudets?

After hours, Léon and Jean-Baptiste and the other students, many from illustrious families of money and privilege, would go to Les Halles for a glass of white wine and a mushroom omelet at one of the pubs open all night on one of the side streets, where the rough and tumble (laborers, streetwalkers, peddlers, and other members of low society) would approach the medical students and ask for advice about their various injuries, sores, and pains. Léon was in his element and studied hard, much to the annoyance of his friend Georges Hugo, who wanted Léon to relax and play. Georges had never shared his friend's intellectual curiosity or ability for sustained effort. Léon also had affairs: furtive encounters with nurses and assistants in the cold, dark corridors of the hospital, with the pretty lasses at student cafés, and sometimes even with prostitutes. But all the while he was secretly in love with Jeanne Hugo, whom he saw each summer at Guernsey accompanied by Georges. Philippe Berthelot was also in love with her—he would not have been surprised if there were others as well. As a testament to how much the matter weighed on him, Léon chose as his thesis subject "Love is a neurosis."

In the spring of 1888, Jeanne Hugo, eighteen years old, suffered an attack of pleurisy. She was officially "followed" by the renowned cardiologist Pierre Potain and his student, Léon. Some whispered that the young medical student and the beautiful heiress were going to be married, but Alphonse and Julia hoped not. They wanted Léon to solidify his future and worried that, without a true fortune of his own, he would be seen as a gold digger. And would the Hugo family ever truly respect him for what he was? After all, Alphonse and Julia confided in Goncourt, Potain himself had presented Léon to the Hugos as the one who would replace him, "the doctor of tomorrow." Léon and Georges were still thick as thieves, although Goncourt for one was struck at how badly the young Hugo was turning out: "He is swollen, bloated like a commoner and unhealthy, fat . . . Alas, he no longer has the delicate, distinguished figure that he once had and promised to have forever." Meanwhile, young Jeanne Charcot, Jean-Baptiste's sister, still quietly pined for Léon. Toward the end of 1886, at a performance of the play *Michel Pauper*, she had maneuvered herself to be seated across the way from the box occupied by Goncourt and Léon in the hopes of attracting the latter's attention. But the love scenes in the play proved to be too much for the young lady, forcing her to spend much of the evening covering up her face in embarrassment, much to the amusement of Goncourt and his young friend.

Jeanne Hugo, meanwhile, was gaining a reputation for being one of the most sought-after, attractive belles in all of Paris. She was known for her incomparable beauty and sweet manners. The great Italian banker and industrialist Henri Cernuschi threw a grand ball in her honor in the spring of 1888 in his Buddha Hall, featuring a giant statue of the religious figure, but Jeanne was too ill to attend. When she led a cotillion at French president Carnot's private reception at the Élysée in February 1888, throwing a toy balloon out at the smiling youths and allowing the one who caught it the privilege of dancing with her, it was featured in society pages around the world. Léon and Jean-Baptiste were both smitten with the young beauty, as was a young Greek cadet at Saint-Cyr military academy, Michel Negreponte. The two had met at a party given by his stepfather, Victor de Lesseps, son of Ferdinand de Lesseps, the Suez Canal founder and longtime friend of Victor Hugo. Jeanne fancied herself in love with Michel, but her mother had more ambitious plans for her and forbade any further courtship. Jeanne had always been a headstrong girl, but she knew she could not disobey her mother in this. She had not been raised to exhibit the sorts of youthful acts of rebellion that young men of her station could indulge in. Well-bred girls like her were monitored constantly—what they read, what they wore, whom they befriended, and certainly whom they might marry. Few could go out without some sort of chaperone.

Most were educated at home or at convents, where the emphasis was less on intellectual improvement than on instruction in wifely arts. Léon and Jean-Baptiste may have crossed paths with a handful of women medical students during their studies, but even if they had, the young men would not have socialized with them, let alone considered them proper potential wives. Jean-Martin even had a woman student, Blanche Edwards, studying under him who successfully defended her medical thesis on hemiplegia. Although by most accounts he was generally supportive of her studies, Jean-Martin reportedly told her in 1889, "I do not see clearly what will be the eventual outcome of such conscientious efforts. What do you plan on doing?" The concept of women actually practicing medicine remained outside his grasp.

During their third year of medical school, Léon and Jean-Baptiste both did their voluntary service as auxiliary doctors. Jean-Baptiste was ecstatic—he loved being out in nature and reveled in the daily tests of endurance and the proofs of fraternal camaraderie. Léon was just glad to be away from his miserable patients and overbearing professors. When not in school or doing his voluntary service, Léon attended his parents' weekly salon, mingling with writers like Marcel Prévost and Pierre Loti, the artist James McNeill Whistler, the photographer Nadar, and of course, their old family friends Émile Zola and Edmond de Goncourt. Jean-Baptiste, meanwhile, attended his father's famous lecture series, the Tuesday lessons, and the gathering of students, friends, and admirers who congregated at the family home afterward.

The political mood in France was tenuous: the Right was angry about the rise of secularism and insisted upon the need for national regeneration, while the Left was unhappy about unrepentant capitalism and an unrepresentative government. Spiritualists preferred to speak with the dead rather than with a corrupt church, while the center seemed to be crumbling, and artists and writers on the fringe dished up an intoxicating and disorienting cocktail of new forms and ideas. The Universal Exposition in 1889 served as a welcome distraction from these tensions as the city filled with tourists and foreigners. A triumphant and wildly successful affirmation of France's power and technological innovation, the exposition, commemorating the centennial of the French Revolution, transformed the city into an enchanted playground for the 300 million people who cruised the Seine in the *bateaux mouches*, admired the vigorous curves of the Eiffel Tower, and sampled the exotic sights and sounds in streets transformed into Moroccan bazaars and Thai villages. The main buildings were illuminated by Thomas Edison's latest invention, the incandescent bulb. Edmond de Goncourt was less impressed by the proceedings, observing that the first symptom of the exposition was an "insupportable odor of musk emanating from the crowd."

Twenty-four hours before the official March 31 inauguration ceremony, Léon Daudet claimed that he and Victor Hugo's grandson, Georges, had crept past the sleeping guards at the base of the Eiffel Tower and climbed up to the top of the iron giant. After an evening carousing on the town, the two young friends—both twenty-two years old—had decided that the magnificent view of the darkened city, illuminated only by brief flashes of lightning from an advancing storm, would be worth the climb. After scrambling up the structure, they found themselves alone at the top with the French flag, which danced and snapped in the strong wind as if struggling to break free. They looked down upon the city, expecting to see the stunning view of Paris at night promised by organizers of the exposition. Instead, they found themselves peering into a dark chasm with no end or beginning in sight. Suddenly the French flag tore from its harness and fell meekly in a pile at their feet. Nothing remained for the two disappointed friends to do but begin the long descent down to the city below, toward a future as murky and ill-defined as the view of the Parisian skyline that stormy evening.

A few months later, Léon had a dream in which Jean-Martin Charcot brought him a copy of Pascal's *Pensées* and had him look inside that great man's brain, which Charcot had brought with him. When he did, he saw that the cells that had once housed great thoughts were now absolutely empty and resembled the cavities of a dried-out hive. Goncourt found Léon's dream delightfully provocative and was struck by "the mixture in him of idiocies, fights with cabdrivers, and at the same time by his intellectual association with high thinkers and his truly original drafts of notes about medical life." The future, Goncourt was sure, lay with this bright young man.

FIVE

In Sickness and in Health

Independent of any incidents or events in her own career, Jeanne
Hugo will ever be a part of the Victor Hugo cult—a cult which is
overshadowed in France only by that of Napoleon.

—Stuart Oliver Henry (1896)

Although the ceremony was not scheduled to begin until six p.m.
on February 12, already by three o'clock the crowds had begun to
gather outside the town hall of the sixteenth arrondissement. By five,
there were five to six thousand Parisians of all classes and ages, patiently waiting in the cool, damp final hours of that February afternoon to catch a glimpse of the great Victor Hugo's granddaughter
before she entered the building to marry.

The 1891 wedding of Jeanne Hugo and Léon Daudet was the
wedding of the year, if not of the decade. Seen as the triumphant
culmination of two great republican dynasties, according to one
observer it had nothing less than "the allure of apotheosis." She was
twenty-one, and he was twenty-three. Reporters sent to cover the
event for the major magazines and newspapers noted with satisfaction the many luminaries from the worlds of politics, the arts, and
letters who were to be in attendance. All aspects of the proceedings
were dissected and analyzed. While anticlerical newspapers applauded
the fact that the ceremony would be a civil one, conservative papers

denounced its agnostic contours (typical of the Hugo family, they agreed, but they had expected better from Alphonse Daudet). Fashion writers lavished detailed commentary on Jeanne's dress, while the gossip columnists speculated about her dowry. A list of all the gifts presented to the young couple was published the day before the ceremony.

For Jeanne and her family, such attention was to be expected. The Daudets were less accustomed to such displays of public interest, and, as the public acclaim rose to a fever pitch in the weeks before the wedding, they felt themselves getting caught up in the limelight with a mixture of trepidation and fascination. And there were other issues about the wedding that gave both Julia and Alphonse pause. They worried that, to outsiders, it would look as if Léon were marrying Jeanne for her name and fortune. And they worried about the wild behavior of Jeanne's brother, Georges, who seemed entirely out of control, with his gambling and women, jumping from one bed to the next with such careless abandon that the elder Daudets feared he could come to tragic ends—felled by a jealous husband, perhaps— if he was not careful. They were also not thrilled at now being so closely allied to that peculiar cult of the old poet, which seemed to have the inevitable effect of turning otherwise sensible men and women into sniveling sycophants. And then there was the problem of Jeanne's stepfather Lockroy's radical politics—the Daudets were republicans, but deeply patriotic ones, and they shared the anti-Semitic concerns of many of their friends. Finally, Julia had heard troubling rumors about Jeanne's having an insane aunt; these rumors, when considered with the well-known insanity of Victor's brother, who had died in an asylum, suggested an undeniably unsettling genealogy.

Jeanne and Léon paid little attention to such details. Léon could scarcely believe his good fortune. When he had called on Jeanne's mother at the end of June 1890 to ask for her daughter's hand in marriage, part of him was sure she would refuse. He was still in awe of her and her family, despite the years he'd spent in such close proximity to them. Instead, she had consented, but only on the express condition that Léon ask Jeanne himself. For two whole days, Léon could not bring himself to do so; and when he finally did find himself before the object of his affection, he could not bring himself to look her in the face. "Mademoiselle, I have loved you since I treated you: will you be my wife?" he mumbled in the general direction of the floor in front of her. Her response—throwing herself into his arms in an embrace at once tender and rapacious—made the whole ordeal worth it. It was, everyone agreed, a storybook romance, this tale of two childhood friends who had fallen in love. But when the engagement was announced, not everyone was pleased. Both Mme Charcot and the socialite Mme Ménard-Dorian had hoped that Léon, a most eligible young bachelor, would marry their daughters. Mme Ménard-Dorian even told Léon outright that her own daughter was wealthier, better educated, and possessed of a greater intellect than Jeanne, who was, she insisted, a nice girl but nothing remarkable. Alphonse was full of paternal pride but could not immediately join in the family celebrations: his hands trembled so violently that the act of writing the letter to Mme Lockroy formally asking for the hand of her daughter on behalf of his son took him three whole hours to complete. He confessed to Goncourt that writing, which had always brought him the greatest pleasure and sense of accomplishment, had become so painful with his illness that he had taken to composing letters in his mind before setting them down on paper, in an attempt to construct letters with the least amount of words necessary.

Edmond de Goncourt was the first one to join the Daudets in celebrating the young couple. He was fascinated by Jeanne and admired her openly as she tentatively accepted her position as a newly engaged young woman. Observing the young couple in the Daudets' salon, he found her breathtakingly beautiful and achingly young. In so many ways they were both still children—Léon in his medical intern's skullcap and Jeanne, never straying too far from her watchful mother. "It is a pretty sight," he jotted down in his journal, "these two lovebirds seated on a sofa, staring into each other's eyes, saying nothing and yet everything." When Goncourt prepared to take his leave, Jeanne kissed him tenderly, and, in spite of himself, the catty old man found himself melting ever so slightly. "Jeanne is really quite lovely," he observed, "with her skin of such dazzling whiteness," standing out against the Pierrot neckline of her beige dress, knotted by a grass-green belt into which an enormous carnation of the most delicate rose color was threaded. A few days later, Goncourt witnessed the young couple unable to stop talking to each other, causing Mme Lockroy to exclaim irritably, "But what in the world can you be talking about? In three months you will have nothing left to say to each other!" Yet Goncourt sensed something within Jeanne that could defy such maternal calls for self-control: "The happiness of Jeanne has an expansion that spreads out over the entire world. She embraces you by throwing her arms around your neck in the carefree fashion of sweet children." He found this childish exuberance surprising and utterly endearing, especially coming as it did from a member of that calculating Hugo clan.

After a few weeks of joyful celebration, Mme Lockroy announced that she planned to take Jeanne away to Guernsey for their customary August vacation. Léon, it was assumed, would stay behind to cram for his medical exams, after which he would join them in Guernsey. But Goncourt and Alphonse found him in tears at the thought of being apart from his beloved. He confessed to them that the previous evening he had gone to the Panthéon with Jeanne to place on the tomb of her grandfather all the flowers that she had received from various well-wishers since the beginning of her courtship. He wasn't sure if it was due to the stress of the past few weeks, the excitement of the engagement, or the simple act of Jeanne's sharing with him the tender gestures of the people's love for her grandfather, but Léon felt overwhelmed by emotion. The two families relented and allowed Léon to join Jeanne and the Hugos at Hauteville House for a few days' break from studying.

When he returned from Guernsey, Léon resumed studying for his examinations—an activity that he had sorely neglected during the emotional whirlwind of the previous weeks. The examination took place in the Salle Saint-Jean at the Hôtel de Ville, beginning at the end of October and finishing in January. Candidates read their compositions before the jury, comprising four physicians, four surgeons, and two obstetricians. Despite his best efforts, despite his intelligence, and despite the assurances that he would pass, Léon failed the exam and had to settle with being named a "provisional intern," that is, an intern for only one year. Instantly he and his family were convinced that some sort of foul play had taken place. Léon, after all, had done quite well on the oral component of the exam, although he had done much worse on the written section. To make matters worse, his friend Jean-Baptiste, the son of the great Charcot, had passed. Léon's mother complained to anyone within earshot that the only reason Léon had failed was that the Charcots were angry that he had picked Jeanne Hugo over their own daughter. For their part the Charcots were indignant that the Daudets would spread such vicious lies. Jean-Baptiste in particular was crushed—no accusation could have been more upsetting to him because deep down he worried that it might be true. He had always been sensitive about being seen as someone who made his way in the world only with the help of his famous surname. The two young men quarreled, and it became clear that their friendship was over. They were each too proud, too sensitive, to forgive the other.

They avoided each other from then on. Léon was first stunned, then humiliated, then furious about the failure. He had always been emotional—his parents called him "passionate"—and had inherited some of his father's southern temper. But he felt a black rage in the face of the injustice carried out against him, the likes of which he had never before experienced. He swore to turn his back forever on medicine, although he kept this decision to himself for the moment for fear of shocking his parents or Jeanne or the exacting Hugo family. The very next day, after learning of his results on the medical exam, he began writing a scathing denunciation of all the wrongs that he saw in the medical profession, allowing his rancor and outrage at all the time he had wasted on such a fruitless enterprise to gush onto the page. During the day he continued to attend classes at the School of Medicine, while at night he went home and outlined the story of *Les Morticoles*, the tale of a young man named Félix Canelon who discovers a strange foreign land where all of the inhabitants live under the tyranny of doctors. The hero starts out as an observer and becomes in turn a patient and then a medical student before finally escaping and returning to the real world. Léon, too, was ready for an escape and had decided that his future no longer lay in medicine but in writing, like his father.

On the morning of the wedding, Goncourt arrived at the Daudet home to accompany the family to the town hall and found Alphonse in a state—agitated, muscles clenched, eyes widened and rolling about as if to find something soothing to settle upon. He confessed to Goncourt that he had been plagued by nightmares about, of all things, the story of the fire at the Schwarzenberg ball. On July 1, 1810, Prince Charles-Philippe de Schwarzenberg, then the ambassador from Austria, had famously given a great ball at the embassy on the rue du Mont-Blanc to celebrate the marriage of Napoléon and Marie-Louise of Austria. In order to accommodate his distinguished guests, including royalty from throughout Europe, he had added a broad hall and wooden gallery, decorated with great quantities of flowers, banners, and candelabras. Just as the emperor, who had been present at the ball for two or three hours, was preparing to leave, one of the chiffon curtains, blown by the breeze, caught fire from a candle. Some of the guests attempted to extinguish the fire by tearing down the drapery and smothering the flames with their hands; but in the twinkling of an eye the curtains, papers, and garlands caught, and the woodwork began to burn. Napoléon and his bride escaped. Though trampled by the crowd, Prince Kourakine, the Russian ambassador, was saved by the thickness of his coat. However, many others perished, including Princess Pauline de Schwarzenberg, wife of the host's brother, who was pregnant with her ninth child. So consumed was Alphonse by this idea of a matrimonial conflagration that when he woke up on the morning of Léon and Jeanne's wedding, he sent a telegram to Lockroy begging him to have someone inspect the lighting in the reception hall where the marriage would take place. He then sent his secretary, Jules Ebner, to the prefecture of police to ask for additional men to be posted. When Alphonse finally stopped agonizing over the myriad catastrophic events that could possibly take place, there was nothing left for him to do but worry about the logistics of his own attendance. How was he going to make it up the grand staircase without his legs giving themselves over to the spasms and sudden moments of weakness that now ruled his days? What if he fell before the hundreds of onlookers? Goncourt assured him that he would remain by his side so that nothing would happen.

The wedding guests, who were only admitted to the proceedings with an access card, began invading the town hall at five p.m. All the most fashionable and esteemed members of the Parisian elite were in attendance. Émile Zola mingled with the great colonialist and statesman Jules Ferry, cabinet ministers with members of the Academy. Those who could not squeeze their way into the main room gathered pell-mell along the banister of the staircase and under the fringed velvet awning. Those who were stuck at the doors found themselves packed so tightly together that they could scarcely breathe, since the authorities had insisted that a clear pathway be established through the middle of the staircase. Outside the town hall, despite the light rain, the number of observers was equally large and dense, and constables struggled to keep the surging crowd under control.

Finally, at six-thirty p.m., the bridal procession arrived and slowly climbed the steps of the town hall. The crowd parted in respect, merely intensifying the crush of people on either side of the young bride, resplendent in her white satin gown. The women in the crowd murmured approvingly about the intricate British lace trim, while the men appreciatively took in her bright eyes and young, full figure. Jeanne smiled serenely, a vision of youthful grace and beauty, nodding at some she knew, shaking hands with others. Her stepfather escorted her through the throng as the various members of the two great families followed. As he had promised, Goncourt was there to help Alphonse Daudet drag himself up the great stairs. It was distressing for Goncourt to see his friend in such a state—his heart pounding, sweat pouring down his neck, his face contorted into an expression of such desperate concentration as he struggled to will his failing body into compliance. Somehow they managed to make it up the stairs and across the great room where the ceremony was to take place so that Alphonse could sink into a chair and attempt to recover. The six bridesmaids and groomsmen had followed gaily behind them, scampering with pert, youthful enthusiasm, oblivious to the two men's struggle before them.

As soon as the bride and her stepfather stepped across the threshold of the marriage hall, the first notes of Saint-Saëns's "Hymn to Victor Hugo" rose triumphantly from the orchestra. When the music finally stopped, the municipal magistrate began the official proceedings. When asked if they agreed to the terms of the marriage, the young couple responded in a single voice: "Yes!" The mayor rose and pronounced a moving statement wishing the newlyweds all happiness. He then recited for the couple and for the audience some stanzas from a poem that Victor Hugo had read at the marriage of his beloved daughter Léopoldine to Charles Vacquerie on February 15, 1843: "Love the one who loves you and be happy in him. / Adieu! Be his treasure, oh you who were ours . . ." How strange for Jeanne to find herself here, the recipient of recycled paeans of affection. It could not be helped, of course, the interchangeable quality that all Victor Hugo's women had in his world. Sister replaced sister, grand-daughter stood in for daughter, lovers replaced wife and other lovers, all twirling in a perfect constellation around the stellar, stunning fig-ure of the great old man. Of course she had grown to love Léon and was delighted at the prospect of being his wife, but it was only a supplement to her identity, an added jewel in her crown. She was and would forever be Victor Hugo's granddaughter. Then the philoso-pher and statesman Jules Simon, who was serving as one of her wit-nesses, rose and spoke to the audience sitting in rapt, reverent silence of his long friendship with the family, particularly with Jeanne's mother, before turning to Jeanne herself: "I am sure, my child," he began, "that you think above all about your grandfather. It is about him that we all are thinking."

> It is for him that all of Paris has come here; for indeed Paris is here. She presses into this room, inundates the stairways and the waiting rooms. Victor Hugo was a great citizen; he was the honor of our cause; but it is not for the republican or the pa-triot that Paris is celebrating. It is the celebration of Homer that we celebrate. It is the spirit of the great poet, who is in the midst of us. Paris understands and remembers; he is today as he was before the capital of thought . . . We all knew his genius, but no one knew as you did his great heart. You, child, who were his last passion, you know what great satisfaction your happiness today would have brought him. This thought touches all those who at this moment press around you.

Alphonse and Julia knew that their son's marriage to Jeanne would necessarily come with a certain amount of Hugolatry, but this was over the top. Léon and his family had scarcely been mentioned dur-ing the ceremony. And even when, finally, Jules Simon got around to discussing the marriage itself, the Hugo name continued to eclipse all other considerations. "Everything conspires in your favor," Simon told the bride. "You are leaving a house full of genius and glory; and you will also find glory and genius in the house where you are entering. I worry that the road will be too easy for you and that you will not have the occasion to show your greatness of spirit." At this, everyone laughed—how delightful to be so lucky! He closed his remarks with a last piece of advice for Jeanne: "We carry within ourselves, my child, the source of happiness. Outside events can do much less for the goodness or the unhappiness of life than your will. Carry joy into your new dwelling. You have within you a real treasure, and this treasure, my child, you must never exhaust." Such accolades for one so young, for one who had accomplished so little in her life.

The entire discourse left the crowd stunned, enraptured. Everyone agreed it was a truly auspicious way for Jeanne and Léon to begin their life together. The orchestra began merrily playing Mendelssohn's overture to *Ruy Blas*, while the wedding procession passed into a gorgeous salon in the style of Louis XVI and formed a receiving line. In just under an hour, the granddaughter of the greatest poet France had ever known had become Mme Léon Daudet.

At eight p.m. a small party had gathered back at the Lockroy-Hugo household on the avenue Victor-Hugo. Jules Simon held forth and entertained the group, and Goncourt was struck by his intelligent brow and seductive eyes. How unfortunate then, he noted snidely, that Simon's wife was pleasant enough but alarmingly ugly, "like an intelligent monkey." But the person Goncourt watched most closely was Jeanne herself, whose smile and obvious delight were contagious to him and the other guests. Léon, who had spent much of the day in such a state of extreme anxiety that he barely seemed cognizant of his surroundings, had visibly relaxed and now seemed to be basking in a postnuptial glow.

A few days later, Goncourt dined at the rue Bellechasse home of Julia and Alphonse with the young couple. Jeanne, he noticed, had voluptuously dark circles under her eyes, while Léon confided grandly in him that "it is really good to be married." The next time Goncourt saw them, he was again struck by the infectious sweetness of Jeanne, noting, "I do not know a more gently caressing, a more tenderly enveloping affection than that of Jeanne Hugo, when she is seated next to you. She really does have a lovely little heart, overwhelming in its elaborations, in its inclinations towards you, in the graces of her magnetic body, a lovely little heart, which is very rare to meet at this time." How lucky for the two of them to have found each other, he thought, especially after learning the story of Germaine Pillaut, a young woman whom Mme Daudet had originally wanted Léon to marry. Instead, her parents had pushed her into a marriage with a sweet boy whom she did not love. Germaine refused to see her mother for eight days after the wedding. When mother and daughter finally met, the former asked, "Are you mad at me?" And the daughter responded, "Yes, I am mad at you . . . it's a horror! If I had known . . . I would never have gotten married!" Germaine had been raised in absolute ignorance about sex, and her mother, speaking with Mme Daudet, allowed that perhaps it would be better to raise girls differently. And yet, if they knew more about what marriage entailed, she worried that parents wishing to marry off their daughters would meet with insurmountable resistance. At least, Goncourt thought to himself, the marriage of Léon and Jeanne had been a true love match.

Léon had hoped that after the wedding, some of the Hugo hoopla would calm down and that he and his bride would have time to spend enjoying each other's company without the prying eyes of family and well-wishers. But Jeanne's family insisted that her mother accompany the newlyweds on their honeymoon in the south, chosen because Léon had wanted to show his bride the people and places that were important to his own family. They met the famous Provençal poet Frédéric Mistral and visited the mill that had inspired Alphonse's *Letters from My Mill,* the book that earned his place in the pantheon of beloved writers in French literature. Yet even before the honeymoon was over, tensions began to rise between the two families over miscommunications about the financial arrangements of the match. Alphonse confided in Goncourt that he was worried about his son's future happiness.

Alphonse was right to worry, for Jeanne and Léon's wedded bliss was indeed short-lived. When they returned to their cavernous apartment after their honeymoon, they were confronted with the reality of daily life. Jeanne was accustomed to being fussed over and cared for; Léon was used to commanding attention and being admired. The narrator of Alan Sheridan's novel *Time and Place* captured Léon's outsized personality best, observing that he "ate, drank, and talked twice as much as anyone else. At twenty-four he already had the exuberance, the self-assertiveness, the arrogance that were to become more marked as he grew older, but he still had the boyish charm that made such traits more palatable." Ultimately they did not have very much in common. Léon, who was attempting to launch a literary career of his own, was already growing weary of the constant homages paid to Victor Hugo. And Jeanne was unwilling or unable to let any man occupy a greater place in her heart than her grandfather. After a particularly heated argument in which Léon angrily declared, "I have not married a tradition. Enough with your old fart grandfather!" Jeanne stormed out of their apartment and returned to her mother's home for a few days—a fact that was scrupulously kept away from public gossip. Léon also took to baiting his mother-in-law, insisting one night over dinner that one could not exist in society without religion and ending his lengthy tirade with the declaration, "Deep down, I am conservative!" Such an admission was nothing short of heresy in the staunchly republican Hugo household.

But Léon was gaining a newfound confidence, now that he had definitively given up on medicine and announced his new literary aspirations to his family. The publisher Charpentier had even agreed to publish one of his works—as long as Alphonse served as guarantor. And Juliette Adam, the indomitable literary benefactor and head of the influential *Nouvelle Revue*, had agreed to publish extracts of his *Seed and Dust*, a collection of philosophical dialogues that only someone as young and naive and supremely self-confident as Léon could have written. The more Léon came into his own as a writer, the worse his fights with Jeanne became. As it turned out, she had quite a temper of her own and was not afraid to let her husband know how she felt. Outside observers would not have guessed that the pretty new bride possessed such a deep wellspring of resentment. One British writer who spent time at the home of Alphonse and Julia observed that Jeanne was a woman "in the Reubens style, endowed with wit and a warm heart." She was also, he continued, "a brilliant talker" who could "discuss your Balzac or your Ibsen with the best of them." But where once she had been petted and praised for her storytelling abilities, now all of the acclaim went to her husband. Léon, who had inherited his father's quick southern temper, was surprised by his wife's capacity for churlishness. Julia Daudet, despairing at the young couple's bickering, hoped that her daughter-in-law's short temper could be explained by her pregnancy. She was expecting, much to the delight of Léon and his family. Still, the arguments continued. In early September Jeanne suffered a "nervous crisis" and once again returned home to her mother. Léon and Jeanne were both ill-equipped to deal with the pressures from their families and the reality of marriage and upcoming parenthood. At a housewarming party they hosted in December 1891, the tension was palpable.

While waiting to become a father, Léon continued to throw himself into his writing. His preoccupation with inheritance had not diminished. He wrote a novel about atavism, which he entitled *Haeres* (The Heir), in which a young man is torn between the dueling influences of his father, his mother, and his uncle before dying precisely at the moment when he appears to have freed himself from this hereditary vortex. It was serialized in the *Nouvelle Revue* later that summer. Jeanne did not write about her pregnancy—there is no way of knowing how she felt about being bound closer to her husband or the prospect of no longer being the center of attention in their family. On February 5, 1892, Jeanne and Léon's son, Charles, was born. Léon and Jeanne were delighted, and, for a time, their arguments ceased. Shortly thereafter Alphonse wrote a short novel, *Rose et Ninette*, which he dedicated to his son Léon, "to the poet and to the philosopher." Unfortunately, like his son, Alphonse was wont to express his anxiety in literary form: the novel addressed the subject of divorce.

A few months later, Edmond de Goncourt found himself chatting with Jeanne Daudet at a dinner party. She told him the story of a young woman from Reims. This woman was very wealthy and had married quite well, yet after a few years of marriage, she began roaming the streets, confessing to people that she found the life of an honest married woman to be utterly boring. The intensity with which Jeanne queried Goncourt about the lessons to be learned from this story caused the elderly writer to raise his eyebrows in surprise and concern. Surely it was not a good sign that Jeanne took such a keen interest in these tales of womanly indifference to the marital contract, Goncourt must have thought. A few days after this encounter, Léon pulled Edmond aside to complain about his wife's stubbornness and her ability, when provoked, to fall into rages such as he had never seen. Léon claimed that such a willful temperament stemmed from her upbringing, raised as she had been by an indulgent and morally compromised narcissist like Victor Hugo, spoiled and allowed to do whatever she desired.

With his domestic life becoming less and less satisfactory, Léon threw himself increasingly into literature. He was desperate to write and to publish—no sooner had he finished one book or article than he started writing another one. He was also eager to make a name for himself as a literary critic, reaching out to his father's connections for assignments and notice. Given the illustrious names of both his father and his wife's grandfather, failure in literature was simply not an option. But it was also a pursuit that gave him great delight. He had grown up, after all, watching the respect and admiration his father had earned through his writing. He remembered statesmen and royalty queuing up for the chance to hear Alphonse's thoughts on the state of the novel, the history of French literature, or the secrets to the creative enterprise. Here was his chance to be afforded the same respect, to join that fraternal order of men of letters that had so sustained Alphonse even during those days when the physical pain had been almost unendurable. As a boy Léon was told that his elders would "make something" of him. Well, here was his chance to make something of himself, on his own. He began offering his opinions to anyone he met with the authority and decisiveness of an equal, a competitor.

Léon also began to avoid his home, going on nocturnal expeditions with his friends Georges Hugo and Philippe Berthelot. He ate for four and drank as if to obliterate any lingering self-doubt, gradually becoming rounder and rounder. He had affairs—glorious, sweaty, torrid ones—like his father before him. And when he returned home, tired and spent and reeking of wine and perfume, Jeanne would pounce on him, lashing out at him with all of her dumb frustration, as baby Charles wailed in the background. Their violent disputes quickly became the stuff of society gossip. Edmond de Goncourt noted one memorable instance in his journal. Léon and Jeanne were attending the theater with Léon's parents. Léon offered his arm to his father, Alphonse, who was weak from his illness and needed help walking. Goncourt, meanwhile, offered his arm to Julia, Alphonse's wife. "What?" Jeanne hissed furiously. "The granddaughter of Victor Hugo is reduced to entering the theater without the arm of a man?" According to Goncourt, she sulked for three months. Things came to a head when Léon's *Les Morticoles* was finally published in June 1894. It was a great succès de scandale, but it only seemed to drive him and Jeanne further apart. Simple domestic spats quickly spiraled into all-out battles, with the two screaming and hitting like frustrated children, lashing out in inarticulate rage and tears and tooth-gnashing.

It was somehow fitting that the disintegration of the Daudets' domestic life coincided with the chaos on the streets of Paris, as anarchist bombs ripped through popular cafés and government buildings. First there was an attack on the Chamber of Deputies on December 9, 1893, then another bomb at the Hôtel Terminus on February 12, 1894, and another in the Madeleine on March 15. When the president of the Republic, Sadi Carnot, was assassinated in Lyon at the height of his popularity by an Italian anarchist, anxiety and grief seized the nation. By midsummer 1894, tucked beneath the stories of reprisals against Italian nationals living in France and legal commentary about the crackdown against anarchism, the major newspapers were already publishing rumors that one of France's most famous young couples was on the verge of divorce. On December 22 Goncourt received a note from his servant with the announcement that Mme Léon Daudet had quit the conjugal home.

Goncourt rushed over to Alphonse and Julia's home at rue Bellechasse and found Léon silent, lost in his own bitterness and despondency. He showed everyone the note Jeanne had left for him, in which she accused him of tearing down the Hugo name, explained that she could no longer support his abuse and insults, and declared that she was leaving the house with her child. Léon walked through his now empty apartment, mournfully passing from room to room. He knew that his parents and Goncourt were right, that the marriage was no longer working and that ending it was the best solution for all involved. Jeanne had never understood him, never encouraged his literature, he told himself. And yet to be twenty-six and already divorced seemed cruelly unfair. As for Jeanne, she was back where she felt safe, understood—a world in which being a Hugo was all that was expected of her. To be divorced with a baby was not what Jeanne (nor anyone) had imagined for herself, but better to be free of Léon than to wake up one day ten years hence with no means of escape.

On December 26 Jeanne and Léon met face-to-face at a formal reconciliation session. The accusations and insults flew—Jeanne told the official that Léon had called her a bitch. Léon confirmed her account, but said he had done so only after she had spit in his face. He accused her of being violent toward him, enumerating various episodes. She replied that she did not recall those episodes but that, in any case, violence demanded violence. When the official presiding over their case asked her if her husband was a man honest, loyal, and generous she said yes, but when the official began to speak of a possible reconciliation she declared, implacably, "Never!" And with that, the fairy-tale romance came crashing down once and for all.

For both Jeanne and Léon, marriage had seemed like a way out of stifling family life: Jeanne had been curious about life beyond the control of her mother and the shadow of her grandfather, and Léon sought to shield himself from the anguish of watching his dying father suffer. But both came to the wedding with specific, ultimately incompatible models of what marriage should be, and neither had been raised to compromise on anything.

By the end of 1894, Léon's relationships with Jeanne and Jean-Baptiste—two people he had known and loved since childhood—had disintegrated. Only a few years earlier, he and Jean-Baptiste had been embarking on the same path, seemingly destined for shared glory in the field of medicine. Jean-Baptiste was still on that path, still dutifully meeting the expectations of his imposing father and laying the groundwork for a brilliant if expected career as a doctor. But Léon had had enough. Behind his angry, painful renunciation of medicine and his messy divorce lay a sense of bewilderment and indignation that the grand plans he and others had sketched out for his future were now cruelly beyond his reach. He had assumed that the transition to adulthood and the acquisition of authority, such as he had so admired in the "giants" he grew up with, would be automatic. But like other youthful rebels both before and to come, the crumbling of one set of expectations and assumptions ultimately left him strangely liberated to embark on a very different kind of journey.

So in 1894, as Jean-Baptiste was busy fulfilling his destiny and Léon was beginning to search for new ways of distinguishing himself, Jeanne had simply run home to her mother. Three young people who had once seemed destined for similar—if not shared—glory were now spinning off in opposite directions. Their three families now hoped that things could just settle down for a bit. Unfortunately, they would all be disappointed.

{SIX}

Degeneration

After Lamartine, you have been, I believe, the most loved man of our century, the one on whose head have been formed the most legends and dreams.

—Ernest Renan on Ferdinand de Lesseps (1884)

—⊃⊂—

In the summer of 1893, while Léon Daudet was struggling to save his marriage and Jean-Baptiste Charcot was dutifully continuing his medical studies, Jean-Martin Charcot found himself caught up in a national scandal. One moment he had been happily going about his usual routine—crossing the familiar flagstones of the Salpêtrière courtyard, enjoying meals with family and friends, secure in the happy rhythm of lectures and rounds, students and colleagues. Almost overnight he found himself compelled to drop everything, to cross the cold and choppy English Channel, bound for the sleepy town of Bournemouth to gauge the health of a fugitive who may have been the most hated man in all of France.

In many ways it was fitting that Jean-Martin Charcot, one of the century's greatest scientific minds and an embodiment of Third Republic achievement, was presiding over the final gasps of the chain of corruption and deceit that came to be known as the Panama Affair. The whole business had all begun innocently enough. In fact, when it was first proposed, it seemed like such an obvious, unmistakable marriage of the noblest impulses of nineteenth-century romanticism and the utopian promises of twentieth-century modernity. What better symbol of the bridge between past and present than the creation of a canal across the Isthmus of Panama, which would unite the Atlantic and Pacific oceans and spare sailors the dangerous trip around Cape Horn at the tip of South America? Engineers and entrepreneurs had toyed with the idea for years, but it only truly took off when the visionary statesman Ferdinand de Lesseps, the "great Frenchman," as he was known, announced in 1875 his intention to begin this project—one which, he insisted, would make his previous feat at the Suez Canal over a decade earlier look modest by comparison. In the face of such conviction, few voices dared to disagree. For if anyone knew a thing or two about achieving the impossible, it was Ferdinand de Lesseps, who for the better part of the previous fifty years had embodied the sort of fearless heroism that one could usually only find in popular adventure novels. He had always been one of those men who made things happen. Passionate, industrious, talented— more than a man had a right to be, on all fronts—he swept up those around him in his enthusiasm and his unshakable sense of destiny. Jean-Martin Charcot had been as much an admirer of the great Lesseps as the next man, but so much had happened since Lesseps had first raised the idea of a Panama canal at the 1875 Geographical Society of Paris meeting, and Jean-Martin now had the distinct impression of having been stuck with the bill of another man's expensive dinner. Jean-Martin was usually an inveterate traveler, but standing out on the dark deck, as his ship chugged toward the British coast, he found himself wishing very much that he had stayed at home. There was no comfort to be found on this trip and certainly no heroism. As Jean-Martin saw it, the age of heroes now seemed decidedly over.

Ferdinand de Lesseps had belonged to this other, this heroic age. Born in 1805, he came from a long line of men who had distinguished themselves in diplomatic service. His role model and personal hero was his uncle, Barthélemy de Lesseps, who could speak three languages at the tender age of ten and had shocked his fellow Frenchmen by traveling across Siberia to St. Petersburg all by himself while still in his twenties, mostly on dogsled, before returning to Paris. Young Ferdinand grew up with stories of such derring-do—

the dank danger of Turkish prisons, the crisp, crunching sound made by the thousands of lonely footsteps of a retreating army, the unmistakable scent of jasmine laced with gunpowder in humid colonial outposts—and was determined to carry on the family tradition. So, after studying a bit of law, the nineteen-year-old Ferdinand became an apprentice consul to his uncle, who was then the French ambassador to Lisbon. Stints in Tunis, Egypt, Rotterdam, Málaga, and Barcelona followed until, in 1848, he was made minister to Madrid. Ferdinand was just forty-three years old.

He had first become interested in canal building in Egypt in the early 1830s, when he encountered a group of Saint-Simonians—about twenty in all, many of them civil engineers—led by Prosper Enfantin, who had come to dig a Suez canal. Such a project had great religious significance for the Saint-Simonians, a sect of messianic socialists who believed that private property and nationalism were relics from meaner, less enlightened times. Led by a scientific and financial elite, the world would be transformed through massive public improvement projects: highways, railroads, and two great ship canals, one through the Isthmus of Suez, the other through the Isthmus of Panama. Although their plan to build the first canal was an utter failure—after four years, more than half the Saint-Simonians had died of cholera or other diseases—the seed had been planted. Lesseps never abandoned this goal, nourished by his belief in progress, of a vision of East and West joined, the energies of mankind unleashed in unimaginable ways. When in 1853 his beloved wife, Agathe Delamalle, died from scarlet fever, followed shortly thereafter by a son, Lesseps threw himself into his canal studies with renewed dedication and grieving desperation. He finally set to work on the actual digging of the canal in 1859. News of his progress found its way back to France in snippets, and for years, out-of-work Frenchmen could pick up the newspaper in towns like Lyon and Marseilles and find advertisements that promised rewards and riches for those brave enough to tempt fate in far-off Egypt. Until the canal's opening, it was still difficult to imagine anyone pulling off such a feat. Yet on the morning of the grand opening, November 17, 1869, there was Ferdinand, victorious, sailing past the thousands of people lining both banks of the canal. He was sixty-four years old and now a national hero back in France.

For the next eight months, he was wined and dined, fêted and fussed over, hailed as a symbol of French industry and colonial prowess. When out in public, he and his large family—he had recently remarried, to the wealthy and lovely twenty-year-old Louise-Hélène Autard de Bragard, and went on to father another twelve children—were surrounded by crowds of well-wishers and photographers; his picture was sold by boys on street corners. They entertained lavishly at their elegant mansion on the avenue Montaigne, and Lesseps now counted among his friends none other than that other national treasure, Victor Hugo. For a generation of Frenchmen deprived of a traditional monarchy, these two men embodied the best and the finest of French tradition, a symbol of the nation itself. But while Hugo was still extolling the virtues of revolutions past and dreams of the future, true love, and his grandchildren, Lesseps was a thoroughly modern, forward-thinking man, an embodiment of a new kind of energy and dynamism that was quickly overtaking modern society, one galloping along on the back of the dynamo, the telephone, the typewriter. If the automobile and railroad were redefining space, and the world was now moving on steam engines, oil, and coal, Lesseps was most definitely along for the ride.

And then all of this triumphalism seemed to collapse with France's defeat by the Prussians in 1870. After the losses at Sedan, the indignities of the siege of Paris, and the brutality of the Commune, when tens of thousands had died on Haussmann's elegant, sweeping boulevards, many feared that France would never find her way back to her former greatness. Others quickly began seeking a way for France to regain some of her lost dignity. Ferdinand de Lesseps, who despite his advanced years projected an image of health and confidence, seemed to accept this challenge. Upon the suggestion of his friend Victor Hugo, who urged him to "astonish the world by the great deeds that can be won without war," he turned his eyes westward, toward Panama, toward another canal project.

And so, starting in 1875, through a series of conferences and meetings held under the auspices of the Geographical Society, Lesseps charged past the scientific debates and public doubts, his conviction

of the fundamental rightness of the project outweighing his ignorance about the very real logistical problems inherent in the undertaking. Formal work on building a canal in Panama began in 1879,
with Lesseps traveling to Panama for the first time at the end of the
year. He brought along his young wife and three small children so
as to discredit the rumors about the dangers of the Panamanian climate. He spent most of his time at grand banquets and parties, bull-
fights and firework displays in his honor, not examining the rough
realities of digging a ditch across some fifty miles of wild, rocky terrain infested by the deadly yellow fever virus. On his way back to Europe, he stopped off at New York for a banquet at Delmonico's on
March 1, 1880. The main dining room was festooned with French
and American flags and the tables were decorated with centerpieces
that alluded to the accomplishments of the great Frenchman: models
of the steamer *Colon*, in which he had arrived from Panama; a Suez
steam-powered dredging machine; the temple of Luxor and various
obelisks; and a representation of Lesseps himself—in full dress, with
a spade in his hand—at the new Panama site.

If Lesseps was deaf and blind to the problems inherent in this
scheme from the outset, others harbored greater trepidations. Engineers warned that, given the terrain and oceanic conditions, a lock-
system canal was the only sensible course, but Ferdinand insisted on
a sea-level canal as he had built in Egypt. His own son, Charles, had
begged his father to forgo his plans, asking:

> What do you wish to find in Panama? Money? You will not
> bother about money at Panama any more than you did at
> Suez. Glory? You've had enough glory. Why not leave that to
> someone else? All of us who have worked at your side are en-
> titled to a rest. Certainly the Panama project is grandiose . . .
> but consider the risks those who direct it will run! You suc-
> ceeded at Suez by a miracle. Should not one be satisfied with
> accomplishing one miracle in a lifetime?

But Ferdinand would hear none of it, declaring "I maintain that
Panama will be easier to make, easier to complete, and easier to keep
up than Suez," and advising investors that the work would be com-

pleted by 1892. There were few who argued with the old man—
certainly not Charles, who, despite being in his forties, still ran after his father with exaggerated filial deference. While his father's
charisma and strength only seemed to grow with each new challenge
that presented itself, Charles—now nearly bald, with dark brows
and a thick, dark beard—lacked his father's stamina and glamour.
He had never fully recovered from the death of his only child, "Little Ferdinand," of cholera in 1865 when the family was at Ismailia,
Egypt. He did not know how to cordon off personal tragedy from
matters of global importance, as his father seemed able to do. He,
too, had risked great things for his father's vision—but he could not
imagine it any other way, so much did he idolize his father.

To finance the enterprise, the company—Compagnie Universelle
du Canal Interocéanique de Panama—began offering shares to
the public at five hundred francs each. News of the company's progress, published in a newsletter called *The Bulletin of the Interoceanic
Canal*, offered regular assurances of imminent success from Lesseps
himself. Frenchmen rushed to invest in the company. French newspapers were filled with stories about the work in Panama; men from
around the country had rushed to join the teams of workers, hoping to make their fortune and partake in some of the Lesseps legend. The painter Paul Gauguin was one such enthusiast: after
spending a particularly lean year in Paris, in 1887 he went to Panama
to work as a laborer. "Paris," he wrote, "is a desert for a poor man.
I must get my energy back, and I'm going to Panama to live like a
native." Yet native living was hardly as palatable as he had imagined.
He became sick with fever and was dismissed after only two weeks.
Gauguin was one of the lucky ones, the survivors—between 1881,
when the excavations began, and their suspension in 1889, untold
thousands of native laborers and hundreds of French engineers died
of malaria and yellow fever, whose transmission by mosquitoes was
not yet understood.

Yet few stories of such hardship found their way into the newspapers. Certainly no one spoke of Jules Dingler, who in the fall of
1883 had brought his family with him to the isthmus when he became director of operations at the canal company. A rather unimpos-
ing, middle-aged man, with a soft, round face and short, stooping

appearance, Dingler hardly seemed cut out for swashbuckling adventure. But he was absolutely dedicated to making the Panama project a success and so eager to prove naysayers wrong that, before sailing from France, he reportedly boasted that once in Panama he would prove that "only drunkards and the dissipated take the yellow fever and die there." He arrived in the dry season, installing his family into a large house atop a hill and taking them out on excursions in the surrounding countryside. He had also brought with him a magnificent team of horses—one photo showed his daughter, Louise, a pretty, dark-haired girl of about eighteen, sitting sidesaddle in a full skirt and Panama hat atop one of them.

But in January, when the wet season commenced, Louise contracted yellow fever and died within a few days. The young woman's death had a profound impact on everyone: canal officials, workers, and locals wept openly at her funeral in the crowded cathedral and afterward during the large procession to the cemetery, with Dingler and Louise's fiancé riding at the head. A month later Dingler's twenty-one-year-old son died of yellow fever, followed shortly by the daughter's fiancé. By summer forty-eight officers of the canal company were dead of the same disease. According to one American naval officer, laborers were dying at a rate of about two hundred a month. A despondent Dingler wrote to Charles de Lesseps, "I cannot thank you enough for your kind and affectionate letter. Mme Dingler who [knows] that she is for me the only source of affection in this world, controls herself with courage, but she is deeply shaken . . . We attach ourselves to life in making the canal our only occupation." When Mme Dingler herself died of yellow fever on New Year's Eve 1884, something in her husband finally snapped. He appeared at his desk at work the next day at the usual hour, but was silent and unnaturally still. After the funeral he led all the family's horses, including his own, into a mountain ravine and shot them. By late August 1885, close to physical and mental collapse, Dingler resigned his position and sailed for France, never to return to the spot in which his entire family lay buried. Such violent tragedies were discreetly and determinedly kept out of the newspaper headlines.

The board of directors of the Panama Canal Company had by this point grossly overshot its budget and depleted its funds. But in order to access further government subsidies and to float additional loans, it was vital that all talk of setbacks and failures remain out of public knowledge. Desperate for time and for cash, they turned to a consortium of shady—and, some observers noted pointedly, predominantly Jewish—speculators, who began paying off an entire network of journalists and key politicians. Leading this operation were one Baron Jacques de Reinach, a German-born French national with an Italian barony, and his deputy Cornelius Herz, a French-born naturalized United States citizen. Yet despite the best efforts of those spearheading the project, reality soon overtook the grand dream of the Panama Canal: in 1889 the company collapsed and was liquidated. And so, that year, the year of the Universal Exposition in Paris, France witnessed two things it had thought impossible: the creation of the Eiffel Tower and the downfall of Ferdinand de Lesseps.

Thousands of small investors lost their money as a result of the company's failure: overall one billion francs were lost, and 800,000 private investors, French men and women, were affected. Those who had believed they were buying a piece of the glory of France ended up losing everything. The bankruptcy of the Panama Canal Company in 1889 caused more than the ruin of thousands of investors. In political circles alone, when the chain of bribes, slush funds, and influence peddling was traced to its end, 104 legislators were found to have been involved. Yet over the next few years, the scandal surrounding it touched an ever-widening number of individuals and institutions and fundamentally altered people's perception of the leaders and values that they had once taken for granted.

It began in 1892, when Édouard Drumont's right-wing newspaper, *La Libre Parole* (The Free Word), published a series of revelations about the scandal. Drumont was a minor civil servant turned journalist who, in 1886, had published *La France Juive* (Jewish France). The book, comprising two volumes and over a thousand pages of hate-filled innuendo and suspicions about the dangers posed by Jews, became a runaway success and by the end of its first year had sold over a hundred thousand copies. Almost overnight Drumont became wealthy and famous, although he demurred that there was nothing particularly extraordinary about what he had done, insisting that the book's "only merit had been to put into print what everyone was thinking." *La Libre Parole* had been only moderately successful until September 1892, when Drumont broke a series of stories entitled "The Secrets of Panama," which purported to expose a secret "Jewish plot" at the heart of the Panama disaster. He was, of course, alluding to the shenanigans of two men: Baron Reinach and Dr. Cornelius Herz, or "the alien Jew and fake Frenchman," as Drumont called them.

The more outrageous Drumont's accusations, the more readers he attracted. Soon Drumont's allegations were being discussed in other newspapers, in salons, and in cafés throughout the nation. The more they read, the more the public seethed. Baron Reinach stunningly committed suicide, while Cornelius Herz fled to Bournemouth, England; a shaken Chamber of Deputies was forced to set up an investigating committee. In an effort to save face, the government prosecuted Ferdinand and Charles de Lesseps, the company directors, and a few of the politicians most flagrantly involved in the cover-up. De Lesseps père and fils were found guilty and sentenced to prison, although Ferdinand, who was eighty-seven and quite ill, was not compelled to serve. In fact, the great man was only vaguely aware of the commotion, and did not leave his room at the family estate, La Chesnaye, until his death on December 7, 1894. He would not have known, then, that during the trial, the prosecuting attorney charged both the de Lessepses with having deceived France with "beautiful illusions." He would not have known that his son, Charles, who had warned him about the folly of the enterprise from the beginning, was forced to spend a year in prison and to pay a steep fine. Among the other casualties of the scandal was the famous engineer Gustave Eiffel, whose reputation suffered mightily despite the guilty judgment against him eventually being reversed, and the fifty-two-year-old leftist politician Georges Clemenceau, who, as the combative editor of *Justice*, it was revealed, used funds supplied by Cornelius Herz. It took Clemenceau years to work his way back into the halls of government.

For many contemporaries the Panama Affair was a sign that there was something fundamentally shaky about the nation's very core. Thirty-four-year-old Jean Jaurès, then a young socialist deputy, declared in a speech in the Chamber of Deputies that in unraveling the intricacies of the case, "we are witnesses to a kind of social decomposition . . . This is not a narrow trial in a courtroom against several men, it's the beginning of the trial of the dying social order, and we are here to substitute for it a more just social order." The poet Stéphane Mallarmé, writing in Britain's *National Observer*, admitted to being fascinated by the catastrophe that had undone so many great men, while Friedrich Engels, writing to Friedrich Adolph Sorge in 1892, wondered if what he called "the Panama business" was not in fact "the beginning of the end of the bourgeois republic and may soon bring us into very responsible positions." Theodor Herzl, a thirty-three-year-old Jewish reporter covering Paris for the Vienna *Neue Freie Presse*, was riveted by the events. He had gotten to know Drumont at Alphonse Daudet's regular salon and was, despite himself, fascinated by the boldness of the no-torious anti-Semite's outlook and by the irrational political style he advocated, which was free from the tired constraints of old-fashioned liberal and parliamentary politics. "I think we'll have a revolution here this coming year," Herzl wrote to the writer Arthur Schnitzler on January 2, 1893, joking, "And if I don't get away on time, I am liable to be shot as a bourgeois, a German spy, a Jew, or a financier."

Léon Daudet, eager for any distraction from his increasingly stormy domestic life, followed the public debate with fascination, as did Alphonse. Édouard Drumont was a close family friend—Alphonse had helped him secure a publisher for *La France Juive*—and to see him personally take on the entire republican establishment was breath-taking to behold. It was exactly the sort of thing Léon was then trying to accomplish with his first book, *Les Morticoles*. Jean-Martin Charcot, however, was less impressed with the public outcry. He had nothing against the man personally, but he didn't approve of how Drumont conducted his business—it was little more than a chaotic, messy witch hunt. People no longer cared for a rational assessment of the facts, he grumbled. At least, Jean-Martin consoled himself, it had noth-ing to do with him. He had his patients and his students, his family and friends—he cared little for the mundanities and scandals upon which newspaper editors depended. Jean-Martin was therefore most unhappy when he was asked to travel to England with Paul Brouardel to verify the diagnosis of Cornelius Herz, one of the figures at the heart of the bribery scandal, who had fled from France in the middle of the night on December 19, 1892. The French government had sought his extradition, but the British presented a certificate from a British doctor declaring Herz to be too ill to be transported. So now Charcot and Brouardel, then the chair of legal medicine at the School of Medicine in Paris and almost as esteemed a doctor as Charcot himself, had been charged with assessing the patient on behalf of their government. Brouardel and Charcot made the journey to London and then on to Bournemouth in mid-June 1893. When they finally arrived at the seaside hotel, they found Herz in bed in his suite overlooking the sea, covered with furs and blankets. After a careful examination, they also determined that his cardiac troubles and diabetes really did make him too ill to be moved. The French press was outraged and declared that these famous doctors either were idiots or, much worse, had been bought off by venal and corrupt politicians who feared what sort of bombshells Herz would release if brought back to trial in France. Cornelius Herz was never extradited from England, and died in seclusion at his seaside hotel in Bournemouth in 1898.

All this excitement did not sit well with Jean-Martin Charcot. He was shocked and outraged that the lay public was now questioning his motives and his methods. Where had it come from, this aura of insubordination? Where once he had enjoyed being the undisputed master, now he saw challenges from all sides. All in all, Charcot was in desperate need of a break. As temperatures rose that summer, he grew increasingly fatigued. His heart, long overburdened by its owner's decadent tastes in food and drink—dinner parties at his home were known to consist of six or seven courses and be accompanied by four different kinds of wine, numerous desserts, and after-dinner liqueurs— had had enough. Nearly three years earlier, after a particularly sumptuous meal on New Year's Eve, that overworked heart had threatened to give out entirely. Léon Daudet, still a medical student at the time, was among those in attendance that evening. One minute Charcot was relaxed, affable, happy to be surrounded by friends and young people; then suddenly he let out a muffled groan, clutched at his chest, and became very pale before falling without a word onto a chair. The dinner guests—many of whom were medical students—quickly organized, while Léon ran across the street to his mentor, Dr. Potain, a cardiologist, who opened to Léon's knocking in a nightgown with a candle in his hand. Apprised of the situation, Potain murmured, "*Ah! Diable!*" and hurriedly threw on pants, a vest, a fur coat, and a white silk scarf before running out into the icy night to help his colleague. When he arrived there, Potain sent the others away, only to reemerge in half an hour and announce that the attack was nothing but a simple stomach upset. But Léon was not convinced. As Léon walked Potain back to his home, the latter turned to him and explained quietly, "I had to reassure him. He thought it was *angor pectoris.*" After another moment of silence, he continued in the same soft voice, "He's not wrong."

"How long, sir?" Léon asked, with a mounting sensation of dread.

"Two years, two and a half, at the very most. But silence, all right, my friend?"

The next day, Charcot seemed completely fine, smiling at all his visitors and scoffing at his own anxiety about the previous evening. But of course Charcot was not fooled. He had, on occasion, issued such bland assurances, designed at easing the sting of bad news. He did not quite know the severity of Potain's diagnosis, but he knew that his heart was weak. So later, in 1893, when he thought of the long, hot summer lying before him, after a particularly exhausting spring, he decided to clear his head and take in some fresh country air by hiking in the hilly Morvan region in Burgundy for a few days before heading back to his villa in Neuilly for a more complete rest. His wife, Augustine, was eager for him to leave, finding that her husband had grown increasingly exhausted and irritable. Discovering the countryside of the Morvan, learning about its art and archaeology, she hoped, would be just the thing to distract him from his medical work. She was reassured that he would be accompanied by two of his former students, Drs. Debove and Strauss, and also by René Vallery-Radot, the son-in-law of Louis Pasteur.

They left on Friday, August 11, with Charcot decked out in his traveling garb—a cape and a bowler, with a leather satchel for his pencils, watercolors, and sketchbooks. Once in the Morvan, they wandered about the countryside like schoolboys on vacation. One day, they rented a carriage to take them to the castle, enjoying the verdant surroundings, reading out loud passages from Mme de Sévigné's letters or testing one another's knowledge of the local history and architecture. At the local inn in Montbard, they enjoyed a sumptuous meal and sampled various local wines. In the middle of the meal, a shepherd's daughter, who had heard that doctors from Paris were dining, stopped by to ask for advice about breastfeeding.

The next morning, it was Charcot who awakened last. He seemed distracted and distinctly annoyed to be the one responsible for the late start for the day's expedition. He said nothing throughout the short carriage ride to the small village of Saint-Père-sous-Vézelay. For lunch they stopped at another hotel and sat down to yet another well-appointed table. Because they had much to see that afternoon, they ate quickly, but when Vallery-Radot offered his arm to Charcot, he brusquely refused, saying "I am not as sick as that." But he was out of breath and was forced to make frequent stops during the afternoon's walk. On the way down through the deserted village, they met a young man who approached the doctors. "You looked after me at the Salpêtrière," he said to Charcot. "You cured me, and now I am a painter . . . and I am very happy to have seen you." Charcot demurred that he had really done nothing extraordinary, but he clearly enjoyed the praise.

The next day, Charcot again woke up exhausted. This lack of energy annoyed and surprised him. He had thought himself beyond such things . . . the summer heat, the discomfort of carriage rides on rocky, dusty roads. He did not wish to say anything to his companions—they would only fuss over him and treat him like an old man. Only when they arrived at Quarré-les-Tombes, where they encountered peasants from throughout the region who had come for the village festival and vespers, did he feel a little more like himself. It made him think of Lourdes, the famous pilgrimage site and the subject of an article he had just written, "Faith That Cures." Some of his colleagues may have raised their eyebrows at Charcot's decision to take on such a subject—Charcot argued that the faith healing that occurred at Lourdes was the result not of miracles but of hysterical responses to an emotionally fraught experience. Moreover, in the article he admitted that he could not entirely explain how some diseases were "cured" there. All he could offer was the vague assertion that even these cases must follow "natural laws" and that, from time to time, he had even condoned his own patients' seeking help there. He ended the article with this surprising admission of the limits of scientific knowledge:

> Can we then affirm that we can explain everything which claims to be of a supernatural origin in the faith-cure, and that the frontiers of the miraculous are visibly shrinking day by day before the march of scientific attainments? Certainly not. In all investigation we have to learn the lesson of patience. I am among the first to recognize that Shakespeare's words hold good today—"There are more things in heaven and earth, Horatio, than are dreamt of in thy philosophy."

As it turned out, "Faith That Cures" was the last article Charcot would ever write. The final words he uttered before going to bed later that evening were about how he was feeling a bit better. He was found dead the following morning, August 16, 1893. The cause was acute pulmonary edema. He was sixty-eight. It was two years and eight months since Potain's prognosis.

His body was returned to Paris and placed in a coffin in a chapel of the Salpêtrière, where it was watched over by the stunned and weeping supervisors and nurses of his service. The following morning, all the inmates of the asylum—mostly old women and the insane patients—filed by his coffin. Some of them were carried in on stretchers—a veritable procession of misery. According to his wishes, there were no speeches at his funeral, which was held under the great dome of the Salpêtrière. His body was then laid to rest in Montmartre Cemetery. The major newspapers printed prominent, glowing accounts of the great professor's life and work. Le Temps declared that with his death "one of the glories of French science has disappeared" and praised him for being the first "orthodox scholar" to have dared to cross the threshold of the unknown and to have succeeded in drawing simple and comprehensible lessons out of the mysterious darkness in which neurological and mental disorders had been obscured.

Jean-Martin's family was overcome with grief. Jean-Baptiste was actually sailing on his yacht off the coast of La Rochelle when news

of his father's death arrived in Paris. The train ride back to the capital after hearing the news was the longest of his life. Jean-Baptiste
had been left alone with his disconsolate mother after his sister,
Jeanne, married Alfred Edwards, the famous director of the newspaper *Le Matin* in 1881. The rhythms of Jean-Martin's life had imposed an order on the lives of his family. Now they all felt adrift as
the hours seeped into one another, undifferentiated cavities of sadness and confusion. Jean-Baptiste tried to be strong for his mother,
his sister, Jeanne, and his half sister, Marie, but he was in many ways
the most affected. Although already twenty-six-years old, he still felt
like an adolescent, still more at home as a student, an apprentice, a
cutup and comedian. His father had been the serious one, the great
one. To even pretend to model himself after his father felt awkward
and inappropriate—like trying to squeeze into another man's shoes.
But the sadness he now felt, the seriousness that seemed to follow
him everywhere, precluded any return to the lightheartedness of his
youth. At first Jean-Baptiste tried to drown himself in work. When
that failed he embarked on an ill-conceived affair with a nurse at the
Salpêtrière, which produced an illegitimate child, a daughter named
Marion. But that only led to more heartache when, shortly after
childbirth, the mother died. Jean-Baptiste sent Marion to be raised
by his sister, Jeanne, and continued with his work and his reading,
feeling more alone than ever before.

The night of Charcot's death, Léon, who was taking the waters at
Uriage, was woken up at around three in the morning by a strange
phenomenon. He perceived a presence at the door, and it slowly
moved across the length of the room. It was his old teacher, Jean-
Martin Charcot, and he was wearing a shirt of an impossible whiteness. The shirt was open at the neck, and the man was clutching at his
heart. "I knew immediately . . . that something bad had happened
to the great man, whose silhouette and work had so strongly made
an impression on my youth," he later recalled. The next day, Léon
learned that Charcot had died suddenly. He was asked by *Le Temps*
to write an article about the esteemed doctor. He bitterly refused.
The old man had caused him enough grief when he was alive, Léon

thought to himself. There was no reason to give him any satisfaction now that he was dead.

Another one of Jean-Martin's former students, Sigmund Freud, was hundreds of miles away, in Vienna, when he heard of his teacher's death. He, too, was asked to write an obituary, in his case for the *Wiener Medizinische Wochenschrift*, which he readily agreed to do. Since leaving Charcot some eight years earlier, Freud had retained his deep appreciation for his French mentor, translating Charcot's lectures into German and giving conference papers that cited his ideas. When he moved to his new offices on Berggasse 19, he proudly hung up an engraving of André Brouillet's painting *Une leçon clinique à la Salpêtrière*, which depicts Charcot presenting a female hysteric before a rapt audience at the Salpêtrière. Freud had even named his first son Jean Martin (known as Martin, born in 1889) after Charcot.

In his obituary Freud began by recalling with great fondness the intellectual vigor and personal sociability of his teacher, his unusual ability to circumvent received ideas in order to seize upon the bold theory. Yet he ended the obituary on a more questioning note, observing that Charcot's therapeutic methods had recently been challenged and that his understanding of the phenomenon of hypnosis—Charcot and his school considered that the hypnotic state could only be produced in hysterics, while a rival school in Nancy argued that hypnosis was no more than a matter of suggestion and therefore could be produced in anyone, not only hysterics—had become outdated. Most of all, Freud concluded, "the aetiological theories supported by Charcot in his doctrine of the '*famille névropathique*,' which he made the basis of his whole concept of nervous disorders, will no doubt soon require sifting and emending." By overestimating heredity, Freud felt, Charcot had left no room for the acquisition of nervous illnesses.

Although heredity and degeneration became standard operating paradigms for understanding various illnesses, Freud pointed out a number of potential problems inherent in them. First, it failed to give any primary etiological role to the bacteria and microbes recently discovered by researchers in the new field of microbiology. A new breed of doctors like Pasteur and Koch had, by the closing decades of the century, isolated and identified bacteria responsible for many infectious diseases. One of the leading pioneers in this area was the syphilographer Alfred Fournier in Paris, who suggested that syphilis was responsible for subsequent diseases of the central nervous system, such as locomotor ataxia and general paralysis. In the mid-to-late 1880s, Fournier, seconded by the German neuropathologist Wilhelm Erb, was vigorously defending his position against Charcot, Magnan, and others who denied that syphilis was the specific and necessary cause of tabes and paralysis. Syphilis, Charcot argued, functioned merely as an agent provocateur. The disagreement was a generational one: Charcot and other scientists of his elder cohort disliked the emphasis on external pathogens as found in germ theory, preferring instead to keep medical theory and nosography within the human body.

Freud first openly challenged Charcot in the footnotes to his translation of Charcot's *Leçons du Mardi* into German in early 1892. In these footnotes Freud essentially rejected the doctrine of the *famille névropathique*, which referred to the tendency of nervous and mental diseases to transform into one another as they were transmitted from one generation to the next. By this time Freud had begun to consider acquired factors, particularly disorders in sexuality or sexual trauma, as the crucial cause of neuroses. In a stern response, dated June 3, 1892, Charcot categorically disagreed with his former student's footnotes, drawing on his own extensive clinical research, particularly his more recent research into the hereditary nature of diabetes. For good measure, he also reminded Freud of the prevalence of inherited diseases in Jewish families—a comment that gnawed at Freud for some time. The two men drifted apart, with Freud turning his attention to the writing of his first major work, *Studies on Hysteria*, an important step in his path toward developing his theory of psychoanalysis, which was published in 1895. Just three years after the death of his former mentor, Freud lost his own father, an event that he would later come to understand as "the most significant event, the most decisive loss, of a man's life."

Freud was not the only former student of Charcot to grapple with the lessons imparted by the "Napoléon of Neuroses." The popularization of the theory of degeneration was largely due to one man, Max Nordau, a Hungarian gynecologist turned journalist and cultural critic who had also studied with Jean-Martin Charcot. Born in Budapest, Nordau had come to Paris in 1880, where he undertook medical research under the direction of Charcot and defended his thesis—on the topic of female sterilization, a practice he deplored—on July 19, 1882. He remained very involved in the Charcot circle, while also being plugged into various other intellectual, political, and scientific circles through his work as the Paris correspondent for the Viennese *Neue Freie Presse.* In 1892 he published in Germany a book that rocked European intellectual and literary circles: *Degeneration.* Drawing on his own clinical knowledge of medical pathologies, he applied his medical expertise to European culture and society more generally. He essentially transferred Morel's theory of degeneration from the insane asylum to the avant-garde literary and artistic salons of the fin de siècle, arguing that the cultural avant-garde was atavistic and even regressive in its preoccupation with disease and sexual deviance. In doing so Nordau provided his bourgeois readers with a theoretical armature for understanding the threat of such bogeymen as anarchism, socialism, class struggle, and alcoholism as the products of degenerate forces within society. Although he took great pains to identify the degeneration of all contemporary European nations, Nordau located in France the most virulent and extensive form of the disease. Such historical events, he argued, as the Napoleonic Wars or even the more recent Franco-Prussian War and the Commune had exacerbated an already uniquely "Gallic predisposition" to what he could only characterize as a kind of national "neurasthenia." So thoroughly did Nordau's account of degenerating culture become accepted that even Émile Zola, one of the Hungarian's favorite targets, willingly submitted to medical checkups to produce scientific proof of his normalcy.

A growing body of work used the new scientific knowledge to describe a society that was hopelessly decadent, the patresfamilias impotent and riddled with disease now inevitably giving rise to a generation of pale, nervous aesthetes. Young critics, like Maurice Barrès, began preaching a new *culte du moi* (cult of the self), having determined that the old value system was bankrupt and, unable to nourish individual fulfillment, brought only decadence and disillusion. As the previous generation—the Victor Hugos, the Ferdinand de Lessepses,

the Jean-Martin Charcots of the world—became ill or infirm and began to die, these newer voices began to drown out the lessons and
received wisdom of the past. One such new voice belonged to Léon
Daudet, who began to take out his anger, which could not be directed against his adored father or his complaining wife, against
those institutions and figureheads that, he proclaimed, had propa-
gated dangerous falsehoods and betrayed his generation. He had
begun writing *Les Morticoles* around the time of his former mentor's death as a way of getting revenge against the medical establishment—embodied by Jean-Martin Charcot—for betraying both him
and his father. He wrote the book quickly and with great gusto as
his father's health continued to deteriorate and as his storybook
marriage quickly began to disintegrate. "I wrote this large book,"
he later explained, "with a veritable joy of liberation, evasion, and intense pleasure to say right to the faces of the powerful people at the
School of Medicine exactly what I thought of them, both good and
bad." Léon began to read excerpts of *Les Morticoles* in public and
decided to dedicate the book to Edmond de Goncourt, to "the glorious patron of *Lettres françaises*." For his part, Goncourt found it
"an abundance of ideas, a richness of images, of horror . . . but an
amusing horror, and a style smashed, full of life, in the midst of a ferocious irony, an irony in the style of Swift." Léon was only twenty-
seven when it was finally published in 1894, giving him his first taste
of literary celebrity. He was hooked and quickly set about writing
his next book—the story of another great man, a writer with a monstrous ego. Was it his ex-wife's grandfather, Victor Hugo? Was it his
former mentor, Jean-Martin Charcot? Was it a generation of great
men whose time, Léon and his friends were fast deciding, had come
to an end? Jean-Baptiste Charcot, Léon Daudet, Sigmund Freud,
and Max Nordau—these four young men, trained by one of the
leading representatives of triumphant nineteenth-century science—
all found themselves casting about for new answers for darker times.
If the idols of their youth had begun to fall, the weight of their tradition and their expectations continued to press upon them. And
having been in their fathers' shadows for so long, the young men
confronted the prospect of striking out on their own with both excitement and dread.

⁌ SEVEN ⁌

Degradation

We were heroes. We must say so quite simply, for I do not believe that anyone will say it for us.

—Charles Péguy, *Notre Jeunesse* (1909)

Our vanquished generation was sad, disillusioned, sardonic, and, finally, powerless . . . The young people who speak and write today doubt that there could really be any mysterious links between the deplorable social state that they encounter and the literature of their elders. —article in *Le Figaro* (1897)

A heavy snowfall blanketed the streets of Paris on the morning of January 5, 1895. The entire city seemed muffled, stilled by the wintry weather. Only the children appeared unaffected by the dreary conditions, darting merrily between the figures of the adults wearing overcoats and somber, expectant expressions as they milled about outside the gates of Morland Courtyard at the École Militaire with growing impatience. Farther on, some spectators had climbed trees— some had even scaled the golden dome of Les Invalides—all in an attempt to catch a glimpse of the spectacle that was about to be performed below. Various newspapers later put the crowd of spectators at several thousand, although to those attending, it felt as if the entire city were there. Twenty-seven-year-old Léon Daudet, standing with the writer Maurice Barrès among the select group of journalists and dignitaries within the courtyard to observe the morning's proceedings, sensed something almost festive about the occasion, an energy that electrified and united the disparate groups of people who had gathered in twos and threes around him. They were joined by nearly four thousand troops, who stood silent and at attention, lining the square's periphery. For Léon it was a large assignment, one of his first, entrusted to him by the editor of *Le Figaro*. All the major French dailies had sent someone to cover the morning's event; the international press was there as well.

Suddenly a murmur raced through the crowd and the staccato drumroll sliced through the air. All eyes swung to the far corner of the courtyard as men and women craned their necks to catch a glimpse of the man whom they had come to see publicly humiliated. Captain Alfred Dreyfus, the thirty-nine-year-old Jewish officer found guilty of treason, was now forced to endure a public degradation. As the clock struck nine, Captain Dreyfus emerged out of the darkness of the doorway, escorted by a brigadier and four gunners. He walked resolutely, head high, and although he stumbled midway, he quickly recovered. The entire group halted at the center of the courtyard as the general rose in his stirrups, raised high his sword, and pronounced the official words of degradation: "Alfred Dreyfus, you are no longer worthy of bearing arms. In the name of the people of France, we dishonor you." Dreyfus, in a voice clear and desperate, shouted: "Soldiers, an innocent man is being degraded; soldiers, an innocent man is being dishonored. Long live France! Long live the Army!" The crowd in the public square beyond the courtyard rumbled and hissed. Some of the more emboldened onlookers answered with catcalls and boos, jeering, "Dirty Jew!" from outside the railings of the parade ground. Then, as drums began to roll, one of the officers proceeded to strip Dreyfus of his badges of rank, shred his clothing, and break his saber. Finally, Dreyfus was led away, forced to file past the troops, who now abandoned their stoic silence and heckled him mercilessly.

The sight of this disassembling whipped many in the crowd into an even greater frenzy, a thirst for violence and dismemberment that recalled the horrific spectacle of the guillotine. Barrès, reaching even further back into history, observed with a certain grim satisfaction that it resembled nothing less than a "parade of Judas." But for at least two observers in the crowd, the spectacle was something altogether different. The forty-four-year-old critic and journalist Max Nordau and the thirty-four-year-old journalist Theodor Herzl, both representing the Austrian *Neue Freie Presse*, felt as if they had stumbled into a horrific nightmare. Death to Jews? Who were these people? They may have appeared like ordinary Frenchmen, but their strangled voices and hard faces seemed possessed by base and ancient hostilities. Neither man had believed that these forces could exist in the country they both considered not only their home, but also a flourishing testament to modern, cosmopolitan life. Hadn't they left such hatred behind, in the pales and ghettos of their families' distant past? Neither wished to acknowledge what they both sensed with a wearying certainty—that something had undeniably and irreversibly shifted. "Those . . . who had actually witnessed the degradation ceremony left in a curious state of agitation," Herzl explained in oddly muted language in his article for the *Neue Freie Presse* that appeared the following day. "The strangely resolute attitude of the degraded captain had made a deep impression on many eyewitnesses."

Léon, too, was disturbed, but for very different reasons. "The wretch is not French," he had muttered moodily to Barrès, before turning and walking home slowly, lost in thought. At dinner that night with his parents and the Zolas, Léon struggled to keep track of the conversation—idle gossip about who had just published what, who had just dined with whom—when all of a sudden he interrupted, unable to remain silent any longer. "If you had seen this Dreyfus fellow go to the degradation, head high, military march, you would have been revolted like the crowd. They do not know what it means to be dishonored, that race . . ." Zola was shocked by Léon's statement—a smart boy like Léon should have been wary of the violent emotions of the crowd. Moreover, Zola continued, no matter what Drumont and the blaring headlines of his newspaper insisted, the question of Dreyfus's guilt was still a matter of debate. At this point Alphonse jumped in on the side of his son and insisted that if seven officers of a council of war found Dreyfus guilty, he must be so. They couldn't all be wrong . . .

As the table burst into a cacophony of different opinions, Léon quietly excused himself and went up to his room to write his article, which he entitled, simply, "The Punishment." The next day, readers of *Le Figaro* were given Léon's firsthand account of the degradation ceremony: how the captain appeared before the crowd like "a walking corpse . . . a zombie on parade." Although Dreyfus was "frail to all appearances," Léon dramatically insisted that the traitor was "magnified by the overwhelming shame and hatred that he evoked." And yet, Léon explained, some good had come out of this unforgivable treachery. The French people had at last come together in their shared condemnation of this external threat—although Léon was careful not to use the word "Jew" a single time, his meaning could not have been lost on his audience. "His face is ashen . . . without appearance of remorse, surely foreign, a wretch of the ghetto . . ."

As Léon mulled over the facts of the case and wrote about his feelings, he felt more invigorated than he had for some time. He was not alone. An economic depression was exacerbating social and political divisions in French politics, with the parliamentary center increasingly under pressure from forces on both the right and the left. Throughout the 1880s a new nationalist right, still obsessed with France's 1870 defeat at the hands of Prussia and the subsequent loss of Alsace-Lorraine, began organizing themselves with renewed energy and focus. In 1882 the Ligue des Patriotes was formed, which preached an authoritarian nationalism organized behind a single leader. In 1887 they had placed their hopes of overthrowing the republic on General Georges Boulanger (1837–91), a handsome, charismatic officer whose belligerent attitude toward Germany—his nickname was "General Revenge"—and wild popularity among the masses made him seem like the perfect candidate to move France to the right. Yet when given the chance to march on the seat of government in an audacious coup d'état, Boulanger failed to show up. Having missed his sole window of opportunity, a few months later, on April Fool's Day, he fled to Belgium, where he committed suicide at the grave of his former mistress, who had recently died of tuberculosis. The Panama scandal had also proved a boon to the right-wing cause, focusing attention on government corruption and the supposedly corrosive influence of Jews. In 1890 Édouard Drumont, hot on the heels of his publishing success with *La France Juive*, founded a French anti-Semitic league. Léon had been a member of Drumont's anti-Semitic league since its beginning, but more out of friendship for Drumont than out of any particularly well-developed sense of anti-Semitism. Otherwise, he had thus far remained somewhat aloof from politics, although his deteriorating relationship with his former in-laws—particularly his former stepfather-in-law, the outspoken radical politician Édouard Lockroy—had made him much more bitter about the current state of republicanism. But as his novelist's imagination set about ordering the various acts of the crime and punishment of Dreyfus, Léon felt more ardently about his country than he had ever before.

The whole business with Dreyfus had started late in 1894, when a charwoman at the German embassy who was secretly a French spy discovered an unsigned note offering to sell the Germans five secret documents about guns and mobilization. She handed the document over to Colonel Henry, a leading figure in the French counterespionage service. Captain Dreyfus, an officer on the army's General Staff, was quickly accused of being the traitor and was arrested on October 15. News of the treachery was first announced on November 1, in an article in Drumont's right-wing newspaper, *La Libre Parole*, entitled "High Treason: The Arrest of the Jewish Officer A. Dreyfus," which incorrectly asserted that Dreyfus had made a full confession when in fact he had not. Then, on December 19, Dreyfus was tried by secret court-martial; since the actual evidence against him had been almost nonexistent, the national counterespionage team had concocted a "secret dossier" of incontrovertible "proof," which was handed to the military judges when they retired to deliberate. He was quickly found guilty of treason and was sentenced to exile and life imprisonment on Devil's Island, a former leper colony off the coast of French Guiana.

Despite the excitement and outrage surrounding the revelation of Dreyfus's spying and his subsequent degradation, the story eventually seemed to recede as daily life in the capital resumed its usual rhythms. While some continued to be skeptical about Dreyfus's guilt and thought further inquiries should take place, the story seemed destined to become just another shameful *fait divers* for those complicated modern times. Even Léon, despite his initial enthusiasm, found his mind drifting toward other matters. There was always writing to be done, and he desperately wanted to get away from Paris and from the headache that was his rapidly dissolving marriage: Jeanne had left their home on December 22, 1894, and the divorce was pronounced in January 1895. And so he left France and traveled, as young men of his means and station were wont to do. First he traveled to Holland and Sweden with his younger brother, Lucien, and his good friend Georges Hugo. Then they joined the rest of the family in London, where Alphonse caught up with his old friend Henry James and wandered happily through the British Museum and the grand parks of the city with Léon. At night father and son listened, enthralled, to the stories of the explorer Henry Morton Stanley as Léon forgot about his failed marriage for a few hours and Alphonse's mind managed to wander away from his own disease.

After returning to Paris in the early summer, Léon traveled with Georges to Guernsey—making sure, in advance, that Jeanne would be far away—to work on his next book, a nonfiction work about Shakespeare. Léon portrayed the bard as a young man who leaves behind his wife and two children and takes a great journey to northern Europe, where he becomes aware of his genius. In Léon's mind he and his subject shared the same passionate enthusiasms and taste for physical love, an admiration for the more earthy writers like Montaigne and Rabelais, and the same greedy hunger for knowledge. In so fashioning his subject in his own image, Léon, it could be argued, was taking literary criticism to new heights of solipsism. When *The Voyage of Shakespeare* was published by Fasquelle in early 1896, though, it was a commercial and critical success. One young critic, Charles Maurras, mused about the author in a review: "This hunger is the mark of a real candidate for genius . . . One guesses that he is similar to his hero: life intoxicates him, he loves life, he wants to multiply life."

But seething just below the surface of this manic appreciation for life was a growing churlishness, even anger. Goncourt wondered if Léon was in such a bad mood because of the announcement of his ex-wife's upcoming marriage to his former friend Jean-Baptiste Charcot. It is true that the news was a difficult pill to swallow, but that was only part of it. Despite his burgeoning literary success, Léon felt restless, agitated. His life was not turning out the way he had expected, and his seeming powerlessness both alarmed and frustrated him. Having abandoned his home on the avenue de l'Alma after the divorce, he took refuge at his parents'. Chaos followed him there as well: his room was quickly overrun by books and papers, which spilled haphazardly onto the floor. He drowned his sorrows and frustrations in food and drink, and the weight quickly accumulated on his five-foot-five frame, until his former boxer's physique became rotund.

In the fall of 1896, feeling that his entire world was falling in around him, Léon decided to go to the Hôtel de France et d'Angleterre in Fontainebleau to clear his head and get some writing done. By then he was finishing his novel *Suzanne*. He walked into the salon and happened upon Marcel Proust, a twenty-five-year-old aspiring writer who had first been introduced to the Daudet family by the composer Reynaldo Hahn a couple of years earlier. Proust had been born in Auteuil, near Paris. He was the son of an eminent doctor, Adrien Proust, and his wife, Jeanne Weil, who hailed from a well-to-do Alsatian Jewish family. Despite his professed literary aspirations, much of Proust's time and energy in 1896 seemed to be devoted to frivolous pursuits and in the courting of fashionable friends. Of the various members of the Daudet clan, it was to Lucien, Léon's younger brother, that Proust had initially been drawn. Sixteen years old and possessing the sort of languid beauty and precise, discerning aesthetics that appealed deeply to Proust, Lucien quickly became one of his favorites. Although Proust was initially shocked by the "appalling materialism" of the Daudet couple, particularly of Alphonse's wife, Julia—"How bourgeois!" he exclaimed after meeting her—there was something about Alphonse that stirred him deeply. Even if he found the older writer's work a bit passé—Proust observed that if Alphonse did indeed possess an "acute power of observation," it nonetheless smelled rather "musty"—Proust was able to collapse the distinction between the man and his work. He found enough poetry in the man himself to satisfy his own Romantic needs. With his great head, bohemian locks, and wizened body, Alphonse was, in Proust's view, simply and exquisitely "a pure spirit still shining across the shadows and swells of his nerves, a small star on the sea." The elder writer and the young Marcel shared not only a passion for literature but also an obsession with their own deteriorating health: while Alphonse was suffering through the last agonized stages of tertiary syphilis, Proust was already displaying the classic symptoms of neurasthenia that would remain with him throughout his life. He would later compare his own health struggles to Alphonse's, writing, "I was unable to understand how he managed to go on producing. Above all, I was reminded of how my own sufferings, so slight compared with his that he would no doubt have enjoyed them as a respite, had made me indifferent to other people, to life, to everything that was not my unfortunate body, to which my mind remained obstinately turned, just as a sick man in bed remains with his head turned to the wall."

Proust had clearly made quite an impression on the older writer. In a June 1896 letter, Alphonse thanked Proust for a basket of flowers, offering him a copy of his book, *Burial of a Star*, in exchange for a copy of Proust's recently published *Pleasures and Days*, which he described as "your youth—dreams, music, and thrills." "Save for me a small corner of your friendship," Alphonse concluded. "It is very precious to me, for the sensitive, tender types are very rare in youth today." Alphonse understood Proust's aesthetic sensibilities in ways Proust's own father, Adrien, never could.

Alphonse, with his poor health and fragile nerves, and Lucien, with his exacting taste and effete finesse, seemed like kindred spirits to the young Proust. Léon was another matter. He was bold, brash, loud, and, in Proust's eyes, almost impossibly macho. So when the two young men found themselves at the same hotel in Fontainebleau, they were understandably ambivalent about each other. Yet since they were acquaintances, dining together was unavoidable. Léon, arms and elbow akimbo, in a collision course with bystanding stemware, dove into his food with relish, all while peppering Proust with questions about his interests, literary goals, and influences. Almost in spite of each other, the two men talked for hours, dining together in a corner of the room, arguing about literature and life while course after course was brought to them long after the other guests had retired.

For all his bluster and noise, Léon was actually an acute observer of human nature—he and Lucien shared that trait, as well as their wicked gift for impersonation, with Proust. Léon was not blind to

Proust's unhappiness and did his best to look after his new friend, sometimes taking him on moonlit walks or carriage rides through the forest, during which Proust told him about his literary projects. Léon described him as "the most charming, the most whimsical, the most unreal of companions," who seemed oblivious to that which was obvious to everyone else and yet seemed to have a special insight available only to him. He also found Proust to be sensitive to the point of seeming "flayed alive," although he noted that despite Proust's "scars" he was nonetheless at work on a "meticulous tapestry, of admirable brilliance." The work in question was the novel *Jean Santeuil*, which Proust had already begun but would later set aside.

When Proust and Léon both left Fontainebleau and returned to Paris, the Dreyfus Affair had returned to the front pages of the newspapers. On November 10 *Le Matin* published a photograph of a facsimile of the *bordereau*, the memorandum sent by the spy in the French army to the German embassy and one of the key pieces of evidence against Dreyfus. Its publication came as a shock both to its true author (the real French spy), Commandant Marie-Charles-Ferdinand-Walsin Esterhazy, and also to the French General Command that had forged a secret dossier against Dreyfus. At the same time, due largely to the efforts of Alfred Dreyfus's brother, Mathieu, a small but potent group of men had begun to rally around the idea of Dreyfus's innocence and began working to reverse the guilty verdict. There was the thirty-one-year-old Jewish critic, editor, and polemicist Bernard Lazare, who had already gained attention for his vigorous defense of anarchists a few years earlier. In 1894 Lazare had announced the end of anti-Semitism in his succès d'estime *Antisemitism: Its History and Causes*, a historical analysis of anti-Semitism from ancient Greece until the end of the nineteenth century. With bifocals that accentuated his intense gaze, Lazare had always been a merciless, righteous critic. Now he found himself roused from his initial indifference to the troubles of a wealthy Jewish man by the sheer viciousness of the public's response. Witnessing Drumont's roving gangs of young troublemakers, the willful refusal by officials to acknowledge the trumped-up nature of the case, and the vitriolic haranguing that had replaced reasoned argument on editorial pages persuaded Bernard Lazare that he had been wrong, and that anti-Semitism in fact remained an endemic feature of French society. He was the first intellectual to mobilize on behalf of Dreyfus and to argue that Dreyfus had been arrested, sentenced, and condemned as a Jew.

Current events were causing similar reappraisal by Max Nordau and Theodor Herzl, who had both witnessed the degradation ceremony. Nordau and Herzl had been friends since 1892—Nordau had even become the personal physician of Herzl and his family. When Herzl wanted input on his latest book, *The Jewish State: An Attempt to Solve the Jewish Question*, in November 1895, he naturally went to Nordau's apartment, where the two friends read, discussed, and argued for three days. Finally, Nordau rose and opened his arms to his exhausted, trembling friend: "If you are insane, we are insane together. Count on me!" They had concluded that their primary allegiance no longer lay with their adopted country but rather with the Jewish people. It was an especially cruel blow for Nordau, who had lived in France for fifteen years and who had felt supremely comfortable in her culture, so much so that he could even write a book like *Degeneration* and diagnose his adopted country with the coolly clinical assurance of a doctor assessing an ailing patient. Herzl, too, had moved unencumbered through French society: he dined at the Daudets' home once a month, where he met Joris-Karl Huysmans and Proust and even Édouard Drumont, whose energy he admired. But all that was shattered by the Dreyfus case, by the haunting memory of the degradation ceremony and the unshakeable hatred of that crowd. Herzl would later declare that the Dreyfus trial made him a Zionist. In 1896 Herzl published *The Jewish State*, which presented for the first time a coherently developed thesis of the creation of a Jewish state as the sole solution to the Jewish question. The following year the first Zionist Congress was held in Basel.

While these men found in the developing Dreyfus Affair a force that shook the very bedrock upon which their belief systems stood, others took a little longer to become engaged. Proust had returned to Paris from his stay at Fontainebleau with Léon, despondent about his literary prospects and uncertain about what step to take next. Although his book *Pleasures and Days* had received mostly lukewarm reviews, one critic, the notorious *éthéromane* (ether addict) and homosexual journalist Jean Lorrain, published a belated review in the newspaper *Le Journal* that was so scabrous that Proust felt compelled to challenge him to a duel. Besides disparaging the young Proust's literary dabblings, it also implied an unsavory relationship between him and young Lucien Daudet. The duel took place in the Bois de Meudon on Saturday, February 6, 1897. Proust's anxiety was intense and his hands shook visibly. He was so unaccustomed to dueling etiquette that he would have shaken hands with Lorrain before the duel if his seconds hadn't stopped him. Although two shots were fired, nobody was hurt. Proust's friends were surprised at his resolve, his coolness, and Proust certainly surprised himself.

In November 1896 Léon Daudet's novel *Suzanne* had been published in serialized form in *Le Journal*. At the age of twenty-nine, he was now a well-established writer, confident in his abilities, and yet his sensibilities were still somewhat undefined. He even recognized it about himself. Even as critics began to herald him as a promising new literary voice, Léon felt as if he had not yet come into his own. Would he ever feel as assured in his own literary gifts as his father? In any case much of his time was now taken up by more carnal pursuits. He embarked on a series of affairs with several actresses and opera singers, like Mlle Lucienne Bréval, a handsome, voluptuous brunette with a piercing gaze and imposing stature. Her critics, noting the distinctive costume she wore for her role as Brünnhilde in Wagner's Ring Cycle, insisted she looked like a rather massive rock lobster. But Léon found her sheer volume entrancing.

On the afternoon of May 4, 1897, Léon stepped into a cab on the Champs-Élysées on his way to yet another amorous encounter. He was in an excellent mood. It was a beautiful late afternoon, and for the next several hours he would be enjoying the delights and attentions of a well-known actress with whom he had become intimate. All of a sudden, he noticed that there were not many other carriages about, and then his attention was drawn to a crowd gathering on the side of the avenue Montaigne. A large cloud of smoke billowed up in the distance, and he could see enormous flames shooting up over the rooftops. He jumped down from the cab and ran over toward a crowd of people who were standing and pointing at the ghastly sight. "The Charity Bazaar is burning!" someone screamed.

The Charity Bazaar had been organized by some of the city's most sought-after and fashionable women. Underneath a huge, striped canvas tent on a vacant lot, surrounded on three sides by buildings, the ladies had set up various counters where they sold luxury items and colorful novelties. As an added attraction, a giant movie projector had been mounted high above the stands to project a new film, *The Disappearance of a Lady at Robert Houdin's*, by Georges Méliès. Stretching across the top of the tent was a vast awning meant to shield those assembled from the light and heat. Onlookers gathering in the street outside gaped as streams of elegant ladies and gentlemen descended from their carriages and swept into the tent in a cloud of soft muslin, cologne, and feathers as the event got under way. Everything was proceeding as expected when a fire broke out suddenly by the projector and flames spread quickly across the awning. Warning cries of "Fire" gave way to terrified screams and moans as smoke filled the tent. Most of the crowd ran away from the fire and toward the back of the tent, where the exit was blocked. Men and women, their clothes aflame, rushed about in panicked frenzy, spreading the fire to their companions as people began to die from asphyxiation and bodies piled up. One woman, Geneviève Straus, who was a friend of Marcel Proust and hostess of one of Paris's most exclusive salons, somehow knew that the only way to safety lay in walking straight into the fire. By doing so she managed to make her way to the front exit and to survive the inferno. By the time the flames had been extinguished, 140 lives had been claimed from the close ranks of Paris's most elite, glittering members of society.

Later that evening Léon went to the Grand Palace, where he ran into Paul Mariéton, an old family friend. Both of them entered the vast, cavernous, and dimly lit room where many of the bodies pulled out from the fire had been placed. Léon could not believe his eyes. Corpses, twisted and charred, lay everywhere. Shreds of burned gowns clung weakly to bodies only recently brimming with life; faces that earlier in the day had registered excitement at the novelty of the film had been shrunken into grimacing expressions, empty eye sockets expressing horrible pain. He could hear the wailing and sobbing of the victims' families and friends as they came upon the charred remains of a daughter, wife, sister, or friend. After he left he walked for a long time in the deserted streets, unable to escape the violent images that now weighed down upon him. It was difficult not to find in the catastrophe an ominous sign of some great dislocation in the world and an unwelcome reminder that even the finest members of society are vulnerable to the ravages of chance. The priest at the well-attended memorial service at Notre Dame on May 8 took it a step further, explaining that the cause of the fire was God's terrible anger at the newfangled scientific and social ideas of the young Third Republic and the rise of secularism.

A pall descended over the city. Léon's father seemed increasingly depressed these days. Some of his close friends—Goncourt, Timoléon Ambroy, and Paul Arène—had died recently, and his own health continued to deteriorate. Zola and Anatole France decided to organize a new monthly dinner to replace the "Group of Hissed Authors," which they baptized the "Balzac Dinner." The Dreyfus Affair, which had been circling these literary comrades for some time, finally chose this inaugural dinner to assert itself in their midst. Alphonse, while secretly sympathizing with much of what his friend Édouard Drumont had had to say on the subject of Jews, was loath to join the political fracas. For the most part, he had always found the line of demarcation between the literary and political worlds both useful and fairly easy to maintain. Having always considered himself a staunch republican, he was made nervous by the reactionary forces that seemed to lurk behind the many late-night brainstorming sessions and impassioned café meetings that his son Léon attended with increasing regularity. Of course it was inevitable that, when so many informed men got together, Dreyfus would be discussed. At that first Balzac dinner, which took place at the restaurant Durand at the place de la Madeleine, Alphonse and Léon, Maurice Barrès, François Coppée, and Paul Bourget took the side of the military judges who had found reason to strip Dreyfus of his rank and throw him into prison, while Anatole France and Émile Zola expressed their doubts about the captain's guilt. What had begun as a mellow evening among friends descended into a fierce shouting match. Alphonse was livid, insisting, "We must not write anything else on this subject. One must not, owing to the evil that it does to this country." Later on Alphonse told his son that he suspected this would be their last dinner with Zola. "But what a hatred of the uniform in this brave Zola! What has the army done to him?" For

Alphonse and others like him, the actual fact of Dreyfus's innocence or guilt was less relevant than the dangerous precedent that could be set by doubting the integrity of the nation's leaders.

But as much as Alphonse and others may have wished it to go away, the Dreyfus Affair limped on, with new allies of the Jewish captain emerging every day—and from unlikely sources. Colonel Marie-Georges Picquart, the youngest lieutenant colonel in the French army, had become head of the counterespionage department in July 1895 and soon became convinced that Dreyfus was innocent. Believing the real traitor to be Commandant Esterhazy, Picquart began pressing for a review of the original trial that had sent Dreyfus to Devil's Island. He met indignation and obstruction from his superiors, who forged damning "evidence" against Dreyfus in case a review should ever occur. In the meantime the military powers-that-be began a campaign against Picquart, which culminated in his transfer to Tunisia.

Before he left, though, Picquart turned over his information about Esterhazy to his lawyer, Louis Leblois, who in turn showed it to Auguste Scheurer-Kestner, vice president of the Senate and a founder of the Third Republic, who had secretly doubted Dreyfus's guilt for some time. One of the great lions of the Republic, a dignified, elegant man with a high forehead and severe white beard, Scheurer-Kestner was horrified when he learned that the army had suppressed evidence proving that Dreyfus was innocent. He sought an audience with President Félix Faure and with Minister of War General Jean-Baptiste Billot, but neither man was willing to stake his political reputation on Scheurer-Kestner's suspicions and instead quickly set about undermining their old friend. Undeterred, he continued his campaign, incurring the wrath of the right-wing press, who showered him with insults, calling him "the gray eminence of treason," "slime that had to be washed into the sewer," and "a valet of the Germans." He finally took his case before the Senate, delivering a statement on December 7, 1897. The writer Romain Rolland, who was present that day, recalled the tall, white-haired old man climbing the steps of the Tribune "with a jerky stride as if he were climbing to the scaffold." The other senators booed and heckled him, while outside the howling crowd filling the Luxembourg Gardens rendered the heavy, foggy weather even more oppressive. After reading his statement, he stepped down into a cruel silence. A month later, in the annual reelection for officers of the Senate, Scheurer-Kestner was defeated for the vice-presidency. When the prime minister confidently declared, "There is no Dreyfus Affair," many truly believed that the case was closed.

If anything, the defeat of yet another old man of the Republic merely showed that no one was immune in this political battle. One by one the most unlikely individuals found themselves caught up in the affair. Georges Clemenceau, who had been out of office since the Panama scandal, was won over by Scheurer-Kestner and dived into the fight with gusto, penning nearly five hundred articles denouncing those who seemed hell-bent on condemning Dreyfus, with little regard for justice or the truth. Even pallid, prissy young Marcel Proust, who had been largely unmoved by the Boulanger crisis of 1889 or the Panama scandal of 1892, found himself swept up in the heady currents of pro-Dreyfus politics. His friend Geneviève Straus, widow of the composer Georges Bizet and wife of the wealthy Jewish lawyer Émile Straus, had become one of the city's most sought-after hostesses. In October 1897, a few months after the Charity Bazaar that almost claimed her life, she and her husband invited their longtime friend Joseph Reinach, a politician and lawyer and the son-in-law of the disgraced Baron de Reinach of Panama scandal infamy, to the salon, where he revealed to those attending that Commandant Esterhazy was almost certainly both the spy and the author of the *bordereau*. Four regular guests among those assembled—the painter Edgar Degas, Jules Lemaître, Jean-Louis Forain, and Gustave Schlumberger—left in disgust, never to return. From that moment on, the Straus salon became a center of Dreyfusard activity, and Marcel Proust became one of its most loyal attendees.

Proust and his friends were also inspired by the increasingly scathing, urging articles of Émile Zola. After witnessing the horrible treatment of Auguste Scheurer-Kestner, Zola, now fifty-seven years old, had published his first article in *Le Figaro* about the affair, concluding his vigorous defense of the old man with the sentence that soon became the slogan for the Dreyfusards: "Truth is on the march, and nothing can stop it." His second article appeared on December 1 and had a similar tone. It was aimed at youth and scolded those students who had demonstrated against Dreyfus in rowdy, rough marches through the Latin Quarter. "So there exist fresh young brains and souls that this idiotic poison has already deranged?" he asked. "How very sad, and how ominous for the coming twentieth century! . . . Who if not you will join the lists, will stand fast against overwhelming odds, will break a lance for justice? Are you not ashamed that we old men are the ones who have become impassioned? That the generous madness of youth has inspired not you but your elders?"

The evening of the article's publication, Proust and his friends Daniel Halévy, Fernand Gregh, Louis de la Salle, and Jacques Baignères met at Weber's Café in the rue Royale, just around the corner from Proust's apartment, and discussed the growing controversy until one-thirty a.m. They determined that it was no longer possible to escape into the ideal world of art, and they decided to enlist distinguished public figures to come to Dreyfus's defense. On the way home, Gregh told Halévy about a scene he had witnessed the previous day, when he had stopped by the offices of Le Figaro. Léon Daudet and Maurice Barrès, both increasingly adamant anti-Semites, had come to pressure the newspaper's director, Ferdinand de Rodays, to adopt a "neutral" editorial stance by closing the paper's columns to Zola and anyone else who questioned Dreyfus's guilt or the integrity of the army. A few days later, Zola's third and final article in Le Figaro appeared: the newspaper responded to the pressure and to a rash of canceled subscriptions by refusing to publish any more articles critical of the army. Meanwhile, Proust and his friends worked to collect signatures from prominent men willing to support Zola's efforts on behalf of Dreyfus. Early on Proust succeeded in getting the illustrious Anatole France to sign their petition. Proud of his success, he promised his friends that he would try to obtain all possible signatures. However, he argued against Halévy's proposal to ask Alphonse Daudet. He said that such a request would be insensitive, given the author's chronic pain, but he told Halévy that he would speak to Daudet privately about signing. Even Jean-Baptiste Charcot, who had remained largely on the outskirts of the sort of political activities and debates that had increasingly mesmerized Léon and Proust, could not help but respond in writing to Émile Zola's rousing calls for justice. On December 1, on the very day that Zola's second article had appeared on the front page of *Le Figaro*, Jean-Baptiste, who at the time was still involved in medical research, wrote the older writer a brief letter, explaining the "great pleasure" he took from the article and congratulating the author on the courage he had shown. He felt confident, he continued, in conveying the reaction that his father, now dead for some four years, would certainly have had to Zola's role in the Dreyfus Affair. "How many times did I hear my father, who had for a long time been preparing a major medico-philosophical work that he planned to call 'Israel,' fulminate against the anti-French horde of anti-Semites."

A few weeks later, on December 16, Léon rushed home, late for dinner. His father was waiting for him in his study, and Léon took Alphonse by the arm and helped him to the table. They spoke of idle family matters, of the final dress rehearsal of *Cyrano de Bergerac* that would take place the next day, of the latest articles printed about the Dreyfus case. Alphonse confessed how much he enjoyed the playwright Edmond Rostand. Then the valet came in to serve the soup. Alphonse lowered his spoon into the plate when all of a sudden, in the midst of a brief and terrible silence, they heard a low rattle, followed by another rattle. His wife, Julia, cried out and the entire family rushed to Alphonse, whose head was thrown back while a cold sweat beaded upon his great brow. Julia was sobbing and murmuring, "Don't leave us," while Léon and Lucien struggled to lay him out on the floor before sending off for Dr. Potain and the *curé* from Sainte-Clotilde. Léon tried to keep his father alive with artificial respiration, until old Potain took over. Daudet's eyelids mechanically fluttered, but that was all. Alphonse was gone; he was fifty-seven years old.

The outpouring of grief and mourning was tremendous. *Le Matin* gravely announced, "The sudden death of M. Alphonse Daudet leaves a great empty place in contemporary French literature." *Le Temps* marveled that, although he had devoted his life to the "exclusive and jealous" world of letters, he had no enemies, for everyone knew of his illness and of the thousand daily moments of agony that he had endured for years. Léon was beside himself and kept bursting into tears before the mourners who had begun dropping by the family home to pay their respects. Marcel Proust and Reynaldo Hahn hurried over that same evening and did not leave their friends Léon and Lucien for three days. They, along with Georges Hugo, also accompanied the Daudet family to the funeral, as did the political opposites Émile Zola and the anti-Semitic journalist Édouard Drumont, each of whom now served as pallbearer for their fallen friend. An enormous crowd turned up for the funeral, which included government ministers, members of the Académie Française, Sarah Bernhardt, Maurice Barrès, Robert de Montesquiou, Stéphane Mallarmé, Rodin, Monet, Renoir, the painter Carolus-Duran, and the composer Jules Massenet. The assembled mourners at Père Lachaise Cemetery ignored an icy rain. Zola pronounced the funeral oration, declaring that the dead writer's Realism placed him at the forefront of a century-long quest for the truth and invoking the camaraderie and fellowship of their former gatherings at the Group of Five. At the end Léon stepped forward and embraced Zola affectionately.

When Léon returned with his family to their home, the pride he had felt in the illustrious and celebratory ceremony could no longer keep his sense of unending loneliness at bay. Alone with his thoughts in the drawing room, Léon simply could not imagine a life without his father. They had shared thirty years together, and for much of that time, Léon had been nimbly orienting himself toward his father's tastes and demands. In these past few years, it seemed as if Alphonse leaned on Léon more and more—but, looking back, Léon realized how much he, too, had depended on his ailing father. He finally felt like an adult—but not as he had felt standing at the altar with Jeanne or holding his son, Charles, for the first time. There was no sense of accomplishment or satisfaction with this sensation of new maturity, no sense of excitement at the new experiences and opportunities that would soon be his. Rather, there was the realization that, the more time we spend on this earth, the more we are forced to witness the decline and eventual demise of the ones we love, forced to abandon the unrestrained hopes of youth in favor of the sober pragmatism of adulthood. This maturity had a heaviness, an oppressive weight that made Léon long for a time when death and disease, venality and disappointment, were kept hidden. He was thirty years old and, quite suddenly, he felt very old.

While Léon numbly attempted to pick up the pieces after his father's death, the Dreyfus Affair lurched forward. In early January

1898, Esterhazy had gone before a court-martial as a way of erasing any lingering questions about his guilt. And after only three minutes of deliberations, he was unsurprisingly found innocent. He stepped down the front steps of the Cherche-Midi prison to the resounding cries of "Hats off to the martyr of the Jews!" and happily strode into the midst of his cheering supporters. Mathieu Dreyfus, Marcel Proust, and the other Dreyfusards were devastated: they had really believed that justice would prevail this time. How could it not? The campaign to secure a review of the Dreyfus case and to once and for all establish his innocence now seemed doomed. Among the Dreyfusards, only Émile Zola was not surprised. He was furious. He had watched the events unfold with growing alarm and indignation, and now that justice had been miscarried once again, he made a decision about what needed to be done. He told his wife of his plans but no one else, and then locked himself in his study for twenty-four hours. When he emerged, he had in his hand a four-thousand-word text that would change the course of the Dreyfus Affair. He took it over himself to the offices of *L'Aurore*, and the next day, January 13, it was published as "Letter to M. Félix Faure, President of the Republic" but came to be known simply as "J'accuse," an open letter in which he accused the high command of an anti-Semitic conspiracy to pervert justice. The publication of Zola's open letter electrified French readers and transformed the ongoing debate into a question of urgent national importance: here was a moment to define what sort of country France would be in the new century. In writing his letter, which included not only an account of what had been happening since Dreyfus's arrest in 1894 but also specific accusations against named members of the military high command, Zola knew he was risking civil or even criminal proceedings taken against him. Yet he thought that the inevitable publicity surrounding his own trial would force the issue of Dreyfus's innocence to remain in the public eye, while the trial itself would compel evidence to be put on the record.

It was a great risk to take for the man whom Flaubert had dubbed a "colossus with dirty feet, nevertheless a colossus." The year before, Zola's fame had peaked upon publication of the final novel of his twenty-volume Rougon-Maquart series. He had been fêted and praised by the greatest politicians and celebrities—even if many ordinary Frenchmen were put off by the brutal Realism of his works. He also hated politics, and as late as November 1897 he dismissively told a reporter from *L'Aurore*, "Politics leaves me completely indifferent." But the writer in him sensed something dramatic in the story of Alfred Dreyfus. And then, after a lunch with Scheurer-Kestner on November 13, Zola realized that, right before him, there was an opportunity for him to make a grand intervention in the affairs of the city, of the nation. Perhaps he could even be the Victor Hugo for the coming generation.

From the moment "J'accuse" was published, the question of Dreyfus's guilt or innocence ceased to be merely an academic exercise. The fifty-eight-year-old writer had effectively thrown down the gauntlet, and in doing so he divided a younger generation of would-be writers and poets—men like Léon Daudet, Marcel Proust, Charles Péguy, André Gide, and Daniel Halévy. The day after its publication, Léon and Georges Hugo went to Zola's to see how he was faring. Zola welcomed them eagerly, insisting that the anti-Dreyfus characters he had just excoriated were worthy characters for one of Léon's novels. But while the two younger men were polite to Zola's face, once they left they could not help mocking the anxious self-righteousness of the older writer, who, Léon later claimed derisively, clearly believed his role in the Dreyfus Affair to be akin to Voltaire's defense of a Protestant shopkeeper in the famous Calas Affair, or Hugo's writing of *Les Châtiments* at the height of Napoléon III's Second Empire.

For by this point, freed from the hesitancy of his father's republicanism, Léon had become increasingly involved in anti-Dreyfusard circles. And so, rather than defending the actions of his father's friend, Léon simply watched with a satisfied smirk as the attack against Zola was mounted. The bestselling author soon found himself pilloried in the press and in ditties sold on street corners. He was mailed packages of excrement and was burnt in effigy. Denounced as a "foreigner," in reference to his Italian father, Zola was formally sued for his criticism of the government's handling of the case. His trial opened on February 7, 1898, and lasted sixteen days.

Zola's trial was a circus. Every day, Marcel Proust climbed up to the public gallery of the Palais de Justice on the Île de la Cité, bringing coffee and sandwiches so as not to miss anything. He took notes obsessively, and much of what he observed made its way into the book he was still writing, *Jean Santeuil.* Édouard Drumont had paid people from the street forty sous a head to stand outside the windows and jeer. The atmosphere inside was hardly better—each time Zola or his lawyer, the volatile young Fernand Labori, or that master debater Georges Clemenceau, representing the newspaper *L'Aurore,* tried to make a statement, they were greeted by roars and boos from the crowd. Jean Jaurès was there, too—his short, stocky body characteristically encased in a haphazard array of clothing, his big head and rough beard giving him the appearance of a workingman, not a rising politician. Everyone was on edge—while waiting to testify at Zola's trial, Jaurès paced up and down the corridors as Anatole France recited seventeenth-century poetry. At one point Zola's legal team seemed to be gaining the upper hand—their arguments were convincing, and it was rumored that the jury was inclined to acquit. But then Édouard Drumont's *Libre Parole* newspaper published the names of the jurors, warning that vengeance would be sought if the "Italian" was acquitted, and the army began pressuring those involved in the case. In his closing speech, Zola staked his entire career and reputation on Dreyfus's innocence. "By all that I have conquered, by the name I have made for myself, by my works, which have advanced the cause of French letters abroad, I swear that Dreyfus is innocent." Yet after a mere thirty-five minutes of deliberation, the jurors found him guilty with a vote of 7–5 and condemned him to a year in prison and a three-thousand-franc fine; the crowd outside roared with approval. After Zola's condemnation, on February 24, Léon and Lucien sent Zola a telegram with their condolences, explaining their "profound and respectful affection" even though his ideas were "not at all ours in this affair."

When news of the verdict became known, the nation howled in a twin flare-up of delight and despair. Mobs descended upon the offices of *L'Aurore* and smashed the windows of Zola's house. Foreigners locked up their shops and made themselves scarce, and more anti-Semitic riots were orchestrated in Orléans, Nancy, Lyon, Bordeaux, Toulouse, and Marseilles. These reached their zenith in Algiers, where the looting of the Jewish quarter lasted four days, with people carrying banners reading "Death to Zola" and "Death to Dreyfus." Even some of Zola's closest friends turned on him—Henry Céard, a former protégé from the Médan days, when he and other young naturalist writers gathered for regular dinners at Zola's house outside Paris, published an open letter in *Le Gaulois* in which he chided Zola for having "written sentences capable of provoking catastrophe and of stirring up wretched humanity, all to evil effect."

But others—students, fellow writers, socialists—were truly galvanized by Zola's open letter and his subsequent prosecution. The Dreyfusards formed the League for the Rights of Man and drew up a petition called the "Protest of the Intellectuals," which began appearing each day in *L'Aurore* with successive signatures. It was organized by Marcel Proust and his brother, Robert, the philosopher Elie Halévy and his brother, Daniel, and Jacques Bizet, son of the composer. All were young men in their late twenties, and this was their battle. During the Esterhazy trial, they had begun meeting every evening in the Café des Variétés to discuss how to campaign for Dreyfus's release. They convinced Anatole France, the leader of the members of the Academy, to sign. When Adrien Proust heard of his sons' involvement, he was so outraged and embarrassed—many of his friends held high government positions—that he refused to speak to either of them for a week. Initially, there were 104 signers, but by the end of the month there were three thousand, including André Gide, Charles Péguy, Louis Pasteur, the geographer Élisée Reclus, the historian Gabriel Monod, and Claude Monet, whose signature so incensed his friend Edgar Degas that they did not speak again for years.

Writing about this heady time in his diary, thirty-two-year-old Romain Rolland confessed, "I would rather have this life of combat than the mortal calm and mournful stupor of these last years. God give me struggle, enemies, howling crowds, all the combat of which I am capable." Others shared this boredom with peace, with listening to the wise and wizened council of their elders. Charles Péguy would later revert to martial imagery, arguing that the very existence of an "Affair" around the struggle over Dreyfus's guilt or innocence could "only be explained by a need, the same one, by a need for heroism that seizes an entire generation—ours—by a need for war, for military war and military glory, by a need for sacrifice up to and

including martyrdom, perhaps (doubtless) by a need for sanctity."
Even twenty-seven-year-old Marcel Proust, the dreamy and effete
young writer, could not help but get caught up in the drama. And
the Dreyfusards were not alone. The anti-Dreyfusards had their
own contingent of young followers, who congregated at the Café
Weber in the rue Royale, where Léon Daudet, who had begun writing weekly diatribes against the Dreyfusards shortly after Zola's first
trial, held court with like-minded people such as Claude Debussy
and Puvis de Chavannes. They joined up with the older and more established leaders of the anti-Dreyfus movement at the salon hosted
by the Comtesse de Loynes on the Champs-Élysées, where Jules
Lemaître reigned.

This was a time of extreme views, in which the middle ground
had all but vanished. "Every conscience is troubled," wrote *Le Petit
Parisien*. "No one reasons any more, no discussion is possible; everyone has taken up a fixed position." Where once Léon had been
welcome at the homes of Fernand Labori and Octave Mirbeau, he
now found those doors closed to him. Léon joined the Ligue de la
Patrie Française, headed by Jules Lemaître and including among its
committee Maurice Barrès and Alphonse's old friend the Provençal
poet Frédéric Mistral. At the Ligue's first meeting, there were fifteen thousand people in attendance, including a very enthusiastic
Julia Daudet and her son Léon; within the first month it had gained
thirty thousand members. Barrès, Drumont, Rochefort, and Paul
Déroulède were the real driving spirits. The zeal and determination
of these men was thrilling to behold, and Léon found himself utterly baffled by what Zola and the others were thinking in throwing
their lot in with the Jewish traitor. As he explained in one of his
articles, behind all of the arguments over legal details and handwrit-
ing analyses "could be heard the tramp of the barbarian legions."
Dreyfusism was nothing less than the foreigners preparing to storm
the citadel. Anyone who thought differently, he concluded, was either unpatriotic or a fool.

Zola remained nervous but steadfast, even as the insults and attacks grew increasingly vicious and personal. It became clear to
Zola and his legal team that subsequent legal appeals would be
fruitless. The government wanted to stifle the writer by throwing

him into prison. On July 18, 1898, Émile Zola and his wife, Alexandrine, fled to England. He would remain in exile for eleven months.

In the meantime, though, the tide of revisionism seemed to be gaining the upper hand. The minister of war, Godefroy Cavaignac, had decided once and for all to put to rest the revisionist case. He reviewed all the evidence, convinced himself that, although Esterhazy was involved, Dreyfus was indeed guilty, went before the Chamber of Deputies on July 7, and announced that he was completely certain of Dreyfus's guilt. He personally vouched for the authenticity of the documents, and the deputies leaped to their feet in acclaim. The very next day, Juarès published an open letter to Cavaignac in *La Petite République*, the first of a series, refuting each one of the minister's "proofs." Thus did the Dreyfusards, with Jaurès at their head, mount their counterassault. To answer Jaurès's charges, Cavaignac ordered another examination of the documents, this time by an officer not previously involved in the case. This officer discovered the forgery upon which the army's case rested, and Cavaignac was forced to admit that the case upon which he had staked his reputation and for which he had won national acclaim was a fraud. He ordered the arrest of the forger, Colonel Henry, who was taken to the same Cherche-Midi prison where Dreyfus had been held. During the night of August 31, Henry committed suicide by slicing his throat in prison. Max Nordau, while giving the key address at the second Zionist Congress in Basel, spoke of the unavoidable conclusion to be drawn from the years of fierce fighting: "The Dreyfus Case has simply drawn aside veils and exposed moods of thought that had been hidden till then. It raises itself as an admonition and a lesson in the face of those Jews who still persist in believing themselves to be definitely and without reserve received into the national comradeship, at least of the most advanced Western countries."

In 1899 President Félix Faure died suddenly—in the arms of his mistress, as it turned out—and was replaced by Émile Loubet, president of the Senate and a known Dreyfus sympathizer. Within five days of his election, on the day of Félix Faure's funeral, Paul Déroulède, joined by fellow members of the Ligue des Patriotes, unsuccessfully attempted a coup d'état. He was arrested instead. From that moment on, the tide swung in favor of the Dreyfusards, who wanted a revision of Dreyfus's original conviction. After several months of investigation, on June 3, 1899, a full revision of the case was officially ordered. It took place in Rennes, a quiet regional city in Brittany, in the auditorium of the local lycée. By the time the trial came around, however, Rennes looked like a city under siege, with troops and gendarmes everywhere. The air reverberated with the sound of horses moving, sabers rattling, boots on the pavement. Barrès described the trial as the Rubicon: it was either Dreyfus or the army, a foreigner or France. The locals were becoming increasingly hostile and regarded all strangers with wary, darting looks. "Check out the horrible head of that guy. He's part of the Dreyfus gang," two locals remarked about Max Nordau, who was there as a reporter for the *Vossische Zeitung*, as they passed him in the street. When the assembled spectators finally saw Dreyfus, the mere sight of him—gaunt and startled—being brought into the room was a tragedy in and of itself. For years so much hatred and pity, anger and devotion, had been awarded to this man, who had become a mythical abstraction. Now, before all of these eager onlookers, he looked desiccated, not of the living. His hair had gone white and he was very pale; his trousers flapped against his scrawny, skeletal legs. He had padded his uniform and taken stimulants. For a moment even Barrès was moved,

> At that moment we felt nothing but a thin wave of pain breaking over the auditorium. A miserable human rag was being thrown into the glaring light. A ball of living flesh, fought over by the players of two teams and who has not had a minute's rest for six years, comes rolling from America into the midst of our battle.

It was somehow clear to all who attended that no absolute victory would be conferred by this trial. Midway through the trial, shortly after six a.m. on August 14, Fernand Labori, the irascible, eloquent attorney for Dreyfus who "looked like Hercules and pleaded like a boxer," was shot in the back while walking toward the courtroom with Picquart along the banks of the Vilaine River. The bullet stopped mere inches from his spine, but Labori was back in court eight days later. Marcel Proust sent Labori a telegram, expressing his relief that the "good invincible giant" had escaped serious injury.

Despite all the new evidence, the military court would not admit their error and found Dreyfus guilty once again on September 9. Due to "extenuating circumstances," he was sentenced to ten years of detention, instead of a mandatory life sentence. It was an absurd sentence, and the response was swift and overwhelming. There were anti-French demonstrations in Antwerp, Milan, Naples, London, and New York. Some called for the World's Fair, which was about to open in Paris, to be boycotted. At Evian on Lake Geneva, Marcel Proust came upon the Comtesse de Noailles weeping and crying, "How could they do it? What will the foreigners think of us now?" Nordau left Rennes heartbroken—it was the last straw, and he was now ready to turn his back on France for good.

Ten days later, on September 19, 1899, Alfred Dreyfus was pardoned, although he was not fully rehabilitated by the army until 1906. By then Émile Zola had been dead for four years. He died at the age of sixty-two during the night of September 29, 1902, due to carbon monoxide poisoning caused by a stopped chimney. When word of his death got out, many believed that he had been assassinated by right-wing nationalists for his role in the Dreyfus Affair. Such paranoid speculation might not have occurred before the affair, but something had become unhinged during those years of angry politicizing and posturing, when men were forced to fight for their ideals in ways that they never had. Years later, in *Remembrance of Things Past*, Proust described the Dreyfus Affair as a kind of "social kaleidoscope" that required even those social hierarchies once thought to be immutable to adapt and evolve. For his character Mme Swann, who because of her scandalous past as a cocotte begins her social ascent at the very bottom, the Dreyfus case proves to be a godsend, allowing her to associate with women from the best circles.

The Dreyfus Affair also served as a kaleidoscope of sorts for the actual men and women who lived through it. By the time the Dreyfus Affair was over, Victor Hugo, Jean-Martin Charcot, and Alphonse Daudet were all dead, and the ideals they had each represented seemed part of a distant memory. The affair was the final nail in the coffin of unquestioning adherence to the tenets of nineteenth-century republicanism, an adherence that had already been shaken by France's defeat by Prussia and subsequent social and political dislocation. Léon, Marcel, Jean-Baptiste, Jeanne, and others like them were part of the first generation in a hundred years to see no uprisings or revolutions, no barricades or serious bloodshed in the streets during their early adulthood in the 1880s and 1890s. Yet their anxieties were no less prevalent for it. The optimism and security of their parents were called into question as, one by one, the great men of the Third Republic fell—some quietly, claimed by sickness and infirmity, others spectacularly, brought down by scandal—and the foundations they had struggled so valiantly to lay seemed suddenly feeble. The eruption of the Dreyfus Affair had only exacerbated and prolonged the sense of unavoidable social disintegration. Out of the rubble, Marcel Proust would go on to create a new idiom for conveying the psychological and social evolution of his generation, and Theodor Herzl would begin laying the intellectual foundation for modern Zionism. Meanwhile, Léon and Jean-Baptiste would attempt to create new traditions of their own.

EIGHT

The Heiress and the Polar Gentleman

Great things are done when Men & Mountains meet;
This is not done by Jostling in the Street.

—William Blake (c. 1808–12)

Will we succeed? And will we manage to justify the confidence of those who supported us and helped us? It is a difficult game that we play and the critics who were so greatly prodigious at our departure will be even more so upon our return if we return empty-handed.

It is not even a matter here of "triumph or perish," we must succeed at any price, for our failure itself would justify all that could have been said and would not make up for the consented sacrifices. If the Expedition returns, how many, alas! of these brave comrades now so full of life and ardor, so happy to throw themselves into the adventures of the unknown, will still respond to the call?

It is a formidable responsibility that I'm assuming, and about which I feel today more than ever the enormous weight; I have not only a goal to achieve, but also I must conserve the nineteen existences of those who accompany me.

These and a host of other fears and anxieties flooded thirty-seven-year-old Jean-Baptiste's thoughts as he and his men left the shelter of Orange Bay in the South Shetlands, about 120 kilometers north of the Antarctic Peninsula, and headed out once again into the swirling waters that would carry them ever closer to their final destination. It was January 27, 1904.

Jean-Baptiste could still scarcely believe it. He had always dreamed of having far-off adventures on uncharted seas, but those had always been childhood dreams for a distant future. He was not even a professional sailor and had only really been pursuing this passion since his father's death more than ten years earlier. Even then, it had never been with the aim of ending up here, at the ends of the earth. At first he had simply found being out on his small boat soothing. Jean-Baptiste was still struggling with the question of what to do with his life. He could not shake the almost crushing sense of responsibility for carrying on the family name in medicine after his father's death. Although he worked his way up to being clinic chief at the Salpêtrière, there were too many painful memories of his father there, so he left the hospital to go to the Pasteur Institute, where he studied cancer with the doctors Émile Roux and Ilya Metchnikoff. He enjoyed his laboratory work but never found the same inspiration in taking care of patients as Jean-Martin had. Instead, he looked forward to summertime, when he could take his yacht out on pleasure cruises. The rhythmic swaying and creaking of the craft as water lapped gently against the side when all was calm eased the tension that crept through his body after long days spent in the lab or seeing patients. And nothing exhilarated him more than the challenge and chaos of rough waters—it was this delicate, uncertain dance between his own physical dexterity and the power of forces far greater than himself that he found intoxicating and actually quite liberating. At times, he observed, the farther from land he found himself, the easier it was for him to breathe, as if the requirements and demands of his family, of his world, had no hold on him.

He spent hours carefully going over ship designs and mapping out the course for his next trip. He also designed a flag to represent his name and spirit out at sea. It was black and white and featured a large question mark at the center for *"Pourquoi Pas?"* (Why not?). Eventually, the excursions became more than mere exercises. First there were trips to the coast of Holland, then the southern coast of

England. In early 1898 Jean-Baptiste had spent three months sailing down the Nile as the personal physician of the American millionaire Cornelius Vanderbilt on his yacht, *Catania*. In the summer of 1900, he toured the waters around Ireland. Then it was off to the Faroe Islands between Scotland and Iceland, with a seven-man team. He continued practicing medicine for a brief time, but soon decided to devote his full attention to his childhood passion: exploration. By 1902 he felt ready to try his hand at a true expedition. He would go north, to the island Novaya Semlya in the Barents Sea, southeast of Spitsbergen, an area still largely unmapped by cartographers, or perhaps to Greenland itself. In any case it would be somewhere in the Arctic, a hostile but attainable region that had held a particular sway over him for the past several years after he took shorter voyages to Jan Mayen, Norway, in his beloved schooner, the *Rose-Marine*. And he was determined that his next trip would be no mere pleasure cruise but a proper scientific expedition, with the latest equipment and devices. It was a bold and massive undertaking for someone with relatively scant experience at sea, and certainly for someone so new to the treacherous, icy waters to the north. Few in his immediate circle could understand: his mother begged him not to go, while his wife, Jeanne, listened in stony silence to his enthusiastic descriptions. But Jean-Baptiste had decided that he would not rest until he had done something truly great, and what greater challenge was there for someone who loved sailing than to join the ranks of those who could call themselves polar explorers?

He quickly discovered that transforming his boyhood fantasies into a real-life expedition would be an expensive undertaking. He approached the famed shipwright Père Gautier to come up with plans for his new boat—which he had mischievously decided to name the *Pourquoi-Pas?*—at the shipyards in Saint-Malo. He liked nothing better than dropping by Gautier's to check up on the progress being made and experience the briny smell of the sea mingling with the unmistakable scent of freshly cut wood, smoke, and tar. He needed a larger, specially equipped vessel, and convinced the famed Belgian explorer Adrien de Gerlache to advise him and Père Gautier about the design. But although Jean-Baptiste was a wealthy man, even he had difficulty coming up with the vast sums required to support his planned undertaking. To fund the outfitting of a laboratory suitably supplied with scientific instruments, he had to sell one of his most prized possessions, a painting by the eighteenth-century master Jean-Honoré Fragonard. Even with that sale, he ran out of money. In the end the mighty ship was equipped with a secondhand and underpowered 125-horsepower engine.

The initial preparations went forward unnoticed, but finally, in late 1902, a few reporters got wind of Jean-Baptiste's intentions. Articles began appearing in the papers about a French expedition to the Arctic—the first such expedition led by a Frenchman—and soon Jean-Baptiste was inundated by inquiries about his plans. One morning he was working at his home at the imposing mansion at 80, rue de l'Université, which he shared with his family, when a servant came and announced that a young man, a Monsieur Pléneau, was at the door and would not leave until he had spoken with the master. Jean-Baptiste reluctantly had the stranger brought before him. He told Jean-Baptiste that his name was Paul Pléneau, and that he was thirty-three years old and an engineer. The previous evening, he had been in bed reading the newspaper when he came across an article— "Good Blood Always Tells"—announcing that the son of the famous professor of the Salpêtrière was planning an expedition to the North Pole. After reading the article, Pléneau had felt electrified. Like Jean-Baptiste, he was not yet ready to give up on his boyhood fantasies of adventure. Now he was here to beg for a spot as an engineer on the expedition.

Listening to the young man's breathless offer, Jean-Baptiste felt a smile tugging at the corners of his mouth. He gently explained that the Arctic expedition was, at that point, more a wish than reality, but Pléneau would not be put off. He asked Jean-Baptiste if he could call on him every Sunday at ten a.m. to be kept abreast of his plans. Jean-Baptiste thought about this proposal for a moment, then smiled, stuck out his hand, and said warmly, "It's a deal."

Over the next several months, Jean-Baptiste solidified these plans. He continued seeing patients and conducting his medical research, but in the evenings he came home to study older travel accounts and pore over maps. He began reaching out to more experienced sailors and consulting with scientists about the sort of research that could and should be undertaken. At first Jean-Baptiste worried that no one would take him seriously, but he soon found that his last name was enough to open most doors, while his enthusiasm and intelligence then quelled any lingering misgivings. Although he did not admit it to anyone, Jean-Baptiste envisioned this trip as merely an initial foray into polar waters—a test of his abilities. After four or five months, he would have the experience needed to mount a subsequent and more significant Antarctic expedition. The thought of such an undertaking—of the honor and esteem it would bring to his family and to his country—made his heart pound.

But then came the news that changed everything. An expedition headed by the great Swedish explorer Otto Nordenskjöld, which had departed for Antarctica in 1901, was declared missing. The news swept through the small but enthusiastic world of polar explorers and made headlines in newspapers throughout the world. The Swedish government mobilized to send a rescue mission there, as did Argentina. Jean-Baptiste decided that France, that *he*, should also participate in the search. Now was no time for timidity, he reasoned, or for trial runs. All thoughts of going to Greenland were set aside as Jean-Baptiste set about recalculating his budget and consulting whatever maps he could find of the area—they really were little more than sketches, illustrated approximations of lands too far off and too little frequented to be measured with any accuracy. He quickly sent Paul Pléneau, who had, as promised, been calling every week for updates, a letter, explaining the new plan: "Instead of going north, we should go south! In the south we are certain to succeed, for very little exploration has been done . . . We have only to get there to achieve something great and fine . . . The north is an unknown quantity; the south is success."

Both men knew that underneath those few, quick, bold assertions lay a host of dangers and challenges. But now was the moment when they needed to cross that line, to have faith in their dreams and take action—not as a doctor and an engineer, but as would-be conquerors.

"Wherever you like. Whenever you like. As much as you like.— Pléneau," replied the young man by telegram. Jean-Baptiste responded the following day with his own telegram: "I was sure of it. Thank you.—Charcot."

Although Jean-Baptiste projected outward confidence in his plans, he had plenty of reasons to feel anxious: little was known about Antarctic travel in 1902. For Europeans of the late nineteenth and early twentieth centuries, polar adventures held the fascination and terror of the exploration of outer space. After the "scramble for Africa," polar regions were the last great question marks on maps, the last frontiers that man could hope to conquer. The area loomed large in the imagination of the age. In the year before he finally succumbed to his illness, a dying Alphonse Daudet, kept awake by the pain radiating throughout his body, remained awake at night reading accounts of polar exploration, gingerly turning the pages in the hope that these tales would help him forget his degenerating body. In *The Interpretation of Dreams* (1900), Sigmund Freud referred to the experiences of Nordenskjöld and his men when discussing the phenomenon of an increase in frequency and intensity of dreams in adults who are transferred into the midst of unfamiliar and extreme conditions. In fact, polar exploration had been involved at the very inception of Freud's work on dream interpretation. As he was working through his initial theories about dreams, in 1898, he wrote to his friend Wilhelm Fliess that his entire household was deeply in the throes of "hero-worshipping" over the exploits of the Norwegian explorer Fridtjof Nansen, whose book, *In Night and Ice*, had recently been published in German. "I shall be able to make some use of Nansen's dreams," Freud explained, "they are practically transparent . . ."

Between 1888 and 1903, several great polar expeditions were launched, and future generations would look back on this as the era of "Heroic Exploration." In the north Nansen followed up his triumphant 1888 trek—on skis—from east to west across Greenland by becoming the first to cross the Arctic Ocean. Then, in 1902, the Englishman Robert Scott went down with Ernest Shackleton across the South Pacific Ocean to explore Ross Sea and Victoria Land, making a daring raid across the great ice barrier. These men traveled to the ends of the earth, through unknown waters where they were forced to endure unimaginable hardship—freezing conditions, isolation, and the near constant threat of shipwreck. The stolid, familiar names they chose to christen the places they discovered—Ross Sea, Graham Land, Coats Land—seemed expressly designed to eradicate all memory of the privations and the desperation that lay behind their discovery.

Why did they do it? Like the generations of explorers who came before them, they were responding to the siren call of immortality—personal glory, honor for country, fame, and accolades. Sometimes their aims were more venal—a desire for power and influence that could be gained by handing new territory to motherlands still eagerly scrambling for mines and slaves, open markets and salvageable souls. But Antarctica was different. The rewards for gaining mastery over it were less tangible and more primal. The poles were true *terras nuevas*, still shielded from prying human eyes by the extreme conditions and great distances. They were uninhabited, unexplored, truly unknown. Scientists had begun to speculate that these regions were essential for understanding global weather and various phenomena of terrestrial magnetism, and statesmen in Europe invoked with increasing frequency the strategic importance of controlling their territories and waterways. But for the hardy few who actually made the journey, the reward was priceless. They were hailed as supermen, applauded in capitals across the globe, and besieged by invitations to speak at black-tie galas and scientific symposia. Roald Amundsen, the steely Norwegian explorer who, during the course of his career, would tackle both North and South poles, put it best when he observed:

> Whatever remains to man unknown, in this world of ours, is by so much a burden on the spirits of all men. It remains a something that man has not yet conquered—a continuing evidence of his weakness, an unmet challenge to his mastery over nature. By the same token, every mystery made plain, every unknown land explored, exalts the spirit of the whole human race—strengthens its courage and exalts its spirit permanently. The trail breaker is an indispensable ally of the spiritual values which advance and sustain civilization.

Jean-Baptiste, who had always been such a good and grounded young man, such an obedient and dutiful son, finally found himself daring to imagine such greatness for himself. Soon a future in medicine, where any achievements he might make would inevitably and forever be overshadowed by his father's, became unthinkable.

Now that his expedition had taken such an ambitious, even grandiose, turn, Jean-Baptiste also decided to rename his ship the *Français*—a proud and patriotic name, befitting his maiden voyage and hopefully suggestive to his own government that it should pay attention to what he was doing. He began casting about more actively for formal government support, eventually obtaining the backing of French president Émile Loubet and the Academy of Sciences, the Geographical Society, and the Museum of Natural History. Of even greater immediate usefulness were the 150,000 francs raised by a public appeal organized by the Parisian newspaper *Le Matin*, whose owner, Alfred Edwards, just happened to be married to Jean-Baptiste's sister, Jeanne. When some other private contributions were added to the mix, Jean-Baptiste was left with a working fund of 450,000 francs, a significant sum at the time but far less than that of other similar polar expeditions. The plan was for him to explore the west coast of Graham Land from the north, venture south to Adelaide Island and, if possible, Alexander Island, and chart the coastline and gather botanical, zoological, hydrographic, and meteorological data along the way. His sponsors also wanted Jean-Baptiste to determine whether Antarctica was a continent or a group of small islands surrounded by ice and to spend the winter there, thereby providing valuable information about the logistical challenges that other explorers would face.

In August, after four months of frenzied preparation, Jean-Baptiste's Antarctic expedition was ready to depart. Throughout the final days before their departure, Jean-Baptiste moved from one task to the next like a man possessed. Jeanne, meanwhile, watched. Charcot's men barely acknowledged her. He knew she was not used to such oversight, and it pained him to see her deal with the disappointment by turning her back resolutely on the proceedings. Jean-Baptiste had tried to convince her of the excitement and the glory it would earn for their family name, but she knew that he was doing this for himself, and that any glory he obtained in pursuit of his prize would reflect little on her.

Jeanne had married Jean-Baptiste in 1896, when she was twenty-seven and he twenty-nine. Unlike her first wedding, with its throngs of well-wishers and massive guest list, her second was attended by only a few close family friends; her fairy-princess gown of white satin had been replaced by a more mature brown suit lined with fur. When the brief, simple ceremony had concluded, the mayor of the arrondissement, M. Rissler, could not help but add how "honored and happy he was to have united two such illustrious names." Everyone agreed that it was a very beautiful, a very hopeful event. Jean-Baptiste, who had loved Jeanne from afar for so long, was over the moon. In some ways it was his first taste of true independence, of becoming a husband rather than merely being a son.

In growing up as the ideal granddaughter of France's most revered idol, Jeanne was unprepared for the blemishes of reality—nothing is more disappointing than finding flaws in perfection. Nor were the men in her life prepared. The flaws had only really revealed themselves once she had left her home and started out in her new life with Léon. But she had reason to hope that things would be different with Jean-Baptiste. He was kind and handsome and had known her from the happier days of childhood. Jeanne may have believed that because Jean-Baptiste had known her as she had been then—the apple of her grandfather's eye—he would allow her to continue in that role a bit longer. Jean-Baptiste, at least, seemed less arrogant than Léon, less ambitious. And unlike Léon, Jean-Baptiste was a doctor, not a writer, and would never dare to presume that any jottings he made could ever be considered in the same realm as Victor Hugo's magnificent body of work.

But as Jean-Baptiste's pursuit of his childhood passion emboldened him with each day that passed, it left little room in his life for Jeanne, who had a young child to tend to and no interest in exploration, nor in a husband who would potentially be willing to leave her for months, even years, on end. Her grandfather had made her the subject of his work in a way that bound them together and provided her with an identity, a purpose, for years. But each of her two husbands had kept his own work separate from her—Léon his writing and Jean-Baptiste his medical career and dreams of exploring. About marriage and motherhood, she knew little. She never got used to signing her name "Jeanne Charcot." She tended to sign it "Jeanne Charcohugo" . . . eliding the final "t" of Charcot and the initial "H" in Hugo. In some respects she had felt best during that brief time between her two marriages when she was simply referred to as "Mme Jeanne Hugo."

Jean-Baptiste was infinitely more patient with Jeanne's attachment to her former life than Léon had been, but it must have pained him to witness her unwillingness to commit to creating a new life with him. Jean-Baptiste tried to interest her in his work, telling her and little Charles animated tales of exploration and—his new favorite—polar adventures. His eagerness made her wary; she feigned boredom at his descriptions of harrowing ocean crossings, strange animals, and gleaming icebergs. But she, too, had once been fascinated by such matters. When she was only eleven years old, the great Swedish explorer A. E. Nordenskjöld, uncle of the Antarctic explorer Otto Nordenskjöld, had presented her with a paper knife made from the tooth of a walrus inscribed on one side with "J.H." and on the other with "From the expedition of the Vega to the Polar Sea." She still remembered how smooth and pale it looked and how exciting it was to think that an object from such a cold, faraway place was now sitting in her warm, child's hands. But that was a different time.

Neither she nor her brother Georges could let go of their extraordinary childhood. Jeanne had been a spoiled and indulged child, then a socialite adored for her handsome features and fine clothing almost as much as for her illustrious name. Such attention had never felt burdensome or false—she had always been loved for being pretty, been encouraged by her grandfather in her incessant preening and prancing. He had appreciated her, needed her youthful, innocent beauty to bring balance and softness to his ancient, craggy visage. But while Jeanne had thrived on this attention, Georges had squandered it. He did not know how to be a Hugo, Jeanne decided. Over the years his boyish good looks had faded and then disappeared outright. He was corpulent and pale and dissipated. She had watched him, first admiringly, then with disdain, as he and Léon got into all sorts of scrapes together—they were so smug, those two, brawling and carousing without a care in the world. But it went further with Georges—for the drinking inevitably led to gambling, which led to debts and horrible rows with the family about loans and promises of repentance. He would not listen to their mother, Alice, and he abhorred their stepfather, Édouard Lockroy. The family had hoped he would settle down, do something, anything, of some distinction. He eventually married well, at least—although it was difficult not to question the sanity of any woman who wished to put up with such a lout. After many sincere promises of good behavior, in 1894 Georges finally secured the hand of Mlle Pauline Ménard-Dorian, daughter and heiress of one of the greatest shipowners and merchants of Marseilles. Fortunately for Georges, Pauline's mother, Mme Ménard-Dorian, was eager to align herself with such an illustrious family and was therefore inclined to overlook the colorful past of her future son-in-law. But when Pauline finally refused to put up with Georges's extravagant ways and his attempts at bullying her family for money, he treated her so horribly that she was obliged to apply for a divorce in 1899, which she had no difficulty in obtaining, along with custody of their two children, Jean and Marguerite. Georges then fled to Florence, where he lived on an allowance paid to him by Gustave Simon, on behalf of his aunt Adèle, on the condition that he stay put and out of trouble. He eventually got married again, to Dora Dorian, the cousin of his former wife—as if the Hugo family needed any more romantic scandals for public consumption.

He behaved just as horribly with Jeanne. When his sister announced that she intended to seek a divorce from Léon Daudet, she drove a wedge between herself and her brother. Divorce in that day was far from common, having only been reestablished in 1884. Most women, particularly women from the best sorts of families, usually remained in unhappy marriages, suffering in quiet, dignified silence, masking their misery behind jewels and fancy frocks and lovers and children. Victor Hugo's wife, Adèle, had never considered leaving the man who, though father to her children, had jumped in and out of beds under her nose and under her roof. Nor had Julia Daudet ever considered leaving her Alphonse, whose notorious womanizing and extreme sexual preferences had left her speechless, aghast, even prostrate on many occasions. But Jeanne, like her brother, had grown up believing herself to be exempt from the rules that applied to everyone else—so when she had had enough of marriage, she simply ended it. A few years later, in mid-May 1898, both brother and sister found themselves at the Odéon Theater for a performance of one of

Victor Hugo's posthumous plays, *The Grandmother*. There is some disagreement over what, precisely, was said, but according to one journalist, during the intermission Georges "took advantage of the situation to apostrophize Jeanne in the coarsest and most insulting manner." Since this was not the first time Georges had confronted his sister in public, loudly, sometimes almost violently, Jean-Baptiste decided that it was finally time for him to intervene. Walking over to Georges, he asked his brother-in-law to kindly lower his voice and refrain from hurling any further insults at Jeanne. When Georges ignored the request, Jean-Baptiste knocked his brother-in-law down with a solid blow to the face. Georges, known more for his penchant for gaming and drink than for his physical prowess, fell to the ground in a heap, stunned. A tense silence fell over the crowd as it waited to see what might happen next. Upon regaining his feet, Georges began to lunge at Jean-Baptiste with his cane, but was prevented from achieving his revenge by the police, who removed both gentlemen from the establishment.

Unfortunately for all those involved, the fight at the Odéon Theater did not end that evening. The following day Georges challenged Jean-Baptiste to a duel. For the sake of his wife and his new in-laws, Jean-Baptiste refused. Georges, now even more outraged, sent a letter to all the major newspapers calling Jean-Baptiste a coward in the hope that his charges would be widely published. They refused. As a last resort, Georges then called Jean-Baptiste before the courts, which ordered him to pay a nominal fine of fifty francs for the beating and instructed Georges to behave more "discreetly" in the future. Everyone agreed it was most unfortunate that the brother and sister should be dragging the family name through the mud in such a way, or, as one journalist put it, "slowly drifting away from the loving traditions of the venerable poet." By now, though, even the most devout Hugo-worshippers would agree that the great poet's angelic grandchildren were in possession of some rather tarnished halos.

Nor did Georges improve with age. He was already a laughing-stock in some circles for making an application to the French government in 1902 for permission to assume his grandfather's name. "Georges" was no longer a sufficiently grand name for him, even with the title "Count" that he used in conjunction with it. Most observers drily suggested that such an application should be denied on the grounds that the younger Hugo had most emphatically done nothing to render himself worthy of the great name, which his grandfather had won for himself throughout the world. Apparently the French government was of the same opinion. His brief career in the navy—his stepfather, Édouard Lockroy, was minister of the marine, after all—ended when Georges was asked to leave due to misconduct. He tried his hand at writing, too, with a novel and then, in 1902, a florid and self-flattering account of his childhood with his grandfather.

Jeanne never wrote her own memoir about her childhood or her grandfather, although she did help her brother Georges when he was working on his. Instead, in so many ways, she continued to live in her memory. When he was old enough to read, Jeanne often asked her son, Charles, to read to her out loud, almost always choosing certain passages from her grandfather's oeuvre, particularly *The Art of Being a Grandfather* and *The Terrible Year*. As little Charles read out loud the indicated passages, Jeanne would slowly close her eyes and remain still, occasionally murmuring, "Continue, continue . . ." when Charles's voice began to drop off. Jeanne had never been good at school, but she had managed to memorize a few of Victor Hugo's poems by heart, and she would repeat these to her son in a state of semidetachment:

> With age all human passions pass away;
> One carries off its dagger, one its mask,
> As bands of traveling players disappear
> Over the hill, still singing at their task.

On August 14, 1903, the day before the departure of the *Français* from Saint-Malo, Jean-Baptiste and his officers enjoyed a final meal together with their families. They sat on the veranda of a seaside restaurant, ribbons on the little girls' dresses fluttering in the wind. The men stood tall, proud, anxious, their eyes already eagerly scanning the horizon over the water despite the sighs and worried glances of their wives and mothers, the uneasy coexistence of anticipation and anxiety casting an awkward pall on the muted conversation. The

following day, on August 15, 1903, as the *Français* left the port of
Le Havre, Jean-Baptiste stood on the bridge, pensively surveying
the preparations. The day was stormy, although that did not deter
the thousands of locals who lined the docks, jostling one another.
Some newspapers estimated the crowd to be more than twenty
thousand strong. The boom of cannon shots punched through the
cries and applause of the crowd, crashing through the strains of
"La Marseillaise." Jean-Baptiste thought about all the obstacles he
had overcome to get to this day, all the niggling self-doubts he had
been forced to brush aside and the uncertainty he had been forced to
ignore in order to arrive at this perfect moment. He turned to Maignan, a young sailor (nicknamed "Biscuit") standing next to him.
"What will our return be like after such a departure?" Jean-Baptiste
asked him, grinning in amazement before turning back to the waving crowd. A few minutes later, he heard a horrible grinding sound,
then a crack—the tow rope had broken loose of its cleat and struck
Maignan, killing him instantly. The faces of the members of the crew
dissolved from elation to disbelief to horror. Jean-Baptiste quickly
assumed a mask of clinical calm, although he, too, felt rattled to the
core as he stared down at the limp, mangled figure of the boy. He
had been around sailors long enough to adopt some of their super-
stitions, and this death at the very onset of their expedition did not
bode well for the enterprise. Jean-Baptiste insisted on personally taking the body to Maignan's widow, who sat there, stiff and awkward
as she rocked herself back and forth, slowly keening. "He loved you
so . . . ," she whispered to Jean-Baptiste, and though there was no
hint of reproach in her voice, her words burned. He joined the estimated five thousand people who attended the young sailor's funeral
and tried to keep calm, but for the first time he felt truly frightened,
not for himself but for those he had convinced to join him in this
risky enterprise. They set sail again on August 27, this time with no
accidents.

But it was a wrenching loss for the small crew, which was com-
prised almost entirely of volunteers (there were also two naval officers, Lieutenant André Matha and Sublieutenant Joseph-J. Rey). For
this reason it came as a great blow to the men's morale when Adrien
de Gerlache, who had been serving as a close advisor to the inexperi-

enced Jean-Baptiste, decided during the crossing that he wished to drop out of the expedition. Citing his recent engagement and upcoming nuptials, he declared his intention of disembarking in Brazil and returning to Europe. Two of the expedition's scientists decided to do the same. Jean-Baptiste sensed he was losing control of the situation and feared that, without de Gerlache's assistance, he would be unable to fulfill his planned program. Could it be that it was all over before they had even really begun?

Jean-Baptiste's worries were exaggerated, for the remaining crew members gave him their unstinting support. They wanted to believe in his vision of a grand expedition in which each of them would play a noble role. And so the ship continued on to Buenos Aires, arriving on November 16. Once docked, captain and crew learned of Nordenskjöld's rescue by an Argentine relief expedition—Nordenskjöld's ship, the *Antarctic*, had not fared so well, having been crushed in the ice in February. With no ship to carry them home, the beleaguered crew had been left under the leadership of the great Norwegian seaman Carl Larsen and endured a punishing winter on small, volcanic Paulet Island, subsisting primarily on penguin eggs, until the rescue ship finally found them. But where others might have viewed in Nordenskjöld's tale a sobering warning, Jean-Baptiste and his men saw only an inspirational lesson about tenacity and survival. There was no question of canceling the *Français*'s expedition, and so they set about making their final preparations for departure. Nordenskjöld himself was eventually invited aboard the *Français*, and he was so impressed with Jean-Baptiste's plans that he generously presented the French expedition with five Greenland huskies. As he told them stories about his own expedition, Jean-Baptiste and the crew began to have more of an idea of the tremendous risks they were undertaking. But they were also quietly thrilled at the prospect of joining such illustrious ranks. With the addition of the two replacement scientists, J. Turquet and Ernest Gourdon, their expedition team now counted twenty men, among them a scientific staff that boasted an impressive array of expertise—from astronomy to zoology and including glaciology, hydrography, meteorology, magnetics, and photography. There was even an Italian alpine guide—Pierre Dayné, who was the first professional mountaineer to go to Antarctica—and a pig named Toby.

When the *Français* left Buenos Aires on December 23, 1903, another cheering crowd had assembled to see the tense, pale Europeans nervously set out for the dangers of the south. As they sailed farther and farther south, Jean-Baptiste's excitement mounted, although alone, at night, nagging doubts and fears flooded his thoughts, confirming his belief that, mid-ocean, alone between sky and sea, one thinks more during the night. With a deliberate self-consciousness that he hoped would steady his nerves, he wrote in his journal, "It is a new page of my life that I turn slowly and gravely, and in the stillness of this night, under the shadow of the steep cliffs of Magellan Land, I cannot foresee what is to be."

The *Français* reached Tierra del Fuego at the southernmost tip of Argentina on January 26, 1904, and sailed for Antarctica the next day. Once they passed the False Cape Horn, thirty-five miles northwest of the real Cape Horn, they encountered the heavy swell of open water. Even the most experienced sailors became seasick in the rolling waves of the Drake Passage, where the swift and strong southern ocean waters are squeezed between the continental landmasses of South America and Antarctica and where storms frequently whip the ocean into a dark, heaving mass of water. On February 1, near the South Shetland Islands, still some sixty miles from the Antarctic Peninsula, the men saw their first iceberg. Each one of them had imagined this moment a hundred times, but their wildest fancies couldn't have prepared them for the real thing. It was thirty to forty meters high, an ice mountain of such exaggerated angularity and whiteness that its glacial mass seemed both sublime and sinister. Others followed, of all different shapes and sizes, like gigantic crystals from some enchanted region. "We have before us a decor too magnificent in its ominous grandeur which gives the impression that one feels with the pain caused by an exaggerated pleasure of the senses," Jean-Baptiste wrote, struggling to find the words to convey what he was witnessing, distracted by the crystalline rustling of the ice groaning under the caresses of an almost hot sun as he attempted to describe the symphony of sounds and colors. (Everything he wrote in his journal, he thought, seemed at once too breathless and too clinical, too vague and too formal.)

Those first days in the Antarctic were deceptively mild. As the *Français* advanced deeper into Antarctic waters, she was eventually joined by giant whales, whose massive forms seemed like majestic links to antediluvian times. Jean-Baptiste was struck by their gentleness, the placid satisfaction expressed in their large, deep, peaceful sighs. With each nautical mile that the *Français* slipped deeper southward, Jean-Baptiste and his crew were confronted with increasingly unknown conditions. Strange noises—the far-off crackle and breaking of ice shearing from the face of an iceberg, the sucking noise of water being pulled under—could be harmless novelties or harbingers of imminent disaster. The ship, which had seemed invincible in the cool, calm waters off the coast of France, often struggled to withstand the harshness of Antarctic conditions. She had trouble negotiating the ice floes, her beams straining under the pressure of solid and liquid. At times, she would slam into blocks of ice, causing the entire boat to shudder and each man on board to feel a rising ball of dread in the back of his throat. At these moments Jean-Baptiste and his men felt like they were walking forth without a harness.

Their first real reminder of how vulnerable they were in the midst of this icy wilderness occurred a few days later, on February 6, 1904. While the ship was off Anvers Island, off the northwest coast of the Antarctic Peninsula, pipes leading to the boiler began to give out, causing an alarming loss in engine pressure. With the propeller turning and jerking sporadically, Charcot was forced to navigate through the icebergs to seek shelter. On February 19 they found an ideal natural harbor on the southwest coast of nearby Wiencke Island, which they named Port Lockroy after Édouard Lockroy, Jeanne Hugo's stepfather and the current minister of the marine, for his help with the expedition. They also discovered their first rookery of penguins, whose presence they were alerted to by the smell—a strong gust of ammonia—which Jean-Baptiste drily described in his notebook as "very sui generis." For the next few hours, the glaciers echoed with the laughter of Jean-Baptiste's men and the indignant squawks of penguins.

By the end of February, it was late in the season. Temperatures began plummeting as conditions worsened, with the wind howling from the northeast, and the enormous sea unfurling in cruel, cold waves that smashed against the sides of the ship. The intense fog seemed to gather into a solid mass that threatened to swallow them whole. Even the snow felt like a weapon, becoming hard little jagged crystals, fine needles that pierced their skin and their eyes, inflicting considerable pain. Everything was icy to the touch—it was a cold unlike anything that Jean-Baptiste or his men had ever experienced. On March 3 they arrived at Port Charcot, their chosen winter station on Wandel Island. At 65°5'S they had made it as far south as de Gerlache and one degree farther south than Nordenskjöld had wintered on the other side of the Antarctic Peninsula, and it was here that they decided to wait out the winter. The island was formed by two great massive rock faces whose summits soared overhead. It was covered entirely with a thick layer of glacier snow and ice, with only the occasional boulder of rock, rounded and dark or sometimes stained with yellow or orange lichen. They moved their base of operations off the ship, building several structures on the island to accommodate the crew and scientific instruments, jauntily raising a French flag upon each of them. A track, which they christened avenue Victor Hugo, had been cut from the ship to the south side of the island, so that the sledges were able to reach the various structures. By early April scientific studies were well under way: Lieutenant Matha and Rallier du Baty, a naval apprentice, were busy with astronomical and topographical observations, while Turquet set about collecting zoological samples. Gourdon, the geologist, was classifying minerals and rocks, and Pléneau worked on the engine and on creating a photographic record of the expedition. The conditions were less than ideal and they had to be creative in carrying out their scientific experiments: Jean-Baptiste installed different bacteriological devices, constructing a hot filter out of an empty box of tinned food and a funnel, while two cases of biscuits, one placed in the other and covered by a lid, were transformed into a sterilizer heated by small gas lamps that he had designed.

To sustain them in their work, they were fortunate in having brought with them an excellent cook from Buenos Aires, Rozo, who had joined the ship at the last moment. Very little was known about him—not his real name or age. He was impervious to the cold, walking around with his bare feet thrust into dilapidated slippers on even the coldest of days. He seemed to have been everywhere, read everything, and seen everything, so much so that Jean-Baptiste liked to joke that none of them would have been surprised if one day Rozo announced that he happened to know of a very good way to the pole. Throughout the winter Rozo baked fresh bread every other day and even made cakes and croissants on Sundays. Before starting the expedition, Charcot had gone to great lengths to ensure that his men would be provided with good food. There was wine at each meal (a double portion on Sundays) and all the tea and milk they desired. They also ate penguin (declared to be excellent) and seal, from which they made a blood sausage and ate the liver, which became the special meals for festival days. A typical day's menu would start with coffee, bread and butter, maybe even some chocolate on Sundays, and continue with a lunch of soup, seal, peas, and dessert. Tea was served at four with more bread and butter, and dinner would once again start with a soup before moving on to some sort of meat (beef or penguin), green beans, and perhaps prunes or fruit. There was a special meal for every holiday or birthday. "I can say without flattering myself," Jean-Baptiste wrote, "that there is not another polar expedition where the provisions were chosen with so much care; they are varied, of good quality, and abundant."

Although Jean-Baptiste loved working beside his men and reveled in the camaraderie of mealtime, he also enjoyed his solitude and looked forward to retiring to his cabin, which was so small that he could barely turn around in it, but in which he could relax and reflect upon the day's events. Sometimes he read the old authors that, as a young man, he had found tedious and whose works he had quickly skimmed to avoid getting a bad grade or a punishment: Homer, Sophocles, Aeschylus, Euripides, Montaigne, Dante, Cervantes, Swift, Hugo, Saint-Simon, Michelet, Dumas père, Rabelais, and Shakespeare. Now all the lessons from these works, which to his schoolboy self had seemed either hopelessly quaint or quixotic, came alive for him. Sometimes he simply stared at photos of his loved ones—his wife, his sisters, his father and mother, especially his father, who was never far from Jean-Baptiste's mind and from whom he was still seeking approbation.

The Antarctic winter continued. In early May they inaugurated school on board, which commenced each night after dinner and continued for an hour and a half. Paul Pléneau, for example, had one student who could neither read nor write; Jean-Baptiste had one who could read but not write; Gourdon had three students whom he was helping with spelling, arithmetic, history, and geography. On other nights Jean-Baptiste would give classes in English to members of the crew. The men also took turns reading one another the stories of Jules Verne and Dumas père. There was nothing Jean-Baptiste liked better than to hear the laughter of men, amusing themselves frankly, teasing one another without meanness. Schoolwork was usually followed by games or cards, with the men generally going to bed by midnight, except for Jean-Baptiste, who usually stayed up until two a.m. poring over maps and charts or carefully recording the day's activities.

Despite their best efforts, none of these diversions could block out the reality of the worsening conditions among the crew of the *Français*. Pléneau used his camera to capture their transformation— once dapper, tanned gentlemen-sailors, they had gradually degraded into pale, hairy, rough explorers with sunken, almost haunted eyes. And the changes were not merely superficial: one night in April, an hour after going to bed, Jean-Baptiste's right finger swelled up, becoming cold and white like ivory and causing him to lose sensation. It happened the next morning at breakfast as well. He didn't want to tell the others—it could only hurt morale if the captain was seen to be succumbing to the stresses of their polar environment—and his greatest fear was that it could develop into something more debilitating. About a month later, Jean-Baptiste woke up to discover that he had edema in his eyelid. "What is going to happen to me? Will I die suddenly, gradually weaken, or become impotent?" he asked his journal with frustration. He'd rather die than be infirm, withering away like an old man.

He was not the only one to worry about his mortality. One of the men, Le Bosco, approached him to say that if he died he would like to be buried on top of the summit, which they had named "Jeanne," because he felt that he would do very well there. Jean-Baptiste tried to make light of the request, thanking him for choosing that spot, since it would ensure that any grief felt by his comrades would be quickly eclipsed by their annoyance at having to haul his body up such a punishing ascent. But then Jean-Baptiste's friend and second-in-command, Matha, fell ill with myocarditis and no amount of joking could lessen Jean-Baptiste's fear. Matha had been one of the first members of the team, brazenly volunteering his services without knowing anything about Jean-Baptiste or much about the expedition itself, and he had quickly become one of Jean-Baptiste's favorites. When he heard the news of Matha's condition, he rushed into his friend's cabin and stayed with him, watching him sleeping peacefully in spite of the ragged breathing. This was the first time that Jean-Baptiste really had to face the prospect of losing one of his men, and the weight of this horrible responsibility was suffocating. Looking distractedly around Matha's little cabin, Jean-Baptiste's eyes fell on the sole decoration: a small photograph of Matha's mother. Jean-Baptiste didn't think he could live with himself if he had to bring back the news to her that her son had died so far from home. Matha eventually recovered and death was, for a time, averted.

By the middle of December, southerly winds had cleared much of the ice from their wintering bay. The men worked diligently to create a channel through the remaining ice so that they could continue their exploration. The excitement at the approaching departure was marred only by the death of the pig Toby, the ship's unofficial mascot. He had been given to them by the men of the *Uruguay*, and he had gone with his previous owners on the search for Nordenskjöld. Charcot had already had to perform surgery on Toby once before when, trying to steal some fish from a basket, he had swallowed half a dozen fishhooks. The crew of the *Français* devotedly fed him spoonfuls of condensed milk for hours on end, but still Toby could not be saved. The men felt the loss keenly, but were cheered up considerably when finally, at Christmas, the ship was freed. The men celebrated their success and the holiday by exchanging presents and eating a special meal. Jean-Baptiste decided to take the gramophone ashore to play popular music for the penguin colony, with the jangly sounds of violins providing an unexpected accompaniment to the animals' usual solitary squawking. The next day, the *Français* began sailing south again. Although the engine still wasn't working properly, it was enough to drive the ship.

Disaster struck at eight a.m. on January 15, 1905, when the ship hit a submerged rock at full speed. Jean-Baptiste and Matha were chatting on the bridge when they felt a horrible shock that nearly knocked them off their feet. The bow reared up almost vertically with a sinister cracking, and the masts swayed as if they would fall in. Jean-Baptiste scrambled to the telegraph to signal to the machine room

"Full astern!" but before this could happen the ship fell back by its own weight onto an even keel with a dull groan. Men who had been sleeping below tumbled up to the deck, half-dressed. Jean-Baptiste felt all eyes turn toward him. "Breathe," he told himself as he straightened his hat and buttoned up his coat. Then water began pouring in, and they all sprung to action. Jean-Baptiste gave the order for Matha to try to steer the ship through the ice closer to hospitable land, knowing that if they started sinking in open water they would barely have one chance in a thousand to make it to the islets off Wandel Island. Meanwhile, two crewmen below deck prepared clothing and provisions in case they would have to abandon ship. Then came word from below that the air pumps were finally working, but they had to be operated by hand. Moreover, the only way to reach the pumps was to break through the watertight compartments sealing them from the rest of the ship. Jean-Baptiste came down to inspect to find Libois, the shipwright and stoker, up to his waist in icy water. In the midst of the chaos, one thought remained in the background of all the men's minds: they understood that any hope of continuing their discoveries had vanished. When they were out of immediate danger, Jean-Baptiste went to his cabin to catch his breath. "To risk a second winter is now impossible," he admitted. Alone, he cried like a child. The realization of how many lives lay in his hands and yet how much he still wanted to accomplish overwhelmed him. For the remainder of the expedition, the *Français* was only kept afloat by hand-pumping for forty-five minutes in every hour. The men's hands froze and many of them began to cough up blood.

They headed north as quickly as possible, reaching Port Lockroy on Wiencke Island by January 30, where they remained for ten days to make what repairs they could before heading back across the brutal Drake Passage. They arrived in Puerto Madryn, Argentina, on March 5. The crew was exhausted and stood on the deck, gazing in bewilderment at the houses, the railway, the men in dapper clothing—at all the trappings of civilization that had suddenly been thrust back into their view. Then a feeling of anxiety swept over the crew—they had received no news from Europe in many months and were afraid of what they might hear. Pléneau was sent to a neighboring town that had a telegraph to get news and returned three days later. He had one telegram in hand but would not let Jean-Baptiste read it in front of the others. Gently leading the captain to the mess room, Pléneau handed him the telegram. It informed Jean-Baptiste that during his lengthy absence his wife, Jeanne, had decided to separate from him. Jean-Baptiste stared down at the piece of paper, unable to speak. He then began to cry. He cried for the youthful fantasy of everlasting love that was no more. At the end of his great journey, perhaps the most awesome feat he had ever accomplished, he felt alone and abandoned. He heard more bad news in the days that followed. He learned that his brother-in-law, Pierre Waldeck-Rousseau, was dead and that his sister, Jeanne, had gotten a divorce from her husband, Alfred Edwards, the owner of *Le Matin*. But these were minor tragedies compared to the other news he learned. A few days earlier, an officer from the Argentine navy had related to Jean-Baptiste with great enthusiasm details of the Russo-Japanese War and of battles in which thirty thousand to forty thousand men had fallen. It was all too overwhelming. "I felt a sensation of anguish in hearing this talk of thousands of dead," he wrote. "A few minutes before, in arriving at the port, I had been so happy, so proud, to see on the bridge of the ship, although exhausted, pale, even sick, but nonetheless living, the nineteen men who had confided their existence to me."

On March 15 the expedition reached Buenos Aires to a warm welcome—all the ships in the port were "dressed" in their honor. The *Français* was placed in dry dock, where it was discovered that twenty-two feet of its false keel had been torn away—they had only narrowly avoided catastrophe. The following days passed in a blur of official meetings and receptions. Jean-Baptiste was back in a suit with a pocket handkerchief. He walked about stiffly in his dress shoes, half expecting to hear the crunch of snow underfoot, to feel the ground swaying beneath him. The Argentine government bought the ship from Charcot for use as a supply vessel to its new meteorological stations, and so Jean-Baptiste and his party returned to France on the liner *Algérie* accompanied by seventy-five boxes of specimens, equipment, and journals. In total, over six hundred miles of coastline had been charted.

As his divorce proceeded at home, Jean-Baptiste moved into his sister's apartment on avenue de l'Alma. There he began to go through the results of the expedition and to publicize his voyage through articles, conferences, and speaking engagements. Overnight he had become something of a celebrity, *the* French specialist on all things polar and a world-renowned expert in the field of Antarctic exploration. His grace and humility, his refusal to become embroiled in international rivalries, led the great Antarctic explorer Sir Robert Scott to dub him "the Polar Gentleman." But the more Jean-Baptiste spoke about his voyage, the further he found himself succumbing to an unexpected nostalgia and to what he could only describe as "this strange attraction to these polar regions, so powerful, so tenacious, that after returning home, one forgets the moral and physical fatigue and can only dream of returning to them." He felt distant from those around him. He missed his fellow sailors, who had also seen another side of the earth, the apparition of new worlds, the surge of waters so dark and cold that they seemed to extend into another universe. He had lived in a world of extremes—where breaking ice could announce a gorgeous spectacle or be a sign of approaching peril. Now, in a world of grays, of moderation, everything felt subdued.

Bit by bit, he stopped seeing great distances between himself and others, and he once again began to enjoy the feel of solid ground underfoot. This readjustment was due, in part, to time, but also to a new woman in his life: Marguerite (Meg) Cléry. He had known her years earlier when she was just any other little girl—all great, unblinking eyes and taffeta bows and impish curiosity about everyone and everything she encountered. Then he met her again, at a party at her father's house, when she was nineteen. The little girl had grown up. He recalled years later that they had played with a train set—the memory always made him smile, for how many proper young women would get down on the floor and play with a train set during a party? Certainly not most of the women he knew. Not his former wife, Jeanne. There was a frankness and forthrightness about Meg that made Jean-Baptiste feel at home. She was accomplished in her own right as well—she played the harp and painted lovely landscapes and had even won some awards for them. Their relationship deepened during long walks in the park while he told her about his first encounter with an indignant penguin, the sight of the sun rising over a bay of icebergs, and the chilling sensation of being utterly alone at the end of the world in a place not meant for human beings. She fell in love with Jean-Baptiste the man, not the boy struggling to get out from under his father's shadow. And he loved her for that. Their romance was uncomplicated and direct, and on January 24, 1907, they were married at the Church of the Trinity, in front of various dignitaries. The one cloud on the horizon was a promise she had been forced to make to him: never to oppose one of Jean-Baptiste's expeditions. But of course, she never would have dreamed of doing such a thing—she understood him too well. Even their honeymoon in England and Norway was a working vacation—Jean-Baptiste wanted to study different types of ships in preparation for his next expedition. When they returned, Meg formally adopted Jean-Baptiste's daughter, Marion. Soon she was pregnant with their own child.

Even as Jean-Baptiste was busy building a new life for himself, he had already begun thinking about returning to Antarctica. In the solitude of Antarctica, he had felt so viscerally bound to his native country that he felt as if his most intimate thoughts must somehow be sensed by loved ones in France, despite the distance. Similarly, now that he was back in France, he found he could not stop hearing the creaking of the masts and the far-off thunder of falling icebergs. His resolve only grew in light of the acclaim he received from the scientific community over the results of his experiments and discoveries in Antarctica. He submitted a plan to the Academy of Sciences, which formed a special committee and quickly approved his new program. Now research facilities and organizations were falling over themselves to assist the heroic Dr. Charcot, and he ended up receiving money from the French government as well as from the Geographical Society of Paris, the Paris Municipal Council, and the Chambers of Commerce of several large French cities. The prince of Monaco even offered the expedition a complete oceanographical outfit.

Once again Jean-Baptiste turned to Père Gautier, the masterful shipwright from Saint-Malo who had been so successful in building the *Français*. Construction of the *Pourquoi-Pas?* began in September 1907 and took less than a year. She benefited greatly from Jean-Baptiste's experience in Antarctic waters. Her rigging was that of a three-masted barque and her masts, sturdy but short, had been selected at great expense from among the finest specimens in the Brest arsenal. Everything was made about three times as strong as on an ordinary ship of the same tonnage. All who saw her agreed that she was one of the finest ships they had ever seen.

The second French Antarctic expedition left Le Havre on a clear, bright day, August 15, 1908. Twenty thousand people attended the ship's departure. In order to ascend the gangplank, Jean-Baptiste had to wade through a sea of eager well-wishers who called out his name or simply tried to touch his sleeve with their outstretched hands. There were men in bowler hats and smart ties, dockworkers with unkempt mustaches and calloused hands, women in crisply starched shirts and colorful skirts—and they had all come to see the famous polar explorer, to admire his crew and his ship, and to be a part of something that was bigger than anything they would ever experience for themselves. For Jean-Baptiste it felt like something of a homecoming—eight out of the twenty-two crew members had served aboard the *Français*, including Chollet, who had been his navigator for years, and Gégen, a sailor who had been on four expeditions with him. Jabet and Libois had been on three. Two hundred and fifty men had applied for the few available positions on the expedition, and Jean-Baptiste was pleased with the energy and devotion of those he had picked. He derived even greater satisfaction from the knowledge that his wife, Meg, would accompany them across the Atlantic. She was by his side when they arrived at Rio de Janeiro on October 12 and did not leave until they reached Punta Arenas at the southernmost tip of Chile. Here she said goodbye to her husband and began the long, lonely journey back to France. It was a difficult moment for Jean-Baptiste, who had been delighted to have finally found a woman, a partner, who could embrace his life's work. "My own thought was to labour for my country and for the honour of a name made illustrious by my father and rendered still more dear to me by her who, in adopting it as her own, was willing to aid me in sharing its responsibility."

The *Pourquoi-Pas?* left Punta Arenas at nine a.m. on December 16, in the midst of fine, calm weather. But once again they encountered the rough and stormy waves of the Drake Passage, with most of the crew suffering from horrible, lurching seasickness. For six days they battled the waves and their stomachs until at last they arrived at Smith Island in the South Shetlands. Continuing southeast, they reached Deception Island on December 22, where they came upon a thriving colony of Norwegian and Chilean whaling ships—thanks to maps drawn on his first expedition, the whalers had been able to extend their operations farther south along the Antarctic Peninsula. Although Jean-Baptiste and his men had known that there was a likelihood that they might run into other vessels, particularly farther north, the sight of this fleet was almost uncanny. This sensation only deepened when they entered the island's basin.

Suddenly they found themselves in the midst of a veritable flotilla of boats, as if they were in some busy European port and not at one of the farthest outposts in the world. But here the industry and activity took on a rather more macabre aspect. "Pieces of whale float about on all sides, and bodies in the process of being cut up or waiting their turn lie alongside the various boats," Jean-Baptiste wrote in his journal. "The smell is unbearable." The *Pourquoi-Pas?* made its way with difficulty through the carcasses of the whales, some of which exploded with gases, sounding like the report of a cannon. The shore of the bay was tinged red with blood and littered with skeletons and remains of the whalers' catch. For the next few days, the *Pourquoi-Pas?* remained at this dark, volcanic island, where vents violently ejected streams of hot steam, causing the edges of the basin to sizzle and gurgle, while the stench of death hovered over everything. Their grim surroundings, however, stood in marked contrast to the gracious, if not exuberant, hospitality of their hosts. The whalers were eager to show their new tricks and techniques to the man whose careful mapping had allowed them to expand their hunting grounds. And although Jean-Baptiste worried that these animals had been hunted "without mercy" and generally abhorred the needless killing of animals, he initially felt some pride in what small role the *Français* expedition had played in reviving the whaling industry in the Antarctic and subantarctic region. He was fascinated by what the whalers could accomplish with their new technology. They no longer had to set out in a boat to "stick" their prey with a harpoon fastened to a long rope, towing the boat as the animal desperately fled. Now they had a cannon, which discharged a harpoon attached to a strong grapnel rope. When the animal was hit, the two shanks of the harpoon opened and exploded a small shell. The body was hauled back by means of a steam windlass, fastened alongside, inflated to prevent it from sinking, and towed to the melting house. The station did not actually process whale blubber—that was done on the ships—but instead took the carcasses and boiled them down to extract additional whale oil, and stored the results in iron tanks. There was a cold, brutal efficiency to the operation, something about the uncanny enormity of those metal cylinders grinding these once living giants into so much unrecognizable, liquefied matter, that seemed tragically out of place in this basin of snowy peaks and placid water. Was this what modern man had brought to Antarctica?

But there was scant time for such moral musings, and Jean-Baptiste's scientific crew quickly got to work: Jules-Alfred-Pierre Rouch made meteorological observations, while René-Émile Godfroy mapped the contours of their anchorage. Gourdon collected geological specimens, while Senouque was busy working on magnetism studies. They left soon after, on Christmas Day 1908, reaching Booth Island on December 29 and anchoring in the bay where the *Français* had wintered in 1904. Jean-Baptiste surveyed the bay, marveling at how, for nine months, they had "lived, worked, hoped, sometimes almost despaired, and often sorrowed" at this very spot. This time he was back under much better conditions, with a stronger ship, more precise and advanced equipment, and the invaluable experience from his previous trip. His eyes were struck by the same familiar objects and the same buildings; his ears caught the same sounds from the rookeries of penguins and cormorants, which gave off the same powerful odor. "I could believe that I never left the spot." He felt as if he had come home.

On New Year's Day they celebrated by eating some fresh grapes, which had been presented to them in Punta Arenas. Jean-Baptiste's thoughts flew to Meg, who not merely allowed him to do his duty, but further had encouraged and helped him to do it. He remembered once trying to soothe her, when she was speaking sadly of anniversaries that they would spend apart, by telling her that all days are alike. He realized now how far from the truth that was. "Too many memories," he concluded, "of family gatherings, some joyful, others saddened by the vanishing of a loved one, are stirred up by these dates for them to be otherwise than like steps on life's great stair, whereon the mind halts to look back on the way already come, fearing with the dread of the unknown, to take the next step."

In early January Jean-Baptiste, the geologist Gourdon, and Lieutenant Godfroy set out in the ship's launch to cross the narrow strait to Cape Tuxen on the Antarctic mainland. They studied the coastline and the nearby Bertholet Islands for a possible route to the south. Once their observations were completed, the men sat down to a meal before starting their return to the ship. By the time they started to head back, it was ten p.m. and snow had begun to fall. The channel was no longer open; the narrow pathways they had made were now blocked by freezing floes. Three days and three nights went by before they heard a siren and saw the *Pourquoi-Pas?* coming to their rescue. The relief among staff and crew when the three men were finally back on board was palpable—beneath the icy monotony of winter lurked an unshakable sense of vulnerability and fear. After a hearty meal, the men felt that the ordeal was behind them and declared themselves eager to face the next challenge.

But less than twenty-four hours later, history repeated itself: the *Pourquoi-Pas?*, like the *Français* before her, ran aground. One moment they were slipping smoothly through quiet coastal waters; the next they felt a shock so forceful it overturned glasses and made the doors of the wardroom bang violently. The gaiety and relief of the previous evening vanished in an instant. The men stared in horror and dread as pieces of the hull were torn away and floated to the surface. The stern deck was underwater and the bow remained pinned down.

Jean-Baptiste and his men worked all day long to lighten the bow and shift the weight to the stern. He struggled to stave off the mounting feeling of despair. For the moment there was no danger to the crew—they were close to land with no icebergs in sight—but if the damage was bad enough, the expedition would be at an end after barely just beginning. All his efforts would be fruitless, and the page that he had dreamed of adding to the history of French explorations would never see the light. At midnight they put the engine full speed astern. "The *Pourquoi Pas?* vibrates as though she wished to shatter herself; but nothing happens," Jean-Baptiste explained. At last they swung a little to starboard, then back astern, only to be greeted by violent shocks and an ominous cracking sound. They were repeating the maneuver when suddenly, with an interminable grinding noise, the ship finally tore free. Surprisingly, the damage did not appear to be too extensive.

After the accident, the icebergs seemed more numerous, more threatening. When the engine could not get them out of the way fast enough, the crew had to get ready with poles and thick planks in an attempt to stave off the enormous mass or at least to break the shock of impact. And yet blocks of ice were constantly ramming against the side of the boat, making it sometimes impossible for Jean-Baptiste to continue writing at his desk. The sight of an iceberg breaking and capsizing was so impressive that Jean-Baptiste struggled to find the words to describe it: "Enormous spurs of glaucous hue jump out of the water, and even rocks are uplifted as if by a submarine mine; the sea boils fiercely and in a few seconds its surface far and wide is covered by debris of all sizes . . ."

And still the expedition continued. In January 1909, the *Pourquoi-Pas?* crossed the Antarctic Circle and sailed south while the men charted the coastline, islands, and other geographic features, naming new lands and landmarks as they went: Marguerite Bay, Jenny Island, Fallières Land, and so on. One notable discovery they made was that Adelaide Island, which had previously been thought to be only eight miles long, was in fact over seventy. They did their best to explore the area as systematically as they could, although dense ice pack prevented them from making the sorts of inroads they had hoped. As the days progressed, the coal supply dwindled. Jean-Baptiste confessed to "a fit of the blues" because they had not yet found good winter quarters. At the end of January, Jean-Baptiste realized that worsening conditions would force them back north to spend the winter in the harbor of Port Circumcision on Petermann Island. Jean-Baptiste was hugely disappointed— "It was a great, almost a desperate, blow to me to have to leave this region where, with more luck, we might have accomplished such interesting work," he mournfully wrote in his journal. He wanted them to push farther south, to push farther into unknown territory. But the men were tired, the ship was unsteady, and the island before them possessed a well-populated penguin rookery, which would provide material for study and food. They quickly set about enclosing the harbor with a system of chains to direct encroaching icebergs away from the ship and built four huts on the island as scientific observatories, each linked by wires to the ship's generator for electricity. It took them nearly a month, working in the midst of strong gales from the northeast and snow, to have the whole winter quarters set up.

They marked the time the only way they knew how. They had access to more than fifteen hundred books in the ship's extensive library and to back issues of *Le Matin*, issued daily. Jean-Baptiste and his officers offered courses in grammar, geography, English, and navigation, while the ship's assistant doctor and zoologist gave classes on first aid. Lieutenant Rouche attempted to write a romantic novel, *The Typist's Lover*—he read each chapter out loud as soon as he had finished it. Sometimes they organized games and skits, making costumes out of whatever odds and ends they could find. They could also listen to the gramophone, and some of the men even founded a musical society that gave concerts on Sundays.

Even as winter gave way to spring, they continued to suffer from the punishing Antarctic conditions. Jean-Baptiste became ill from polar anemia. His legs were badly swollen, and his breathing became increasingly difficult. Eventually the weather became too extreme for excursions. The crew began to suffer from scurvy and Jean-Baptiste authorized a seal hunt, although he forbade the killing of any females. One day the men fetched him to look at a newly born seal. "Nothing could be more moving in the midst of these sinister, seemingly lifeless, surroundings than this little creature, so uncannily human, dainty in appearance and proportion beside its mother's clumsy bulk . . ." The sight of that small, helpless creature, so trusting, made him think about home and about the family he had left behind. He turned away so that the other men would not see the tears welling up in his eyes. He had not felt these tugs of regret on his first trip to Antarctica, and he did not quite know what to do with them now.

When they returned to Deception Island in late November to stock up on coal, Jean-Baptiste and his men heard about the astounding latest developments in polar exploration, specifically Ernest Shackleton's making it to within ninety-seven miles of the South Pole (surpassing the previous "farthest south" point) and the American Robert E. Peary's claim to have reached the North Pole. They also learned that while they had been gone, one of their compatriots, the Frenchman Louis Blériot, had made the first powered flight across the English Channel. Charcot's men were taken aback at the thought of other expeditions proceeding, so lost had they been in their own world. One evening, Charcot was invited to dine with M. Andresen, manager of the Magellan Whaling Company, and his wife. "For the occasion," he noted in his journal, "I got into civilized garb, with a linen shirt, a starched collar, cuffs, tie-pin, and all the rest. I must confess, moreover, that I found myself immediately at my ease and that I mechanically put into my pockets the useless objects I had given up for so many months."

With the *Pourquoi-Pas?* now leaking steadily, a Norwegian diver was sent down to inspect the damaged hull. He discovered that a large section of the keel had been torn away. Although the Norwegians were adamant that the Frenchmen should sail for home right away, Jean-Baptiste would not hear of it. To his mind, nothing less than the honor and glory of his nation—as well as his own personal reputation—was at stake. Keeping the grim diagnosis from his men, Jean-Baptiste directed the *Pourquoi Pas?* south again in early January. On January 11, 1910, they were sailing near Alexander I Land (Alexander Island) at 70° S, 76° W when they saw something that caused Jean-Baptiste to race up to the crow's nest and eagerly scan the horizon through his binoculars. He was looking at unknown land, which Jean-Baptiste insisted on naming Charcot Land, after his father. Although they attempted to approach the landmass, the ice was too thick and they could not risk further damage to the ship. With weather conditions worsening and their fears for their damaged vessel mounting, they turned the ship north and headed toward South America on January 22.

As they began their return, Jean-Baptiste's head filled with nagging worries. "I left my home and happiness of my own free will to do what I considered my duty," he wrote. "What shall I find on my return?" Would it all have been worth it? All the sorrow his absence had caused for his family? All the danger he had required his crew to face? Then, as if in answer to his question, he caught sight of the ship's motto on the poop deck—"Honor and country"—and looked up to see the ship's ensign on the flapping flag: Why not? The ship was back in European waters by early June and finally reached Rouen on June 5.

As a result of the crew's efforts, 1,250 miles of new coastline had been charted, and enough scientific data—including extensive observations of magnetism, atmospheric electricity, bacteriology, and polar flora—had been collected to fill twenty-eight volumes. Thousands of photographs had been taken. The maps Jean-Baptiste and his men drew were so precise that they would be used for the next twenty-five years by sealers and whalers.

But Jean-Baptiste himself was disappointed by the expedition. The telegram he sent to the Academy of Sciences said it all: "We dreamed of more. We did the best possible." And to Prince Albert I of Monaco he explained, "Our results will appear negligible next to the impressive exploits of Shackleton, and yet I am aware that we accomplished a great deal even if I had dreamed of doing something more sensational for my country." Even if Jean-Baptiste privately doubted the importance of his achievements, he had successfully created a name for himself, independent from his father's. If his father's noble science had come to be seen as an emblem of the last century, Jean-Baptiste's scientific endeavors seemed to represent the potential of the twentieth century, when human determination coupled with technological innovation could conquer the final mysteries of the planet. He had gotten the attention of the world. He was the esteemed Jean-Baptiste Charcot—captain, leader, teacher, mentor—to a group of men whose very survival depended upon him. And, most important, he had entered into an international fraternity of explorers. Such multinational camaraderie was rare at a time when international hostilities seemed on the brink of boiling over. "Above the polar circle, there are no longer Frenchmen, nor British, nor Danes; there are only polar explorers, there are only men," Charcot observed with obvious satisfaction. Of course, not everyone was eager to do away with such distinctions.

NINE

The Polemicist

The danger of being a halfhearted individual in these times in
which we live . . . is that one risks quickly becoming spineless.
There is a weakness, I would go so far as to say a cowardice, in
moderation, and this comes from these tragic hours.

—Léon Daudet, in *Le Gaulois* (1901)

On Thursday, December 8, 1904, while Jean-Baptiste Charcot was
thousands of miles away in a foreign world of water and ice, Léon
Daudet was enjoying a leisurely Thursday afternoon. After lunch
with his wife, Marthe, he headed back to his study for a few hours
of work. At around four p.m., he left his house and began making
his way on foot to the editorial offices of the newspaper *Le Gaulois*.
As he was nearing his destination, Léon ran into a colleague, Gaston Jollivet, who quickly grabbed him by the shoulder and asked,
"You know the news?"

"What news?" Léon asked.

"Syveton is dead. They're saying he was murdered."

Léon could scarcely believe his ears. The nationalist deputy and
founder of the anti-Dreyfusard group Ligue de la Patrie Française,
Gabriel Syveton had only recently gone after the war minister, General Louis André, who, in an attempt to purge the army of officers dis-
loyal to the Republic, had begun gathering information on officers'

religious beliefs and attendance at church and church schools. One
of the officers on André's staff, a Captain Mollin, had enlisted the aid
of the Masonic Grand Orient, which kept extensive records on just
such information in their offices. Long accused of being a bastion
of anti-Christian and occult activity, the Masons had, along with the
Jews, become one of the favorite targets of the right-wing Action
Française. Earlier in 1904, Syveton had bought a large collection of
these Masonic files from an employee of the Grand Orient, providing the nationalists with ample ammunition to create a full-scale political scandal and causing the government to be excoriated first by
the press and then in the Chamber of Deputies itself. But Syveton
still feared a government cover-up, and so during a particularly
heated session of the Chamber on November 4, he publicly slapped
the sixty-six-year-old war minister, hoping to prevent the issue from
being closed by a vote. The stunt backfired horribly: the public was
outraged and Syveton was ordered to appear in court to explain his
actions in a trial. For his part, Léon was delighted by the bravado of
his friend, declaring in an article in *La Libre Parole* that the slap had
taken on a symbolic valor and represented nothing less than "the indignant national frankness that castigates the Jewish and Masonic
treachery." His fellow right-wing journalists and activists, however,
were cooler in their appraisal and withheld their support until they
could better determine how damaged Syveton's political career
truly was. The deputy's trial had been set to begin on December 9,
the day after his sudden death.

Léon pulled away from Jollivet and hailed the next taxi that
passed, directing it to the Syveton residence, 20 bis, avenue de
Neuilly. Even as his emotions whirled in a ferocious torrent, Léon's
mind was already thinking through the implications of this stunning
news. This capacity to think on his feet when it was most necessary
had always held him in good stead. Léon may have looked like a character from a Daumier cartoon—the very picture of merry ineptitude
manifested in his cherubic cheeks and Buddha belly—but he was as
agile and ruthless as a cobra. In the taxi on the way to his friend's
home on that brisk November afternoon, Léon was already coming
up with all kinds of questions and theories. Syveton had been warned
that getting involved in the sort of politics he espoused could anger
important people. But would his enemies really have killed for this?

When Léon finally arrived at the Syveton residence, he came upon a ghastly and surreal scene. Syveton's body was still sprawled out on the floor in the study, near the fireplace, covered in a copy of the newspaper *L'Intransigeant*. Léon cast his eyes about, looking for signs of hidden disturbance aside from the corpse. He took in the scrapes on Syveton's forehead and the wild, horrified expression on his now lifeless face. He also noticed that his wife, Mme Syveton, was dry-eyed and seemed distant and strangely unmoved, while Syveton's stepdaughter, Marguerite, was not even present. The police who were at the scene pointed out how Syveton's head was posed near the open gas taps—the easier for him to breathe in the gas, they guessed. But if this really was the scene of a suicide, Léon wondered, why had the study door not been locked from the inside . . . and why was there a freshly filled pipe and a loaded revolver next to the body? No, this was a police crime, he thought to himself, and the thought made him more proud than nervous, as if Syveton's murder were a confirmation of the importance of the cause they had both championed, of the stakes involved in the political game they were playing.

The next day, Léon attended the autopsy of Syveton's body at the morgue. The doctor concluded that he had died by carbon monoxide poisoning—just like Émile Zola, who had died two years earlier, amid whispers that he had been done in by anti-Dreyfusards—and gave permission for the body to be buried. The funeral services took place at Saint-Pierre de Neuilly, then at Montparnasse Cemetery, as a large, rowdy crowd looked on. Léon de Montesquiou, grandson of the governess of the king of Rome and now an ardent critic of the Republic, cried out at one point, "Down with the murderers!" and was promptly arrested. Thirty-seven-year-old Léon Daudet and the thirty-six-year-old journalist Charles Maurras both served as pallbearers. In the days immediately following the funeral, Syveton's right-wing compatriots held their fallen comrade up as a hero, a victim of republican persecution. But Syveton's posthumous status as tragic martyr quickly faded when tongues began to wag about some of the more unsavory details of his life. Soon the papers were printing the rumors that he had raped his stepdaughter, Marguerite, who had confided as much to her husband and mother. Mme Syveton had then confronted Syveton, who initially denied everything and then finally broke down and confessed his misdeeds.

It was said that Mme Syveton then decided to separate from her husband, who, realizing that the gossip would destroy his chances before the courts, decided to kill himself. It was later alleged that Syveton had been embezzling monies from the Ligue de la Patrie Française. Despite these upsetting revelations, Léon never swayed from his developing conviction that Syveton had been the victim of a "Masonic crime," as he put it in the title of another article for *La Libre Parole*. Power-thirsty republicans and anti-French Jews were also part of the conspiracy, he explained to his readers: "It was absolutely necessary that Syveton's mouth remained closed, and by any means. Syveton is dead, and this death, which overwhelms us, saved Israel from a great worry."

The rapidly expanding Syveton scandal was the final, fatal blow for the Ligue. But it marked the beginning of a new stage in Léon Daudet's life. At Syveton's funeral he met the man who would be his closest friend and colleague for the rest of his life—Charles Maurras. For two hours Léon and the royalist talked and took stock of each other, discussing a range of topics, from their literary preferences to their disappointment in the French political system. Léon found something irresistible in this slight, stern man. A few weeks later, at a nationalist meeting, Léon took the stage and publicly declared his adherence to Maurras's political ideas and the royalist cause.

Léon and Charles Maurras had known of each other for a few years, having frequented similar social and cultural circles. But the two men were quite different. While Léon had been born into a privileged family in the heart of Paris, Charles Maurras was born to a modest family in a small town in the south between Arles and Marseilles. He had arrived in Paris only in 1885, at the age of seventeen. Charles Maurras had come to Paris to make a name for himself and to take advantage of the opportunities presented by the capital's famed literary circles. He sought out other Provençals and soon became a familiar in the circle of Provençal poets, artists, writers, and politicians. As he made his way in the crowded literary world, he learned more about the city and its inhabitants.

The origins of Maurras's political nationalism and royalism lay in these early days in Paris. He was repulsed by the crass materialism and decadence he witnessed, by the streets teeming with swift-moving men and gaudily dressed women. He was stunned by what he saw as the overwhelming influence of foreigners, whose presence made him wonder out loud, "Were Frenchmen still at home in France?" Barbarism, he concluded, was everywhere, and he was determined to impose a new kind of order in his life. But the current vogue for foreign writers, the chaos of city life, the jangling sounds of street music and public transportation were just the superficial signs of a deeper economic, political, and even spiritual malaise. The connection between cultural and political decadence was obvious to Maurras, but not necessarily to others. He drifted away from provincial writers and moved toward circles inhabited by Maurice Barrès and Juliette Adam, people with conservative political goals like his.

It was not a particularly good time to be a member of the Right, however. After the political tumult of the Dreyfus Affair, in which the conservative forces had effectively lost, the new government of President Pierre Waldeck-Rousseau was determined to consolidate its power and defend the Republic against the reactionary right wing and the Church. The new, staunchly anticlerical view was swiftly codified into legislation under the government of the next president, Émile Combes, culminating in the formal separation of Church and State in 1905. And when Émile Zola died in 1902, he was hailed as a hero of the Republic, much to the horror of conservative Frenchmen throughout the nation. Some fifty thousand people accompanied his casket to the cemetery in Montmartre, including other veterans of the affair such as Alfred Dreyfus and Bernard Lazare. Miners chanted *"Germinal, Germinal,"* and all heard a moving funeral oration by the Dreyfusard novelist Anatole France, in which he declared that out of Zola's courage "has emerged a new order of things based on sounder justice and on a deeper knowledge of everyone's rights." It was the revenge of the Dreyfusards, who, in the eyes of their opponents, wielded their new power with all the subtlety of a battering ram.

The more Maurras observed and read and discussed with others who were equally unhappy with the current political climate, the more he knew that only a profound change could save the nation. He gradually came to believe that political action—even at the local, provincial level—could only happen from above, and that the best form of government for achieving this was a monarchy. The French

needed to reassert their national identity in order to lessen the impact of foreigners, and France needed to find the strength and forti-
tude that had been lost with her provinces in 1871 and had remained
dormant during the subsequent years of republican dominance.
What his countrymen needed was a king, a figure around whom
they could all rally in unity and pride, a man capable of quelling the
social and political strife that had been tearing the country apart since
the Revolution.

In 1899 thirty-year-old Maurras met fellow nationalist Henri
Vaugeois, then a thirty-four-year-old professor of philosophy and
descendant of an important republican family. The two decided that
other political groups were not moving fast enough to counter the
dangerous forces at work in France, and they agreed to attempt to
create something different. On June 20, at a public lecture, Vaugeois
proudly introduced their new organization, which they christened
the Action Française, to a room full of nationalists. They said that
its aim was to create a closer relationship between the masses and
the men of high culture in order to stimulate "the revival of more
honest politics." Despite their lofty intentions, they were quickly
forced to deal with political realities: the group's first steps were
made in an atmosphere of overwhelming public indifference. Other
nationalist and royalist groups faltered in this atmosphere of grimly
determined unity, and if the Action Française ultimately survived
where others failed, it was due to their ability to combine and reconcile the popular radicalism of nationalism with the reactionary elit-
ism of royalism.

When the dust settled on the Dreyfus Affair, Léon found himself
on the losing side, but he had also found for himself a career and a
passion. He would follow in his father's footsteps and make his living with the pen, but unlike his father, he would also take on the
political questions of the day. In 1898 he published a moving and
highly personal portrait of his father, *Alphonse Daudet*; otherwise,
he focused mainly on writing articles and reviews for various publications, such as *La Libre Parole*, *Le Gaulois*, *Le Journal*, and *Le Soleil*.
His writing was eclectic and encyclopedic, robust and erratic. He
worked in short, intense bursts, becoming consumed with a subject
until an editor's deadline or a social commitment required him to

stop. When Léon wasn't working, he was enjoying himself as a man-about-town, flitting about from an evening at the opera to lavish dinners and raucous nights barhopping. He slept with opera singers and not so secretly pined for an up-and-coming poetess named Anna de Noailles. This antic schedule—the soirées and dinner parties, the amorous intrigues and the social gossip—continued for some time, until one day he realized that he had finally had enough. Despite his outré antics and his love of rowdy, randy bachelor ways, he still very much wanted a wife, and a traditional one at that—not that he ever intended marriage to be a deterrent to extramarital activities. Like other well-to-do sons of important families, Léon had absolutely no problem preaching the values of bourgeois domestic responsibility while also indulging his more carnal tastes away from the matrimonial bed. It had worked for his parents, after all: Julia and Alphonse had been literary partners, soulmates of a sort, while Alphonse kept up his sexual side projects until his failing health got in the way.

The woman Léon eventually chose was twenty-two-year-old Marthe Allard, his first cousin, the product of the marriage of his father's sister to his mother's brother. Léon had spent summers with her at the family estate in Champrosay, but as she had been eleven years his junior, he had never really noticed her when they were growing up. But then he spent the summer of 1901 with her and the rest of the Allard-Daudet clan in Chargé in Touraine, and their relationship became something different. He spent his days walking with his younger sister Edmée and Marthe, taking them to eat cheese and drink Vouvray in local inns, enjoying their nervous giggles, their naive excitement at their own imagined daringness. What drew Léon to Marthe now? She was attractive without being distractingly beautiful, intelligent, active, knowing beyond her years. Whereas Jeanne Hugo—and his various paramours—had all been voluptuous, temperamental creatures, Marthe was thin, almost brittle, and self-composed, with a tendency to furrow her brow and purse her lips when considering something. But that was not to say that she was docile. In fact, her political ideas were already well formed—certainly more firmly than Léon's. She was one of the first members of the Ligue de la Patrie Française and was a committed and ardent Catholic and royalist. She also had a dowry of a hundred thousand francs.

When they returned to Paris, they continued to see a lot of each other, taking long walks along the Seine and in the Jardin de Luxembourg while discussing politics. Léon was neither a particularly committed Catholic nor a royalist, and Marthe lectured him about his anarchical and lazy republicanism, his morally dubious fiction, his excessive drinking and carousing. And, for once, he seems to have listened. He was impressed by her, writing to a friend that she was a "masterpiece of nature" and that he appreciated her powers of "lyrical and satirical invention." He in turn impressed her with his tales of dueling and travel, his enthusiasm and his gusto. The tempestuous Léon liked her steady certainty, whether about the role of religion in society or the proper texture for a well-cooked soufflé. Her competence, he sensed, could be a useful asset to him, while her calm stability could nourish his dreams and aspirations. Theirs was an affair of the mind, as well as the heart—so different from his whirlwind relationship with Jeanne, which had never evolved past the initial, impetuous acquiescence to libido and youthful emotion. He asked Marthe to marry him, and as a testament to his devotion to a new era of domestic bliss, he even voluntarily broke things off with his mistress, the superb and opulent Lucienne Bréval. Léon and Marthe were married on August 3, 1903, in Chargé Church, in a very religious ceremony before family and a few friends. Among the witnesses were Colonel Marchand, the hero of the Fashoda Crisis (an 1898 incident during which competing colonial claims over an inconsequential parcel of land in eastern Sudan almost catapulted France and Great Britain to war), and Édouard Drumont, France's leading anti-Semite. The sermon was filled with stirring, patriotic appeals, and guests called out "Long live the king!" as the young couple left the church.

His married life with Marthe, whose nickname, thanks to the literary critic Jules Lemaître, was Pampille, was marked by new levels of sedate domesticity. As Julia had done for Alphonse, Marthe ruled over the running of the household with steely efficiency, making sure that everything she surveyed—from the food to the furnishings to the shine on the stemware and the drape of the tablecloth—coexisted in perfect harmony. Léon, who had for so long led friends like Georges Hugo, Philippe Berthelot, and Jean-Baptiste Charcot through endless nights of debauchery, could on most nights now be found read-ing or writing at home, 8, rue Saint-Simon, by the fire.

And he had much to write about. The nation was in trouble and, with the help of Marthe, Léon was becoming increasingly well versed in conservative politics. The Dreyfus Affair had awakened him to a new sense of political engagement and had provided several high-profile opportunities for his own personal brand of colorful com-mentary. His anti-Semitism had not been particularly well developed before the scandal and owed more to his family's personal relation-ship with Édouard Drumont than to any deeply held political beliefs of his own. But the arguments in Drumont's bestselling *La France Juive*, the acrimony dredged up by the Dreyfus Affair, and the war-ring factions that had emerged had clarified things for him. For the first time, something outside of himself was really at stake. Léon wanted to believe that these political decisions had a life-or-death importance. He was taken with the romance of being an instrument for something larger than himself. As the scandal wore on, Léon's anti-Semitism deepened and hardened and he became convinced that Jews and their coconspirators were hurting the French body politic. With Marthe's encouragement he began attending the famed salon of Mme de Loynes, on the Champs-Élysées, where the leading lights of the Ligue de la Patrie Française congregated. It was at one of these meetings that Léon had become reacquainted with Syveton, a former classmate who had gone on to become a university profes-sor. After being fired from his academic position for his violent ex-pressions of anti-Dreyfusard sentiment, Syveton had become a deputy in Paris and secretary-treasurer for the Ligue. Léon and Syveton got on famously from the get-go, reveling in their memories of various childhood pranks they had performed in school and sharing, as adults, the same pugnacious and irreverent *joie de vivre*. And of course, Léon had ambitions for himself within the Ligue and jumped on any opportunity to raise his profile among its members.

After the Ligue de la Patrie Française went into decline follow-ing the resolution of the Dreyfus Affair, Marthe drew Léon to the Action Française. The more Léon came to know Charles Maurras, the more he admired the man and the writer. Soon after Syveton's death in November 1904, he and Marthe—upon Maurras's urging—

traveled to London to meet Philippe, the exiled Duke of Orléans, at his residence in the Savoy Hotel. He and his family had been living in exile since his great-grandfather, Louis-Philippe, King of the French, had abdicated and was exiled from France in 1848. Upon the death of his father, Philippe, Count of Paris, in 1894, the duke became the Orléanist claimant to the French throne. It was love at first sight for Léon, who stammered, sweated, and trembled like a teenage girl: "After an hour of the interview, I was conquered forever," he admitted. The duke fondly kissed Léon on both cheeks and asked him to lunch. Léon, in a state of sheer ecstasy, later confessed that if the duke had asked him to jump out of the window he would have gladly obliged. He returned to Paris the most ardent of monarchists and spent the rest of the year getting to know the leaders of the Action Française better, reading and rereading Maurras's *Inquiry on the Monarchy* and other political texts. He was finally, as he put it, "entering into the light," after spending his whole adult life in philosophical and political obscurity. His first public profession of his monarchist faith appeared in *Le Gaulois* on September 3, 1904, in an article in which he announced that a king alone could be an arbiter because he is beholden to no one: "A century ago, clever and villainous men persuaded the French people that they could liberate themselves by chopping off the head of their king. By listening to this pernicious advice, the people decapitated themselves."

Léon's new political life started out each day at the headquarters of the Action Française, a small office at 42, rue du Bac, where Maurras, Vaugeois, the former journalist Maurice Pujo, and others would gather to discuss, argue, and print the small bulletin through which they hoped to spread their ideas. In these unassuming, cramped offices, Léon had the daily opportunity to bandy arguments and ideas off men who seemed to breathe in politics like other men required air. It was a glorious fraternity that reminded Léon of the stories his father had told him about his meetings with the Group of Five. But there were also practical matters to attend to. For their part Maurras and the others recognized that Léon would never be more than a mediocre diplomat, but that his bullish enthusiasm, coupled with his fun-loving bonhomie, could actually work in their favor. He was insolent and brutal, ferocious in an argument, generous with friends and admirers around the dinner table. And they soon discovered where his true strengths lay—public speaking. Maurras, who was partially deaf, had a low, hollow voice; Pujo stammered and tried to hide behind his handwritten notes; Vaugeois was charming but ineffectual and always disappointing with a crowd. So it was left to Léon to be the spokesperson, the public face of the Action Française. He quickly became the public's favorite—he was amusing, seductive, inspiring, threatening. "It is one of the greatest known pleasures to make love to a crowd and to see it become animated, then leap about and roar," Léon mused, and when he found himself standing before a crowd of twenty thousand in Saint-Rémy-de-Provence a few months later, he could scarcely believe it. To witness his own power over that mass of people, to feed himself on their energy, was perhaps the most powerful sensation Léon had ever known.

But the movement still lacked a political organ, a voice for spreading their beliefs. Here again Léon—and his new wife—proved their utility. When Mme de Loynes died in January 1908, she left Marthe Daudet 200,000 francs to be used for the royalist cause. Marthe and Léon in turn used the funds as the core of the original capital needed to found a newspaper. On March 21, 1908, the first issue of the daily newspaper *Action Française* went on sale. Despite initial enthusiasm the newspaper's editors were already calling for capital within seven weeks of its launch; within another seven months, the funds had dried up again. But such base practicalities were hardly of concern for Léon, who had now found a way of uniting his two great passions—writing and politics.

The months leading up to the launch of their newspaper passed in a blur for Léon. But once the money had been spent, the new editorial offices rented and set up, journalists and other editorial collaborators identified, Léon could finally step back and survey the results. He was delighted with what he saw before him—it was as if he had created for himself an entirely new universe. Even though his family's wealth had often granted him social clout and insider status, Léon had always possessed a peculiar contempt for those whose exalted status he deemed to be undeserved. Perhaps it was the result of the years he had spent watching Alphonse be overlooked by men who regarded his talent as second-rate and inconsequential, while men like Zola, sycophants and social climbers in Léon's mind, achieved a level of fame unknown to most writers. Léon had thus always been eager to defy convention, despite his privileged upbringing. But now the resentment that had once been merely a gut reaction to Léon's unconfirmed suspicions about the fundamental falseness of society found validation in his companions at the Action Française. With them he found evidence for his long-held belief in some fundamental unfairness. He was now able to see the true inner workings of French society: politicians who piously proclaimed their fealty to the Republic while they secretly whored themselves to German interests, the police and mainstream journalists who were in their pocket, and the vast, slumbering public who could not be bothered to care about any of it. With the Action Française, he became a modern-day Cassandra, brave truth-teller and victim at the same time, destined to be shunned by those whose secrets he revealed.

Léon's education in royalism and political activism occurred at these daily meetings at the Action Française offices or at one-on-one meetings with Maurras at the latter's home on the rue de Verneuil, where Léon would spend hours peppering his friend with questions. For the Action Française, there were two guiding principles. First, France would only regain her former glory if she returned to the divinely ordained form of government that had been so brutally exterminated in 1791. Second, those who currently led France were—wittingly and unwittingly—placing her citizens in grave danger by either willfully ignoring or basely abetting the threat posed by Germany to the east. These ideas appealed to conservative French men and women throughout the country, those who believed in the fundamental rightness of the family and the army and the Church, those who agonized over the 1905 separation of Church and State, and those for whom the angry hysterics of the Dreyfus Affair, and its final, ignominious end with the victory of the Dreyfusards, had served as a sad reminder of how far the nation had fallen. For these men and women, the Dreyfus Affair had been the ultimate confirmation that France was being destroyed from within by an unacceptably high proportion of "foreigners."

Léon was now a monarchist, too. And he took this message out to the people, harangued them from torch-lit stages in countless, nameless meeting halls in midsize hamlets and cities throughout the nation. But when he sat down alone, at night, he thought of even greater dangers . . . to the nation, but also to himself and his comrades. It was this Léon who, late at night, reflected anxiously on Gabriel Syveton's death, who went over the details, again and again, trying to discover the one clue or hint that would confirm his suspicions that a murder—or, worse, a political assassination—had in fact been committed. And when he woke up in the morning, he would head into the offices of the Action Française, where he, Maurras, Pujo, and others would fume and rant and lecture at each other until finally each retreated to his own desk in his own corner of the offices, and once there, began the arduous, exhilarating task of transforming those fears, that outrage, that certitude into the speeches, essays, and columns that had slowly begun molding public opinion.

The first issue of *Action Française* appeared on March 21, 1908, and featured a lead article signed by Léon, Vaugeois, Maurras, and the other directors, calling on all good Frenchmen to turn against the Republic. They found their news by combing through the *faits divers*—throwaway gossip items featured in most of the main newspapers—to see if any of them could easily be exploited to serve their cause. Léon compiled dossiers on anyone who might be important—politicians and prominent businessmen—with an eye to any past or future scandals. Given Léon and Maurras's interest in literature, the newspaper also contained a healthy dose of literary criticism. Although the circulation of *Action Française* was insignificant compared to that of the other major Parisian newspapers—it boasted only about twenty-three thousand readers, while traditional republican newspapers like *Le Journal* and *Petit Parisien* had over a million—it counted among its readership some of the leading figures in the literary and intellectual worlds, who were drawn to the intellectual pedigree of the paper's editors and the sheer audacity of its opinions. *Action Française* gave readers access to arguments that most conventional journalists and politicians would not dare say. And since they were not merely attempting to increase circulation, but also to build a political movement, the editors of *Action Française* organized regular conferences in Paris for the longtime faithful and for new recruits. They also regularly left the capital to raise public consciousness in the provinces, with as many as thirty or more public lectures or meetings a year.

Over the next several years, Léon's involvement with the Action
Française only deepened. He hurried about Paris like a man electrified, bustling from a rally in the Latin Quarter to editorial meetings
to dinners with potential benefactors. Even at night, when other men
might have collapsed wearily into bed, Léon still burned with political passion, which he would set down meticulously in fierce essays.
Léon embraced his new identity. He was no longer the dutiful son
of received wisdoms; he was a reactionary, a polemicist. Later, in his
extended essay *Le Stupide XIXe Siècle (The Stupid XIXth Century)*
(1922), he defended the label, writing, "The term Reaction, unjustly ridiculed, disparaged, and held in contempt, must be salvaged
and boldly reclaimed if we are to chase away bloodthirsty error, restore true peace, and destroy the dead ideas and institutions that
were honored during the nineteenth century. I have not written
this truthful and sincere book for any other reason than to give
heart to Reaction, which is to say, to the rebuilders in all areas and
planes of life."

What made the Action Française stand out from other right-
wing groups, what transformed it into *the* predominant force on
the nationalist Right in the early years of the twentieth century, was
the result of a specific convergence of factors. First, it had a core of
younger, devoted militants whose contempt for status quo politics
and parliamentary democracy was coupled with a commitment to
order and traditional, conservative values. Second, it received considerable support from the Catholic Church, now under attack from
successive governments who distrusted its traditional support for
reactionary politics. Third, in marked contrast with the internation-
alism and antimilitarism of many groups on the Left, the Action Française's unwavering and uncompromising nationalism attracted those
Frenchmen who were growing increasingly nervous about German
militarism.

The cause of the Action Française was also helped by a group
of young toughs, the *camelots du roi*, that Léon and Maurras had
at their disposal. Although officially charged with distributing the
newspaper, they were better known for their combative, thuggish
behavior, which was frequently unleashed on the group's opponents.
Within a year of the group's formation in late 1908, there were sixty-

five sections of *camelots* throughout France and some six hundred members in Paris alone. Léon was particularly enthusiastic about the idea of leading a vanguard of the young, explaining in a later account of his political transformation that it was an error to think that young people were less apt than adults to deal with civic struggle and controversy. "My generation ignored these duties to public matters and wasted, in childishness or puerility, or vain quarrels, her thirst for the royalist movement," he sternly noted.

These royalist youths had first flexed their muscle at the June 4, 1908, ceremony transferring Zola's ashes to the Panthéon, although their rowdy behavior was overshadowed when a journalist from *Le Gaulois* by the name of Grégori shot at Alfred Dreyfus, wounding him in the shoulder. They were then prominently involved in an ongoing action against a professor of history at the Sorbonne, François Thalamas, whom they accused of being a "half-breed" after he dared to question the purity of Joan of Arc in a lecture. For several months in 1908, fifty *camelots* would turn up at the Sorbonne every Wednesday to disrupt Thalamas's lectures, throwing eggs at the teacher and his students and shouting insults until the university had to call in the police. On a few occasions, they even managed to forcibly expel Thalamas from the lecture hall and would submit the remaining students to strident and frequently incoherent lectures on the history of royalism. Léon watched this new generation with great interest, and was convinced that their skirmishes with left-wing activities in the streets of Paris—or even in the hallways and classrooms of the Sorbonne—were preparing them for the inevitable, righteous battle for the soul of the nation.

The year 1911 proved to be a watershed for Léon and his burgeoning movement. Léon was in the thick of things, fighting four duels that year alone, haranguing the readers of the *Action Française* newspaper in his column each day and at the regular conferences he gave. But there were two events in particular that afforded him the opportunity to shine a spotlight on both the threats facing France and the Action Française's role in defeating them. It all began in mid-February. The Théâtre-Français was preparing for the production of a play by the noted playwright Henri Bernstein: *Après Moi*. The play seemed poised to be another success when an article in *L'Oeuvre* appeared reminding people that Bernstein had deserted his military service in 1897 at the military hospital Saint-Mandé. The article went on to note that he had been condemned in absentia, although it failed to mention that he had then been amnestied in 1901. Gustave Téry, author of the article, then launched into a violent anti-Semitic attack, suggesting that "if the Jew Bernstein wants to be performed at the Comédie-Française, he should first finish his military service."

The premiere of the play was scheduled for February 18. The day before the premiere, Léon reprinted in *Action Française* a letter that Bernstein had written eleven years earlier, boasting of his avoidance of military service by fleeing to Brussels, to a well-known pacifist. Léon added his own commentary: "Everything in this [letter] is Jewish, hideously Jewish." Although the final dress rehearsal took place without any disruptions—and was even positively reviewed by many critics in the following days—other conservative newspapers began repeating Léon's objections. As Charles Maurras summed up, "One must do with [Bernstein] what one must do to all the Jews of France, microbes of the State." And then the Action Française really swung into action. On opening night all the posters in Paris and on the theater itself were pasted over with Action Française stickers denouncing "the Jewish Deserter." *Camelots du roi* assembled in front of the theater, calling out, "Down with deserters! Long live the army!" and "Down with the Jews!" Maurice Pujo had planted royalist activists in seats throughout the theater, from which they catcalled and hurled insults at the actors, the director, and anyone who attempted to stop their antics. Their interruptions were so forceful that they frequently drowned out the play. The fact that Bernstein's youthful peccadillo had been officially forgiven and essentially forgotten no longer mattered. And a few weeks later, Bernstein was forced to take down his play. The nationalists were ecstatic. "Yesterday the Latin Quarter carried Paris with it," wrote Xavier de Magallon in *La Libre Parole*. "Youth is with us. The future is ours." Inevitably, the matter ended up on the dueling field, with Léon going up first against Georges Claretie, son of Jules Claretie, director of the Comédie-Française and a friend of Bernstein. Then, on July 21, 1911, during an evening of wilting heat, Léon and Henri Bernstein faced each other at the Parc des Princes. Before a crowd of photographers and journalists, they tried to fell each other, first with pistols and then with swords—an indication, noted a journalist from *Le Figaro*, of the severity of the disagreement. Although the duel ended when Léon was wounded on the arm, the journalist from *Le Figaro* praised him for providing "a truly impressive spectacle," adding, "M. Daudet, once again, has displayed his energy and courage beyond a shadow of a doubt." Defying gentlemanly custom, they left the ground without shaking hands.

Another great opportunity for the Action Française to demonstrate its growing influence occurred later that year, when it was reported that the famed Polish-born scientist Marie Curie, who with her late husband, Pierre, had won a Nobel Prize in 1903 for physics, was willing to be nominated for election to the Academy of Sciences. If she had been chosen, she would have been the first woman to enter into that illustrious body. Among the most vocal opponents to Curie's candidacy were Léon and his colleagues. For them the issue of merit could hardly even be broached: the true issue was what such a gesture would indicate to the world at large. Once again the lurking undercurrents of anti-Semitism and xenophobia came welling up to the surface, where they were joined by the Right's peculiar ambivalence about women, especially women who dabbled in science. (Léon's own mother had declared years earlier, in a letter to a friend, that "science is useless to women.") Observers on the Right cast the matter in terms of the Dreyfus Affair, insisting that the academics and scientists promoting Curie's candidacy were nothing more than a "cabal of Dreyfusards." As the controversy surrounding Curie's nomination swelled, the physicist Édouard Branly was put forth as another possible candidate the week before the election. Léon himself captured this struggle best in an article that appeared on the day the Academy of Sciences was to take its vote. In "Dreyfus Against Branly," he declared, "The imbeciles who go around insisting that the Dreyfus Affair has been buried should take notice: it is so unburied, this epic struggle of the national genius versus the foreign demon, that on every fashionable, sportive, literary, dramatic, musical, scientific, social, political, and economic occasion it begins again in a thousand forms, with actors who are always basically the same." If the supporters of Marie Curie opposed Branly,

Léon opined, it was because he had left the Sorbonne to teach in the Catholic Institute; thus their quarrel was not with the man's credentials or his science but rather with his beliefs. Soon other journalists caught on to this line of argument. They also repeated the worried whispers and cutting innuendo mouthed about Marie Curie by Action Française leaders: that her husband, Pierre, had done all of their work; that she might be Jewish; that she had loose morals.

The January 23, 1911, vote was made before a crush of curious, often impassioned observers. Despite her world-renowned accomplishments, including a shared Nobel Prize in 1903, and support from prominent researchers in her field, she was defeated by Branly, 28 votes to Branly's 30. The following day, Léon proudly declared that the vote was nothing less than "the defeat of Dreyfus." *The New York Times* saw it somewhat differently, its headline bluntly declaring: "Mme Curie Defeated: Fails Election to the Academy of Sciences Because of Her Sex."

A few months later, Marie Curie became the target of yet another campaign in the press. This time it was a matter about her private life—her relationship with her colleague Paul Langevin, who had experienced marital problems for some time and had recently left his wife. Newspaper reports named Curie as the cause of the split. In the midst of the melee, she got word that she had been awarded the Nobel Prize in Chemistry. News of the latest honor bestowed upon her, however, was virtually ignored amid salacious speculations about her personal life. When private letters between Curie and Paul Langevin were published, Léon once again went on the attack. There was no proof that the accusations made against Curie were true and the authenticity of the letters could have easily been called into question, but in the heated atmosphere there were few who thought clearly. Here was a liar and a cheat, a foreigner, stealing the husband of an honest Frenchwoman. Quoting Antoine-Quentin Fouquier-Tinville's notorious words, which had sent the chemist Antoine Lavoisier to the guillotine during the French Revolution, Léon darkly declared, "The Republic does not need any scientists." In November two highly publicized duels were fought as a result of the scandal—first Léon was challenged by the editor of the newspaper *Gil Blas*; then Langevin fought a duel with Gustave Téry, a right-wing journalist who had referred to the former as "a boor and a coward."

Curie was quietly informed by the Swedish Academy of Sciences that it would be better for all involved if she did not accept the prize until the charges against her were proven to be unfounded. Wounded and indignant, she maintained that the value of her scientific work should not be cast into doubt by malicious gossip concerning her personal life. The Nobel Committee relented and, on December 11, she was allowed to deliver her Nobel lecture in Stockholm. It was a Pyrrhic victory at best: soon afterward Curie collapsed from the physical and mental strain she had endured, and she did not recover for some time.

For Léon, however, the year had been a triumphant success. His penchant for what he called "heroic medications," miraculous cures for the seemingly incurable, which had begun while observing his father's illness, was now fully realized in his new political enthusiasms. He had had enough of moderation and compromise; he was ready to fight for what he believed in because he believed it was truly a matter of life or death for his country. Léon had become one of the most visible and effective leaders of a loud and belligerent minority opposed to the Republic. The Action Française group and its newspaper specialized in violent, insolent smear campaigns, successfully grafting nationalism on the formerly antiquated monarchist movement and recruiting young adherents and intellectuals back into the folds of Catholicism. In the Action Française, Léon found an extended family, where he was eagerly welcomed, side by side with his friend Charles Maurras, as a revered, if explosive, patriarch. But the violence in Léon Daudet's new life was no longer merely rhetorical. The duels, the brawls, the confrontations with the police—these were just natural extensions of his acid-dipped pen.

As 1911 rolled on, Léon found increasing evidence that he and the Action Française were needed by his country. On July 1, 1911, the Agadir Crisis, during which a German gunboat dropped anchor in the Bay of Agadir off the coast of Morocco, caused England and France to consider the possibility of war. The tone in the press and even in the halls of the republican government became increasingly patriotic and aggressive. As tensions between France and Germany grew, and the ominous clouds of war gathered on the horizon, the Action Française became the chief exponent of French nationalism, with their caustic yet effective combination of printed and spoken invective. Their leaders, particularly Léon Daudet, were willing to back up their violent rhetoric with actual violence. As the year came to a close, Léon decided to begin investigating the activities of German and German-Jewish "spies" within France who, he alleged, were secretly preparing the way for the enemy invasion of France. Throughout the next few years, he unveiled to his appalled readers the extent to which German agents had come to control essential industries. He then published the story of his campaign to unmask this stealth German pre-invasion in March 1913 under the portentous title *L'Avant-Guerre*. It proved to be his greatest publishing success to date: as historian Eugen Weber archly observed about the book, "Eleven thousand copies had been sold by the beginning of the war, 25,000 by January 1915; by 1918 it had passed through fifty printings, and the men it pilloried had suffered the torments of hell." Léon became the most vocal proponent of the idea that no individuals or businesses with any connection to Germany could be trusted, and he was hellbent on rooting out—and publicizing—any cases of treachery. One company that fell into this dubious category was Maggi-Kub, an international dairy-products firm, which, although headquartered in Switzerland, also had significant holdings in Germany as well as France. Léon and his comrades leaped into action. They claimed to have documents that were incontrovertible proof of treason occurring at the Maggi dairies. In July the company sued Léon for libel. His documents were proven to be forgeries, and Maggi won its libel suit. But the Action Française's steady barrage of innuendo and anti-German baiting had done its job, and a cloud of suspicion hung over Maggi-Kub until the end of World War I. When Maggi outlets in France were pillaged a few months later, the police stood by and did nothing on the grounds that the company was "German."

When war was declared in August 1914, the stakes were raised even higher. For a time, political differences and personal ambitions were put aside. Jean-Baptiste Charcot was enlisted to hunt down and destroy German submarines, first as commander of a Q-boat for Britain's Royal Navy in the northern seas off the coast of Scotland and the Hebrides, and then as captain of two antisubmarine ships, the *Meg* and the *Meg II* off the coast of Normandy. His courageous conduct restlessly trawling the coasts of England and northern France earned him a Distinguished Service Cross. But his military activities were no substitute for the thrill of exploring in icy waters at the ends of the earth, and as the war continued from year to year he began to wonder if he'd ever see another iceberg again.

Léon meanwhile eagerly embraced the idea that France was waging a "total war" involving every aspect of national life—"A total war: them or us," he announced in the March 11, 1916, edition of *Action Française*. Léon, who was too old and too fat to fight, waged another kind of war at home. He and his colleagues at the Action Française rallied to the cause of the *union sacrée*, an agreement to bury traditional Right-Left political and ideological differences in the name of national unity and defense against German aggression, and focused their attentions on those they deemed insufficiently patriotic. They decided to go after some left-wing publications whose pro-peace stance they considered to be too defeatist—and therefore dangerous. Their main target was *Le Bonnet Rouge*, founded and edited by Miguel Vigo-Almereyda. In July 1917 the paper's business editor was arrested while trying to cross into France from Switzerland. He was holding a large check—drawn from a German account, no less. Even more important to members of the Action Française, the paper had received private financial support from former premier Joseph Caillaux and public subsidies from the Radical-Socialist Louis-Jean Malvy, minister of the interior since June 1914, who resisted calls for dissenters to be rounded up after the outbreak of the war. Both men had been seen as political enemies of the Action Française well before their names were dragged into this most recent scandal of Léon's own making. It was the opportunity Léon and Charles Maurras had been waiting for—to expose the government as being led by a cabal of corrupt and hopelessly inept politicians—but there was some danger, too, that pursuing these allegations could destroy the fragile wartime truce between Right and Left. Nevertheless, the members of Action Française were determined to keep up their attacks, and for months, in countless articles and public speeches, they relentlessly hounded *Le Bonnet Rouge*, Caillaux, and Malvy. By early summer 1917, the attacks were clearly taking their toll. "Daudet's campaign against me is making me ill," one staffer from *Le Bonnet Rouge* complained to a reporter. "It's driving me mad. All the journals where I used to get work are closed to me."

During a secret session of the Senate in July 1917, the radical politician Georges Clemenceau openly accused Malvy of betraying French interests, and Malvy was forced to resign on August 31, 1917. Vigo-Almereyda had been arrested at the beginning of August and was found dead in his cell less than a week later, strangled with some kind of narrow cord. The official cause of death was suicide, but the Action Française declared that he had been assassinated to prevent him from incriminating high-placed government officials. Léon's charges against Malvy, which he had written in an inflamed letter to Président Poincaré, were read before the Chamber of Deputies on October 4. "Monsieur le Président," it read, "I address myself to you because it is important that you be informed about what is no longer a secret to many people, and also because you have a great role to play and can save France . . . M. Malvy, former minister of the interior, is a traitor." The letter caused a furor. "For the last six hours," a socialist complained, "in this overexcited hall, we have argued on a question brought up by Léon Daudet. On one side, a calumniator, a professional defamer, on the other the Chamber and the whole country. What is this person who can thus occupy the country's representatives for six hours? What is his importance? What is his power? I cannot find an explanation consistent with the dignity of this Assembly!"

Yet such was Léon's power at this precarious moment. *"Vive Léon Daudet"* began to appear scribbled on Paris walls, and the leaders of the Action Française could smell victory in the air. *Action Française* was ultimately fined for defaming Malvy, and its offices were searched by the police. But when Georges Clemenceau, known as "the Tiger," became prime minister in November, the tide changed once again: Clemenceau adopted a ruthless approach to all those he believed to be guilty of defeatism. As German bombs fell on Paris, Malvy and Caillaux were both arrested and charged with treason. Léon was ecstatic. On August 7, 1918, the Senate, sitting as a High Court of Justice, acquitted Louis Malvy of a higher charge but condemned him to five years' exile for "culpable negligence in the discharge of his duties." On April 23, 1920, it condemned onetime premier Joseph Caillaux to three years' imprisonment (which was commuted), five years' exile from Paris, and loss of civic rights for ten years on the charge of having "impeded prosecution of the War." In a sign per-haps of the inherently forgetful nature of politics, both men would resurface several years later and hold prominent political positions. Although France had paid dearly for it, her victory in the war was vindication for conservatives and nationalists such as Léon. The Right made major gains in the general election of 1919, with the Action Française's own Léon Daudet earning a seat in the Chamber of Dep-uties. It was a new age of extremes. The same year that Léon was elected a deputy, Raoul Villain, who had been in prison throughout the war, was finally brought to trial for the assassination of Jean Jaurès. On March 29, 1919, to the surprise of many and the outrage of the Left, he was acquitted on the grounds that he had killed the social-ist leader in a "patriotic passion." Clearly the rules of the game had changed.

TEN

Sins of the Father

The storm has died away and still we are restless, uneasy, as if the storm were about to break . . . We think of what has disappeared, we are almost destroyed by what has been destroyed; we do not know what will be born, and we fear the future, not without reason . . . But among all these injured things is the Mind. The Mind has indeed been cruelly wounded . . . It passes a mournful judgment on itself. It doubts itself profoundly.   —Paul Valéry (1922)

The relation of a boy to his father is, as we say, an "ambivalent" one. In addition to the hate which seeks to get rid of the father as a rival, a measure of tenderness for him is also habitually present. The two attitudes of mind combine to produce identification with the father; the boy wants to be in his father's place because he admires him and wants to be like him, and also because he wants to put him out of the way.

    —Sigmund Freud, "Dostoevsky and Parricide" (1928)

⸺⊸⊂⸻

On Sunday, November 25, 1923, Léon Daudet stared down in anger at the dead body of his eldest son. He had arrived at the hospital to confirm that the body in question was indeed that of his Philippe. Charles Maurras, his close friend and political ally, accompanied him. Léon didn't have to be there—the family doctor had already visited the Lariboisière hospital, identified the body, and performed the ghastly task of informing Léon and his wife that Philippe was dead at fourteen years of age, apparently by a self-inflicted gunshot wound to the head. But Léon needed to see it for himself.

The spectacle of death was nothing new to him. Before the war Parisians from all walks of life had eagerly queued up in front of the city morgue for the public viewing of unclaimed bodies, ostensibly for the purpose of identification but really out of fascination at the chance to see the meticulously arranged bodies of those hapless victims of disaster, self-induced or otherwise. In this way death became a spectator sport, the danger witnessed from a tantalizingly close distance. And then, of course, there had been the war—the "war to end all wars," as they hopefully called it. Death never looked the same after that. It had lost some of its individual novelty, its delicacy, during those days of mass-produced and indiscriminate annihilation. With it, death had surged through the cage doors and was now roaming the streets, looking for its next victim.

But none of those deaths had prepared Léon, fifty-six years old, for this death. He fell to his knees and began to pray: "This unhappy child has not spared his mother or me any sadness." He then forced himself to his feet and began carefully examining the entire body, using his medical training to create an emotional buffer between himself and his son. He observed the red, swollen mark at his right temple. The long, fine hands, which later, he would remember, showed no trace of gunpowder. Philippe had always been a big boy, his bulky frame belying an emotional fragility, which Léon, who abhorred weakness of all sorts, must have found embarrassing. It was called a suicide, and so it appeared. But what a thing for his son to do, when it so expressly went against everything that he and his entire family stood for: devotion to the nation, the Church, the king. In spite of himself, Léon found himself thinking about what this death meant for his own public image. How would he explain this to his followers, or, worse, to his enemies? Such thoughts of political responsibility were the only thing that kept Léon from plunging headfirst into a darkness that he had not known since his own father had died. It would have been quite difficult, at any rate, for a man such as he to keep the personal and the political entirely apart. In fact, it would have been unthinkable.

The war had been worse than anyone could have imagined, and the country was still reeling, proud to have won and grateful that it was over but still unable to face all that had been lost. During the war a thousand Frenchmen were killed each day, nearly one out of every five men who had been mobilized. In total, approximately 1.4 million French lost their lives and over one million returned as invalids, having been gassed, mangled, and disfigured during the course of the four-year conflict that was only supposed to have lasted a few months. By 1918 there were 630,000 war widows in France, and many thousands of women who had been deprived of the chance for marriage. And those were just the obvious scars. The Great War was supposed to have been a noble crusade that would restore moral values such as honor and discipline and revive people's faith in progress. But the realization that bungling bureaucrats and bellicose statesmen had led an entire generation into mechanized slaughter the likes of which none had ever imagined had caused those older values to collapse. Everywhere were signs of what people could only describe as a national weariness and a general agreement that future war must be avoided at all costs. Many sought an escape from the painful memories in a frenzied hedonism. Dadaists banged on tin cans, Josephine Baker dazzled audiences with her banana skirt, and American jazz musicians jived and trilled until the early-morning hours in hot, smoky jazz clubs where men and women drank gin and thought of sex. As the literary critic and writer Elisabeth de Gramont noted, "We all wanted to forget the war; while eminent men were discussing its consequences, we were dancing." Léon had now become one of those "eminent men." Fifty years old when the war ended, he would have seemed like a relic from another era to the young people flirting and arguing about politics in the city's cafés. To some he had passed over into farce. On January 23, 1920, the twenty-four-year-old Romanian Dadaist Tristan Tzara decided to launch the first of a series of public Dada gatherings in Paris with an evening of poetry and dissonant music culminating in his humorous—and heavily accented—reading of one of Léon's recent speeches from the National Assembly. Tzara cut up the speech and dropped the pieces in a hat before pro-

ceeding to pull random scraps of paper out and read them as if they
were a poem, while from the wings André Breton and Louis
Aragon nearly drowned out his voice with loud electric bells.

The year 1923 had been difficult. Germany was coming apart
at the seams, plagued with strikes, unemployment, and violence. In
early November a war veteran named Adolf Hitler, supported by the
former German army officer Erich Ludendorff, had attempted a
coup in a Munich beer hall, and hyperinflation in Germany reached
its height. In France the year started off well for the royalists, with
the government led by Poincaré seeming to adopt their platform by
arresting communist leaders and, at long last, occupying the Ruhr.
But then on January 22, Marius Plateau, one of the royalist movement's most active young leaders, was murdered by a twenty-year-
old anarchist named Germaine Berton. The young woman's target
was initially Léon Daudet—she had attempted to gain access to both
his home and his office—before she arranged to have a meeting with
Marius Plateau at the Action Française offices. At the end of their
meeting, as Plateau was walking to open the door, she pulled out a
gun and shot him five times. When the victim's friends and cowork-
ers came rushing over, Germaine Breton cried out, "I have avenged
Jaurès and Almereyda! I wanted to get Daudet."

The members of the Action Française were furious and wanted
their revenge. The *camelots* took to the streets, rioting and demonstrating and wrecking the headquarters and printing shops of rival
newspapers and political organizations. Then, in June, three well-
known politicians, on their way to speak at a meeting protesting
Poincaré's German policy, were attacked by *camelots*, beaten, and
doused in coal tar and printer's ink. The royalist group was quickly
denounced—*Time* magazine declared they were "emulating Facismo," while Édouard Herriot of the French Radical Party stood up
the day following the attack in the French Chamber of Deputies to
announce, "We have had enough!" on behalf of communists, socialists, and members of the moderate Left. Marc Saugnier, one of
the deputies who had been attacked by the *camelots*, warned his fellow deputies about giving the Action Française too much influence:

Too many of our colleagues seem to fear the Action Française
press campaigns . . . too many fear to say openly what they

think of certain acts of the Action Française . . . they fear—
oh, how wrong they are!—I know not what reprisals . . . The
importance attributed to the Action Française is factitious,
and I think I can assert that the daring of [Daudet] comes
only from the cowardice of many others.

The stakes had been raised, and this was precisely what Léon and
Charles Maurras wanted.

But Léon and his family were ripped from political strategizing
later that year, when catastrophe visited their home. They had first
realized that Philippe was gone on Tuesday, November 20, when he
failed to return from school. Léon's wife, Marthe, had invited a friend
to dinner and had lost track of the time—it was well past seven p.m.
when she realized that her son was still not home. She put on her
hat and coat and hailed the first taxi she saw. When she arrived at
Philippe's school—the prestigious Louis-le-Grand, which Léon had
attended years earlier—she was told that he had not showed up at
all that day. She returned to her gracious home on the rue Saint-
Guillaume, where she, Léon, and their friend pretended to eat the
remains of their sad, silent dinner. Later that night they noticed that
an envelope containing a thousand francs was missing—now they
knew that Philippe had run away. He had done so before, running
off to Marseilles for a few days when he was twelve. At the time,
Léon had tried to shrug it off as a lark: hadn't he himself once been
young, once impatiently ignored his father's admonitions, longed for
the sort of freedom and adventures that one read about in schoolboy novels? But soothing and familiar as this narrative of harmless
youthful rebellion might be, there had always been something a bit
off about Philippe, and Léon and Marthe had struggled to understand *why*—why he was so unlike other children, why he had disappeared like that. Now they were anxious.

When Philippe had run off to Marseilles, the shock of arriving in
a strange city, of being alone in unfamiliar surroundings, had brought
him quickly back to his senses. He sought out a family friend who
lived there, who had promptly telegraphed Marthe and Léon and arranged to send the boy back to Paris, where he was reunited with his
parents amid tears and hugs and promises never to run away again.
So this time the Daudets told no one at first: Marthe was worried

about the "disreputable types" at the police who might use Philippe's disappearance in order to extract some revenge from Léon. After two days with still no sign, Léon added to the end of his November 23 article in *Action Française* a postscript addressed to "a traveler in the south": "I advise you to return, it is the most simple thing." Marthe, however, had a feeling in the pit of her stomach that he was not in the south, but rather still in Paris. That evening she had a nightmare that she was sitting before a cloudy mirror, arranging her hair. Each time she passed the comb through her hair, it fell out in clumps, like tufts of grass. She began praying constantly.

Philippe had been born on January 7, 1909, making him fourteen years and ten months old when he disappeared. He was the oldest of Léon's three children with Marthe: François had been born in 1915 and Claire in 1918. By all accounts he was an intelligent and talented boy, but he was also secretive and prone to emotional out-bursts and fugues of varying duration. Some even whispered that he might suffer from epilepsy. Friends and acquaintances spoke of his broad-shouldered six-foot-tall frame, which disguised such youth, such gentleness. He had grown up in the strident environment of his father's politics, and had frequently taken part in the demonstra-tions and rallies of the Action Française. He was immersed in that world, devouring the newspapers that his father read every morning, buttressed by accounts of the often vicious verbal sparring that took place between his father and his enemies. And he had witnessed first-hand the dangerous physical implications of Léon's political pas-sions, including his father's tense preparations for duels. Sometimes the tension was simply too much to bear, and Philippe would burst into tears at the thought of what could happen to his father, just as, years earlier, a young Léon had wept openly when Alphonse left to settle scores on the dueling field. Philippe would wait by the win-dow through the duel, fear dissolving into relief upon the sight of his father—out-of-breath, disheveled, victorious, and, for the time being at least, unscathed—returning home.

Every morning for eight days, Marthe snuck a peek at the newspaper, waiting cautiously until Léon had finished reading it. Léon sensed her anxiety and could not help but be irritated by such overt displays of concern, which undermined the untroubled facade he had been try-ing to maintain for both their sakes—and for others as well, since he knew that any potential scandal in his domestic life would have re-verberations within his political circle and beyond. For over a week, Léon had spent much of each day standing by the window, looking out onto the street, waiting for signs of a disaster.

That Sunday morning something compelled Marthe to turn im-mediately to page 3 in the newspapers, where the *faits divers*, those brief news items that veered wildly between gruesome and fanciful, were to be found. One item in particular caught her eye, and she showed the piece to Léon, convinced that it described their son: "A young man, appearing to be in his twenties, placed a bullet in his head in a taxi on the boulevard Magenta. Serious condition. At Lariboisière."

Léon preferred to believe otherwise: surely their son could never be mistaken for a man in his twenties! But Marthe's fears would not be allayed, and she quietly cut out the piece and slipped it into an en-velope with a note addressed to their family doctor, Lucien Bernard, asking him to go to the hospital and gather information about the wounded young man. Later that day, as Léon and Marthe were meet-ing with a private detective, the doctor arrived. Taking in his pale, drawn face, Marthe knew immediately that her son was dead. She uttered a hoarse, guttural cry and slumped to the floor. Léon stood in silent disbelief.

Dr. Bernard quickly told them what information he had gath-ered about the circumstances surrounding Philippe's death. Philippe had been brought to the hospital by a taxi driver named Bajot, who told police that he had picked up the boy at the place de la Bastille. Philippe wanted to be taken to the Médrano circus, located in Mont-martre. Bajot heard the shot, which at first he mistook for the sound of a blown tire, at approximately four-thirty p.m., as they were arriv-ing at the top of the rue de Maubeuge. The driver, accompanied by a policeman, took the bleeding boy to the hospital, where he died at six p.m., having never regained consciousness.

First, Léon went to the hospital to identify his son's body for himself. When he returned home, he confirmed what Dr. Bernard had told them. Marthe, unwilling to believe the awful truth, in-sisted on viewing the body herself the next day, writing afterward to her mother, "I just saw my handsome Philippe . . . He still smiles a little. All is well. May God's will be done . . ." The funeral was set for Wednesday morning, November 28. Officially, the cause of death was spinal meningitis, but word was already spreading of a darker cause. Lucien Daudet, Léon's younger brother, told Abbé Mugnier, a Catholic priest who acted as a kind of confessor to the rich and mighty, that Philippe's suicide was the inevitable consequence of an entire line of conduct. "Nothing good ever came out of hatred," Lucien declared. He had never warmed to his brother's politics, finding the rhetoric of the Action Française coarse and hateful and its actions thuggish. Despite the rumors, Dr. Bernard was able to obtain a certificate affirming that Philippe was not responsible for his act, which allowed the family to have a Christian service at St. Thomas Aquinas, followed by burial at Père Lachaise Cemetery. On a bone-chilling day, when rain and snow swirled around the mourners, Léon marched up the rue de la Roquette, which leads from the place de la Bastille to the cemetery, just as he had done twenty-six years earlier for the funeral procession of his father. As he staggered behind the coffin, eyes fixed on the white shroud laden with white flowers, Léon felt a particular sense of pride piercing through the desolate sadness—pride at the sight of the *camelots du roi* serving as pallbearers, carrying their fallen comrade to his final resting place, their tricolor armbands a reminder of an ideal that meant more to them than all else.

On Saturday, December 1, Marthe was resting in her room after lunch when the doorbell rang. It was the mailman with a registered letter sent by Georges Vidal, administrator of the *Libertaire*, one of the primary anarchist newspapers in Paris. She stood by the window reading the note, in which Vidal informed her that her son had sought him out in the hopes of making an anarchist attack. "Believe me, Madame," he wrote, "that it is profoundly upsetting for me to mix politics and tears, but I could not act otherwise. The few days that I spent with Philippe made me love him, and I too would have preferred to cry without noise." In her memoir about Philippe's death, Marthe would later recall that as she read those vile words she had "the physical sensation that a hyena had just sneaked up and that it was trying to devour the body of my son." She ran to Léon's office and threw the letter on the table before him, declaring, "They killed him!"

That same day the *Libertaire* published an article entitled "Léon Daudet Smothers the Truth," detailing their alleged encounter with Philippe and announcing to the world that the son of France's most famed and feared royalist was, in fact, a committed anarchist, willing to sacrifice his own father to make a strike for the cause. In the article they accused Léon of being a tyrant. They also published a copy of a letter that Philippe had left for his parents:

> *My dear mother,*
> *Forgive me for the pain that I cause you. I have been an anarchist for some time without daring to say it; now the cause has called me and I believe that it is my duty to do what I am doing. I love you very much. Kiss the children for me.*
> *Philippe*

There was no allusion to Léon in this letter.

Léon reacted first with disbelief, then with rage. But there was something else, too. Relief. Comprehension. The suicide of his son was not something that made sense. But this, murder, revenge—it was the sort of thing he understood best. Religious faith, solid and unshakable, was the only thing, he felt, that kept one from having the sort of nihilistic—*"macbethéenne,"* as he called it—view of life: "A tale told by an idiot, full of sound and fury, signifying nothing." But if this senseless death of his son was bound up in the power struggles that had defined Léon's adult life, then it was another matter altogether. If the anarchists were involved, then surely so were the Germans, the Jews, the Freemasons, and the police. If Philippe was killed as a way of getting at his father, then Léon would find a way to avenge his son's death.

In the days that followed the realization that Philippe was dead, Léon and Marthe had wandered around their house listlessly, but now they sprung into action. On December 2 an article in the *Action Française* announced, "An Atrocious Revenge: Philippe Daudet Has Been Murdered." By whom? German agents, of course, eager to strike a blow against France by attacking the Action Française. The next day, Léon entered a formal complaint with the public prosecutor claiming that "corruption of a minor" and murder had occurred. Judge Barnaud was immediately charged with the investigation and the *"Affaire Philippe Daudet"* began in earnest.

A few years later, Léon recalled, "In the greatest sadness of my life, the murder of our good little boy Philippe, I remained, for many long months, inaccessible to physical beauty, to color, to all aspects of art and nature. There was inside of me a vast 'emptiness,' a sort of retreat from all that was not the injured soul." It seemed to him that nothing else would ever be as important as discovering the truth about his son's death and proclaiming it to the world. The first order of business was to reconstruct those four days between the time Philippe left his parents' home and his death in the taxicab. Court-appointed investigators determined that Philippe had left his home as usual on the morning of Tuesday, November 20, but instead of going to school, he had headed to the Saint-Lazare train station, where he boarded a train for Le Havre, a busy port town on the Atlantic and a gateway to the world beyond France. He checked into the Hôtel Bellevue under the name of Pierre Bouchamp, claiming to be an electrician and paying eight francs a day for his room. According to witnesses, he spoke of his wish to travel to Canada, but he did not have enough money to book a passage across the Atlantic, and without proper identification papers or any real skills he was unable to find work to pay his way. At a loss, the boy spent his remaining time in Le Havre holed up in his hotel room, smoking heavily, reading, and writing. Among the items he left behind when he finally checked out of the hotel a few days later were fragments of a letter he had attempted to write to his parents. The letter read:

My dearest parents,
Pardon, oh forgive me for the immense pain that I caused you. I am nothing more than a miserable thing, and a thief. But I hope that my repentance will erase this stain. I am returning to you the money that I haven't spent and I beseech you to forgive me. By the time you receive this letter, I will no longer be living.
Adieu, I love you more than anything.
Your desperate child

Philippe
Kiss Claire and François for me, but never tell them that their brother was a thief.

Philippe's erratic behavior only intensified once he returned to Paris on November 22. Upon exiting the Saint-Lazare train station, he was not fifty meters from the offices of the Action Française on the rue de Rome, where his father and his father's friends would be waiting to take him home, scolding him fondly for his prank. But instead of entering that familiar edifice, he hailed a taxi and sped over to the offices of the anarchist review *Le Libertaire*, where he found one of its editors, twenty-year-old Georges Vidal, a thin young man with the sort of pale, gaunt face, wire spectacles, and long hair that marked him instantly as a bohemian and intellectual. According to Vidal, who was interrogated at great length by the police, Philippe declared himself a follower of anarchist ideas and asked if there was anyone in particular the anarchists would like eliminated—Poincaré, Millerand, maybe Léon Daudet? Vidal, hardly the bomb-throwing type, tried to dissuade the young visitor, who had not revealed his true identity, from harboring such thoughts.

Philippe's new anarchist friends invited him to join them for dinner at a neighboring restaurant, Au Rendez-vous du Garage. Then he attended a meeting for anarchist youth on the rue de Bretagne with Vidal and nineteen-year-old Jean Gruffy, a painter and designer. When the meeting ended at around midnight, Philippe, who claimed he had no place to stay, went back with Gruffy to his tiny apartment in Montmartre. Gruffy later told reporters that, although the stranger appeared to be calm, before going to bed in the adjoining room he asked Jean where the best means of exit was "in case the police come." The next day, Philippe confessed that he had come from Le Havre "to kill Léon Daudet," repeating this last phrase twice before continuing, "If I can't have Léon Daudet, I want Maurras or Réal del Sartre . . ." Philippe confided that his father beat and punished him too harshly, that he wanted to escape, that he wanted revenge. "I left my parents' home," Philippe reportedly told him, "because I wanted to live my life and to have the freedom to think as I like." Investigators who later examined Gruffy's lodgings found Philippe's sack, containing a shirt, two detachable collars, a blank notebook, and a pair of leggings.

The next day, Friday, Philippe went out in search of a gun. He then paid a visit to the explorer Louis-Frédéric Rouquette, whose writings on Alaska and the Northwest Territories of Canada in works like *The Great White Silence* (and his work as editor of the review *France-Islam*) captured the imagination of schoolboys everywhere. Philippe explained that he wanted information about Canada, Alaska, and polar regions, and confessed his own desire to explore. Rouquette was kind, but did not offer the boy any encouragement. This was not the first young man with adventure in his heart and a few francs in his pocket who had approached him about joining the ranks of those heroes of the newspapers—Scott, Charcot, Shackleton—but Rouquette had no wish to encourage such folly. Later that day Philippe returned to the *Libertaire* and handed Vidal a sheaf of poems and a sealed letter that Vidal was to open if anything should happen to him. Among the poems—derivative, moony musings reflecting the timeless adolescent yearning for self-determination—was one called "Départ." It included the lines: "My soul thrills with pleasure at the idea of all that it will taste . . . No one will understand why I have left. No one will guess the sentiments that drove me . . . Like a bird on its first flight, I will leave for faraway lands, new sentiments and adventure." Unfortunately, those dreams of exotic adventures would never materialize for Philippe.

The next morning—Saturday, November 24—Philippe visited the bookshop of another anarchist, Pierre Le Flaoutter, at 46, boulevard Beaumarchais, near the Bastille, where he asked for Baudelaire's *Les Fleurs du Mal.* Philippe appeared breathless and fitful, as if pre-occupied with something, and Le Flaoutter encouraged him to tell him what was on his mind. Philippe told the bookseller that he had come from the provinces to "strike a blow" and that he planned to murder an important political figure, perhaps Poincaré, Millerand, or Léon Daudet. Le Flaoutter, who was also a police informer, first attempted to dissuade the boy and then, thinking Philippe's confession might be a setup, passed the information along to his superiors at the Sûreté. They were sufficiently concerned by the story to send several policemen to keep watch at the bookstore and wait for the potentially dangerous criminal who had so brazenly declared his intent to commit violence. The winter afternoon deepened into evening, but their target did not reappear.

A few blocks away, at a little before half past four, a young boy, tall and sturdy, hailed a taxi and asked to be driven to the Médrano circus. The driver, named Bajot, turned his vehicle down the boulevard Beaumarchais, past Le Flaoutter's shop and toward the boulevard Magenta. As he was nearing the Gare du Nord, Bajot heard a crack like a blowout. He quickly peered into the cab and saw his passenger slump over, bleeding profusely from a wound in his head. He stopped, got out to check on the boy, and found a policeman who drove with him to the Lariboisière hospital. The boy died there without ever regaining consciousness.

This, in any case, was the version of events that the judge accepted, after a long and exhaustive investigation, after the body had been exhumed and minutely examined by the doctors Paul, Socquet, and Balthazard, and after the police's efforts to find clues—at the offices of the *Libertaire* (9, rue Louis-Blanc) and at the home of M. Georges Vidal (6, passage de Clichy)—resulted in nothing. Léon and his friends at the Action Française meanwhile sought proof that Philippe had been murdered, discovering so-called "witnesses" to the crime (all of whom were later discredited) and brandishing "evidence" of various conspiracies and cover-ups in the headlines of their newspaper and in the meetings they held throughout the city. Philippe, they insisted, had been trying to infiltrate the anarchists in the hopes of exposing their criminal activities. When the police discovered this, they allowed their informant Le Flaoutter to lure him to the bookshop with the promise of assistance and a gun, and then cornered the boy. The plan had been to frame Philippe, and thereby to threaten and undermine his father. But something went wrong—someone panicked or tempers flared—and Philippe was shot, put into a taxi, and later "found" as a suicide. Or had it been one of the police subordinates who deliberately shot Philippe? Or had it been someone else? Given the number of enemies the Action Française and Léon in particular had made over the years, the possibilities were truly endless. Where others might have seen a far-fetched story strung out of coincidences, Léon saw in this narrative of conspiracy and corruption a dramatic confirmation of his suspicions and his politics. From the first months in 1924, Léon started going after Bajot, hounding the taxi driver in increasingly violent articles in *Action Française*, accusing him of bearing false witness. If he could get Bajot to crack, Léon was sure that the real culprits could no longer remain in obscurity.

Throughout the investigation, whose every new development was splashed across the pages of newspapers and shouted above the din of cars and trams by vendors on street corners, the question of politics was, unsurprisingly, never far from the headlines. The ins and outs of the case were dissected at dinner tables and in cafés throughout France. When Léon decided that the wheels of justice were spinning too slowly, that his impassioned pleas in his newspaper columns were not being heeded, he took his fight for the truth to the Chamber of Deputies, where he had been a member since 1919 and where, in March 1924, he introduced his charges that the suicide was merely a cover-up for murder. But for many observers, this was just another Daudet stunt. As the left-wing newspaper *L'Humanité* reminded their readers, "M. Daudet has a particular taste for scandal. He seeks it out, he creates it, out of need. He thrives there." Apparently their readers—and the Parisian voters—agreed. In the May 1924 elections, Léon lost his seat as a deputy representing Paris. Léon was disappointed, of course—outraged, really—but even this political reversal seemed unimportant in comparison to the mystery of his son's death. He kept going at a frenzied pace, pouring all his anguish and frustration into his work. In quick succession he came out with four books, whose broadly ranging themes captured the voluble, quasi-incoherent nature of the author's intellectual interests: a novel with spiritual overtones, a medico-psychological study, a volume of literary criticism, and a political pamphlet dedicated to Philippe entitled *The Agony of the Regime.*

In January 1925, after eighteen months of being harassed and heckled by Léon and his friends, the taxi driver Bajot enlisted the help of a lawyer, Louis Noguères, to enter a suit of defamation before the correctional tribunal. When Bajot finally sued Léon for slander, he gave the grieving father exactly what he wanted: his day in court. The defamation trial began on October 26, 1925, and included nineteen sessions in total, with well over a hundred witnesses. Léon was determined that the defamation charges would be a secondary component of the trial, which he hoped would allow him to prove, once and for all, that his son had indeed been murdered. The anger and confusion of the past two years seemed to have reached a point of combustion on the opening day of the trial. The atmosphere in the courtroom was acrid and angry, and Léon had the sense that he was experiencing "the hottest and most bitter battle" of his life. Each day, drawings of the witnesses appeared in the newspapers: lanky, pensive Georges Vidal; the valet from the Hôtel Bellevue in Le Havre, whose wounds from the war had left him with an "extreme emotionalism" that perhaps explained the connection he felt with the strange young man with a "lost air" who had stayed briefly at his hotel. Cross-examinations occasionally descended into scuffles, and witnesses were frequently reduced to tears.

But perhaps the most outlandish moment of the trial came with the announcement that one of the sessions would take place at Le Flaoutter's former bookstore. The objective, Léon's legal team insisted, was to discover whether or not a revolver shot from the basement of the bookstore could be heard at the loge of the concierge or in another part of the house. It was an unprecedented decision. So, on the afternoon of October 30, the participants in the trial—from the plaintiff and defendant to the seven witnesses, thirteen jury members, lawyers, and judges—took taxis over to the bookstore at 46, boulevard Beaumarchais. They huddled around in the chilly dusk, the lawyers' robes flapping quietly in the breeze. The principal players descended the great stairs of the Palais de Justice and got into awaiting cars as an enormous crowd looked on. First came Léon, accompanied by his brother-in-law and two friends, then the magistrates in red robes and the clerk carrying a voluminous dossier, and finally two bailiffs in black robes, followed by the lawyers and the members of the jury. Photographers and cameramen took their positions in anticipation of capturing this historic moment. The new owner of the bookstore, Mme Arfeuil, quickly set out a display of books in the hopes of making a windfall from the throngs. There was also a display of postcards of famous military figures, artists, and politicians . . . including Léon Daudet. Léon himself stepped in to take part in a reenactment. Not surprisingly, the re-creation did not make things any clearer.

Finally it was time for Bajot's lawyer, forty-four-year-old Louis Noguères, to make his concluding remarks. Knowing that he would have to do more than merely remind the jury of the facts if he was going to pierce the hothouse emotionalism of Léon's theatrics, he decided to go down an unusual route. If Léon Daudet had the audacity to publicly impugn the character and good name of his client, an innocent taxi driver, a man without means, then Noguères would put Daudet's own conduct—his entire life, actually—on trial. As Léon sat there in the defendant's chair, Noguères described the difficulties the young Léon had faced watching his father's health fail, and how the latter's demise contributed to Léon's ongoing fear of heredity. He then turned to Léon's first marriage, and to its breakup amid revelations about Léon's violent temperament, a breakup which led to Léon's rupture with the republican circles of his youth and his turn toward reactionary figures then involved in anti-Dreyfusard campaigns. Noguères then analyzed the marriage of Léon to Marthe—he reminded the courtroom that they were first cousins—who initiated him into royalist circles and who was herself as much of a devotee of extreme royalist notions as her husband, if not more of one. This was not, Noguères insisted, the ideal or even the typical French family. This was a family in whose blood politics coursed, a family where everything was subordinated to a reactionary, often violent, cause. Leading the family was Léon, a man whose lyricism frequently veered into fanaticism and whose imaginative leaps were harmless enough in his works of middling fiction, but were enormously destructive in real life. Léon's warped mind transformed ordinary men and women into devious criminals. And so Philippe Daudet's dissociative fugue states could be seen not merely as epileptic manifestations—although yes, Noguères insisted, the boy *did* suffer from epilepsy—but also as a search for peace and calm, an escape from life with one of the most combative and vigorous polemicists of the day.

This line of argument was breathtaking in the sheer scope and scale of its accusations. Léon sputtered and fumed and looked ready to explode, but Noguères was not close to being finished. Again and again Noguères returned to the idea that the real culprit in the case was the Daudet family and their sordid history. This was, he argued, a family trapped by heredity. To see evidence of this, one only needed to turn to Léon's own writing, which was so heavily influenced by the lingering illness of his father. In works like *L'Hérédo* and *Le Monde des Images*, Léon had sought to refute prevailing assumptions that heredity was inescapable. Instead, these works introduce the notion of a "moi" bounded by the laws of heredity but offset by the "soi," which was a freestanding and independent part of human identity. Even inherited pathology might be overcome in Léon's theory, since one parent's healthy blood may balance out the impurities of the other parent. And yet if Philippe had been driven to suicide, Noguères contended, the reason most likely lay in his family medical history. To underscore his point, Noguères turned to an account in the published journal of Jules Renard of an 1891 encounter with Alphonse Daudet, in which the latter spoke of his fears that his children would inherit his sickness. The effects of this tainted lineage could only have been encouraged by the fact that Philippe was the product of a marriage of two first cousins—Léon and Marthe. The court should not be surprised, Noguères continued, that Léon did not wish to admit that Philippe had committed suicide. That would be tantamount to admitting that his son had been contaminated by the illness of Alphonse Daudet, which meant admitting that he was as well.

In their great effort to hide the troubles of the family, Noguères charged, Léon and Marthe had created a story of political intrigue that all but eclipsed the most important person in this whole sad affair: their son. Philippe was not, Noguères maintained, simply the favored son of a distinguished and famous family, an enthusiastic champion of his father's political activities, an ardent royalist-in-training. Nor was he merely a committed anarchist. He was, first and foremost, a mentally unbalanced boy, whose wandering episodes and penchant for violence—against himself and others—could easily be explained as a by-product of the epilepsy from which he suffered and the violent, ideological world of the Action Française in which he grew up. The only real mystery, the lawyer declared, was why on earth Léon and Marthe told no one when their son went missing, and how they could have gone about their usual business: Léon writing his diatribes against the government, Marthe writing a newspaper advice column on the perils of aging. Finally, Louis Noguères turned to the members of the jury and implored that they recall that the suicide of Philippe did not, must not, allow the boy's father to attack and dishonor innocent bystanders.

On November 14, 1925, the final day of the trial, the courtroom was packed, and feverish throngs of people at the doors strained to squeeze in. Many of them had been waiting for hours outside in the damp foggy cold. Before the jury was excused to deliberate, the defense had a last opportunity to make its case. Then Léon rose and begged the court to forget his political, literary, or philosophical roles. Only one thing counted in life: "natural sentiments," of which he had many. He explained,

> I loved my father passionately. I was his cane in old age. I was the confidant of his intimate thoughts. It was he who taught me all that I know, it was he who made me who I am. He called me his little brother, and this friendship, at once filial and fraternal, I hold above everything else, except for faith and nation. What my father did for me, my dream was to do it for my Philippe. The fates did not wish it to be so.

"You are justice," he implored. "Forget everything, only see before you a devastated father." He next addressed the claims that heredity played a factor in Philippe's death. Based on his own medical expertise, he insisted that a man could redeem himself from the sin of heredity. Heredity had not killed his son. Georges Claretie of *Le Figaro* declared that he had never before heard anything more poignant in the courthouse. The entire room fell silent at the sight of the devastated man and the sound of his trembling, sobbing voice. There was not a dry eye in the room.

But it was apparently difficult to ignore the lack of solid evidence in Léon's favor, for, after two long hours on the evening of November 14, 1925, the jury returned with guilty verdicts on all counts. Then the judge read the sentence against Léon: five months' imprisonment and a 1,500-franc fine. Joseph Delest, the business manager of *Action Française*, was sentenced to two months' imprisonment and a 300-franc fine; both men were ordered to pay Bajot joint damages of 35,000 francs. Suddenly there was a cry, "Long live Daudet!" and the crowd in the courtroom rushed toward him. The calls continued out into the street, where the crowd grew to be so large that it prevented trams from passing.

And so the Philippe Daudet Affair came to a conclusion, after two years of instigating the kind of public interest and political debate that France had not seen since the heady days of the Dreyfus Affair. Many observers breathed a heavy sigh of relief that the drama was finally over. But for the Daudets and their supporters, this miscarriage of justice was just further confirmation that their country had been hijacked by amoral forces. Others saw only the human tragedy in the chain of events. Georges Claretie, who had been following the case, wondered if the simple taxi driver would understand the "greatness and the tragic beauty" of this father fighting for his son, noting how magnificent Léon was during his testimony, eloquent and ardent, by turns violent and ironic, dominating the tumult, filling the room with his great voice, responding to the insults addressed to him, all while holding back tears. "What a handsome fighter and in what a fight! A father for his son! There is no greater drama!" *Le Figaro* also published an open letter protesting the Action Française leader's imprisonment, signed by such literary luminaries as Paul Bourget, Anna de Noailles, Paul Valéry, and even his old enemy Henri Bernstein.

With the death of Philippe, the very idea that family is sacred— a cornerstone of Léon's whole conception of what French society ought to be—was destroyed. He was fighting to save his family, but it was also the fight for a specific idea of family, in which sons revere and worship their fathers, and fathers bestow patronage and life lessons upon their sons. But even in the midst of his personal defeat, Léon could not help but continue fighting for his political convictions. On June 9, 1927, instead of turning himself in at the Santé prison, Léon, along with Joseph Delest, barricaded himself in the *Action Française* offices on the rue de Rome. In so doing he hoped to inspire the sympathy and outrage of the French public, but it aroused their amusement instead. Huge crowds gathered outside the offices, blocking traffic and confounding police and government officials. At dawn on June 13, after three days of siege, the prefect of police appealed to Daudet's high principles as a Frenchman to avoid the shedding of French blood. Daudet patriotically agreed, and he and Delest, along with the pale, hairy *camelots* who had been guarding them, emerged and were driven off to serve their prison terms in the Santé. Less than two weeks later, on June 25, the *camelots* managed to trick the director of the Santé into releasing Daudet and Delest. They hid in a fifteenth-century château outside Paris for a time and then, with Mme Daudet, slipped across the border into Belgium, where they lived in a suburb of Brussels for two and a half years. But even while in Belgium, Léon's thoughts were never far from his beloved Paris. He wrote a topographical diary of the city he knew, traveling from neighborhood to neighborhood, explaining the events and experiences he had at each place. He would not return to the city until 1930, when he was sixty-two years old.

If Léon's theory about Philippe's murder always seemed improbable, the explanation of suicide nonetheless still left some questions unanswered. First, there was the missing bullet that killed Philippe and left no trace on the wall of the taxi; the cartridge ejected by the revolver was only found six days later. There were other inconsistencies, too. When Philippe had left home, his clothes had been carefully labeled; yet the labels had been removed by the time he died. Had he removed the tags himself or had someone else? Why had so many police been mobilized on the basis of some youthful crackpot's threats? And how had they all managed to miss their target? As *L'Humanité* observed, "If judicially, the Philippe Daudet affair is closed, mysterious aspects are still unexplained. The child's death remains an historical enigma."

There was yet another expert who weighed in on the Philippe Daudet Affair. In 1924 Sigmund Freud received a manuscript about Léon entitled *The Obsessed: A Drama of the Libido*. It was written by a former colleague of Léon's from the Action Française named André Gaucher, who had since taken an extremely critical stance against his former friend and colleague. In the book Gaucher doggedly pursued the hereditary thesis to explain both Philippe's suicide and Léon's obsessive fixation on it, citing the medical authority of Pierre Janet, a pioneering psychologist and former student of Jean-Martin Charcot. When it was finally published, *The Obsessed* also included Freud's response in two letters. In the first letter, he praised Gaucher's essay as "so rich in ideas" and written "in a stunning style," and remarked that during his several months in Paris, he had the opportunity of often seeing Léon at the Charcot residence. "He was then the inseparable friend of young Charcot and the father referred to him as 'the little Tartarin.'" But in a second letter, sent to Gaucher on June 10, 1925, shortly before the publication date of *The Obsessed*, Freud added some qualifications to his initial praise of Gaucher's work. While he agreed that, since the work of the renowned syphilis expert Fournier, it had become accepted that advanced syphilis in a parent can create a host of complications, including psychological ones, in the offspring, he nonetheless felt that Gaucher's argument was oversimplified in its attempt to explain everything by Léon's obsession with heredity and love of his father. Perhaps Freud was thinking of his former teacher's favorite saying—"Theory is fine, but that doesn't prevent facts from existing." One could speculate endlessly about the reasons why Philippe had killed himself, or one could simply acknowledge that sometimes sons lose their way.

ELEVEN

The Final Voyage

Everything is calm. We are going to leave this morning after having received the weather report . . . We are going to leave. What
will this crossing be like?   —Jean-Baptiste Charcot (1936)

───◁▷───

Jean-Baptiste paused and looked up from the letter he was writing
to his secretary. It was seven-thirty a.m., September 15, 1936. His
cabin was perhaps the only place on board that wasn't abuzz with
activity. The *Pourquoi-Pas?* would set off from Reykjavík at one p.m.
for Copenhagen, and all were busy preparing. "What, indeed, will
this crossing be like?" Jean-Baptiste mused. Though everything was
calm, it was the kind of eerie, unsettling calm that masked turbulent
waters underneath. For months now he had felt that something was
going to happen. He could not explain why. Was it a premonition?
A gut feeling? He was not afraid, exactly. But it did weigh on him,
making even the most seemingly trivial interactions with those he
knew feel fraught with meaning.

He had a feeling that this trip would be his last. As he had observed to his friends, the *Pourqoui-Pas?* was aging, and so was he.
But it was about more than just old age. Increasingly, Jean-Baptiste,
now sixty-nine years old, felt as if his voyages were becoming obso-
lete. The world had changed, and no one cared about an old man and
his old boat. The world's attention was drawn elsewhere: to Moscow

and Spain, to film stars, and to fanatical dictators marshaling the powers of new technology in terrifying new ways. Yet Charcot had little patience for this world, with its feuding politicians and angry workers, where men seemed driven to destroy one another with ever greater intensity. In the months before his departure, he could not shake the impression that ominous forces were at work. In March, Hitler stunned the world by violating the Versailles Treaty and reoccupying the Rhineland, and civil war seemed inevitable in Spain. Jean-Baptiste was also deeply distressed by the social unrest in France as violent internal political passions and partisan battles drew his countrymen's attention away from exterior perils. The very events and debates that gave Léon's days a sense of purpose and energy felt foreign and jarring to Jean-Baptiste. Complaining to Brian Roberts, from the English expedition to Graham Land in Antarctica, Jean-Baptiste wrote, "I suppose that you have access to the newspapers, etc., and that you are informed about the agonizing situation in Europe . . . Politicians ought to spend a few winters in Antarctica! It would also be beneficial for most of my compatriots to go there as well, and for many of them to remain there!" The joy and excitement he usually felt before a voyage were saturated by this sense of foreboding. And in letters to friends and colleagues, he exhibited a dark conviction of the probability of his own imminent demise. "If I am still alive . . ." was a frequent refrain. And again, to another young explorer, Fred Matter, Jean-Baptiste wondered what would happen to "Poor France."

> God knows that I, grandson of workers, having worked all my life in a manner disinterested, almost ashamed of the small fortune coming from the work and the value of my father, I sympathize with the people, and want to see everyone happy! But a wind of madness blows through all of the classes of Frenchmen, who are no longer French, furthermore. They all struggle for their own particular interests; two sentiments dominate everything: egoism and heinous jealousy. They all want happiness—which is natural, and believe that they will find it in the satisfaction of their appetites. It is however so simple to achieve through mutual esteem, with the ideal of service, with

Honor, and Country . . . I loved my country to the point of frenzy . . . I had for her such an adoration, such an admiring esteem that I believed that one could only be worthy of serving her in following the path of honor, morally and materially . . .

He ended with a small, soft lament for his own fate:

In three weeks, I will go out again on the old ship: I will attempt to aid your ex-camarades, all in hoping that it will not be to the detriment of the personal work of my own crew. It will probably be my last voyage: the PP is getting old, me too, and then above all, the world doesn't give a hoot and my last resources are exhausted.

That sense of exhaustion was particularly acute on the morning of September 15, as Jean-Baptiste slowly finished the letter and addressed it for the post—his last letter back home before the ship's departure. And a few hours later, as the *Pourquoi-Pas?* slowly glided out of the port of Reykjavík, Jean-Baptiste turned back to observe the comforting silhouette of the city, the light-colored buildings, squat and low and trimmed with black. He had come to love this country and its people, with their steely, frank appreciation of the world around them, born out of the irrefutable reality that they were alone out there in the middle of a raging ocean. Yes, this is why Jean-Baptiste loved them—a people that understood and acknowledged their dependence on the seas and oceans that surrounded their tiny island.

He took one last look at the quietly receding horizon of Iceland. Everything seemed calm. He sighed and returned to his cabin to work. Perhaps, he thought fretfully, he was just tired after a summer spent in these Arctic waters. They had always been dangerous—that very summer the North Atlantic had been a perpetual tempest, which had caused numerous wrecks. Yet even this tumult was deceptive, for, as if to compensate, the ice floe that had encircled the coast had disappeared almost completely, something that seasoned Greenland experts had never before experienced. So Jean-Baptiste and his crew had found themselves in the strange position of being able to navigate in zones previously thought to be impenetrable. For weeks on end they had glided deep into silent fjords, weaving in and out of icebergs so hulking and massive and immutable that they forgot the squalls and spray of the passage over, forgot the moments when, through the din of rattling pans and straining beams, through the bitter, churning sensation of bile rising up in their throats, they cursed whatever folly had enticed them to venture so far into that inhospitable drink. This most recent trip to Greenland was thus a strange mixture of discovery and disappointment, risk and inaction.

For Jean-Baptiste the past decade spent in these northern waters had been particularly turbulent, with the usual elation of exploring new places and making new discoveries constantly tinged with the shadow of disaster. It had been that way since his first summer there in 1925, almost eleven years earlier, when the Norwegian explorer Roald Amundsen—perhaps the single greatest living explorer in the world—had gone missing. Amundsen and his crew had taken off by plane—the latest rage in polar exploration—from Spitsbergen on May 21, in an attempt to be the first to fly over the North Pole in a hydroplane. Soon after, he disappeared. As he had when Otto Nordenskjöld was declared missing in 1903, Jean-Baptiste offered his services in search of a fellow explorer.

In 1925 Jean-Baptiste was almost sixty and had already begun to sense himself fading into obsolescence. Of course he was still quite active, traveling to international conferences and giving lectures around the country for colleagues and for the interested public. By all accounts he was an excellent public speaker. He would stride up and down the stage, recounting all that he had seen and experienced, while behind him giant black-and-white projections of images of icebergs and penguins chased his words, thrilling the audience. Sometimes these presentations were so full of people that he had difficulty getting to the front of whatever smoke-filled meeting room or town concert hall he happened to find himself in. On Sundays he tried to stay at home, where, as his father had done on Tuesdays before, he and Meg received friends and admirers. The gaiety of the family, the work involved in presiding over the Yacht Club of Paris and in leading shorter teaching and scientific expeditions in the English Channel, the North Sea, and the North Atlantic—all this would have kept many a man occupied. But he was still restless with the kind of nervous energy that had years earlier pushed fellow explorer Robert Scott to insist to him that his own upcoming marriage "does not stop my plans for my work . . . which is as well, for I tire of this life of regularity."

So in the summer of 1925, when his offer of assistance in the search for Amundsen was accepted by the minister of the marine, Jean-Baptiste eagerly gathered together a crew and set off for Arctic waters to do what he knew best. En route, the *Pourquoi-Pas?* received a cable that Amundsen and his crew had been miraculously found by a seal hunter; they were given new instructions, and their mission became one of navigation and geography, limited primarily to Iceland and the nearby island of Jan Mayen. Upon arriving at Jan Mayen, Jean-Baptiste and his men were told that a Danish expedition had gone deep into Scoresby Sund, a massive fjord cut into the eastern coast of Greenland, and had not been heard from in some time. Here was another chance at a rescue mission, so Jean-Baptiste decided to disobey his orders—much to the delight of his adventure-hungry sailors—and go in search of the missing Danes. They set sail for the eastern coast of Greenland, and at midnight on July 31, Jean-Baptiste finally saw once more the icebergs that he had not seen in years. In his delight he scampered up the crow's nest like a young man half his age, staring deeply at the proud, hulking masses standing in silent sentry on either side of his ship. He had forgotten what it felt like to behold these figures—they simply took his breath away. For the next twenty-eight hours, the *Pourquoi-Pas?* patiently pushed its way through the ice pack, slipping in and out of the fog in utter silence. Jean-Baptiste was again struck by how very small men and their ships are. When the fog finally lifted, the crew was greeted with a beautiful sight: a horizon of rose-and-gold-tipped mountains, dusted with snow, appeared before them. Greenland had revealed herself to them in all her splendor.

"Do you believe in God, Commander?" one of his sailors asked him quietly.

"Yes!" Jean-Baptiste replied. "But above all in moments like this."

As they entered the bay of Rosenvinge, they saw a large house still under construction and several smaller, scattered cabins. Six hairy men appeared at the door: they had found the Danish expedition members. Their leader, Bjerring Petersen, had died of scurvy, and he had been the only one who knew Morse code. After putting them in contact with a Danish ship that would come and fetch them, the *Pourquoi-Pas?* gave the Danes some champagne and cigarettes and then headed off toward Jameson Land, some twenty miles from the station, to gather fossils before heading back toward Iceland and arriving in Reykjavík on August 5.

It was the first time that a French vessel had arrived at the majestic east coast of Greenland. Jean-Baptiste found his brief time in Greenland that summer intoxicating, and for the next decade he would return often in the summer to explore. Greenland, the largest island in the world, so close to the North Pole, had never been a welcoming place for humans. A vast and inhospitable desert of ice and snow covers much of the landmass, and a dense belt of pack ice hugs its eastern coastline. Most of the Eskimos who lived there did so along the fjords of the southwest area of the mainland. Scoresby Sund, the largest fjord in the entire world, sits like a gash in the eastern side of the island: starting off as an arm of the sea, it then divides into two branches that further multiply into four secondary fjords. From year to year, Jean-Baptiste and other explorers could never predict what conditions would be like in the fjords and canals—one year the waters could be cold and clear as far as the eye could see, an uninterrupted mirrorlike surface, while the next year they could be congested with sheets of ice, punctuated by craggy ice formations, like smashed-up fists. Much depended merely on the will of the waves, the wind, the ice. Navigating it was the sort of challenge that required both daring and technical experience—the sort of challenge that Jean-Baptiste loved. They moved down narrow, sinuous canals of water surrounded by soaring, icy mountains that seemed to reach the sky. While Antarctica was almost uninterrupted ice and snow, so cold and remote as to feel almost alien, the banks of the fjords in Greenland seemed less hostile, revealing turbid, springy tundra straining for the first beams of the sun that rose behind the reddish-brown mountains as icebergs cast long, angular shadows. Jean-Baptiste had become very attached to this immense and dangerous coastline, with its grandiose demeanor and difficult access. And for ten years, he pushed himself and his boat through these punishing, choppy waters, training younger sailors, conducting scientific research.

Even back then—ten years ago, Jean-Baptiste thought now, as his ship pulled away from the Reykjavík port on the morning of September 15, 1936—things were changing. When Shackleton had emerged from his death-defying expedition on the *Endurance* in 1917, he had, naturally, been hailed as a hero. But the dangers and sacrifices of his expedition had been dwarfed by tales of the war. Since then, a new generation of explorers—led by the indomitable Amundsen—had taken to the sky, as if trying to sail above the land that had produced such horrible memories. The present and future lay in airplanes, which could provide transportation at much greater speed, at altitudes from which one could see great distances. They were capable of landing on snow, ice, and water. In short, they were the key to resolving many of the mysteries that still remained about the poles and the darkly uninhabitable land that surrounded them.

Together with Fridtjof Nansen, Amundsen had made Norway the birthplace of the greatest polar adventurers. While Nansen had gained fame for his heroic 1888 ski trip across Greenland and later his brash—and brilliant—winter on the *Fram* in the frozen ice pack of 1895, Amundsen initially garnered attention when, in 1903, he became the first man to sail through the Northwest Passage in his forty-seven-ton sloop. But he only truly gained worldwide fame as leader of the first expedition to reach the South Pole on December 14, 1911, at the age of thirty-nine, narrowly beating the famed British explorer Robert Scott. Amundsen had notoriously concealed his intention to make an attempt on the South Pole until he was already en route, informing Scott with a terse telegram of the new plans: "Beg leave to inform you *Fram* proceeding Antarctic. Amundsen." After recording some scientific data, Amundsen's team began their return journey on December 17 and arrived back at their base at the Bay of Whales on January 25, 1912. Scott, meanwhile, had reached the South Pole on January 17, only to see the Norwegian flag flying gaily where he had hoped to hoist the British one. "Great God! This is an awful place and terrible enough for us to have laboured to it without the reward of priority," Scott wrote in his journal that night, devastated by the realization that Amundsen had beaten his team to their goal. During a difficult return journey, Scott and all his men perished. As controversy raged over Scott's untimely death and Amundsen's questionable exploratory etiquette, Jean-Baptiste remained characteristically diplomatic. Assuming, he explained, that both reached the South Pole, the question of who arrived there first is of little importance. "If one wishes to pronounce one greater than the other, the preference must go to him who surrounds this magnificent result with the greatest number of discoveries and scientific observations."

For a time, after his return to Norway, Amundsen basked in the glory of his recent triumph, but soon he was thinking about what to do next. A fortuitous encounter with Lincoln Ellsworth, an adventure-hungry son of a wealthy American industrialist, solved his financial worries, and so Amundsen once again set his sights on the Arctic. Having sensed the shift away from sea exploration, Amundsen made his move toward air travel and, in May 1925, with Ellsworth, pilot Hjalmar Riiser-Larsen, and a small crew, attempted to become the first plane to fly from Spitsbergen, Norway, to the North Pole and then over to Alaska in the hope of discovering new land. Although the expedition ultimately failed—they made it to within 150 miles of the pole—it marked the first attempt to fly an airplane there. Newspapers around the world printed breathless articles about the small, heroic crew, which had flown over 120,000 square miles of previously unexplored territory. It was the northernmost latitude reached by a plane at that point in time. Amundsen was hooked.

In 1926 Amundsen and Ellsworth were at it again, this time with an airship called the *Norge* piloted by a slight, boyish forty-one-year-old Italian engineer named Umberto Nobile. Amundsen was now convinced that airships had a greater range than airplanes. They were more stable and safer, since repairs could be made in the air. The flight, which began on May 11 and flew from Kings Bay to Teller, Alaska, by way of the North Pole, lasted seventy hours, forty minutes. And while they were not the first to fly over "the top"—an American expedition led by Richard Byrd had just claimed to have reached the pole by airplane a few days before Amundsen's expedition was due to depart—they nonetheless claimed the honor of being the first to fly over the pole in a dirigible and having made the first crossing of the entire Polar Sea. It also made Amundsen the first person to have visited both the North and South poles.

But what should have been a heroic triumph for the three men—the trip was popularly referred to as the "Rome to Nome" flight—quickly descended into one of the more bitter feuds in the history of exploration. Nobile, egged on by his supporters in the Fascist government, was quick to claim as much credit for himself as he could, relegating Amundsen and Ellsworth to the role of passengers. The voyage had convinced the grizzled and taciturn Amundsen that the age of exploration that he had helped to define was now coming to a close, and when interviewed by reporters he frequently hinted that he would soon retire. For Nobile, on the other hand, the expedition only fueled his ambition to prove to the world what Italy and her people could do in long-distance flight. In this ambition he was enthusiastically supported by the Italian government, helmed by Benito Mussolini. So confident was Il Duce in this new mode of transportation that he declared that, thanks to air travel, "the most impenetrable continents will be opened to the knowledge of man, to the throbbing fervor of his traffic and to the intellectual and material exchange among peoples." And on Nobile's speaking tour of America, organized by the Fascist government, the young explorer repeatedly declared that Il Duce himself had originated the idea of the *Norge* flight.

And so it came as no surprise when, in 1928, Nobile announced his plan to mount a new expedition on the dirigible *Italia*, during which he planned to chart a little-known area north of Russia and Siberia, to examine the region between Prince Albert Land, Baffin Land, and the pole, and to remain several weeks anchored near the pole itself conducting scientific experiments. After departing on May 23 from Kings Bay, Nobile initially seemed destined for yet another success. The *Italia* hovered over the pole for a few hours—to mark the occasion, Nobile had his men wind up the gramophone in the cabin and play the Italian national anthem, while all the Italians held up their hands in the Fascist salute—before turning back. But strong winds slowed down the vessel, and unfortunately, the turbulence made it too bumpy for them to drink the champagne they had brought. And then disaster struck.

Unbeknownst to the giddy travelers, ice had begun to form on the envelope, the stabilizer planes, the rudders, and the propellers.

They were traveling at a height of 1,500 feet when suddenly the *Italia* became heavy and began an extremely rapid fall, striking the ice less than two minutes later. The cabin part of the structure was torn off and smashed, while the dirigible was carried rapidly away by the wind in an easterly direction. At the time of the crash, nine crew members—including Nobile—were in the main cabin gondola and were thrown onto the ice. One additional crew member was in the rear engine gondola and was also thrown to the ice, but was found dead. Six crew members were inside the envelope and disappeared when the envelope, relieved of the weight of the gondola, floated away in free flight.

When the *Italia* disappeared from radio contact, the entire world took notice, and the first massive air-sea rescue operation in the far north was launched. It took a dynamic turn when Roald Amundsen himself insisted that he be allowed to take part in an aerial expedition in search of the *Italia* crew. Amundsen's rescue mission left at four p.m. on the afternoon of June 18, bound for Spitsbergen. Ground control heard news again from the crew at six-forty-five p.m. Then there was silence. After twenty-four hours of silence, the mission's organizers had to consider that a new catastrophe had occurred: now four Frenchmen and two Norwegians could be added to those already missing. The rescue operation gained even greater urgency.

Jean-Baptiste had watched the developments from the sidelines with great anxiety. His offer to aid in the search for Nobile had initially been ignored, and he had felt the slight most keenly. Finally, after Amundsen's disappearance, his offer was accepted, but, much to his annoyance, he was placed under the command of the cruiser *Strasbourg*'s fifty-five-year-old commander, who treated him like a relic with little to nothing to offer. Although Jean-Baptiste attempted to find some humor in the situation, he was clearly put out by the condescension. The *Pourquoi-Pas?* left France on July 10 to the acclaim and applause of an enthusiastic local crowd. Jean-Baptiste insisted to reporters that he had every confidence that the men would be found: "With men like Amundsen and Dietrichson one is never lost on the ice floes." But privately he was less confident. "These people think that we are going to do something extraordinary," Jean-Baptiste wrote in his dairy, adding glumly, "I do not share their illusions."

So there he was, on another rescue mission, this time in search of Amundsen, as years earlier he had been for Nordenskjöld. Two of his former officers, Paul Pléneau, who had accompanied him in 1903–1905 in Antarctica, and Ernest Gourdon, who had taken part in both Antarctic expeditions as well as in two Arctic cruises, abandoned their current employment and demanded to join Jean-Baptiste's team, despite the hazards that another adventure could bring. As the *Pourquoi-Pas?* made its way to the spot where Amundsen and his crew were presumed to have gone missing, they met a shiphandler in Bergen, Norway, who gave them news that the *Italia* had finally been saved but that Amundsen, his French pilot René Guilbaud, and their crew were still lost. The shiphandler said something that struck Jean-Baptiste: "It is distressing about the youth, but for Amundsen who is old . . . it is a beautiful death!" he explained, adding for emphasis, "The old should know to go off when it is time!" Amundsen himself had said as much earlier that year, telling a journalist, "If only you knew how splendid it is up there, that's where I want to die." As for himself, Jean-Baptiste found the sentiment both true and terrifying. When, in late July, Jean-Baptiste and his crew were given orders to search the waters off the eastern coast of Greenland, he was gripped by an inexplicable wave of anxiety. While acknowledging their principal goal of searching for Amundsen—as well as conducting whatever scientific work they could—he returned again and again to his concerns about the welfare of those on board. "I have thirty-five people who depend on me, and *they* are young," he grimly reminded himself. It was a rough, horrible trip with storms and howling winds, and the spirits of the demoralized crew could not be roused. They felt death all around them; their role was not to save people but to search for the debris of the airplane—the role of mortician, Jean-Baptiste wrote in his journal.

In the meantime the entire world continued to follow the saga of the *Italia* and the search for Amundsen. What made this wreck even more riveting than previous ones was that, thanks to the radio, people everywhere were able to tune in. While Scott had died a silent, agonizing death at the ends of the earth, radio allowed this latest saga to unfold instantly, dramatically, with daily reports of brutal ice conditions and suspenseful rescue attempts. *The New York Times* declared, "Next to the devotion with which both explorers and rescuers risked and flung away their lives, the incident is signalized as a supreme test of three great modern inventions—the airship, the airplane and the radio."

On September 1 news that one of the floats from Amundsen's plane had been found shot across the world. With this news, all hope of finding the explorer alive quickly faded. Despite an exhaustive search that covered approximately ten thousand miles and ranged from Franz Josef Land, an archipelago in the far north of Russia, in the east to Greenland in the west, the remains of Amundsen and his companions were never found. It was described as the "greatest tragedy in the history of modern Polar exploration." It was a bitter end to a frustrating and worrisome adventure for Jean-Baptiste, who wrote in his journal, "I can now say it: what they wanted to make us do was the most dangerous thing in the world. Despite all of our precautions, there was a greater chance that we would remain there than that we would return . . . The nightmare of this awful responsibility is dissipated . . ." What must it have felt like for Jean-Baptiste to give up on Amundsen, whose discipline and commitment to polar exploration had made him a kind of kindred spirit? What Amundsen had written in his autobiography bears repeating:

> Whatever remains to man unknown, in this world of ours, is by so much a burden on the spirits of all men. It remains a something that man has not yet conquered—a continuing evidence of his weakness, an unmet challenge to his mastery over nature. By the same token, every mystery made plain, every unknown land explored, exalts the spirit of the whole human race—strengthens its courage and exalts its spirit permanently. The trail breaker is an indispensable ally of the spiritual values which advance and sustain civilization.

This appreciation of the ineffable value of exploration was close to Jean-Baptiste's own feeling.

Eight years later Jean-Baptiste found himself in the midst of another summer of turbulent winds and fierce waves in the dangerous waters between Iceland and Greenland. He and his crew had left from Saint-Servan, just south of Saint-Malo in Brittany, on July 14,

1936. They had spent the day before their departure with their families, all of whom had come to see their boys off. Since Jean-Baptiste's birthday was on July 15, they organized a party for him—a festive dinner full of gifts and jokes and stories about past glories. As, one by one, the men pushed back from their tables, stood up, and led the group in increasingly drunken toasts in Jean-Baptiste's honor, a storm raged outside, uprooting trees and causing dangerous flooding. So grim was the weather, in fact, that they decided to push back their departure by a few days. They arrived at Reykjavík at five a.m. on July 31, and set off once again the following day for Greenland. As they made their final approach to that great island, all their troubles with bad weather seemed to be behind them. The sea was absolutely calm, the sky gray, pale, and pearl-like. When finally they saw their first icebergs of the trip, Jean-Baptiste felt his heart skip, as it always did at the sight of them, sentries guarding a secret realm.

Indifferent, they allow to pass the little ship that is penetrating in the domain of which they are sentinels. We others, the men who drive it, must feel quite small. Me above all, perhaps, because more accustomed to this spectacle, knowing the power of the elements of this decor, drawn by the desire to penetrate this mystery, I believe that I grow larger in affronting them and, each time, a little more, I realize that the teeming and vain humankind is nothing more than tolerated dust that nature could disperse with a breath of scornful impatience . . .

That summer, in addition to their navigational exercises and scientific studies, the crew of the *Pourquoi-Pas?* had another mission—to deposit provisions for the young anthropologist Paul-Émile Victor and his team at Angmagssalik and then take them a hundred kilometers north to Kangerdlugssuaq, where they would spend the winter studying the indigenous populations. Paul-Émile Victor saw Jean-Baptiste for the last time on August 10 while aboard the *Pourquoi-Pas?*. With his twenty-five companions, their thirty dogs, and materials they neded for their winter studies in Kangerdlugssuaq. That evening he went to Charcot's cabin and knocked on the door. Jean-Baptiste was sitting, writing.

Paul-Émile thanked him. Jean-Baptiste rose and took Paul-Émile's hand between his two hands. "Do not thank me, little one," Jean-Baptiste insisted. He called them all his "little ones." "I did what I could to help you."

They stood there for a moment, facing each other, the silence creeping to fill up the space that seemed to widen between them. Paul-Émile noticed that the old man's eyes were not laughing like they usually were.

"If it weren't for my family, I would prefer to die at sea . . . ," Jean-Baptiste said, dreamily, almost as if he had forgotten who was standing there in front of him. Then he shook his head and went to find a bottle of good wine and another of rum and stuffed them into Paul-Émile's pockets.

"Goodbye, my little one," he said fondly, and then suddenly embraced the young man strongly.

The next day, the *Pourquoi-Pas?* deposited its passengers and proceeded further into the fjord for some final dredging. The weather was horrible—torrential rain and fierce winds—and Jean-Baptiste found it all, quite simply, sinister. The following day they were back in the sea.

During their return they were dogged by bad luck and worse weather. On August 30 the ship developed boiler trouble while they were traversing the Denmark Strait between Iceland and Greenland. By the time they got back to Reykjavík, they had spent a horrible thirty days exploring. The trouble with the boiler, which required them to take the last leg of their trip with sails, was more serious than they had suspected, forcing them to delay their departure. This development worried Jean-Baptiste, since the greater the delay, the greater the chance that they would get caught up in the notoriously hairy weather of the upcoming bad season. On September 11 he fell on board; and although his injuries weren't serious, the fall merely served to confirm in Jean-Baptiste's mind that their luck was running out.

What would this crossing be like?

He was once again sitting in his office a few hours later when one of his men came to fetch him. He would have gone up anyway—the weather, which had seemed to be clearing up just in time for their departure, had begun to get rough. Rain started pouring down.

They continued along their southern route, past Cape Skagi, and began turning south along the extreme southwest of Iceland, when the wind picked up speed. The barometer tumbled, the ship began to pitch and rock, and the rain was slamming up against his porthole in angry rivulets. They had stumbled into a nasty storm, but such storms were common that time of year, especially in the angry waters of the Denmark Strait. They kept moving forward, slower and more laboriously than before. The wind only blew harder, and the waves swelled to monstrous proportions. It was time to turn back and search for shelter on the other side of Cape Skagi. But the wind had become a veritable tempest—unbeknownst to them, a great depression was arriving from the south of Greenland, with hurricane-force gales. At three a.m. they saw through the veil of foam the beacon from the lighthouse at the rocky point of Akranes, the northernmost point of the Hvalfjord. Despite their best efforts, they were unable to turn into the fjord—their last hope of shelter. The situation was becoming more dire with each second that passed, yet the crew exhibited an exemplary calm. Many of them had already survived storms and much worse—they executed the orders given to them with full confidence in their commanders. Among the officers, however, a sinking sense of dread had descended. They could see that they were close to land—about two miles out—but this proved to be only more dangerous. Hurricane-force winds whipped the water and the air filled with foam as the ship drifted precariously close to the jagged rocks and boulders of the point. The whole ship strained and shuddered as if trying to hold itself together. A loud groan and sudden crack, like the crunch of bones, and the foremast snapped in two. The wireless antenna was broken when the mizzenmast fell at around four-thirty a.m., cutting them off completely from the world and from help. In the early morning light, the crew could make out the sad sight—the ship was ringed by reefs that were breaking it, and a powerful current was pushing it dangerously toward land. The engine of the *Pourquoi-Pas?* strained uselessly against the superior natural forces as the ship swirled helplessly back toward the shore, up north, past the port of Reykjavík. It was being hammered by rain and buffeted by gale-storm winds like a toy. Throughout the evening and into the night, Jean-Baptiste and his crew struggled desperately to maneuver out of the storm.

The Akranes lighthouse and the coast, bristling with reefs, were in view. They all felt the end was near. At five-fifteen a.m., with the beam from the lighthouse beckoning to them, the crew of the *Pourquoi-Pas?* felt a sudden jolt and a terrifying, grinding sound alerting them that they had hit a reef. The engine exploded. In a final, desperate attempt, Jean-Baptiste and Commander Le Conniant ordered anchors dropped on either side of the ship to keep it in place. But a new wave slammed the ship against another reef, and this time the shell could not withstand it. The sea was now penetrating the hulking interior in rivers. It was no longer possible to avoid the obvious—their fight was over. The call to abandon ship was made, and dinghies were launched.

Jean-Baptiste watched helplessly as the horrifying spectacle unfolded—his beloved ship, once a haven to him and so many men, was now the source of their doom. His men, whom he viewed as sons, were now scrambling throughout the ship, trying desperately to save their own lives. He watched helplessly as some were sucked overboard into dark and angry waters, where they would drown or be smashed against the sharp and slippery rocks and reefs. He felt calm about the fate that lay before him, but the desperate movements of his sailors during their final, frightened struggle were too much to bear. "Oh, my poor children!" he murmured, and then turned to the cage of the seagull and ship's mascot, Rita, giving her one final caress before sending her far away from the carnage.

While this desperate battle between man and nature, life and death, raged, an Icelandic farmer and his son watched aghast from a nearby beach. They came to that spot on the beach after every stormy night to observe the debris brought forth by the powerful waves. They had not expected to be witnesses to ongoing disaster. Suddenly they spotted a motionless figure clinging to a ladder wedged within some nearby boulders. It was Eugène Gonidec, the young master helmsman from the *Pourquoi-Pas?*. The younger farmer then saw the figure begin to slip into the turbulent water. He lunged onto the rocks, struggling to stay on his feet despite the sea's backwash. Supported by his father, he managed to grab onto the inert body, which was already beginning to slip back into the sea. Father and son dragged the limp seaman out of the water and across the flagstones.

They scanned the water to see if there were any other men they could save, but saw nothing.

When Gonidec woke up several hours later, he was in a bed surrounded by farmers—silent, sturdy peasants who spoke a foreign tongue. The atmosphere in the farmhouse was calm—very different from the frenzied activity that was taking place just a short distance away by the beach. Gonidec did not know that scores of farmers were gathering on the beach, tugging pieces of the wreckage from the water, pulling out bodies and attempting artificial respiration whenever it seemed remotely hopeful. He did not know that all that was left of the *Pourquoi-Pas?* was a piece of the grand mast sticking out from the rocks.

The same storm that sank the *Pourquoi-Pas?* was so severe that it virtually cut off Iceland, blowing down telegraph and telephone lines throughout the country and sending the usually fearless local sailors scurrying back into harbor for safety. The storm continued for several days, making any search-and-rescue operation extremely difficult, if not impossible. The French consul arrived on the scene, as did several journalists, alerted to the news that the great French explorer may have perished in a dreadful catastrophe. They walked among the wreckage on the beach, picking up pieces of scientific equipment, boxes of scientific samples, soaked documents, pieces of Jean-Baptiste's desk. One of them came across Jeannot Lapin, a stuffed rabbit that one of Jean-Baptiste's daughters had given him years ago and that, under her instructions, had accompanied him on every voyage. There were other toys, too—dolls and stuffed animals bought by the crew, almost all of whom were fathers, as presents for their children back home.

While the men did what they could to find out more about the wreck and to search for any survivors, Gonidec was cared for in the farmhouse. Initially, horrified by the ordeal he had just experienced, he refused to remove his wet and cold clothes. Only when the woman on the farm warmed up her husband's clothes in the coal oven and placed them in his hands did he finally agree to change. Even once his sailor's uniform was cleaned and dried, he refused to put it on again. The farmer's wife and a neighbor's daughter were instructed to watch Gonidec and make sure he did not go near the beach, as the bodies of his crewmates were beginning to wash ashore and were gradually being laid out in a grisly line. But Gonidec managed to sneak past them and make his way to the shore, where he beheld the ghastly sight: a beach strewn with his friends. With a strangled cry, Gonidec rushed toward the water, toward the lifeless, blue-tinged bodies that lay stewn before him.

When he was returned to the farmhouse, Gonidec looked so stricken that the farmer's daughter felt desperate to help him. They were the same age—twenty-nine—and she wanted to console him, to tell him that everything would be all right, to hold him until some of the pain had gone away. But she spoke no French—and he no Icelandic—so she just sat there, mutely, looking at him. Then she remembered the one thing she knew in French, and began to sing to him "La Marseillaise," the French national anthem, just as they had taught her in school.

When the consul arrived, he escorted Gonidec to the beach in order to help in the identification of bodies. Gonidec, who had known them all intimately; who had eaten with them and sung songs with them; who knew the details of their marriages, the birthdays of their children, their hopes and their fears—now it was up to him simply to provide the correct spelling of their names, their positions on the crew. The following day, news of the tragedy was reported in newspapers around the world. Even in death Jean-Baptiste was remembered as his father's son. As *The New York Times* explained, "A medical career that promised to equal that of his illustrious father was broken off abruptly when Dr. Jean Charcot forsook his profession and succumbed to the lure of exploration . . ."

The first of many tributes to the fallen sailors occurred on September 30 in Reykjavík, with a funeral procession winding up from the port to the severe Catholic cathedral on the hill overlooking the city. The streets were lined with locals wearing black.

Then the bodies were transported back to France, arriving at Saint-Malo on Saturday morning, October 10. Church bells rang sadly throughout the region as an enormous crowd gathered at the maritime train station. The majority of the crew had been Breton sailors. Their countrymen came to mourn their sons, their brothers, their fathers, their friends. The entire city seemed to be in mourning. This was, after all, the ship's hometown. The region had lived in a kind of symbiosis with the sea for centuries. Just as the Icelandic people pointed proudly to their Viking forebearers, so the men and women of Brittany were descended from a long line of corsairs and navigators. Black flags waved in the windows of all the houses and the ramparts and docks were covered with people—government representatives, Charcot's family, the families of the sailors—as the bodies were lifted by crane from the boat and taken to a chapel next to the maritime train station. For the rest of the day and throughout the night, more than twenty thousand people filed before the bodies, watched over by officers and by the sole survivor, Gonidec. One very young and pregnant woman, wearing the traditional Breton headdress, groaned and staggered between the sailors on guard like an injured butterfly banging against a window. She begged to be allowed to have her husband's body for one night at home, but it was forbidden. She spent the night clinging to his coffin at the station. On Sunday morning the twenty-two coffins were taken from the station to the esplanade Saint-Vincent and lined up before a grandiose cenotaph. The "Honor and country" plaque, which had been found in the wreckage, was propped up against it, underneath the names of the sailors. One by one the names of the dead were read out loud, followed either by "Having died for France" for those whose bodies had been recovered, or "Disappeared at sea," for those whose remains were lost forever. At one p.m. a special train set off with the coffins for Paris, arriving at seven p.m. on Sunday, October 11.

The official state funeral for Jean-Baptiste Charcot and his men took place on October 12, 1936, at Notre Dame Cathedral in Paris. Crowds swarmed along the neighboring streets—they were silent, mute, as if frozen or in a stupor. The newspapers remarked at how, despite ongoing political and ideological battles, everyone seemed to have called a sort of truce. The president of the Republic, Albert Lebrun, addressed a few words to Gonidec, who stood alone amid twenty-two empty chairs representing the twenty-two bodies that had been found. Another eighteen bodies were never found. Forty families were devastated. Mothers lost sons, sisters lost brothers, wives lost husbands, and no amount of speeches or accolades could ever make things right.

Jean-Baptiste Charcot could have been just another daddy's boy.
He could have been a respectable doctor with a pastime of yachting.
But he always wanted to be something more. He wanted to be a
hero, even though, by the end of his life, such talk of heroism had
become decidedly démodé. Ironically, one of the places where such
traditional values were still promoted was in the Action Française,
whose newspaper ran a series of stirring, laudatory articles, first about
the shipwreck and then about the funeral preparations for Jean-
Baptiste and his men. It stressed his patriotism in bringing the French
flag to Antarctic waters and then in chasing submarines in World
War I, and his heroism for going in search of Amundsen in 1925.
The paper also faithfully reprinted the official government eulogy,
which both compared Jean-Baptiste to the conquistadors of old and
placed him at the forefront of the most exciting new scientific research in various fields, including meteorology and biology.

Even within the world of explorers, Jean-Baptiste lived at the
border between two epochs—that of the golden age of exploration,
of Scott and Shackleton and Amundsen, and that of the twentieth
century, whose heroics were due to radios and radar. His struggle
to navigate between these two paradigms gave his achievements an
air of poignancy. He entered the field too late to be truly pathbreak-
ing, and outlived his contemporaries—Scott died in 1912 at the age
of forty-four, Shackleton in 1922 at the age of forty-seven—to witness the next generation assume dominance as the race to the poles
took to the air. Yet perhaps it was this duality that allowed him to become the ideal Frenchman—and son—that he had always hoped to
be. While others faltered and doubted or seethed with resentment
as they struggled to keep up with the changing times, Jean-Baptiste
never forgot the lessons of his childhood: that faith in science and
progress can see a man through even the darkest storms.

TWELVE

The Final Chapter

Ah! This matter of Heredity; what a subject of endless meditations.
—Émile Zola, *Le Docteur Pascal* (1893)

Within five years of Jean-Baptiste's tragic death off the coast of Iceland at the age of sixty-nine, both Léon and Jeanne were also dead. In his final years, Léon became increasingly out of step with the prevailing political winds. The coalition of radical, socialist, and communist parties forming the Popular Front in the 1930s incensed his right-wing compatriots and led to a series of crippling strikes, which had devastating consequences for the already fragile French economy. Charles Maurras and Léon fumed—Maurras went even further and called for the murder of the leader of the Popular Front, the Jewish politician Léon Blum, and other deputies, an act that landed him in jail for eight months. A weakened centrist government eventually took power in France, but all eyes were really focused on the international stage, with the rise of Hitler in Germany and Mussolini in Italy.

Léon's focus had been elsewhere for some time. The writer Henri Massis, who had visited him in exile in Brussels, noticed the change in him, observing that Léon had become more cerebral, more prone to discuss literature or philosophy than news reports and political gossip. At no time was this more in evidence than in the pages of

Action Française in the fall of 1936. Amid articles detailing bloody offensives in the Spanish Civil War and the latest communist agitation in the eastern provinces, Léon chose with increasing frequency to reminisce on the peoples and themes from his childhood. Articles such as "Flaubert in the Public Domain" and "The Work and Figure of Zola" promised his readers the sort of intimate, gossipy, and opinionated tale that had made his memoirs so popular when they were published. But while his article on Zola was expectedly cruel and vindictive, the one about Flaubert was full of tender nostalgia. "I am one of those, today rather rare, who has heard the sound of his voice," Léon explained wistfully, as he wondered whether the works of Flaubert would live on in the popular consciousness. He wrote of the magic of those gatherings of the Group of Five. He described doing homework near the table where his mother and father worked when the telegram arrived announcing Flaubert's death, recalling how his father burst into tears while his mother slumped over in distress. He and his friends, Léon explained to his readers, had loved Flaubert so passionately, had memorized so carefully their favorite passages from *Madame Bovary* and, most especially, *Sentimental Education*, that he now no longer had to read the great author "because . . . I know it by heart." Had all the talk of his childhood friend's death at sea caused this meditation on both one of the "giants" from his youth and the transmission of ideas from one generation to the next? Was he already worried about how his own works would stand the test of time?

Although no longer at the forefront of political debates, Léon's uncanny sense of augury still seemed in full force. Already in 1933 he had written of the inevitable upcoming conflict with Germany, one, he warned, that would be exactly the opposite of 1914 and more closely resembling that of 1870: a war of penetration, not of trenches. Such prognostications only heightened people's anxiety—hadn't Léon warned a lax and unaware nation of the dangers of German espionage before the last war, and hadn't he been proven correct? And Léon's warnings about Nazi military might were not limited to vague presentiments of doom: he specified even further that the enemy would attack via Alsace and Lorraine and that not even the famed Maginot Line, the permanent fortifications at the Belgian frontier along the Rhine, would be able to hold them back. After the German invasion of

Poland on September 1, 1939, all of Europe waited nervously for a war they finally realized was unavoidable. Many Parisians tried to pretend that nothing had happened—the theaters and salons remained open, there were raucous parties with frenzied dancing and drinking to the thumps and squawks of the latest jazz numbers. But underneath the usual banter and activity was a hum of desperation, with people scanning the newspaper headlines and sky alike, looking for clues as to what might happen next. After the carnage of 1914–18, which had made France a nation of cripples, women, and the elderly, many Frenchmen did not think they could withstand another war. In 1938 the writer Céline predicted 25 million casualties and "the end of the breed" should another conflict break out, explaining: "We'll disappear body and soul from this place like the Gauls . . . They left us hardly twenty words of their own language. We'll be lucky if anything more than the word 'merde' survives us."

Meanwhile, French troops kept their eyes on the eastern horizon, bracing themselves for a long winter while rain and mist and sleet enveloped their bunkers in the forests along the Belgian frontier. The British government issued gas masks to all Londoners and imposed a nighttime blackout. The world waited and held its breath. On May 10, 1940, this "phony war" in the west suddenly ended when German gliders landed troops that captured a massive Belgian fortress and continued their assault through the Ardennes on the Belgian border. German forces then outflanked French troops assembled along the Maginot Line and began their inexorable march west. By the end of May, the roads of northern France were clogged with retreating British and French troops and with Belgian and French refugees fleeing the battle zones. In the Paris region alone, close to four million people left their homes and fled south, and by the time the Germans entered the city, just one-fifth of the normal population remained. On June 3 and 4 every available English vessel, including fishing trawlers and pleasure boats, evacuated over 300,000 British and French troops from Dunkirk. The French government left Paris for Bordeaux in the southwest, as it had in 1870; and on June 14 the German army occupied the capital. On June 16 Marshal Philippe Pétain, hero of the battle of Verdun in 1916, became premier. The next day, he asked Germany for an armistice. On June 22, 1940, a gleeful Hitler accepted the French surrender in the same railway car where Germany had signed a similar document in November 1918. Hitler danced a jig of joy, and then set out to tour Paris. The Third Republic, which had stumbled from disaster to disaster since it was formed in the wake of military defeat at the hands of the Germans, was officially dissolved on July 10, 1940, when the Chamber of Deputies voted to give full powers to Pétain, who subsequently established the new Vichy State. And with that, the Third Republic, which had provided the framework for the lives of Léon, Jean-Baptiste, and Jeanne, ignominiously crumbled at the hands of their country's mortal enemies.

The initial response by many when Marshal Pétain announced that the government he had just formed was seeking an armistice was relief. After the senseless slaughter of a generation of young Frenchmen in 1914–18, many cheered at the cautious, conciliatory gestures of the new government and its promises of restoring order and ending the fighting. The Action Française saw in France's defeat proof of what it had been arguing all along, namely, that democracy was a hopelessly inept form of government. In losing the war, they argued, the Third Republic had lost its legitimacy and the only way to rescue the country was through counterrevolution. They found the cause of their defeat everywhere they looked: the widespread denigration of the Catholic faith, the existence of Jewish statesmen, short skirts, loud music, birth control, jazz, unbridled individualism, and a lack of respect for elders. Léon, for whom the personal would always be political, penned an article in 1941 complaining that the lack of morality within French families had allowed the nation to become susceptible to defeat. Specifically, he complained about divorce:

A recent statistic shows that, since the passing of the Naquet law, approximately one million couples have split up, which, as it happens, has become the easiest thing in the world for them to do . . . The separation could have been merely temporary. Divorce is a real barrier, and it has given marriage an exit door. It is a venom introduced into good relations. It is against the preservation of the family.

Léon clearly was not one to forgive and forget. But now he, like the other leaders of the Action Française, was hopeful that the era of republican decadence and degeneration was over and that a new era of regeneration and moral order was upon them. And yet he could not muster the same enthusiasm for the current political situation as his friend Maurras. He was not ready to let go of the past, instead preferring to reflect on those moments decades earlier when he had felt himself part of a small, brave band of men against the world. He wrote a memoir of his father, *When My Father Lived*, a sequel to his 1898 *Alphonse Daudet*, in which he lovingly recounted the fatherly advice and intellectual insight his father had given him. In his longing for those heady, turbulent days, Léon found that even those moments of fierce conflict provided him with sentimental memories. The previous year, he had penned an article in which he had reminisced with warm nostalgia about his famous duel with Henri Bernstein in 1911. At the time, Léon had treated Bernstein as nothing less than an enemy of the state—a Jew, a deserter, a degenerate—and had persecuted him accordingly. But years later an older, more mellow Léon recalled that same encounter with such feeling and sensitivity that Bernstein, his onetime target, wrote to thank him for his lively, fond account of their battle. Bernstein marveled at how much time had elapsed since their intense fights. "I was not ready at our meeting in 1911 to admire your great art," Bernstein confessed, "not in the furor of that time . . . for you made my life rather difficult."

Of course he had. Léon had liked nothing better than to be a thorn in the side of convention or complacency. For this reason he also found himself reflecting with some pride at his work on behalf of the Prix Goncourt. Edmond de Goncourt had bequeathed his entire estate for the foundation and maintenance of the Goncourt Academy, which each year was to award a literary prize in honor of his brother and collaborator, Jules de Goncourt. The jury that determined the winner met for deliberations at the restaurant Drouant; and the award, though nominal, quickly proved itself able to ensure the winner a certain measure of celebrity status and a boost in sales. After lunch the youngest member of the Academy would announce the winner to awaiting journalists, and within an hour red bands with the words "Prix Goncourt" would be wrapped around the winning work in bookstores throughout Paris. In 1919 the Prix Goncourt was awarded to Léon's old friend and onetime dinner companion from Fontainebleau, Marcel Proust, for *Within a Budding Grove*. There were many who disagreed with this choice, grumbling that the prize ought to have been awarded to Roland Dorgelès's *Wooden Crosses*. (Dorgelès was a young war hero who had written a bracing novel about the recently ended World War I, while Marcel was a forty-eight-year-old asthmatic who had not fought in the war and who had written a work of subtle social analysis and psychological contemplation.) A few days later, on December 12, 1919, Léon published a front-page article in *Action Française* whose title boldly proclaimed, "A New and Powerful Novelist, Marcel Proust." Since the founding of the Goncourt Academy in 1903, Léon explained, the judges had not yet "crowned a work as vigorous, as new, as full of riches." Suddenly, after years of wheezing and worrying and writing in rarefied obscurity, Marcel Proust was famous. He dedicated his next book, *The Guermantes Way*, to Léon: "To the author of so many masterpieces and incomparable friend in testament to my gratitude and admiration." When Marcel died on November 18, 1922, Léon was one of the first of his friends to arrive and wept openly by the body for a long time. Proust's brother, Robert, thanked Léon for having been so kind to Marcel. "Don't thank me," he answered. "He was more than a century ahead of the rest of us. No one can do anything after him."

Léon was dragged out of his reveries by the realities of war. When France fell to the Germans, Léon found himself facing the same dilemma as millions of other Frenchmen: how to survive. His wife, Marthe, took refuge with friends in Agen, while their son François was made a prisoner of war. At the outbreak of hostilities, Léon happened to be in Saint-Rémy-de-Provence, but he soon made his way to Lyon to join the rest of the Action Française leadership. Under the early days of Vichy, he and Charles Maurras were of a same mind about the best way to handle the defeat. They encouraged their readers and followers to show respect for Marshal Pétain and sympathy for the principles of his National Revolution, and they urged them not to collaborate actively with the Nazi invaders.

But while his colleagues debated the policies of the new Vichy government, Léon felt increasingly distracted. He sensed the anxiety and desperation mounting, could feel the tension between his comrades over their duties toward their country and their country's new masters, but he did not feel like a part of it. The end was approaching, he was certain of it—he could feel his body slowing down, could sense a weakness creeping into his hands and a cooling of his usually impetuous, forceful reactions. It soon became difficult and then impossible for him to write. His articles no longer appeared in *Action Française*. Other voices, shriller and louder, came to the fore. Then, on May 27, Léon suffered a stroke, and he became imprisoned in his own body. He could still speak, however, and continued to urge on his compatriots and followers to stay the course and remain true to the ideals of the Action Française. No one was surprised when, a few weeks later, he died of an aneurism in the middle of the night, on June 29–30, 1942. He was buried on Saturday, July 4, at the cemetery of Saint-Rémy with only a few dozen people in attendance as the hot Provençal sun blazed and the cicadas buzzed. With the war, travel had become difficult for most people. Charles Maurras gave an anguished eulogy, and for the first time in the thirty-odd-year friendship referred to his old friend in the familiar "you" form. Tears streamed down Marthe's face as Charles, Léon's son with Jeanne, listened in passive, strained silence. *Action Française* ran a series of front-page articles with reminiscences about Léon's life and work, an account of the funeral, and an ongoing list of messages of condolence. They even printed the text of a telegram that Pétain himself had sent to Marthe offering his sympathy. But not everyone was sad at Léon's demise. *Time* magazine published a notice about his passing entitled "Death of a Conspiracy," describing him as a "paunchy" and "hook-nosed" character who "spent most of his life in a seriocomic clamor for the return of the House of Bourbon-Orleans to the throne of France." To underscore the over-the-top theatrics of France's best-known royalist, the article reminded its readers that "Léon Daudet's editorials in *Action Française* were slapstick smacks, in which he called his enemies female camels, unfecund sows, burst dogs, humpbacked cats, circumcised hermaphrodites. In a courtroom squabble Daudet once screamed 'liar' at an opponent so long & loud that his nose began to bleed."

After Léon's passing, the Action Française, along with the nation as a whole, plunged into even darker times. After years of preaching intolerance and anti-Semitism from the fringes of the political world, they now found themselves living under a government that embraced their political and ideological views. In Pétain's new government, whose capital was the spa town of Vichy, "Country, Family, Work" replaced "Liberty, Fraternity, Equality" on French coins. The Vichy government proclaimed a "spiritual revival" against "decadence," banning Masonic lodges and divorce while favoring Catholicism. Léon had been well schooled in anti-Semitism from his youth, like so many of the men and women who congregated at his parents' home. But he was also deeply patriotic, and the sight of German boots stomping down the boulevards of Paris would have made his blood boil. He may not have been comfortable, after all, with the logical extension of the Action Française's doctrine of hatred, xenophobia, and anti-Semitism—at least as it was practiced by the Nazis. A law in July 1940 sought to eliminate all Jewish influence on the national economy; then, in October, a series of laws forbade Jews from holding jobs in public service, education, cultural affairs, or professions such as medicine and law. More restrictions and ordinances followed, and it was not long before the persecution became more direct, relentless, barbaric. In July 1941 the Nazis began to prepare for the "Final Solution," with a July 17 Gestapo directive ordering commanders of prison camps in the east to liquidate all the Jews.

Perhaps, had he lived, Léon might have followed his friend Charles Maurras, who began as an opponent of Nazi Germany but soon changed his mind and decided that collaboration was the only path to once and for all suppress the decadent and individualistic morals of modern France. After 1942, when Vichy became a satellite of Nazi Germany, Maurras decided that only a German victory over communism could prevent "the re-emergence of Masons, Jews, and all the political personnel eliminated in 1940." His language about the Resistance grew fiercer as well, and he argued that if the death penalty was not sufficient incentive to prevent their activities, members of their families should be seized as hostages and executed. The Action Française ran stories spewing anti-Semitic, pro-Pétain propaganda, and occasionally even specific hiding places of Jews and other state "enemies," thus facilitating many arrests. Pétain greatly valued Maurras, who provided an intellectual armature for the Vichy government's policies, referring to him as the "most French of the French." Maurras was equally enamored, calling Pétain's rise to power in 1940 a "divine surprise." After the war, however, both Pétain and Maurras found themselves on the losing side of history. Maurras was arrested and convicted for "complicity with the enemy." "It is the revenge of Dreyfus!" he exclaimed when he heard his sentence to life imprisonment in the Court of Justice at Lyon in 1945 (he was not executed because of his age—he was seventy-six years old). He died in a private clinic near Tours on November 16, 1952, while Pétain, who also avoided execution due to his advanced age, died in part without ever having admitted any error. In an odd twist of fate, the presiding judge at the High Court during both men's trials was none other than Louis Noguères, the lawyer who had represented the cabdriver Bajot against Léon's accusations during the investigation of his son Philippe's murder. Noguères had been one of only eighty deputies who had voted to deny Marshal Pétain special powers in July 1940, the act that paved the way for the establishment of the Vichy government and France's surrender.

Seven months before Léon died, Jeanne passed away in Paris on November 30, 1941. When the announcement of her death appeared in *The New York Times*, it read "Victor Hugo's Kin Dies." In life, as in death, Jeanne and her grandfather were inextricably bound. During her final years, she, too, had largely disengaged from the world around her. After divorcing Jean-Baptiste in 1905, she was finally able to marry the man she had always loved, Michel Negreponte. Michel had been born in Alexandria on July 21, 1872, and was the stepson of Victor de Lesseps, the younger of the two sons of Ferdinand de Lesseps by his first marriage. Victor had spent many years in Egypt as the resident managing director of the Suez Canal, and there he met his wife, a sister of the Greek Alexandrian bankers Constantine and Ambroise Sinadino. She was then the widow of Georges Negreponte, whose family had played an important role in the Greek war of liberation in the early nineteenth century. Victor viewed Michel—and his twin brother, Jacques—as his own, and old Ferdinand de Lesseps welcomed the two brothers into his large brood of grandchildren. When Michel was older, he attended the French military academy Saint-Cyr and then entered the Greek army, achieving the rank of captain. Jeanne and Michel had first met as teenagers at a ball. They had danced several dances—both Jacques and Michel had a reputation for being elegant, handsome young men and excellent dancers—and had fallen for each other on the spot. Jeanne's mother, however, had not approved of the match, and it was only years later, after she had already married twice and he once, that they were finally able to marry.

Michel was wealthy and handsome and a lively companion for Jeanne; by all accounts the marriage was a happy one. She converted to Greek Orthodoxy shortly before her wedding and adopted her new religion with surprising fervor. They split their time between Paris and the Hugos' estate in the south, in the countryside near Montpellier; his friends—glamorous expatriates and itinerant demiroyals from Greece and southern Europe—became hers. But their life together was cut short when Michel died on April 4, 1914, as a result of an operation for appendicitis, which could still be deadly in those days. His death took Jeanne entirely by surprise. She had expected him to take care of her for her remaining days—for there had always been someone to take care of her. But with the death first of her mother, Alice, then of Michel, and finally, in 1925, of her brother Georges, the circle of caretakers had grown alarmingly small. What would she do? As one social observer archly suggested, "Once the period of mourning is over she will doubtless take to herself a fourth husband. For nobody dreams of Jeanne Hugo remaining single."

She did not remarry—perhaps she knew in her heart of hearts that it was time to stop looking for someone to fill the void in her life that had originally opened with her grandfather's death. She moved to the elegant neighborhood of Passy, where her son, Charles, attended to her every need. He would read to her and dine with her, and go strolling through the neighborhood with her. Most important, he listened to her reminisce about her family, her childhood, her time in the sun with her grandfather. These accounts were such a ritual they sometimes felt like prayer. Charles's constant attentions and devotion kept his mother's anxiety and overwhelming sadness at being widowed at forty-five somewhat at bay. As her nephew, the artist Jean Hugo, recalled, she tended to wake up late each day and spend a considerable amount of time painting her nails, her preferred color being a deep, dusky rose. She would then slowly, majestically, descend to the dining room at around two-thirty, deigning to grace the day with her presence. Perhaps adhering to such an idiosyncratic schedule reminded her of her grandfather's peculiar timetable. In any case Jeanne Hugo never doubted that she was the sort of woman for whom people wait. But she had her moments of fear and insecurity as well. Although she loved Hauteville House, she only went there occasionally. She had developed a real terror of drowning in a shipwreck. Jeanne had never been wholly comfortable at sea—she had always resisted Jean-Baptiste's invitations to sail with him when they were married—and that feeling had only intensified with her second husband's tragic drowning.

When she emerged from her isolation for the occasional interview or commemorative event honoring her grandfather, she was described by journalists as still being a woman of great beauty and grace. But not everyone was so kind in their estimation of the nation's favorite granddaughter. The year after Michel died, in 1915, her aunt Adèle finally passed away at the luxurious nursing home at Suresnes where she had lived in quiet seclusion since returning to France so many years earlier. When Adèle's death was announced, most of the country was too transfixed by news of the terrible losses of life and limb in trenches to the east. A few newspapers in France and abroad, though, printed articles that reviewed the turbulent saga of Victor Hugo's insane daughter, using her death as an excuse to remind readers of all the sordid rumors about the Hugo clan: the reported insanity of Victor's brother, the eccentric lifestyle at Hauteville House, the poet's radical politics and ravenous womanizing. "Victor Hugo's children, brought up in these fantastic surroundings, were destined to tragedy, though it would perhaps be going too far to say that all their misfortunes were due to their training or lack of training," one writer opined, adding, "And even in the third generation startling eccentricity appears." With no professional or creative achievements to distinguish them, Jeanne and Georges ended up being judged by their personal conduct. As Hugos, they were expected to somehow carry themselves heroically, grandly, like characters in one of their grandfather's novels. Instead, they seemed to have squandered their youth and charisma on misguided amorous adventures and petty schemes for personal fulfillment. "How can you leave your husband?" the press and the public had asked Jeanne incredulously when she left her home with Léon. "How can you divorce a man who may be dead?" they demanded to know when she left Jean-Baptiste. How could she ever explain with any degree of satisfaction? Did they even really want an answer from her, or did they just want her to remain an ideal?

In 1925, at the age of fifty-six, Jeanne spoke about her turbulent life and loves with Abbé Mugnier, a Catholic priest who attended to the spiritual needs of wealthy, well-known Parisians in the early decades of the twentieth century. It is one of the few published accounts in which Jeanne's version of her own life is told, unfiltered by the prejudices and perceptions of the extraordinary men in her life—her grandfather and her first two husbands—and, later, of their biographers. She spoke about things that many might not have wanted to hear. She explained that she had only found the true love of her life after failing at marriage twice before. She spoke of the kindness Jean-Baptiste had shown her when he agreed to divorce her so that she could be with Michel, and about how much she admired his second wife, Meg, and enjoyed their children, who decades later still remembered her as the beautiful lady with the stylish clothing and impressive jewelry. She described a life that had been improvised, imperfectly, perhaps even thoughtlessly—but still it was hers. From an early age, Jeanne learned to find sustenance in the greatness of the men in her life rather than in the cultivation of her own interests or talents. But if her failures and limitations seem almost banal when compared to the mythic dimensions of her grandfather, they are also touchingly human and speak to the obligatory, if frequently painful, negotiation between youth and adulthood.

The world, according to Charles Péguy in 1913, "has changed less since Jesus Christ than it has changed in the last thirty years." Perhaps no three people captured so well the inherent contradictions and confusions of their generation as Léon Daudet, Jean-Baptiste Charcot, and Jeanne Hugo. They had grown up at a time when horse-drawn carriages dominated the streets of Paris, and they ailed as airplanes took to the skies. As children they had heard stories of a not-so-distant Europe ruled by kings and Corsican conquerors, and as aging adults had watched with incredulity and dread as dictators and brown-shirted thugs led a cowed and docile continent into servitude. From the paeans for a unified Europe penned by an immutable Victor Hugo to the anguished verses of Wilfred Owen, from streets lit by gas lamps to gas chambers for the undesirable, they had witnessed the very best and the very worst of what man could achieve. In 1912 Henri Massis, a member of that generation that was later declared to be irretrievably "lost" due to the trauma of the Great War, dismissed Léon, Jean-Baptiste, and Jeanne's cohort as a "sacrificed generation," unable to shed the pessimism and pensiveness of the nineteenth century and unwilling to embrace the energy and activity of the twentieth century.

A sense of disquiet did permeate the lives of the men and women whose youth was spent negotiating the tumultuous and occasionally tortured transition from one century to the next. The uneasiness was there as Jean-Baptiste marshaled the most advanced tools and technology he could find in a quixotic and ancient quest to become a conqueror of new worlds, or as Léon dipped into an arsenal of modern media to extol the virtues of the traditional values of king, country, and family. Even Jeanne's refusal to accept anything but her own specific, exalted vision of romantic love—even if it meant resorting to divorce and the resulting disgrace—can be seen as a sign of her difficulty in detaching herself from the ideals and expectations with which she was raised. But Léon, Jean-Baptiste, and Jeanne were also particularly bound by more private anxieties of influence as offspring of three leading families in contemporary French culture: Would Léon be graced with his father's literary gifts or be afflicted by the taint of his disease? Whose name would resonate more loudly with posterity, Charcot père or fils? Could Jeanne be the one descendant whose life was not thwarted by the burden of growing up a Hugo? While they were not the first nor the last offspring of remarkable parents to confront such dilemmas, their struggle has a poignancy born out of history and circumstance that renders their lives at once recognizable and extraordinary. Their private preoccupations with inheritance were reinforced by a larger discussion then occurring about biological degeneration and its impact on both individuals and society as a whole. Again and again, in the literature, philosophy, and science of the fin de siècle, people articulated growing fears that the progress of the nineteenth century had finally begun to work against itself, creating disorders that led to poverty, crime, alcoholism, moral perversion, and political violence. It was within this perfect storm of anxiety and opportunity, despair and determination, that Léon, Jean-Baptiste, and Jeanne waged their struggle for self-determination, battling with private demons and public expectations to be both worthy of and free from their gilded legacies.

Notes

INTRODUCTION

3 *"They've shot Jaurès!"*: For accounts of the life and death of Jaurès, see François Broche, *Jaurès: Paris, le 31 Juillet 1914* (1978); Harvey Goldberg, *The Life of Jean Jaurès* (1962); Jean Rabaut, *Jaurès Assassiné: 1914* (1984); Madeleine Rebérioux and Gilles Candar, *Jaurès et les Intellectuels* (1994); and Barbara Tuchman, *The Proud Tower: A Portrait of the World Before the War, 1890–1914* (1966).

4 *the nationalist doctrines of Charles Maurras, Léon Daudet, and their royalist and nationalist group, the Action Française:* The best account of the Action Française is Eugen Weber, *Action Française: Royalism and Reaction in Twentieth-Century France* (1962). For a full-length biographical treatment of Léon Daudet, see Michel Bassi, *Léon Daudet: Un Géant de Papier* (1993); François Broche, *Léon Daudet: Le Dernier Imprécateur* (1992); and Eric Vatré, *Léon Daudet, ou, Le Libre Réactionnaire* (1987).

11 *Jean-Baptiste's dream of Antarctic exploration:* Among the sources consulted for the voyages of Jean-Baptiste Charcot are a compilation by the Yacht Club of France, *Jean-Baptiste Charcot, 1867–1936* (1937); Marthe Emmanuel, *Tel Fut Charcot, 1867–1936* (1967); Benoît Heimermann and Gérard Janichon, *Charcot, le Gentleman des Pôles* (1991); Serge Kahn, *Jean-Baptiste Charcot: Explorateur des Mers, Navigateur des Pôles* (2006); Henri Queffélec, *Le Grand Départ: Charcot et le "Pourquoi pas?"* (1977); Gaston Rouillon, *Jean-Baptiste Charcot: Sa Vie, Son Oeuvre, Leurs Prolongements 50 Ans Après* (1986); and Marguerite Verdat, *Charcot, Le Chevalier du Pôle* (1950). Jean-Baptiste Charcot's accounts of his Antarctic exploration include *Journal de l'Expédition Antarctique Française, 1903–1905. Le "Français" au Pôle Sud* (1906), *Deuxième Expédition Antarctique Française (1908–1910)* (1911–14), and *The Voyage of the "Why Not?" in the Antarctic: The Journal of the Second French South Polar Expedition, 1908–1910*, trans. Philip Walsh (1911).

12 *"Why is man bound to do evil":* Jean-Baptiste Charcot, *The Pourquoi-Pas? in the Antarctic* (1911), 63.

1: TUESDAY LESSONS

17 *For there, in Paris, shone the great name of Charcot:* Sigmund Freud, *An Autobiographical Study,* trans. and ed. James Strachey (1989), 10.

18 *"For years, I only dreamed of Paris":* Sigmund Freud, *Interpretation of Dreams,* trans. James Strachey (1954), 259.

19 *"The French are a people of psychical epidemics":* Sigmund Freud to Martha Bernays (December 3, 1885), in *Letters of Sigmund Freud,* ed. Ernst L. Freud, trans. Tania and James Stern (1992), 188.

19 *"the hysteria capital of the world":* Martha Noel Evans, *Fits and Starts: A Genealogy of Hysteria in Modern France* (1991), 9.

19 *"I am now quite comfortably installed":* Freud to Bernays (November 24, 1885), in *Letters of Sigmund Freud,* 184–85.

20 *who already showed signs:* Georges Guillain, M.D., *J.-M. Charcot, 1825–1893, His Life—His Work,* trans. and ed. Pearce Bailey (1959), 4.

20 *"No lifestyle that I know":* Christopher G. Goetz, Michel Bonduelle, and Toby Gelfand, *Charcot: Constructing Neurology* (1995), 7.

22 *"living pathological museum":* Goetz et al., *Charcot: Constructing Neurology,* 64.

22 *"a prison and an asylum of unwanted womanhood":* Guillain, *J.-M. Charcot,* xi.

23 *"It is not on an inert corpse":* Paul Richer and J.-M. Charcot, "Note sur l'Anatomie Morphologique de la Région Lombaire: Sillon Lombaire Médian," in *Nouvelle Iconographie de la Salpêtrière* 1 (1888): 13, 14–15, cited in Debora L. Silverman, *Art Nouveau in Fin-de-Siècle France: Politics, Psychology, and Style* (1989), 94.

24 *laid out like so many altar icons:* Goetz et al., *Charcot: Constructing Neurology,* 64. This work offers the most comprehensive overview in English of Charcot's career and teaching.

25 *more than a passing resemblance to Napoléon:* Jean Thuillier, *Monsieur Charcot de la Salpêtrière* (1993), 17.

25 *"well-constructed rhetorical performances":* Sigmund Freud, "Report on my Studies in Paris and Berlin," in *The Standard Edition of the Complete Psychological Works of Sigmund Freud,* vol. 1, trans. and ed. James Strachey (1953–74), 8.

25 *"a little work of art":* Sigmund Freud, "Charcot," in *The Standard Edition of the Complete Psychological Works of Sigmund Freud,* vol. 3, 17.

26 *"the skill with which":* See Goetz et al., *Charcot: Constructing Neurology;* and Freud, "Charcot," in *The Standard Edition of the Complete Psychological Works of Sigmund Freud,* vol. 3, 11–23. Some of the best descriptions of Charcot's teaching style can be found in A. Joffroy, "Jean-Martin Charcot," *Archives de la Médecine Expérimentale* 5: 577–606; Fulgance Raymond, "Leçon d'Ouverture," *La Presse Médicale* 20: 399–407; and Freud, "Charcot."

27 *coming in at a rate of one a day:* Evans, *Fits and Starts,* 10.

28 *Charcot and his colleagues underscored:* See J.-M. Charcot and Paul Richer, *Les Démoniaques dans l'Art* (1887), 91–106.

28 *"here we have the epileptoid phase":* Jean-Martin Charcot, *Charcot, the Clinician: The Tuesday Lessons: Excerpts from Nine Case Presentations on General*

Neurology Delivered at the Salpêtrière Hospital in 1887–88 by Jean-Martin Charcot, trans. Christopher G. Goetz (1987), 105–106.

29 *"Theory is fine"*: Freud, "Charcot," 13.

29 *the greatest satisfaction a man could have:* Ibid., 12.

30 *a smaller version of the "act of liberation"*: Ibid., 18.

30 *to "untie my tongue"*: Freud to Bernays (January 18, 1886), in *Letters of Sigmund Freud*, 193.

32 *"A magnificent face"*: Freud to Bernays (February 10, 1886), ibid., 208.

32 *"A beautiful mind, respectful of literature"*: Goetz et al., *Charcot: Constructing Neurology*, 291.

32 *"I feel like I'm under a microscope"*: Edmond and Jules de Goncourt (October 19, 1893), *Journal: Mémoires de la Vie Littéraire*, ed. Robert Ricatte (1989), 880.

33 *"it was a paradise for youth"*: Léon Daudet, *Devant la Douleur*, in *Souvenirs et Polémiques* (1992), 151.

33 *"Ataxics and melancholiacs squirmed"*: Ibid.

34 *"It is instinctive, almost a Darwinism"*: Jean-Martin Charcot (November 15, 1887), in *Charcot the Clinician*, 10.

35 *"Man is in the hands of the gods"*: Guillain, *J.-M. Charcot*, 33.

35 *a school of thought that used the concept of degeneration:* See Daniel Pick, *Faces of Degeneration* (1989).

36 *"Herr Dr. Sigmund Freud"*: Peter Gay, *Freud: A Life for Our Times* (1984), 53.

2: THE GROUP OF FIVE

38 *"Victor Hugo is expecting death"*: "Victor Hugo's Last Hours," *The New York Times* (May 23, 1885). In addition to newspaper articles from the era, some of the best accounts of Victor Hugo's death can be found in *Funerailles de Victor Hugo* (1885); Graham Robb, *Victor Hugo* (1997); Raymond Escholier, *Victor Hugo et les Femmes* (1935); and the compilation *Tombeau de Victor Hugo* (1985).

39 *"Here we have the struggle"*: "Victor Hugo's Last Days," *The New York Times* (May 31, 1885).

39 *"Remember everything for me"*: Raymond Escholier, *Victor Hugo, Cet Inconnu* (1951), 328–30.

40 *"Be happy! Think of me"*: Escholier, *Victor Hugo et les Femmes*, 125.

41 *"The death of Victor Hugo is an event"*: The *Times* (London) (May 23, 1885), 11.

42 *"You might never see me again"*: Escholier, *Victor Hugo, Cet Inconnu*, 336.

42 *she kept this talisman:* Ibid.

43 *"without any concern about protocol"*: Léon Daudet, *Fantômes et Vivants*, in *Souvenirs et Polémiques* (1992), 67.

43 *"Surrounded, watched—it was terrible"*: Alphonse Daudet, *In the Land of Pain*, trans. and ed. Julian Barnes (2002), 16.

45 *christened their little club the "Group of Five"*: By far the best accounts of these regular meetings is found in the Goncourts' journal.

46 *they all seemed like giants:* Léon Daudet, *Quand Vivait Mon Père* (1942), 15.

46   *"in order to clear up our ideas"*: Léon Daudet, *Alphonse Daudet* (1898), 26.

46   *"capable of performing the most frightful follies"*: Ibid.

48   could only describe the audience's reaction to the play as *"funereal"*: Goncourt *Journal*, II (March 12, 1874), 573.

48   *"sad and a little surreal"*: Ibid.

48   a man who had a vested interest in the play: Flaubert to Alphonse Daudet (March 17, 1874), in *The Letters of Gustave Flaubert: 1830–1880*, trans. and ed. Francis Steegmuller (2001), 580.

49   *"I feel tears rising"*: Émile Zola, *Le Sémaphore de Marseilles* (March 14, 1874), in *Oeuvres Complètes*, vol. 6, ed. Henri Mitterand (2003), 568.

50   *"with this mixture of naiveté and finesse"*: Goncourt *Journal*, II (March 2, 1872), 499.

51   *"Sustained by the boundless confidence of youth"*: Alphonse Daudet, *Thirty Years of Paris and of My Literary Life*, trans. Laura Ensor (1888), 11.

54   Léon was taught to revere his father's friend: Léon Daudet, *Fantômes et Vivants*, 50.

54   would forever be, *"an old, enraged Romantic"*: Victor H. Brombert, *The Hidden Reader: Stendhal, Balzac, Hugo, Baudelaire, Flaubert* (1988), 7.

54   *"there were no modern subjects"*: Frederick Brown, *Zola: A Life* (1995), 285.

54   His quest for absolute *"impersonality"*: Stuart P. Sherman, introduction to *The George Sand–Gustave Flaubert Letters*, trans. A. L. McKensie (2004), 19.

54   *"your school is not concerned with fundamentals"*: George Sand to Flaubert (December 18–19, 1875), in *Letters of Gustave Flaubert*, 605.

54   *"I aim at beauty above all else"*: Flaubert to Sand (December 31, 1875), ibid., 605–606.

55   *"a dinner deadly for letters"*: Alphonse Daudet to Edmond de Goncourt (Autumn 1874), in Edmond de Goncourt and Alphonse Daudet, *Correspondance*, ed. Pierre Dufief with Anne-Simone Dufief (1996), 20.

55   *"We opened our minds"*: Ibid., 339.

56   *"what a whiner that fat, pot-bellied young fellow"*: Goncourt *Journal*, II (January 25, 1875), 620–21.

56   *"your dreadful and splendid book"*: Flaubert to Émile Zola (December 1, 1871), in *Letters of Gustave Flaubert*, 556–57.

57   *"All has been said before us"*: Émile Zola, "Les Romanciers Naturalistes," in *Du Roman: Sur Stendhal, Flaubert et les Goncourt*, ed. Henri Mitterand (1989), 213.

57   *"Still young, aren't I?"*: Léon Daudet, *Quand Vivait Mon Père*, 15.

58   *"It's purely and simply a masterpiece!"*: Flaubert to Alphonse Daudet (March 1872), in *Letters of Gustave Flaubert*, 559.

58   *"Testiculos habes, et magnos"*: Ibid., 612.

58   *"the delicacy of his wit"*: Guy de Maupassant, *Pour Gustave Flaubert* (1986), 105–106.

58   *"We kept the best of ourselves for those meetings"*: Léon Daudet, *Alphonse Daudet*, 124–25.

59   *"I felt that a band sometimes slackened"*: Goncourt *Journal*, II (May 8, 1880), 862.

60   *"He was the center of all our lives"*: Brown, *Flaubert*, 563.

61   *"Here is the new army forming"*: Goncourt *Journal*, II (April 16, 1877), 736.

61   *"whose brains become the valets of their stomachs"*: Brown, *Zola*, 575.

62 *"like a knife cutting through a banana"*: Goncourt *Journal*, II (April 25, 1883), 1003.

62 *"fully cognizant of what I owe him"*: Brown, *Zola*, 546.

62 *"The timid ones always remain incomplete"*: Léon Daudet, *Alphonse Daudet*, 85.

63 *"like quills upon the fretful porcupine"*: "At Home with Émile Zola," *The New York Times* (April 19, 1885).

3: HAUTEVILLE HOUSE

67 *jewel-like interior:* Plans of the interior and accounts of Victor Hugo's expenses, some of which speak to the decorating of Hauteville House, can be found in "Agendas de Guernesey," in Victor Hugo, *Oeuvres Complètes*, ed. Jean Massin, vol. 10 (1996), 1373–1514. Other descriptions of the decor at Hauteville House include Robb, *Victor Hugo*, 387–394; Corinne Charles, *Victor Hugo, Visions d'Intérieurs: Du Meuble au Décor* (2003); and René Weiss, ed., *La Maison de Victor Hugo à Guernesey (Hauteville-House): Propriété de la Ville de Paris* (1928).

67 *they had a hard time disposing of:* Goncourt *Journal*, III (October 7, 1887), 66.

68 *"Be in fear of error"*: Robb, *Victor Hugo*, 387.

68 *"ingenuous, rosy simplicity itself"*: "Jeanne Hugo Then and Now," *The New York Times* (July 10, 1887).

68 *"Victor Hugo stood behind the child"*: "Jeanne Hugo's Divorce," *Chicago Tribune* (March 24, 1895).

69 *"The real guilty party . . . is I"*: Sophie Grossiord, *Victor Hugo: "Et s'il n'en reste qu'un . . ."* (1998), 76.

70 *"You were very great"*: Henri Guillemin, *L'Engloutie: Adèle, Fille de Victor Hugo, 1830–1915* (1985), 21.

71 *"They accept their solitude"*: Robb, *Victor Hugo*, 352.

71 *"Lord Spleen and Lady Nostalgy"*: Max Gallo, *Victor Hugo*, vol. 2 (2001), 209.

71 *the most attractive woman that he had ever seen:* Leslie Smith Dow, *Adèle Hugo: La Misérable* (1993), 13.

72 *"a young miss, speaking a little English"*: Guillemin, *L'Engloutie*, 37.

72 *"losing my name and giving myself a master"*: Ibid., 38.

73 *Their affair was brief, passionate, soaring:* Dow, *Adèle Hugo*, 39.

73 *"The spirit of Victor Hugo and the body of a twenty-six-year-old"*: Robb, *Victor Hugo*, 358.

73 *"I have none"*: Dow, *Adèle Hugo*, 39

74 *"willfullness and self-centeredness"*: Victor Hugo, *Oeuvres Complètes*, vol. 10, 1283.

74 *"my daughter alone loses her life"*: Guillemin, *L'Engloutie*, 45.

74 *"Adèle has given you her youth"*: Adèle Hugo to Victor Hugo (1857?), in Victor Hugo, *Oeuvres Complètes*, vol. 10, 1282.

75 *"Adèle lives inside herself"*: Guillemin, *L'Engloutie*, 52.

76 *"He was a royalist and British. He was the past"*: Ibid., 78–82.

76 *"She hates me"*: Ibid., 91.

77 *"It would be an incredible thing"*: Frances Vernor Guille, *Le Journal d'Adèle Hugo* (1968), 70.

77 *Victor was mystified by Adèle's behavior:* Gallo, *Victor Hugo*, vol. 2, 265.

78 *The poor child has not yet known happiness:* Guillemin, *L'Engloutie*, 118–19.

79 *One of her first acts:* Gallo, *Victor Hugo*, vol. 2, 322.

80 *"Little Jeanne has imagined a way of puffing out her cheeks":* Victor Hugo, *The Memoirs of Victor Hugo* (2007), 131–48.

81 *"It isn't normal":* Goncourt *Journal*, II (March 18, 1871), 395.

82 *"I saw Adèle. My heart is broken":* Robb, *Victor Hugo*, 475.

82 *as a broken forty-one-year-old:* Dow, *Adèle Hugo*, 161.

82 *a place that "everyone knows":* Henri Gourdin, *Adèle, l'Autre Fille de Victor Hugo: 1830–1915: Biographie* (2003), 291–92.

83 *"She kissed Georges and Jeanne":* Guillemin, *L'Engloutie*, 153.

83 *she confused the generations:* Jean Hugo, *Le Regard de la Mémoire: 1914–1945* (1994), 165.

83 *"the obliviousness of his powerful and rugged good health":* Goncourt *Journal*, II (August 5, 1873), 546–48.

84 *"that is the title of the Hugo family":* Ibid.

84 *reduced to a simple, anonymous obligation:* See Joanna Richardson, *Victor Hugo* (1976), 208; Dow, *Adèle Hugo*, 164; and Gallo, *Victor Hugo*, vol. 2, 401.

85 *He oversaw her education:* Jeanne Hugo, bulletin of exams (October–December; no year), archives of the Maison Victor Hugo.

86 *"all the sick and the poorest people":* Jeanne Hugo, French exam (October 1881), archives of the Maison Victor Hugo.

4: BABIES OF THE REPUBLIC

88 *the event and its journalistic aftermath:* Accounts of the fight can be found in *Le Temps, Le Figaro,* and *Le Petit Parisien* on May 17, 18, and 19.

88 *"We were spared neither admonitions nor remonstrance":* Léon Daudet, *Devant la Douleur*, 263.

88 *suppress an indulgent smile:* Goetz et al., *Charcot*, 270.

90 *"We will make something of you":* Léon Daudet, *Fantômes et Vivants*, 11.

90 *first run of eighty thousand copies:* Broche, *Léon Daudet*, 65.

91 *Champions of reason and science:* Eugen Weber, *France, Fin de Siècle* (1986), 14.

92 *"fought within ourselves the good national sense":* Léon Daudet, *Fantômes et Vivants*, 64.

93 *"The sadness, the alarm of my dear son":* Alphonse Daudet, *Oeuvres*, III, ed. Roger Ripoll (1994), 1267.

95 *"I would always be taken for a papa's boy":* Heimermann and Janichon, *Charcot, le Gentleman des Pôles*, 22.

95 *"they will always know how to amuse themselves anywhere":* Emmanuel, *Tel Fut Charcot*, 14.

95 *the victim was only a scarecrow:* Ibid., 25.

95 *"One doesn't marry at twenty-three":* Thuillier, *Monsieur Charcot de la Salpêtrière*, 254.

96 *After being roundly upbraided by her father:* Goncourt *Journal*, III, 436.

96 *by years of being poked and prodded:* Léon Daudet, *Les Morticoles* (1894), 156.

97 *the odor of dirty feet and carbolic acid:* Broche, *Léon Daudet*, 80.

99 *Silence fell like a shroud:* Léon Daudet, *Devant la Douleur*, 171.

99 *"never suspected this filial treachery":* Léon Daudet, *Quand Vivait Mon Père*, 257.

100 *ask for advice about their various injuries, sores, and pains:* Léon Daudet, *Paris Vécu: Rive Droite*, in *Souvenirs et Polémiques* (1992), 922.

100 *he would be seen as a gold digger:* Goncourt *Journal*, III (May 10, 1888), 123.

101 *"the doctor of tomorrow":* Ibid. (June 23, 1888), 137.

101 *"He is swollen, bloated like a commoner":* Ibid. (March 6, 1889), 236.

101 *covering up her face in embarrassment:* Ibid., II (December 15, 1886), 1288.

101 *The great Italian banker and industrialist:* "Cernuschi's Parties," *The New York Times* (May 19, 1888).

101 *featured in society pages around the world:* These included the major French and American newspapers.

102 *"what will be the eventual outcome of such conscientious efforts":* Christopher Goetz, "Charcot and the Myth of Misogyny," *Neurology* 52 (1999), 1681.

103 *"insupportable odor of musk":* Goncourt *Journal*, III (May 7, 1889), 267.

103 *"the mixture in him of idiocies, fights with cabdrivers":* Ibid. (May 16, 1889), 270.

5: IN SICKNESS AND IN HEALTH

105 *to catch a glimpse of the great Victor Hugo's granddaughter:* Accounts of the wedding appeared in all the major Parisian newspapers, including *Le Temps*, *Le Figaro*, *Éclair*, and *Rappel*.

106 *suggested an undeniably unsettling genealogy:* Wanda Bannour, *Alphonse Daudet: Bohème et Bourgeois* (1990), 166.

107 *"Mademoiselle, I have loved you since I treated you":* Goncourt *Journal*, III (July 8, 1890), 444.

107 *a nice girl but nothing remarkable:* Ibid.

107 *"It is a pretty sight":* Ibid. (July 9, 1890), 446.

107 *"Jeanne is really quite lovely":* Ibid.

108 *"But what in the world can you be talking about?":* Ibid. (July 13, 1890), 449.

108 *"The happiness of Jeanne has an expansion that spreads out":* Ibid. (July 20, 1890), 451.

110 *would remain by his side so that nothing would happen:* Ibid. (February 12, 1891), 539.

112 *"Love the one who loves you":* *Le Temps* (February 13, 1891).

112 *It is for him that all of Paris has come here:* *Le Temps* (February 13, 1891).

113 *"Everything conspires in your favor":* Ibid.

113 *"like an intelligent monkey":* Goncourt *Journal*, III (February 13, 1891), 541.

113 *"it is really good to be married":* Ibid. (February 15, 1891), 542.

113 *"a more tenderly enveloping affection":* Ibid. (April 12, 1891), 571.

114 *"Yes, I am mad at you":* Ibid. (July 12, 1890), 448.

115 *"charm that made such traits more palatable":* Alan Sheridan, *Time and Place* (2004), 384.

115 *"Enough with your old fart grandfather":* Jean Paul Clébert, *Les Daudet: 1840–1940: Une Famille Bien Française* (1988), 262.

115 *"discuss your Balzac or your Ibsen":* Robert Harborough Sherard, *Alphonse Daudet: A Biographical and Critical Study* (1896), 426–27.

118 *reduced to entering the theater without the arm of a man:* Clébert, *Les Daudet*, 262–63.

118 *as anarchist bombs ripped through popular cafés:* See John Merriman, *The Dynamite Club: How a Bombing in Fin-de-Siècle Paris Ignited the Age of Modern Terror* (2009).

6: DEGENERATION

124 *"astonish the world by the great deeds":* David G. McCullough, *The Path Between the Seas: The Creation of the Panama Canal, 1870–1914* (1999), 58.

125 *the tables were decorated with centerpieces:* "The Merchant's Welcome," *The New York Times* (March 2, 1880).

125 *"What do you wish to find in Panama?":* Benoît Heimermann, *Suez et Panama: La Fabuleuse Épopée de Ferdinand de Lesseps* (1996), 93; McCullough, *Path Between the Seas*, 68–69.

125 *"I maintain that Panama will be easier":* Zachary Karabell, *Parting the Desert: The Creation of the Suez Canal* (2003), 267.

126 *"a desert for a poor man":* Paul Gaugin to Melle, in *Correspondance de Paul Gaugin*, vol. 1 (1873–1888), ed. Victor Merlhès (1984), 147.

127 *"only drunkards and the dissipated":* William C. Haskins, ed., *Canal Zone Pilot: Guide to the Republic of Panama and Classified Business Directory* (1908), 194.

127 *one photo:* McCullough, *Path Between the Seas*, 160. Sources on Dingler's tragedy include McCullough, *Path Between the Seas*, 160–61 and 171–72; Haskins, *Canal Zone Pilot*, 194; Heimermann, *Suez et Panama*, 103; Deborah Cadbury, *Dreams of Iron and Steel: Seven Wonders of the Modern Age, from the Building of the London Sewers to the Panama Canal* (2005), 205; and Joseph Bucklin Bishop, *The Panama Gateway* (1915), 94–95.

127 *"about two hundred a month":* McCullough, *Path Between the Seas*, 160.

127 *"I cannot thank you enough":* Ibid., 160–61.

128 *published a series of revelations:* Eventually all the major French newspapers of the day picked up on the story and followed the unfolding scandal closely. Other sources include Jean-Yves Mollier, *Le Scandale de Panama* (1991).

128 *"only merit had been to put into print":* Stephen Wilson, *Ideology and Experience: Antisemitism in France at the Time of the Dreyfus Affair* (1982), 171.

129 *the prosecuting attorney charged both the de Lessepses:* Karabell, *Parting the Desert*, 268.

129 *"witnesses to a kind of social decomposition":* Jean Jaurès, February 8, 1893, in the Chamber of Deputies, in *Les Grands Orateurs Republicains* (1949), 46.

130 *"the beginning of the end":* Engels to Sorge (December 31, 1892), in Dona Torr, ed. and trans., *Correspondence, 1846–1895* (1934), 503.

130 *"And if I don't get away on time":* Ernst Pawel, *The Labyrinth of Exile: A Life of Theodor Herzl* (1989), 171–72.

131 *The French press was outraged:* See articles in *Le Temps* and *Le Figaro*. See also "Herz Too Ill to Be Moved," *The New York Times* (June 23, 1893), 9.

132 *"I had to reassure him":* Léon Daudet, *Devant la Douleur*, 186.

133 *"You looked after me at the Salpêtrière":* Cited in Guillain, *J.-M. Charcot*, 72.

134 *"Can we then affirm":* J.-M. Charcot, "La Foi Qui Guerit," *Revue Hebdomadaire* (December 3, 1892), 112–32.

134 *"one of the glories of French science"*: *Le Temps* (August 18, 1897).
135 *"I knew immediately . . . that something"*: Léon Daudet, *Les Oeuvres dans les Hommes* (1922), 238.
136 *"the aetiological theories"*: Freud, "Charcot," 23.
137 *he also reminded Freud of the prevalence:* Toby Gelfand, "Charcot's Response to Freud's Rebellion," *Journal of the History of Ideas* 50:2 (April–June 1989), 293–307.
137 *"the most significant event, the most decisive loss"*: Peter Gay, *Freud: A Life for Our Time*, 89.
138 *"Gallic predisposition"*: Debora L. Silverman, *Art Nouveau in Fin-de-Siècle France*, 82.
138 *willingly submitted to medical checkups:* Hans-Peter Soder, "Disease and Health as Contexts of Modernity: Max Nordau as a Critic of Fin-de-Siècle Modernism," *German Studies Review* 14:3 (October 1991), 473–87.
139 *"I wrote this large book"*: Broche, *Léon Daudet*, 131.
139 *"an abundance of ideas, a richness of images"*: Goncourt *Journal*, III (April 1, 1894), 935.

7: DEGRADATION

142 *"Soldiers, an innocent man is being degraded"*: Jean-Denis Bredin, *The Affair: The Case of Alfred Dreyfus* (1986), 4–5.
143 *"Those . . . who had actually witnessed the degradation"*: Theodor Herzl, "Account of the Dreyfus Degradation," *Neue Freie Presse* (January 6, 1895), cited in Michael Burns, *France and the Dreyfus Affair: A Documentary History* (1999), 54–55.
143 *"If you had seen this Dreyfus fellow"*: Clébert, *Les Daudet*, 265.
144 *"a walking corpse . . . a zombie on parade"*: Léon Daudet, "The Punishment," *Le Figaro* (January 6, 1895), cited in Burns, *France and the Dreyfus Affair*, 51–52.
146 *"This hunger is the mark"*: Charles Maurras, *La Revue Encyclopédique* (February 29, 1896), cited in Broche, *Léon Daudet*, 150.
146 *Goncourt wondered if Léon was in such a bad mood:* Goncourt *Journal*, III (May 13, 1896), 1281.
147 *shocked by the "appalling materialism"*: Marcel Proust to Reynaldo Hahn, (November 15, 1895), in Marcel Proust, *Correspondance*, vol. 1 (1880–1895), ed. Philip Kolb (1970), 369.
148 *"I was unable to understand . . ."*: Marcel Proust, *Contre Sainte Beuve: Précédé de Pastiches et Mélanges et Suivi de Essais et Articles* (1971), 400.
148 *"It is very precious to me"*: Alphonse Daudet to Marcel Proust (June 1896), in Marcel Proust, *Correspondance*, vol. 2 (1896–1901), ed. Philip Kolb (1976), 79.
149 *"the most charming, the most whimsical"*: Léon Daudet, *Salons et Journaux*, in *Souvenirs et Polémiques* (1992), 505.
149 "meticulous tapestry, of admirable brilliance": Léon Daudet, *Paris Vécu: Rive Droite*, in *Souvenirs et Polémiques* (1992), 988.
150 *"If you are insane, we are insane together"*: Anna Nordau, *Max Nordau, a Biography* (1943), 120. See also Pawel, *Labyrinth of Exile*, 257–58.

151 *Proust's anxiety was intense and his hands shook:* Ronald Heyman, *Proust: A Biography* (1990), 117.

151 *"The Charity Bazaar is burning!":* See articles in *Le Figaro, Le Temps,* and *Le Petit Parisien.*

153 *"We must not write anything else":* Clébert, *Les Daudet,* 286.

153 *"But what a hatred of the uniform":* Léon Daudet, *Au Temps de Judas,* in *Souvenirs et Polémiques* (1992), 536.

154 *"the gray eminence of treason":* Bredin, *Affair,* 201.

154 *"with a jerky stride as if he were climbing":* Ibid., 230.

156 *"So there exist fresh young brains and souls":* Brown, *Zola,* 732.

157 *"How many times did I hear my father":* Jan Goldstein, "The Wandering Jew and the Problem of Psychiatric Anti-Semitism in Fin-de-Siècle France, *Journal of Contemporary History* 20:4 (1985), 521.

157 *"The sudden death of M. Alphonse Daudet":* "Mort de Daudet," *Le Matin* (December 17, 1897).

157 *although he had devoted his life:* "Alphonse Daudet," *Le Temps* (December 18, 1897).

159 *"colossus with dirty feet":* Gustave Flaubert to Edma Roger des Genelles (April 18, 1880), in *Flaubert: Correspondance,* vol. 5, ed. Jean Bruneau and Yvan Le Clerc (2007), 886.

160 *"Politics leaves me completely indifferent":* "Zola Ne Sera Pas Deputé. Chèz l'Auteur *des Rougon-Macquart,*" *L'Aurore* (November 4, 1897).

161 *while waiting to testify at Zola's trial:* Goldberg, *Life of Jean Jaurès,* 226.

161 *"By all that I have conquered":* Brown, *Zola,* 741.

161 *"profound and respectful affection":* in Émile Zola, *Correspondence,* vol. 9, ed. B. H. Bakker (1993), 203 (note 2).

162 *"written sentences capable of provoking catastrophe":* Brown, *Zola,* 743.

162 *"I would rather have this life of combat":* Tuchman, *Proud Tower,* 204.

162 *"only be explained by a need":* Charles Péguy, *Notre Jeunesse* (1933), 220.

163 *"Every conscience is troubled":* Tuchman, *Proud Tower,* 200.

163 *"could be heard the tramp of the barbarian legions":* Daudet, *"Au Temps de Judas,"* in *Souvenirs et Polémiques,* 546.

164 *"The Dreyfus Case has simply drawn aside veils":* Anna Nordau, *Max Nordau,* 145–46.

165 *"Check out the horrible head of that guy":* Max Simon Nordau and Anna Nordau: *Errinerungen: Erzählt von Ihm Selbst und von der Gefährtin Seines Lebens* (1928), 215.

165 *"At that moment we felt nothing":* Maurice Barrès, *Scènes et Doctrines du Nationalism* (1902), 138, cited in Bredin, *Affair,* 405.

165 *"looked like Hercules and pleaded like a boxer":* Tuchman, *Proud Tower,* 224.

166 *"good invincible giant":* William C. Carter, *Marcel Proust: A Life* (2000), 266.

166 *"How could they do it?":* Tuchman, *Proud Tower,* 224.

8: THE HEIRESS AND THE POLAR GENTLEMAN

169 *"Will we succeed?":* Jean-Baptiste Charcot, *Le "Français" au Pôle Sud,* 2.

172 *he came across an article:* Paul Pléneau, "La Gènese d'une Expédition Polaire: Comment J'ai Connu Charcot," *Jean-Baptiste Charcot,* 109.

172 *"It's a deal":* Paul Pléneau, "La Genèse d'une Expédition Polaire: Comment J'ai Connu Charcot," *Yacht Club* (1937), 112.

173 *"Instead of going north":* Ibid., 120.

173 *"Wherever you like":* Ibid., 121.

174 *Sigmund Freud referred to the experiences:* Freud, "The Interpretation of Dreams," in *The Standard Edition of the Complete Psychological Works of Sigmund Freud,* vol. 4, 191.

174 *"I shall be able to make some use of Nansen's dreams":* Sigmund Freud to Wilhelm Fliess (August 20, 1898), in *Letters of Sigmund Freud* (1992), 238.

175 *"Whatever remains to man unknown":* Roald Amundsen, *Roald Amundsen: My Life As an Explorer* (1927), 244.

177 *"honored and happy he was":* *L'Eclair,* November 20, 1896.

178 *"From the expedition":* "Personal," *The Washington Post* (June 11, 1880).

180 *"took advantage of the situation":* "Marquise de Fontenoy's Letter," *Chicago Daily News* (May 25, 1898).

180 *instructed Georges to behave more "discreetly":* "Always Animated Paris," *The New York Times* (July 17, 1898).

180 *"slowly drifting away from the loving traditions":* "French Literature," *Los Angeles Times* (August 14, 1898).

181 *He tried his hand at writing, too:* Georges Hugo, *Mon Grand-Père* (1902).

181 *"Continue, continue . . .":* "En Écoutant Charles Daudet Parler de Sa Mère Jeanne Hugo, la Petite-Fille du Poète," *Vie Heureuse,* n.d., archives of Maison Victor Hugo.

182 *Some newspapers estimated the crowd:* "Antarctic Voyage Delayed," *The New York Times* (August 16, 1903), 1.

182 *"He loved you so":* Jean-Baptiste Charcot, *Le "Français" au Pôle Sud,* 2, 192.

183 *There was even an Italian alpine guide:* William James Mills, *Exploring Polar Frontiers: A Historical Encyclopedia* (2003), 136.

184 *As they sailed farther and farther south:* Marthe Oulié, *Charcot of the Antarctic* (1938), 35.

184 *"It is a new page of my life":* Jean-Baptiste Charcot, *Le "Français" au Pôle Sud,* 3.

184 *"We have before us a decor":* Ibid., 8.

185 *described in his notebook as "very sui generis":* Ibid., 35, 39.

185 *Even the snow felt like a weapon:* Ibid., 62.

187 *"I can say without flattering myself":* Ibid., 116.

188 *He didn't want to tell the others:* Ibid., 135.

188 *"What is going to happen to me?":* Ibid., 152.

190 *"To risk a second winter is now impossible":* Ibid., 305.

191 *"A few minutes before, in arriving at the port":* Ibid., 327.

191 *twenty-two feet:* Oulié, *Charcot of the Antarctic,* 99.

192 *"this strange attraction to these polar regions":* Charcot, *Le "Français" au Pôle Sud,* 317–18.

194 *"My own thought was to labour":* Jean-Baptiste Charcot, *Voyage of the "Why Not?,"* 27.

195	*"Pieces of whale float about on all sides"*: Ibid., 32.
196	*"I could believe that I never"*: Ibid., 60–61.
196	*"Too many memories"*: Ibid., 65.
197	*shock so forceful*: Ibid., 78.
197	*"vibrates as though she wished to shatter herself"*: Ibid., 79.
198	*"Enormous spurs of glaucous hue jump"*: Ibid., 114.
198	*confessed to "a fit of the blues"*: Ibid., 113.
198	*"It was a great, almost a desperate, blow"*: Ibid., 132.
199	*concerts on Sundays:* Heimermann and Janichon, *Charcot, le Gentleman des Pôles*, 107.
199	*"Nothing could be more moving"*: Oulié, *Charcot of the Antarctic*, 128.
200	*"For the occasion"*: Jean-Baptiste Charcot, *Voyage of the "Why Not?,"* 261.
200	*"I left my home and happiness"*: Jean-Baptiste Charcot, *Voyage of the "Why Not?,"* 302.
201	*"As a result of the crew's efforts"*: Oulié, *Charcot of the Antarctic*, 143–44, and Mills, *Exploring Polar Frontiers*, 139.
201	*"We dreamed of more"*: Heimermann and Janichon, *Charcot, le Gentleman des Pôles*, 118.
201	*"Our results will appear negligible"*: Kahn, *Jean-Baptiste Charcot*, 114.
201	*"Above the polar circle"*: Oulié, *Charcot of the Antarctic*, 141.

9: THE POLEMICIST

203	*"Syveton is dead"*: Léon Daudet, *Au Temps de Judas*, 621. The Syveton Affair was featured in the major French and international newspapers of the day. It is also discussed in Goldberg, *Life of Jean Jaurès*; Weber, *Action Française*; Broche, *Léon Daudet*; and Fernand Hauser, *Un Mystére Historique: l'Affaire Syveton* (1905). Weber's *Action Française* remains the most comprehensive study of the history, organization, and influence of the Action Française. Other useful sources that examine the political landscape of the Right during this period include Stéphane Giocanti, *Maurras: Le Chaos et l'Ordre* (2006); Zeev Sternhell, *Ni Droit, ni Gauche: l'Idéologie Fasciste en France* (1983); and Wilson, *Ideology and Experience*.
204	*"the indignant national frankness"*: Léon Daudet, *La Libre Parole* (November 6, 1904), cited in Jean Noël Marque, *Léon Daudet* (1971), 75.
206	*the victim of a "Masonic crime"*: Léon Daudet, "Un Crime Maçonnique," *La Libre Parole* (December 11, 1904).
206	*For two hours Léon and the royalist:* Marque, *Léon Daudet*, 77.
207	*"Were Frenchmen still at home in France?"*: Charles Maurras, *Au Signe de Flore: La Fondation de L'Action Française 1898–1900* (1933), 31.
207	*"has emerged a new order of things"*: Brown, *Zola*, 795–96.
208	*"the revival of more honest politics"*: Weber, *Action Française*, 20.
210	*"masterpiece of nature"*: Broche, *Léon Daudet*, 189.
212	*"After an hour of the interview"*: Léon Daudet, *Au Temps de Judas*, 604.
212	*"A century ago, clever and villainous men"*: Léon Daudet, "Le Pays sans Arbiter," *Le Gaulois* (September 3, 1904).
213	*"It is one of the greatest known pleasures"*: Clébert, *Les Daudet*, 314–15.

216 *"The unjustly scorned, disparaged, despised term"*: Léon Daudet, *Le Stupide XIXe Siècle*, in *Souvenirs et Polémiques* (1992), 1331.
217 *"My generation ignored these duties"*: Clébert, *Les Daudet*, 314–15.
218 *"if the Jew Bernstein"*: Weber, *Action Française*, 113.
218 *"Jewish, hideously Jewish"*: Broche, *Léon Daudet*, 240.
218 *"Jews of France, microbes of the State"*: Ibid.
218 *"Youth is with us"*: *La Libre Parole* (March 14, 1911), cited in Weber, *Action Française*, 84.
218 *during an evening of wilting heat:* The duel was covered in the major Paris and American newspapers, including Maurice Leudet, "Le Duel Bernstein-Daudet," in *Le Figaro* (July 22, 1911), cited in Susan Quinn, *Marie Curie: A Life* (1996), 289–91.
219 *"science is useless to women"*: Clébert, *Les Daudet*, 293–94.
219 *"The imbeciles who go around"*: Léon Daudet, "Dreyfus Contre Branly," *Action Française* (January 23, 1911), cited in Quinn, *Marie Curie*, 289–91.
220 *"Mme Curie Defeated"*: *The New York Times* (January 24, 1911). The controversy surrounding Marie Curie's possible election to the Académie Française and the scandal surrounding her personal life were widely discussed in the French and international newspapers of the day. These incidents are also discussed in many biographies of Marie Curie, including Quinn, *Marie Curie: A Life* (1996), and Barbara Goldsmith, *Obsessive Genius: The Inner World of Marie Curie* (2005).
220 *"The Republic does not need any scientists"*: Cited in Nanny Fröman, "Marie and Pierre Curie ad the Discovery of Polonium and Radium." Lecture at the Royal Swedish Academy of Sciences, Stockholm (February 28, 1996).
220 *"a boor and a coward"*: cited in Goldsmith, *Obsessive Genius*, 176.
222 *"Eleven thousand copies had been sold"*: Weber, *Action Française*, 89.
223 *"A total war: them or us"*: Léon Daudet, *Action Française* (March 11, 1916).
223 *"It's driving me mad"*: Weber, *Action Française*, 103.
224 *M. Malvy . . . is a traitor:* Léon Daudet's letter was reprinted widely in the newspapers of the day, including *Le Figaro* (October 5, 1917). Léon Daudet's prewar and wartime campaigns against political enemies were covered extensively in the French and international newspapers of the time and are also set forth in Broche, *Léon Daudet*, and Weber, *Action Française*.
224 *"For the last six hours"*: Weber, *Action Française*, 106.
224 *three years' imprisonment:* Accounts of the trial appeared in all the major French newspapers, including *Le Figaro*, *Le Gaulois*, *Le Temps*, and *Action Française*, as well as in *The New York Times*.
225 *killed the socialist leader:* "Jaurès Slayer Acquitted," *The New York Times* (March 30, 1919).

10: SINS OF THE FATHER
228 *queued up in front of the city morgue:* Vanesssa R. Schwartz has an excellent discussion of the "spectacularization" of death and the popularity of morgue visits in *Spectacular Realities: Early Mass Culture in Fin-de-Siècle Paris* (1998), 45–88.

228 *"This unhappy child has not"*: Louis Noguères, *Le Suicide de Philippe Daudet* (1926), 231.

228 *showed no trace of gunpowder:* Léon Daudet, *Paris Vécu: Rive Droite*, 953.

229 *nearly one out of every five men:* Eugen Weber, *The Hollow Years: France in the 1930s* (1994), 11.

229 *there were 630,000 war widows in France:* John Keegan, *The First World War* (1994), 6.

229 *"We all wanted to forget the war"*: Elisabeth de Gramont, *Souvenirs du Monde de 1890 à 1940* (1966), 319.

229 *an evening of poetry and dissonant music:* Mathew Gale, *Dada & Surrealism* (1997), 183, and Ruth Brandon, *Surreal Lives: The Surrealists 1917–1945* (1999), 138.

230 *"I have avenged Jaurès and Almereyda!"*: "Une Jeune Fille Anarchiste Tue M. Marius Plateau," *Le Figaro* (January 23, 1923). See also Weber, *Action Française*, 138–39.

230 *"emulating Facismo"*: "Camelots du Roi," *Time* (June 11, 1923).

230 *"Too many of our colleagues"*: Weber, *Action Française*, 143–44.

231 *worried about the "disreputable types"*: Mme Léon Daudet, *La Vie et la Mort de Philippe* (1926), 91.

232 *"I advise you to return"*: Léon Daudet, *Action Française* (November 23, 1923).

232 *sitting before a cloudy mirror:* Mme Léon Daudet, *La Vie et la Mort*, 92.

233 *"A young man"*: *Le Petit Parisien* (November 25, 1923).

233 *slumped to the floor:* Ibid., 95.

234 *"I just saw my handsome Philippe"*: Broche, *Léon Daudet*, 328.

234 *"Nothing good ever came out"*: Abbé Mugnier, *Journal de l'Abbé Mugnier: 1879–1939* (1985), 426.

234 *their tricolor armbands a reminder:* Léon Daudet, *Paris Vécu: Rive Droite*, 936–37.

234 *"Believe me, Madame"*: Broche, *Léon Daudet*, 329.

234 *"the physical sensation that a hyena"*: Mme Léon Daudet, *La Vie et la Mort*, 107.

235 *"My dear mother"*: Broche, *Léon Daudet*, 330.

235 "macbethéenne," *as he called it—view of life:* Léon Daudet, *Paris Vécu: Rive Droite*, 937.

235 *the "Affaire Philippe Daudet" began in earnest:* Brief accounts of the Philippe Daudet Affair can be found in most biographies of Léon Daudet, including Broche, Marque, and Bassi. Eugen Weber also devotes a chapter to the affair in *Action Française*. Examples of works that argue that Philippe was murdered include Mme Léon Daudet, *La Vie et la Mort*, and René Breval, *Philippe Daudet A Bel et Bien Été Assassiné* (1959).

236 *"the greatest sadness of my life"*: Léon Daudet, *Paris Vécu: Rive Droite*, 923–24.

236 *under the name of Pierre Bouchamp:* *Le Petit Parisien* (December 5, 1923).

236 *"My dearest parents"*: Noguères, *Le Suicide de Philippe Daudet*, 220.

237 *"in case the police come"*: *Le Petit Parisien* (December 9, 1923).

237 *"to kill Léon Daudet"*: Ibid.

237 *"I wanted to live my life"*: Ibid.

238 *confessed his own desire to explore:* Ibid.

238 *"My soul thrills with pleasure"*: The *Poèmes en Prose* of Philippe Daudet were published in Noguères, *Le Suicide de Philippe Daudet*, 197–207. Cited in Broche, *Léon Daudet*, 331.

240 *"a particular taste for scandal"*: Marque, *Léon Daudet*, 381.

241 *"the hottest and most bitter battle"*: Léon Daudet, *Paris Vécu: Rive Droite*, 1052.

241 *explained the connection he felt*: Maurice Privat, *L'Enigme Philippe Daudet* (1931), 43.

242 *reminded the courtroom:* "The Daudet Case Stirs Paris Anew," *The New York Times* (November 22, 1925).

242 *transformed ordinary men and women:* Le Temps (November 15, 1925).

243 *his fears that his children would inherit:* Noguères, *Le Suicide de Philippe Daudet*, 216.

244 *"I loved my father passionately"*: Georges Claretie, "M. Léon Daudet Est Condamné à Cinq Mois de Prison," *Le Figaro* (November 15, 1925).

244 *not a dry eye in the room:* Ibid.

245 *since the heady days of the Dreyfus Affair:* Comparisons to the Dreyfus Affair occurred throughout the newspapers of the day, including *The New York Times* (November 22, 1925).

245 *"What a handsome fighter"*: Claretie, "M. Léon Daudet Est Condamné."

246 *"mysterious aspects are still unexplained"*: *L'Humanité* (September 8, 1925), cited in Weber, *Action Française*, 169.

247 *Gaucher's argument was oversimplified:* André Gaucher, *L'Obsédé* (1925), 218.

11: THE FINAL VOYAGE

250 *"Politicians ought to spend"*: Emmanuel, *Tel Fut Charcot*, 216.

250 *"God knows that I, grandson of workers"*: Ibid., 216–18.

253 *"does not stop my plans"*: Roland Huntford, *The Last Place on Earth* (1999), 237.

253 *rose-and-gold-tipped mountains:* Jean-Baptiste Charcot, *La Mer du Groenland, Croisières du "Pourquoi pas?"* (1929), 61.

253 *"above all in moments like this"*: Jean-Baptiste Charcot, *Mer du Groenland*, 62.

255 *"the key to resolving"*: Mills, *Exploring Polar Frontiers*, 5.

255 *"Beg leave to inform you"*: Mills, *Exploring Polar Frontiers*, 15.

256 *"If one wishes to pronounce one greater"*: "Scott, Too, Says Charcot," *The New York Times* (March 9, 1912), 5.

257 *"the most impenetrable continents"*: "Mussolini Lauds Our Air Activity," *The New York Times* (March 25, 1927).

258 *"With men like Amundsen"*: "Swedish Plane Rescues Nobile from Ice, Then Upsets in Attempt to Get Comrades," *The New York Times* (June 25, 1928), 1.

258 *"I do not share their illusions"*: Emmanuel, *Tel Fut Charcot*, 150.

259 *Two of his former officers:* Jean-Baptiste Charcot, *Mer du Groenland*, 167.

259 *"The old should know to go off when it is time!"*: Emmanuel, *Tel Fut Charcot*, 151.

259 *"thirty-five people who depend on me"*: Ibid., 154.

259 *"Next to the devotion"*: *The New York Times* (June 27, 1928).

260 *"greatest tragedy in the history"*: "*Italia* Toll 19; Lundborg Believes," *The New York Times* (July 11, 1928), 1.

260 *"the most dangerous thing in the world"*: Emmanuel, *Tel Fut Charcot*, 173.
260 *"Whatever remains to man unknown"*: Amundsen, *Roald Amundsen: My Life As an Explorer*, 244.
261 *"Indifferent, they allow to pass"*: Emmanuel, *Tel Fut Charcot*, 231.
262 *"Goodbye, my little one"*: Kahn, *Jean-Baptiste Charcot*, 163.
266 *Then she remembered the one thing she knew:* "Naufrage du *Pourquoi Pas?*," *Espace 2*, Radio Suisse Romande (1986).
266 *"A medical career that promised"*: *The New York Times* (September 17, 1936). The shipwreck made headlines around the world.
267 *like an injured butterfly banging against a window:* Marthe Oulié, *Jean Charcot*, (1937), 236.
268 *in bringing the French flag to Antarctic waters:* "Le 'Pourquoi-Pas' Coule au Large des Côtes d'Islande," *Action Française* (September 17, 1936).

12: THE FINAL CHAPTER

270 *"because . . . I know it by heart"*: Léon Daudet, "Flaubert et le Domaine Publique," *Action Française* (October 7, 1936).
270 *not even the famed Maginot Line:* Léon Daudet, *Action Française* (September 15, 1933).
271 *"disappear body and soul from this place"*: Louis-Ferdinand Céline, *L'École des Cadavres* (1938), cited in Robert O. Paxton, *Vichy France: Old Guard and New Order, 1940–1944* (1972), 12.
271 *close to four million people left their homes:* See Hanna Diamond, *Fleeing Hitler: France 1940* (2007).
272 *"since the passing of the Naquet law"*: Léon Daudet, *Action Française* (April 17, 1941).
273 *"I was not ready at our meeting"*: Broche, *Léon Daudet*, 399.
274 *"more than a century ahead"*: Céleste Alabert, *Monsieur Proust* (2001), 360.
275 *"he called his enemies female camels"*: "Death of a Conspiracy," *Time* (July 13, 1942).
276 *"the re-emerence of Masons, Jews"*: Charles Maurras in *Action Française* (May 8, 1944), cited in Weber, *Action Française*, 468.
277 *Pétain's rise to power:* Weber, *Action Française*, 447.
277 *When the announcement of her death:* "Victor Hugo's Kin Dies," *The New York Times* (December 3, 1941).
278 *"nobody dreams of Jeanne Hugo remaining single"*: Marquise de Fontenoy, "The Kaiser's Visit to Baron Mumm," *The Washington Post* (May 2, 1914).
278 *her nephew, the artist Jean Hugo:* Jean Hugo, *Regard*, 310.
279 *"brought up in these fantastic surroundings"*: "The Tragedy of Hugo's Daughter," *The New York Times* (May 2, 1915).
280 *her turbulent life and loves:* Mugnier, *Journal*, 230.
280 *"has changed less since Jesus Christ"*: Charles Péguy, *L'Argent* (1913), in *Oeuvres en Prose, 1909–1914* (1968), 1104.
281 *unable to shed the pessimism:* Robert Wohl, *The Generation of 1914* (1979), 17.

Bibliography

Adam, Juliette. *Mes Premières Armes Littéraires et Politiques*. Paris: A. Lemerre, 1904.

Amundsen, Roald. *Roald Amundsen: My Life As an Explorer*. Garden City, N.Y.: Doubleday, 1927.

Amundsen, Roald, and Lincoln Ellsworth. *First Crossing of the Polar Sea*. New York: George H. Doran, 1927.

Atget, Eugène, Arthur Donald Trottenberg, and Marcel Proust. *A Vision of Paris: The Photographs of Eugène Atget; the Words of Marcel Proust*. Reissue edition. New York: Macmillan, 1980.

Baldick, Robert. *Dinner at Magny's*. London: Gollancz, 1971.

———. *The Duel: A History of Duelling*. New York: C. N. Potter, 1965.

———. *The Siege of Paris*. New York: Macmillan, 1964.

Barrès, Maurice. *La République ou le Roi; Correspondance Inédite (1888–1923)*. Edited by Hélène and Nicole Maurras. Paris: Plon, 1970.

———. *Scènes et Doctrines du Nationalisme*. 2 vols. Paris: Plon-Nourrit et Cie, 1925.

Bassi, Michel. *Léon Daudet: Un Géant de Papier*. Monaco: Editions du Rocher, 1993.

Bredin, Jean-Denis. *The Affair: The Case of Alfred Dreyfus* [Affaire]. New York: G. Braziller, 1986.

Breuer, Josef, and Sigmund Freud. *Studies on Hysteria* [Studien über Hysterie]. New York: Basic Books, 1957.

Broche, François. *Léon Daudet: Le Dernier Imprécateur*. Biographies Sans Masque. Paris: R. Laffont, 1992.

Brombert, Victor H. *The Hidden Reader: Stendhal, Balzac, Hugo, Baudelaire, Flaubert*. Cambridge, Mass.: Harvard University Press, 1988.

———. *Victor Hugo and the Visionary Novel*. Cambridge, Mass.: Harvard University Press, 1984.

Brown, Frederick. *Flaubert: A Biography*. New York: Little, Brown, 2006.

———. *Zola: A Life*. New York: Farrar, Straus and Giroux, 1995.

Burns, Michael. *Dreyfus: A Family Affair, 1789–1945*. New York: HarperCollins, 1991.

Chamberlin, J. Edward, and Sander L. Gilman. *Degeneration: The Dark Side of Progress.* New York: Columbia University Press, 1985.

Charcot, Jean-Baptiste Auguste Étienne. *Christophe Colomb Vu par un Marin.* Paris: Flammarion, 1928.

———. *Deuxième Expédition Antarctique Française (1908–1910).* 4 vols. Paris: Masson, 1914–15.

———. *Expédition Antarctique Française (1903–1905).* Paris: Masson, 1908.

———. *Le "Français" au Pôle Sud.* Paris: Éditions de l'Aube, 1997.

———. *La Mer du Groenland, Croisières du "Pourquoi pas?"* Paris and Bruges: Desclée, de Brouwer, 1929.

———. *Le "Pourquoi-pas?" dans l'Antarctique, 1908–1910.* Preface by Pierre Drach. Paris: Flammarion, 1968.

———. *The Voyage of the "Why Not?" in the Antarctic: The Journal of the Second French South Polar Expedition, 1908–1910.* Translated by Philip Walsh. New York: Hodder and Stoughton, 1911.

———. *Voyages aux Îles Feroë.* Paris: Société d'Éditions Géographiques, Maritimes et Coloniales, 1934.

Charcot, Jean-Martin. *Charcot, the Clinician: The Tuesday Lessons: Excerpts from Nine Case Presentations on General Neurology Delivered at the Salpêtrière Hospital in 1887–88 by Jean-Martin Charcot* [Leçons du Mardi à la Salpêtrière]. Translated by Christopher G. Goetz. New York: Raven Press, 1987.

———. *Clinical Lectures of Certain Diseases of the Nervous System.* Translated by Edward Payson Hurd. Detroit: G. S. Davis, 1888.

———. *Les Difformes et les Malades dans l'Art.* Amsterdam: N. V. Boekhandel & Antiquariaat B. M. Israël, 1972.

———. *Lectures on the Diseases of the Nervous System.* New York: Hafner, 1962.

———. *Oeuvres Complètes de J.M. Charcot.* Paris: Bureaux du Progrès Medical, 1888–94.

Charle, Christophe. *Paris Fin de Siècle: Culture et Politique.* Univers Historique. Paris: Éditions du Seuil, 1998.

Clébert, Jean Paul. *Les Daudet: 1840–1940: Une Famille Bien Française.* Paris: Presses de la Renaissance, 1988.

Cocteau, Jean, Jean Hugo, Brigitte Borsaro, and Pierre Caizergues. *Jean Cocteau, Correspondance, Jean Hugo.* Montpellier, France: Centre d'Étude du XXe Siècle, Université Paul Valéry, 1995.

Crémieux, Benjamin, and Marcel Proust. *Du Côté de Marcel Proust.* Paris: Éditions Lemarget, 1929.

Daudet, Alphonse. *Aventures Prodigieuses de Tartarin de Tarascon.* Edited and with a preface by Marie-Ange Voisin-Fougère. Paris: Librairie Générale Française, 1997.

———. *In the Land of Pain* [Doulou]. Translated and edited by Julian Barnes. New York: Knopf, 2002.

———. *Monday Tales.* Boston: Little, Brown, 1927.

———. *The Nabob* [Nabab]. Crown Gems of France. New York: Werner, 1902.

———. *Oeuvres.* Edited by Roger Ripoll. Paris: Gallimard, 1986–94.

———. *Oeuvres Complètes.* Edited by Henry Céard. 18 vols. Paris: A. Houssiaux, 1899–1901.

———. *Le Petit Chose: Histoire d'un Enfant.* Preface by Paul Guth, commentary and notes by Louis Forestier and Marie-France Azéma. Paris: Livre de Poche, 2008.

———. *Rose et Ninette: Moeurs du Jour.* Paris: Flammarion, 1892.

———. *Thirty Years of Paris and of My Literary Life.* Translated by Laura Ensor. London: J. M. Dent, 1896.

Daudet, Alphonse, and Frédéric Mistral. *Histoire d'une Amitié: Correspondance Inédite Entre Alphonse Daudet et Frédéric Mistral, 1860–1897.* Edited by Jacques-Henry Bornecque. Paris: Julliard, 1979.

Daudet, Léon. *Alphonse Daudet.* Paris: Fasquelle, 1898.

———. *Cloudy Trophy: The Romance of Victor Hugo* [Tragique Existence de Victor Hugo]. Translated by James Whitall. New York: W. Morrow, 1938.

———. *L'Hérédo, Essai sur le Drame Intérieur.* Paris: Nouvelle Librairie Nationale, 1917.

———. *Le Monde des Images. Suite de "L'Hérédo".* Paris: Nouvelle Librairie Nationale, 1919.

———. *Le Poignard dans le Dos: Notes sur l'Affaire Malvy.* Paris: Nouvelle Librairie Nationale, 1918.

———. *La Police Politique, Ses Moyens et Ses Crimes.* Paris: Les Éditions Denoël et Steele, 1934.

———. *Quand Vivait Mon Père; Souvenirs Inédits sur Alphonse Daudet.* Paris: Grasset, 1942.

———. *Souvenirs et Polémiques.* Paris: R. Laffont, 1992.

———. *Souvenirs Politiques.* Edited by René Wittmann. Paris: Éditions d'Histoire et d'Art, 1974.

———. *The Stupid XIXth Century.* Translated by Lewis Galantière. New York: Payson & Clarke, 1928.

———. *Le Stupide XIXe Siècle, Exposé des Insanités Meutrières Qui Se Sont Abattues sur la France Depuis 130 Ans, 1789–1919.* Paris: Nouvelle Librairie Nationale, 1922.

———. *La Tragique Existence de Victor Hugo.* Paris: A. Michel, 1937.

———. *Vingt-Neuf Mois d'Exil.* Paris: Grasset, 1930.

Daudet, Marthe, and Shirley King. *Pampille's Table: Recipes and Writings from the French Countryside from Marthe Daudet's Les Bons Plats de France.* New York: Faber and Faber, 1996.

de Diesbach, Ghislain. *Ferdinand de Lesseps.* Paris: Perrin, 1998.

———. *La Princesse Bibesco, 1886–1973.* Collection Terres des Femmes. Paris: Librairie Académique Perrin, 1986.

———. *Proust.* Paris: Perrin, 1991.

de Lesseps, Ferdinand. *Lettres, Journal et Documents pour Servir à l'Histoire du Canal de Suez (1854, 1855, 1856).* Paris: Didier, 1969.

———. *Souvenirs de Quarante Ans Dédiés à Mes Enfants.* Paris: Nouvelle Revue, 1887.

Didi-Huberman, Georges, and J.-M. Charcot. *The Invention of Hysteria: Charcot and the Photographic Iconography of the Salpêtrière* [Invention de l'Hystérie]. Cambridge, Mass.: MIT Press, 2003.

Dimier, Louis. *Vingt Ans d'Action Française et Autres Souvenirs.* Paris: Nouvelle Librairie Nationale, 1926.

Dow, Leslie Smith. *Adèle Hugo: La Misérable*. Fredericton, New Brunswick: Goose Lane, 1993.

Dowbiggin, Ian R. *Inheriting Madness: Professionalization and Psychiatric Knowledge in Nineteenth-Century France*. Medicine and Society. Vol. 4. Berkeley: University of California Press, 1991.

Drake, David. *French Intellectuals and Politics from the Dreyfus Affair to the Occupation*. French Politics, Society, and Culture Series. New York: Palgrave Macmillan, 2005.

Dreyfus, Alfred, and L. G. Moreau. *Lettres d'un Innocent: The Letters of Captain Dreyfus to His Wife*. New York and London: Harper & Brothers, 1899.

Dreyfus, Alfred, and Philippe Oriol. *Carnets (1899–1907): Après le Procès de Rennes*. Paris: Calmann-Lévy, 1998.

Drumont, Édouard Adolphe. *La France Juive: Essai d'Histoire Contemporaine*. Paris: C. Marpon & E. Flammarion, 1887.

Elwitt, Sanford. *The Making of the Third Republic: Class and Politics in France, 1868–1884*. Baton Rouge: Louisiana State University Press, 1975.

Emmanuel, Marthe. *Charcot, Navigateur Polaire*. Paris: Éditions des Loisirs, 1943.

———. *Le France et l'Exploration Polaire*. Paris: Nouvelles Éditions Latines, 1959.

———. *J.-B. Charcot, le "Polar Gentleman."* Paris: Éditions Alsatia, 1945.

———. *Tel Fut Charcot, 1867–1936*. Figues d'Hier et d'Aujourd'hui. Paris: Beauchesne, 1967.

Escholier, Raymond. *Un Amant de Génie, Victor Hugo: Lettres d'Amour et Carnets Inédits*. Paris: Fayard, 1979.

———. *Victor Hugo, Cet Inconnu*. Paris: Plon, 1951.

———. *Victor Hugo et les Femmes*. Paris: Flammarion, 1935.

———. *Victor Hugo Raconté par Ceux Qui l'Ont Vu: Souvenirs, Lettres, Documents, Réunis, Annotés et Accompagnés de Résumés Biographiques*. Les Grands Hommes Racontés par Ceux Qui les Ont Vus. Paris: Stock Delamain et Boutelleau, 1931.

Evans, Martha Noel. *Fits and Starts: A Genealogy of Hysteria in Modern France*. Ithaca, N.Y.: Cornell University Press, 1991.

Flaubert, Gustave. *The Letters of Gustave Flaubert. Vols. 1 and 2, 1830–1880*. Selected and translated by Francis Steegmuller, with a foreword by Anita Brookner. London: Picador, 2001.

Flaubert, Gustave, Edmond de Goncourt, Jules de Goncourt, and Pierre Dufief. *Gustave Flaubert–Les Goncourt, Correspondance*. Edited by Pierre Dufief. Paris: Flammarion, 1998.

Flaubert, Gustave, and Ivan Turgenev. *A Friendship in Letters: The Complete Correspondence*. Edited and translated by Barbara Beaumont. London: Athlone Press, 1985.

Forth, Christopher E. *The Dreyfus Affair and the Crisis of French Manhood*. Baltimore: Johns Hopkins University Press, 2004.

———. *Zarathustra in Paris: The Nietzsche Vogue in France, 1891–1918*. Dekalb: Northern Illinois University Press, 2001.

Freud, Sigmund. *An Autobiographical Study*. Translated and edited by James Strachey. New York: W. W. Norton, 1989.

———. *The Freud Reader*. Edited by Peter Gay. New York: W. W. Norton, 1989.

———. *The Interpretation of Dreams* [Traumdeutung]. Translated by James Strachey. London: G. Allen & Unwin, 1954.

———. *Letters of Sigmund Freud.* Edited by Ernst L. Freud. New York: Dover, 1992.

———. *New Introductory Lectures on Psychoanalysis.* Edited by James Strachey. New York: W. W. Norton, 1965.

———. *Psychological Writings and Letters.* Edited by Sander L. Gilman. The German Library. Vol. 59. New York: Continuum, 1995.

Freud, Sigmund, and Wilhelm Fliess. *The Origins of Psycho-Analysis: Letters to Wilhelm Fliess, Drafts and Notes, 1887–1902* [Aus den Anfängen der Psychoanalyse]. Edited by Marie Bonaparte, Anna Freud, and Ernst Kris. Translated by Eric Mosbacher and James Strachey. New York: Basic Books, 1954.

———. *The Standard Edition of the Complete Psychological Works of Sigmund Freud.* Translated and edited by James Strachey, in collaboration with Anna Freud, assisted by Alix Strachey and Alan Tyson. London: Hogarth Press, 1953–74.

Freud, Sigmund, and Arnold Zweig. *The Letters of Sigmund Freud & Arnold Zweig.* Edited by Ernst L. Freud. The International Psychoanalytical Library. Vol. 84. London: Hogarth Press for the Institute of Psycho-Analysis, 1970.

Fröman, Nanny. "Marie and Pierre Curie and the Discovery of Polonium and Radium." Lecture at the Royal Swedish Academy of Sciences, Stockholm. February 28, 1996.

Gallo, Max. *Victor Hugo.* 2 vols. Paris: XO Editions, 2001.

Garrigues, Jean. *Les Scandales de la République: De Panama à l'Affaire Elf.* Paris: R. Laffont, 2004.

Gauguin, Paul. *Correspondance de Paul Gauguin.* Edited by Victor Merlhès. Paris: Fondation Singer-Polignac, 1984.

Gay, Peter. *The Bourgeois Experience: Victoria to Freud.* New York: Oxford University Press, 1984.

———. *Freud: A Life for Our Time.* New York: W. W. Norton, 2006.

Gilman, Sander L. *Difference and Pathology: Stereotypes of Sexuality, Race, and Madness.* Ithaca, N.Y.: Cornell University Press, 1985.

———. *Inscribing the Other.* Texts and Contexts. Lincoln: University of Nebraska Press, 1991.

Giocanti, Stéphane. *Charles Maurras Félibre: l'Itinéraire et l'Oeuvre d'un Chantre.* Paris: De Montalte, 1995.

———. *Maurras: Le Chaos et l'Ordre.* Paris: Flammarion, 2006.

Goetz, Christopher G., Michel Bonduelle, and Toby Gelfand. *Charcot: Constructing Neurology.* New York: Oxford University Press, 1995.

Goldberg, Harvey. *The Life of Jean Jaurès.* Madison: University of Wisconsin Press, 1962.

Goldsmith, Barbara. *Obsessive Genius: The Inner World of Marie Curie.* London: Weidenfeld & Nicolson, 2005.

Goncourt, Edmond de. *Paris Under Siege, 1870–1871: From the Goncourt Journal* [Journal des Goncourts]. Edited and translated by George Joseph Becker. Ithaca N.Y.: Cornell University Press, 1969.

Goncourt, Edmond de, and Alphonse Daudet. *Correspondance.* Edited by Pierre Dufief with Anne-Simone Dufief. Histoire des Idées et Critique Littéraire. Geneva: Librairie Droz, 1996.

Goncourt, Edmond de, and Jules de Goncourt. *Journal: Mémoires de la Vie Littéraire.* Edited by Robert Ricatte. Paris: R. Laffont, 1989.

Gourdin, Henri. *Adèle, l'Autre Fille de Victor Hugo: 1830–1915: Biographie.* Paris: Ramsay, 2003.

Gregh, Fernand, and Marcel Proust. *Mon Amitié Avec Marcel Proust: Souvenirs et Lettres Inédites.* Paris: Grasset, 1958.

Guillemin, Henri. *L'Engloutie: Adèle, Fille de Victor Hugo, 1830–1915.* Paris: Éditions du Seuil, 1985.

Heimermann, Benoît. *Suez et Panama: La Fabuleuse Épopée de Ferdinand de Lesseps.* Collection "Les Pionniers." Paris: Arthaud, 1996.

Heimermann, Benoît, and Gérard Janichon. *Charcot, le Gentleman des Pôles.* Rennes and Versailles: Éditions Ouest-France, Éditions du Pen-Duick, 1991.

Higonnet, Patrice L. R. *Paris, Capital of the World* [Paris, Capitale du Monde]. Cambridge, Mass.: Belknap Press of Harvard University Press, 2002.

Hugo, Adèle, Evelyn Blewer, Anne Ubersfeld, and Guy Rosa. *Victor Hugo Raconté par Adèle Hugo.* Collection les Mémorables. Paris: Plon, 1985.

Hugo, Adèle, and Frances Vernor Guille. *Le Journal d'Adèle Hugo.* Bibliothèque Introuvable. Paris: Lettres Modernes, 1968–2002.

Hugo, Georges. *Mon Grand-Père.* Paris: Clamann-Lévy, 1902.

Hugo, Jean. *Avant d'Oublier: 1918–1931.* Paris: Fayard, 1976.

———. *Carnets: 1946–1984.* Arles: Actes Sud, 1994.

———. *Le Regard de la Mémoire: 1914–1945.* Arles: Actes Sud, 1994.

Hugo, Victor. *Oeuvres Complètes: Édition Chronologique.* 18 vols. Edited by Jean Massin. Paris: Club Français du Livre, 1967–70.

Huntford, Roland. *The Last Place on Earth.* Modern Library Exploration Series. New York: Modern Library, 1999.

———. *Shackleton.* New York: Carroll & Graf, 1998.

Huret, Jules. *Interviews de Littérature et d'Art.* Collection Patrimoine. Vanves: Éditions Thot, 1984.

Irvine, William D. *The Boulanger Affair Reconsidered: Royalism, Boulangism, and the Origins of the Radical Right in France.* New York: Oxford University Press, 1989.

James, Henry, and the Henry James Collection. *Essays in London and Elsewhere.* New York: Harper & Brothers, 1893.

Jaurès, Jean. *Action Socialiste.* Paris: G. Bellais, 1899.

———. *Discours à la Jeunesse.* Pages Socialistes. Vol 1. Paris: Éditions de la Liberté, 1944.

Jaurès, Jean, Eric Cahm, and Madeleine Rebérioux. *Les Temps de l'Affaire Dreyfus, 1897–1899.* Oeuvres de Jean Jaurès. Vols. 6–7. Paris: Fayard, 2000.

Jaurès, Jean, and Louis Lévy. *Anthologie de Jean Jaurès.* Paris: Calmann-Lévy, 1946.

Johnson, Martin Phillip. *The Paradise of Association: Political Culture and Popular Organizations in the Paris Commune of 1871.* Ann Arbor: University of Michigan Press, 1996.

Joyau, Auguste. *Adèle Hugo: La Mal-Aimée*. Morne-Rouge, Martinique: Éditions des Horizons Caraïbes, 1981.

Kahn, Serge. *Jean-Baptiste Charcot: Explorateur des Mers, Navigateur des Pôles*. Paris: Glénat, 2006.

Karabell, Zachary. *Parting the Desert: The Creation of the Suez Canal*. New York: Knopf, 2003.

Katz, Steven T., and Sander L. Gilman. *Anti-Semitism in Times of Crisis*. New York: New York University Press, 1991.

Maillot, François. *Léon Daudet, Député Royaliste*. Paris: Albatros, 1991.

Marcel, Pierre, and Charles Péguy. *Correspondance: 1905–1914*. Edited by Julie Sabiani. Paris: Minard, 1980.

Marque, Jean Noël. *Léon Daudet*. Paris: Fayard, 1971.

Maurras, Charles. *Au Signe de Flore: Souvenirs de Vie Politique*. Paris: B. Grasset, 1933.

————. *L'Avenir de l'Intelligence*. Paris: Flammarion, 1927.

————. *Enquête sur la Monarchie / Charles Maurras*. Paris: Nouvelle Librairie Nationale, 1916.

————. *Heures Immortelles, 1914–1919*. Paris: Nouvelle Librairie Française, 1932.

————. *Kiel et Tanger, 1895–1905: La République Française Devant l'Europe, 1905–1913–1921*. Les Écrivains de la Renaissance Française. L'Oeuvre de Charles Maurras. Vol. 1. Paris: Nouvelle Librairie Nationale, 1921.

————. *Lorsque Hugo Eut les Cent Ans: -Indications- / Charles Maurras*. Paris: Marcelle Lesage, 1927.

————. *La Musique Intérieure, par Charles Maurras*. Paris: B. Grasset, 1925.

————. *Oeuvres Capitales*. Paris: Flammarion, 1954.

————. *Quand les Français Ne S'Aimaient Pas: Chronique d'une Renaissance, 1895–1905*. Versailles: Bibliothèque des Oeuvres Politiques, 1928.

Mayeur, Jean Marie, and Madeleine Rebérioux. *The Third Republic from Its Origins to the Great War, 1871–1914*. The Cambridge History of Modern France. Vol. 4. Cambridge, U.K., New York, and Paris: Cambridge University Press and Maison des Sciences de l'Homme, 1984.

McCullough, David G. *The Path Between the Seas: The Creation of the Panama Canal, 1870–1914*. New York: Simon and Schuster, 1999.

McGrath, William J., and Sigmund Freud. *Freud's Discovery of Psychoanalysis: The Politics of Hysteria*. Ithaca, N.Y.: Cornell University Press, 1986.

Merriman, John. *The Dynamite Club: How a Bombing in Fin-de-Siècle Paris Ignited the Age of Modern Terror*. New York: Houghton Mifflin Harcourt, 2009.

————. *French Cities in the Nineteenth Century*. New York: Holmes & Meier, 1981.

————. *A History of Modern Europe: From the Renaissance to the Present*. 2nd ed. New York: W. W. Norton, 2004.

Mollier, Jean-Yves, *Le Scandale de Panama*. Paris: Fayard, 1991.

Monroe, John Warne. *Laboratories of Faith: Mesmerism, Spiritism, and Occultism in Modern France*. Ithaca, N.Y.: Cornell University Press, 2008.

Noguères, Louis. *La Haute Cour de la Libération, 1944–1949*. Paris: Éditions de Minuit, 1965.

————. *Le Véritable Procès du Maréchal Pétain*. Paris: Fayard, 1955.

Nord, Philip G. *Paris Shopkeepers and the Politics of Resentment.* Princeton, N.J.: Princeton University Press, 1986.

Nordau, Anna. *Max Nordau, a Biography.* New York: The Nordau Committee, 1943.

Nordau, Max Simon. *Degeneration* [Entartung]. New York: H. Fertig, 1968.

————. *Écrits Sionistes; Textes Choisis, avec Introduction, Bibliographie et Notes.* Paris: Librairie Lipschutz, 1936.

Nordau, Max Simon, and Anna Nordau. *Erinnerungen: Erzählt von Ihm Selbst und von der Gefährtin Seines Lebens.* Leipzig: Renaissance-Verlag, 1928.

Nye, Robert A. *Crime, Madness, & Politics in Modern France: The Medical Concept of National Decline.* Princeton, N.J.: Princeton University Press, 1984.

Oriol, Philippe. *Bernard Lazare.* Biographies. Paris: Stock, 2003.

Oulié, Marthe. *Charcot of the Antarctic.* London: J. Murray, 1938.

————. *Jean Charcot.* Paris: Gallimard, 1937.

————. *Quand J'Était Matelot.* Collection "La Route." Vol. 2. Paris: A. Redier, 1930.

Paléologue, Maurice. *An Intimate Journal of the Dreyfus Case* [Journal de l'Affaire Dreyfus, 1894–1899]. New York: Criterion Books, 1957.

Pawel, Ernst. *The Labyrinth of Exile: A Life of Theodor Herzl.* New York: Farrar, Straus and Giroux, 1989.

Péguy, Charles. *L'Argent Suite.* Paris: Cahiers de la Quinzaine, 1913.

Péguy, Charles, Romain Rolland, and Alfred Saffrey. *Une Amitié Française.* Paris: A. Michel, 1955.

Pick, Daniel. *Faces of Degeneration: A European Disorder, c. 1848–c. 1918.* Ideas in Context. Cambridge, U.K., and New York: Cambridge University Press, 1989.

Proust, Marcel. *À la Recherche du Temps Perdu.* Edited by Jean-Yves Tadié. Bibliothèque de la Pléiade. Vol. 356. Paris: Gallimard, 1987.

————. *Contre Sainte-Beuve: Précédé de Pastiches et Mélanges et Suivi de Essais et Articles.* Edited by Pierre Clarac and Yves Sandre. Bibliothéque de la Pléiade. Vol. 229. Paris: Gallimard, 1971.

————. *Correspondance.* Edited by Philip Kolb. Paris: Plon, 1970–1993.

————. *Jean Santeuil.* Translated by Gerard Hopkins with a preface by André Maurois. New York: Simon and Schuster, 1956.

————. *Letters of Marcel Proust.* Translated and edited by Mina Stein. New York: Random House, 2006.

————. *Marcel Proust: Selected Letters, 1880–1903.* Edited by Philip Kolb. Garden City, N.Y.: Doubleday, 1983.

————. *Textes Retrouvés.* Edited by Larkin B. Price and Philip Kolb. Urbana: University of Illinois Press, 1968.

Proust, Marcel, and Lucien Daudet. *Mon Cher Petit: Lettres à Lucien Daudet, 1895–1897, 1904, 1907, 1908.* Edited by Michel Bonduelle. Paris: Gallimard, 1991.

Queffélec, Henri. *Le Grand Départ: Charcot et le "Pourquoi Pas?"* Paris: Presse de la Cité, 1977.

Quinn, Susan. *Marie Curie: A Life.* New York: Simon and Schuster, 1995.

Rebérioux, Madeleine, and Gilles Candar. *Jaurès et les Intellectuels.* Patrimoine. Paris: Éditions de l'Atelier/Éditions Ouvrières, 1994.

Richardson, Joanna. *Sarah Bernhardt and Her World.* New York: Putnam, 1977.

Robb, Graham. *The Discovery of France: A Historical Geography from the Revolution to the First World War.* New York: W. W. Norton, 2007.

———. *Victor Hugo.* New York: W. W. Norton, 1997.

Rogger, Hans, and Eugen Joseph Weber. *The European Right: A Historical Profile.* Berkeley: University of California Press, 1965.

Sand, George, and Gustave Flaubert. *The George Sand–Gustave Flaubert Letters.* Translated by Aimee L. McKenzie, with an introduction by Stuart P. Sherman. Whitefish, Mont.: Kessinger Publishing, 2004.

Shattuck, Roger. *The Banquet Years: The Origins of the Avant-Garde in France, 1885 to World War I.* Essay Index Reprint Series. Rev. ed. Freeport, N.Y.: Books for Libraries Press, 1972.

Sonn, Richard David. *Anarchism and Cultural Politics in Fin-de-Siècle France.* Lincoln: University of Nebraska Press, 1989.

Soucy, Robert. *Fascism in France: The Case of Maurice Barrès.* Berkeley: University of California Press, 1972.

Spiquel, Agnès. *Du Passant au Passeur: Quand Victor Hugo Devenait Grand-Père, 1871–1877.* Saint-Pierre-du-Mont, France: Eurédit, 2002.

Spufford, Francis. *I May Be Some Time: Ice and the English Imagination.* London: Faber and Faber, 1996.

Steegmuller, Francis. *Flaubert and Madame Bovary: A Double Portrait.* London: Constable, 1993.

Sternhell, Zeev. *Birth of Fascist Ideology: From Cultural Rebellion to Political Revolution.* Princeton, N.J.: Princeton University Press, 1994.

———. *Neither Right nor Left: Fascist Ideology in France* [Ni Droite, ni Gauche]. Berkeley: University of California Press, 1986.

———. *Ni Droite, ni Gauche: l'Idéologie Fasciste en France.* Paris: Fayard, 2000.

Tadié, Jean-Yves. *Marcel Proust: Biographie.* N.R.F. Biographies. Paris: Gallimard, 1996.

———. *Proust.* Les Dossiers Belfond. Paris: P. Belfond, 1983.

Thuillier, Jean. *Monsieur Charcot de la Salpêtrière.* Laffont Histoire. Paris: R. Laffont, 1993.

Valéry, Paul. *Oeuvres.* Paris: Éditions du Sagittaire, 1931.

Vatré, Eric. *Charles Maurras: Un Itinéraire Spirituel.* Paris: Nouvelles Éditions Latines, 1978.

———. *Léon Daudet, ou, le Libre Réactionnaire.* Paris: Éditions France-Empire, 1987.

Weber, Eugen. *Action Française: Royalism and Reaction in Twentieth-Century France.* Stanford, Calif.: Stanford University Press, 1962.

———. *France, Fin de Siècle.* Cambridge, Mass.: Belknap Press of Harvard University Press, 1986.

———. *The Hollow Years: France in the 1930s.* New York: W. W. Norton, 1994.

———. *My France: Politics, Culture, Myth.* Cambridge, Mass.: Belknap Press of Harvard University Press, 1991.

———. *The Nationalist Revival in France, 1905–1914.* Berkeley: University of California Press, 1959.

————. *Twentieth Century Europe*. The Forum Series in European History. St. Louis, Mo.: Forum Press, 1980.

Wilson, Stephen. *Ideology and Experience: Antisemitism in France at the Time of the Dreyfus Affair*. Rutherford, N.J., and London: Fairleigh Dickinson University Press and Associated University Presses, 1982.

Winter, J. M. *Sites of Memory, Sites of Mourning: The Great War in European Cultural History*. New York: Cambridge University Press, 1995.

Wohl, Robert. *The Generation of 1914*. Cambridge, Mass.: Harvard University Press, 1979.

Zola, Émile. *Du Roman: Sur Stendhal, Flaubert et les Goncourt*. Edited by Henri Mitterand. Brussels: Éditions Complexe, 1989.

————. *The Dreyfus Affair: J'accuse and Other Writings*. Edited by Alain Pagès; translated by Eleanor Levieux. New Haven: Yale University Press, 1996

————. *Oeuvres Complètes*. Edited by Henri Mitterand. Paris: Nouveau Monde, 2002– .

Acknowledgments

My interest in the lives of Jean-Baptiste Charcot, Léon Daudet, and Jeanne Hugo began a few years ago in a master class in biography with the endlessly gracious and witty Hermione Lee. Since then, I have relied on the kindness and generosity of countless individuals and institutions. I am especially grateful to the staff at the following institutions: the Bibliothèque Nationale de France, the Archives Nationales (France), the Maison Victor Hugo, Sterling Memorial Library at Yale University, Bobst Library at New York University, and the New York Public Library. In particular, I'd like to thank, first, Wayne Furman and then the wonderful David Smith for providing me with a writing haven in the Allen Room. I must also acknowledge the insight, assistance, guidance, and friendship I received from friends, colleagues, scholars, and fellow travelers around the world (this book could not have been written without their support—and needless to say, any mistakes it contains are mine alone): Anne-Marie Vallin-Charcot, Adèle Hugo, George Negroponte, Ramon Gutierrez, Serge Kahn, Marie Foucard (and the staff of Grand Nord Grand Large), Stéphane Giocanti, Laurent Bury, Harold and Jeanne Bloom, Ben Kafka, Julie Coe, Laurence Gould, Grace and Ben Reed, Joshua Micah Marshall, Millet Israeli, Daragh Holmes, Laura Merriman, Yeewan Koon, Serena Mayeri, Matthew Francis, Theresa von Fuchs, Alex Hickox, Harvey Rich, Jennifer Boittin, Lien-Hang Nguyen, Helen Veit, Charles Keith, Adrian Lentz-Smith, Angela Ryan, James Delorey, Genevieve Tremblay, Alison Hart, Phil Cohen, Lisa Levy,

Scott Labby, James Gates, Kathryn Pickford, Jennifer McGrady, June Terry, Hinda and Barry Simon, Anne Bohnn, Nancy Manderson, and Bill Coats. Thanks to Mark Lamster, my Allen Room partner in crime, and especially to Dana Goldblatt, Stephen Vella, Francesca Ryan, Kerrie Mitchell, and George Trumbull IV for their spirited and patient friendship (the last two also offered wise critiques of earlier drafts of the manuscript). Anthony Grafton has been an uncommonly generous advisor, mentor, and model for humane scholarship, while John Merriman's patience, good nature, and passion for archival research have always held me in good stead, even when the end seemed nowhere in sight.

At FSG, I'd like to thank Eric Chinski for his brilliant editorial eye and reassuringly wry outlook, the ever-patient and all-around impressive Eugenie Cha, and the lovely Marion Duvert. I am also grateful to have in my corner the enthusiastic Hélène Fiamma at Flammarion, and, of course, my excellent agent, Lydia Wills.

Thanks to the extended Cambor clan—Carolyn and Elizabeth; Steve, Wendy, Wentworth, and Charlotte; Roger, Maryellen, and Spencer; and most especially my parents, Kathleen and Glenn, and my brother, Peter—for their unstinting love, support, and enthusiasm for learning. Finally, thanks to Justin Gullingsrud, whose love, good humor, and companionship mean the world to me.

Index

Index